WORKING THROUGH DERRIDA

Northwestern University
Studies in Phenomenology
and
Existential Philosophy

WORKING
THROUGH
DERRIDA

Edited by Gary B. Madison

Northwestern University Press
Evanston, Illinois

1993

Northwestern University Press
Evanston, Illinois 60201-2807

Copyright © 1993 by Northwestern University Press
All rights reserved. Published 1993
Printed in the United States of America

Library of Congress Cataloging-in-Publication Data
Working through Derrida / edited by Gary B. Madison.
    p.   cm. — (Northwestern University studies in phenomenology
and existential philosophy)
   Includes bibliographical references.
   ISBN 0-8101-1054-7 (alk. paper). — ISBN 0-8101-1079-2 (pbk.)
   1. Derrida, Jacques.   I. Madison, Gary Brent.   II. Series:
Northwestern University studies in phenomenology & existential
philosophy.
B2430.D484W67   1993
194—dc20   93-16218
                                                  CIP

Contents

Acknowledgments

The editor wishes to thank the following for permission to reprint previously published work.

David Couzens Hoy, "Splitting the Difference: Habermas's Critique of Derrida," *Praxis International* 8 (January 1989). Reprinted by permission of the author.

Nancy Fraser, "The French Derrideans: Politicizing Deconstruction or Deconstructing Politics," *New German Critique,* no. 33 (Fall 1984). Reprinted by permission of the author.

John Searle, "The World Turned Upside Down," *The New York Review of Books* (October 27, 1983), and "Reply to Mackey," *The New York Review of Books* (February 2, 1984). Reprinted by permission of the author.

Richard Bernstein, "An Allegory of Modernity/Postmodernity: Habermas and Derrida," in *The New Constellation: The Ethical-Political Horizons of Modernity/ Postmodernity* (Oxford: Polity Press, 1991). Reprinted by permission of the publisher.

Drucilla Cornell, "The Violence of the Masquerade: Law Dressed up as Justice," *Cardozo Law Review* 11, nos. 5–6. Reprinted by permission of the author.

Richard Rorty, "Is Derrida a Transcendental Philosopher?" in *Essays on Heidegger and Others* (Cambridge: Cambridge University Press, 1991). Reprinted by permission of the publisher.

Introduction

Gary B. Madison

Over the course of the last thirty years or so a truly prolific number of texts have appeared bearing the signature "Jacques Derrida." Derrida's texts have, in turn, produced a veritable host of other texts, as is only natural. For, it is in the nature of texts, especially those called "seminal," to produce ever more texts. Texts demand to be read, and to read a text is, in effect, to produce another text. Reading is writing. This is what is called *interpretation*. There is never any end to it. We are all, as human beings, as speaking animals, ceaselessly engaged in the business of interpretation (and thus of text production), since we are all beings who, as thinking beings, are ever seeking understanding. As Italo Calvino said of Mr. Palomar in his novel of the same name: "Not to interpret is impossible, as refraining from thinking is impossible."[1]

Derrida's own texts are themselves mostly interpretations of the texts of others. There is an essential "parasiticality" ("intertextuality," if one prefers) involved in the production of any text whatsoever, and this is nowhere more evident than in Derrida himself. His interpretations of the texts of others are, moreover, "active interpretations," ones, that is, which challenge our accustomed readings of the texts of our tradition. After reading Derrida's reading of others, is there any way we can read these "same" texts as we may have before, before our reading of Derrida? As things stand today, no thinking/reading being—no philosopher, certainly—can refrain from interpreting Derrida, and from interpreting his interpretations of others, no matter how much he or she may regret the obligation thus imposed on him or her by the avalanche of texts bearing the name "Derrida." As Calvino might say, not to interpret Derrida is impossible, as refraining from thinking is impossible.

Interpreting Derrida poses special problems, however. This is because of what he has called *dissemination*—because he himself has appeared to give license to any and all manner of interpretations of his own texts. In his characteristically liberal fashion Derrida once wrote:

> Perhaps the desire to write is the desire to launch things that come back to you as much as possible in as many forms as possible. That is, it is the desire to perfect a program or a matrix having the greatest potential, variability, undecidability, plurivocality, et cetera, so that each time something returns it will be as different as possible. This is also what one does when one has children—talking beings who can always outtalk you. You have the illusion that it comes back to you—that these unpredictable words come out of you somewhat. This is what goes on with texts.[2]

Is it the case, then, that texts can mean anything that anyone in the world wants them to mean? Is the meaning of texts purely and simply "undecidable"—on a par with Nietzsche's enigmatic "Today I forgot my umbrella"? Is it the case that in the interpretation business "anything goes"? Hardly. In contrast to the exuberant excesses of some of his more uncritical epigones, Derrida himself has insisted that there are constraints on reading (one must, he says, recognize and respect the "classical exigencies").[3] And although he insists—and quite rightly so—that "reading is transformation," he fully recognizes that "this transformation cannot be executed however one wishes" and that it requires "protocols of reading."[4] As any experienced reader knows, while a good text will always have multiple meanings, it does not, and cannot, mean just anything at all. If the meaning of a text were not, to some degree or another, "decidable," one could not even begin to "deconstruct" it. Over the years an innumerable number of texts on Derrida and what he means have been written, including ones which have adhered slavishly to his own dictum that in his writings he does not "mean" (*vouloir dire*) anything in particular at all. The pages of our learned journals are now filled with these texts that "mean" nothing. The texts gathered together in this volume are of a different sort, however. They all (or almost all) assume that Derrida does indeed "mean" something, something perhaps extremely significant (or pernicious), and they are out to ascertain, and assess, what it is that he means (to say). This is perhaps especially the case in regard to those essays which attempt to come to grips with the ethical-political implications of Derrida's deconstructive enterprise.

The fact remains, however, that the authors gathered together in this volume speak in their own, quite different, distinctive voices. Some of them are ardent admirers of Derrida; some simply respect him, while maintaining serious differences with him; some do not like him at all— or, at least, would appear to thoroughly regret the influence he has had on the philosophical scene. And they speak from a multitude of different perspectives. This is as it should be. Quite a number of books have already been written in uncritical praise of Derrida—or, even worse, in a thoughtless, Derridaesque, imitative style. And quite a few—among which one can count some genuinely good ones—have also been written in a quite opposite vein. This book is different. It is neither an apologia nor a critique. Rather, it represents an attempt on the part of some of the leading scholars of our time to *come to terms* with Derrida. It is an attempt to *work through* Derrida.

Let me explain what I mean by "working through." *Durcharbeiten* is a Freudian term, related to such other terms as *Traumarbeit* (dream work), *Trauerarbeit* (work of mourning), and *psychische verarbeiten* (psychical working over).[5] Psychical working over refers to the work of integrating excitations by establishing associative links and by transforming the distribution of drive cathexis in a way that binds and masters the stimulus—until it breaks out afresh, as it certainly will, so long as one is alive. Freud believed that the absence or defectiveness of this "working over" was behind each case of neurosis or psychosis. He saw an analogy between the work of the analysand in the treatment and the work of the psychical apparatus itself. "Working through" names the process by which analysis overcomes resistance to its interpretations, a piece of work in the course of which the analysand passes from resistance to recognition of the resistance and its sources. Indeed, working through might be defined as "that process which is liable to halt the repetitive insistence characteristic of unconscious formations."[6]

Now Derrida is, if not exactly a dream, then at least a text which we must now interpretively, "psychically," work through. This dream is yet far from having been "dreamed out," *ausgetraumpt.* As readers of Derrida, we are all still in the position of analysands. To work through Derrida—as the essays here gathered seek to do—would be, in Freudian terms, to engage in the work of recognizing that which we owe to Derrida, and that which we also refuse to accept. It would be to work through his own "ec-centricities." Where there is no "working over," there is only, as Freud said, neurosis, interpretive hang-ups. There is only repetition of the same. But if we really *work* through something (as these essays are designed to help us to do), then we may genuinely *understand* what is at work in that thing. Then we no longer simply repeat, excessively—or simply react, blindly. We learn. And we go on.

But we need to work through Derrida—especially since no one has called into question the entire tradition of Western philosophy in as radical a way as he has. Even—and especially—if we believe that there remains a crucial role for philosophy after the demise of the "metaphysics of presence," even if we believe that subjectivity ("man") cannot be erased, reduced to the transcendent and meaningless play of *différance*, even if we reject as outlandish the accusations made (not without encouragements on the part of Derrida himself) to the effect that Western philosophy—the *logos*, the *ratio*—is nothing but a "Eurocentric" device to enslave the rest of the world, even then we must, if we are going to defend ourselves in a responsible sort of way, *work through* Derrida. This is the task that the writers of the essays included in this volume have set themselves.

Reading Derrida is never easy (although it may, at times, be fun). These essays do not seek to make Derrida easy—they seek to make him a bit more understandable, *abordable*. They are critical essays, in the best sense of the term. They illustrate that and how writing about reading Derrida can be a mode in which to engage in serious philosophical *work*. One can *work* through Derrida.

Of course, the work is interminable. But the essays gathered here demonstrate that more and more English-speaking philosophers are finding it possible to advance their work by working through Derrida and also thereby working through the outworn and counterproductive dichotomy of "continental" and "analytic" philosophy.[7]

1

Difference
Unlimited

Barry Allen

> [W]e are to perceive as "normal" . . . what Husserl believed he
> could isolate as a peculiar and accidental experience, some-
> thing dependent and secondary—that is, the indefinite drift of
> signs, as errancy and change of scene, linking up representa-
> tions one to another without beginning or end.
>
> —Derrida[1]

Aristotle's *De Interpretatione* begins with a statement of the proper order
among things, souls, and signs:

> Now spoken sounds are symbols [*sumbola*] of affections in the
> soul, and written marks symbols of spoken sounds. And just as
> written marks are not the same for all men, neither are spoken
> sounds. But what these are in the first place signs [*semeia*] of—
> affections in the soul—are the same for all; and what these af-
> fections are likenesses [*homeiomata*] of—actual things—are also
> the same.[2]

These three sentences have been described as the most influential
text in the history of semantics.[3] Two ideas with an essential historical
and theoretical reference to it have governed Western thought on language and language's signs.

First, linguistic conventionality: Languages are more like laws or fashions than stellar motion or organic growth. Later, Aristotle defines a noun or name (*onoma*) as "a spoken sound significant by convention" (*kata suntheken*).

Second, a secondary sign: Speech is before writing, images or phantasy before speech, things before mental impressions. Nature always comes before convention and being before representation. At the end of Aristotle's series (writing, speech, affection, thing) we reach a permanently present natural form whose being or self-identical presence is the ontological presupposition of signs, representations, knowledge, and truth; while whether as writing or speech, as phantasms, images, copies, or representations, the being of signs is secondary.

Following Aristotle's lead, Western work on language and its signs from the Stoics to Locke subordinates these typically "conventional" and "arbitrary" contrivances to something whose identity and existence is autonomous of the language in which it is named. The identity of a given sign (*what* sign it is) is determined by the identity of the nonsign it stands for, and language is first of all an apparatus for naming and predication. It were as if signs could not be signs apart from something that is emphatically not itself another sign. In relation to this more original being the identity and existence of signs is derivative, secondary, dependent, accidental.[4]

Derrida proposes "to restore the original and non-derivative character of signs, in opposition to classical metaphysics." One effect is "to eliminate a concept of signs whose whole history and meaning belongs to the adventure of the metaphysics of presence."[5] The formula "nothing outside the text" registers this effect. "Nothing outside the text" does not mean "prison-house of language." Neither does it mean that everything is a sign. But to differentiate signs ontologically from something which is emphatically not itself a sign, something which would have a being of its own, a self-identity or nature unconditioned by the artificial contrivances of nomenclature, is untenable, or at least arbitrary. It has no obvious, self-evident basis in uncontroversial facts about the phenomena of verbal meaning.

As a point of departure for my look at this argumentation I choose the linguistics of Saussure.

Semiological Difference

As the citation from Aristotle with which I began suggests, speech and the spoken, linguistic sign have been understood to depend on a relation between a thing and the vocable that stands for it. In a gesture that compares with Wittgenstein's critique of the "Augustinian" picture of language—"individual words in language name objects, sentences are combinations of such names"—Saussure dismisses this as a fallacious "nomenclaturism." According to the revisionary concept he advances, the identity of a language's signs, or what Saussure calls their "linguistic value," is entirely determined by relations among other signs. Whether we consider a verbal signal (*signifiant*) or a signification or verbal meaning (*signifié*), "what characterizes each most exactly is being whatever the others are not. . . . In a language there are only differences *and no positive terms*." This is Saussure's principle of semiological difference. He went so far as to call it "the absolutely final law of language":

> The absolutely final law of language is, we dare say, that there
> is nothing that can ever reside in *one* term . . . *a* is powerless to
> designate anything without the aid of *b*, and the same thing is
> true of *b* without the aid of *a* . . . both have no value except
> through their reciprocal difference . . . neither has any value
> . . . other than through this same plexus of eternally negative
> differences.[6]

Make this an absolute law and one must conclude that nothing strictly indispensable to the phenomena of verbal meaning depends on anything which is emphatically not itself another, different sign. What signifies are the differences that distinguish physical patterns, and these differences (and therefore the signs they define) have no natural or purely physical existence apart from an arbitrary ensemble of opposed values.[7]

This is unprecedented, on more than one count.[8] First, there is the ontological singularity of the principle. For Plato, "among things that exist, some are always spoken of as being what they are, just in themselves, others as being what they are with reference to other things. . . . And what is different is always so called with reference to another thing."[9] Differences are secondary, derivative, relative to the more original "self-identical being" of a being. Yet for Saussure, language (indeed, the entire field of signs, of the semiological) is a domain where, contrary to the Platonic principle, difference is original and identity (the "being identical to itself" of one sign) secondary and derived.

Saussure's principle is also singular in contrast to earlier work on signs in logic and philosophy. The principle of difference implies that languages function with all their familiar effectiveness without relying on any form of sign/nonsign opposition, whether the postulated nonsign were a substance or *res*, an idea or intention. With one limitation to be noted, Saussure asserts the autonomy of the linguistic sign and the independence of verbal meaning from anything that is not itself another sign. This holds for every part of a language (*langue*), including the so-called categorematic terms where both traditional and modern logic subordinate the sign's identity to the nonsign it stands for.

One must wonder what becomes of reference and truth, although Saussure nowhere considers this question. He has much to say about language and its signs, but nothing of a philosopher's interest in truth. It fell to Derrida to take the measure of Saussure's principle here. But before turning to that, I want to show how even for Saussure the occasional sign remains secondary in relation to a sovereign nonsign.

Only if there is a momentarily changeless and formally closed total distribution of differences does any occasional, empirical, token sign of language have a determinate identity or linguistic value. Saussure refers to this totality or system as a linguistic structure (*une langue*), a static, synchronic language-state (*état de langue*) "from which the passage of time is entirely excluded." Unlike speaking (*parole*), in which linguistic signs circulate (and change their values), a *langue* is a "system of pure values, determined by nothing else apart from the temporary state of its constituent elements." Saussure defines a *langue* as "a system . . . in which the value of one element depends on the simultaneous co-existence of all the others." He claims that "amid the disparate mass of facts involved in language [*langage*]" this synchronic system "stands out like a well-defined entity." It "is no less real than speech, and no less amenable to study." The signs and their system "are not abstractions" but "realities localized in the brain."[10]

In light of the favor of this perspective found in later linguistics it is well to remember that it is less an established result than a stipulation and directive for research.[11] Why does the idea of a synchronic language-state even come into the picture for Saussure? Because he wants the signs of language to have identities determinate in themselves and determinable by a synchronic science indifferent to history. If there is to be the science of language he envisions, there must be something only a synchronic, structural linguistics can get right or be true to, and for that there must be a durable self-identity to the "linguistic structure" of language. This is not a *result;* Saussure *posits* its existence a priori. He takes his philosophy of science from Aristotle: What is first for a science is what it posits, what makes it "positive."[12] With this venture into ontology Saussure gains a sphere of objective reality for his science of language, but also thereby repeats, in a "structuralist" variation, the theme of the secondary sign. For Saussure as much as for Aristotle or Locke, it is finally by reference to something that is not itself another sign that the occasional sign derives its identity as a sign or as language—something "fully present" and "identical to itself"; in this case, *la langue*, "linguistic structure," the fully present totality of a synchronic language-state, which is certainly not itself a sign differing among signs. Thus does the most innovative work since antiquity on language and language's signs nevertheless repeat the "metaphysics of presence" which has always condemned the sign to a secondary, derivative status. *La langue* is Saussure's name for the self-identically present being over against which the occasional sign is newly determined as secondary.

Difference Unlimited

It is possible to detach Saussure's principle of difference from his dream of a synchronic science of language. The assumption that there must be a closed totality of linguistic signs is not motivated by any obvious, uncontroversial phenomena of verbal meaning. Saussure posits it because he no doubt unwittingly follows the oldest ontological tradition of Western philosophy according to which *to be* is to be "fully" determinate and "self-identical." The cash-value of the postulated totality is precisely to guarantee that for the signs of language. But the principle of semiological difference is itself an argument against this classical procedure. To the extent that it is plausible to view signs as essentially contrastive, differentiating and relational, so far is it evident that a sign does not need to be primitively self-identical in order to admit of interpretation or function in the communication of verbal meaning.

This is how I see Derrida's relation to Saussure. He agrees that in language there are only differences (*M*,10), but instead of positing their synchronic totality a priori, he seizes the most obvious implication of the principle of difference, concluding that difference among signs—and not a "purely synchronic" differing but one open to time, at no point nonarbitrarily limited—determines whatever value or identity there is for the occasional sign. Three points summarize the results which follow.

1. A sign attains its identity as the one that it is by differing from other signs. These differences, which elude totalization, which are open to history, give a sign what value it has as a signifier or as a signification. This introduces the need for a far-ranging reconsideration of what

passes for reference in signs. All signs, whether linguistic or nonlinguistic, spoken or written, are now, so far as concerns their reference-value, in the position formerly reserved for the special, limiting case of writing.

Western thought about language traditionally maintains that writing is not itself language but is instead a historical supplement or extension, a convenient instrument for the representation of what is not just accidentally but by nature an originally spoken language.[13] The written sign is thus doubly secondary, a sign of a sign, deferring its identity as language to a pronunciation it anticipates and presupposes. If, however, the differences that condition the entity of a sign are unlimited and nontotalizable, then the prescribed distinction according to which some are signs "of signs" (writing) while others break out of the circle and refer to what is not itself another sign is untenable (*G*, 7). What was supposed to be limited to the written sign (remainder, trace, supplement) becomes the plight of signs without limitation (*G*, 43). An occasional sign, written or spoken, is a trace of the differing that constitutes it, and this, for Derrida, "divides, from the start, every reference." Each occasional sign "begins by referring back, that is to say, does not begin . . . there is not a single reference, but from then on, always, a multiplicity of references, so many different traces referring back to other traces and to traces of others."[14]

The sign is therefore cut off from natural, intentional, or purely formal sources of meaning. The identity of the occasional sign—*what* sign it is and what it does or does not imply—is therefore radically open to nonsemantic, nonformal, historical, social or institutional determination. Later, I shall return to the implications of this for the existence and value of truth.

2. Once the principle of difference is unconstrained by the assumption of synchronic closure the sign becomes radically open to time, historical through and through (*M*, 11). There is then nothing *to* a sign "itself" (or a language "itself")—no identity or determination at any level bearing on signaling/signifying values—that is indifferent to a change of time or context.

It sometimes seems to go without saying that of course there is *something* in signs that is the same regardless of temporal or contextual differences among tokens. For instance, it has become commonplace to describe the occasional sign as a token of an infinitely repeatable type. Besides a type-identity, signs (especially linguistic signs) are supposed to have something like intentional content, truth-conditions or logical form, and this is supposed to be the same, at least sometimes, despite differences of context. But since the differing that determines the value of an occasional sign is unlimited; since nothing *present* (from which the passing of time is excluded) limits this differing, securing totality, imposing nonarbitrary closure; since differing and therefore identity are wide open to historical contingency, there is nothing *to* the occasional sign that functions symbolically and which might simply repeat. Each occasional sign has a historically conditioned, circumstantial effect but not a durable, self-identical content.

Here is a place for two observations on the popular distinction between types and tokens. The idea is familiar enough. A type is the infinitely repeatable form which the occasional token instantiates. The sequence "the cat is on the mat" contains six graphic word-tokens but only five types, the two occurrences of "the" being tokens of the same type. The first point is that linguistic practice, not geometry, determines this count. It is impossible for natural similarity and difference (acoustic, spatial, etc.) to settle the count of tokens and types. One is counting signs, and sameness of sign has nothing to do with resemblance in respects that exist independently of signs or practice. Furthermore, it must not be assumed that repetition in signs is the reinstantiation of a form whose identity is independent of historical differing among contingent tokens. That would subordinate the occasional sign to an enduring, lasting, present being (a type) which is not itself a sign (not an occasional sign or token) but whose transcendent self-identity supposedly conditions the identity of an occasional sign. Nothing "constitutes" that identity except a contingent history of iteration, so there is nothing strictly or finally *constituted* about a sign: no durable self-identity indifferent to time; no self-same signifying form, no type-identity which must remain the same if that very sign is to repeat. The temporary movement from one occasional sign to another, or what Derrida calls *iteration,* "is not simply repetition" (*L,* 53). "Iteration alters, something new takes place" (*L,* 40).[15]

One may object, "But if I say *cat cat cat,* obviously I do the same, say the same, repeat the self-same sign." Compare saying *cat cat cat* to spending $5 in three consecutive transactions: How "same" is a $5 note from one transaction to the next? Within certain parameters of person, place, and time there may be indifference to differences, but this is entirely circumstantial and not grounded in anything about the $5 note "itself." The exchange-value of a note is not "fully determinate" in a way that anticipates its historical possibilities of transaction, and that iterating series of transactions ($5 $5 $5) is far from the simple repetition of a fixed and self-identical form or content. Likewise, the iteration of signs is less a matter of self-identical form contingently reinstantiated than habitual, normative, lawful, contextually controlled indifference to differences. The idea of a "type," like that of "content" and "proposition," merely reifies this indifference, positing something to be the same in each case and construing linguistic competence as a capacity to deploy and re-cognize it. There is nothing *to* the occasional sign which remains indifferent to place and time and simply repeats, contributing a self-same content to a new and different speech act.

3. To abolish the secondariness of signs, to view their identity as historically and intertextually conditioned by differing, does not merely challenge a prevailing conception of signs. If there is no nonsign whose somewhere sometime self-identical presence finally limits the reference from sign to sign, then the distinction between sign and thing, or being and representation, loses its rationale and begins to seem arbitrary.

Saussure's limitation of "original" difference to the sphere of signs, which he separates from a supposedly more primordial order of natural nonsigns, is not motivated by any consideration concerning verbal meaning as such. It derives from his idea of a synchronic, structural science of language and his Aristotelian assumption concerning of the preconditions of scientific truth. Derrida exposes the independence of Saussure's principle, relieving it of a limitation to the specifically semiological, to languages or systems of signs in deference to physical nature. The differing Saussure saw as the essence of the sign, but also tried to limit to the semiological and to totalize in a synchronic state, is unlimited and nontotalizable. There is no limit to what receives its character (poor thing that it is) from difference, and differences do not formally terminate; they do not admit of totality or nonarbitrary closure. The negative, contrastive, *original* difference that was supposed to be limited to signs is all the difference there is.

In other words, "there is nothing outside of the text" (*G*, 158). In *Of Grammatology* (1967), Derrida described this as an "axial proposition." More than twenty years later, in the "Afterword" (1988) to *Limited Inc,* he offers these elucidations:

> the concept of text or context which guides me embraces and does not exclude the world, reality, history. . . . the text is not the book, it is not confined in a volume itself confined to the library. It does not suspend reference—to history, to the world, to reality, to being, and especially not to the other, since they always appear in an experience, hence in a movement of interpretation which contextualizes them according to a network of differences. (*L*, 137)

> the concept of text I propose is limited neither to the graphic, nor to the book, nor even to discourse, and even less to the semantic, representational, symbolic, ideal, or ideological sphere. What I call "text" implies all the structures called "real," "economic," "historical," socio-institutional, in short: all possible referents. . . . every referent, all reality has the structure of a differential trace. (*L*, 148)

So it is not just conventional signs (as opposed to natural non-signs), not just linguistic (as opposed to physical) differences, not just symbols (as opposed to states of affairs) that are "constituted" (such as they are constituted at all) uniquely by unlimited, relational differing. A thing is as much a trace, its identity as differential and as deferred, as that of a sign. This introduces an unconventional element of temporal deferral into ontology. Contrary to a Greek and Scholastic assumption which passed uncritically into modern thought, what we call a "being," something that "is," is invariably less than identical to itself. The actuality or durable self-sameness classical ontology demands of its beings never comes to pass, not fully, not finally. Difference is "older" than identity, while self-identical being is deferred ad infinitum. *Différance* is what becomes of semiological difference once it has been radically un-limited, leaving identity and sameness nowhere primitive or given (*M*, 24). Derrida's neologism fuses the ideas of irreducible, original difference and the interminable deferral of identity which it implies (*M*, 14). What passes for actual or extant or for the same is always less, a simulacrum whose physical presence is a "special effect" (as cinematic motion is a special effect) of the "displaced and equivocal passage from one different thing to another" (*M*, 17).

To take the measure of these arguments, I shall consider their implications first against Heidegger's thought of ontological difference (section 3), and then against the conception of language that Saussure bequeathed to structural linguistics (section 4).

Ontological Difference

In what is supposed to have been the last text he composed before his death, Heidegger writes of "that single question which I have persistently tried to ask in a more questioning manner. It is known as *die Seinsfrage*, "the question of being."" Elsewhere, in a remark directed to "the critics," he asks, "Has the question posed in *Sein und Zeit* regarding the 'meaning of being' (as being) been at all taken up as a question? . . . Have the critics ever asked whether the question posed is possible or impossible?"[16]

To frame this question of being, Heidegger needs the idea of what he calls ontological difference. This is the singular difference between, on the one hand, *das Seiende*—entities, the beings that there are (whatever they may be)—and on the other, *das Sein*—the being or presencing (*Anwesen*) of whatever happens to be. Heidegger writes, "Being *is* not. There is being as the unconcealing of presencing."[17] That is, being is not entity, not something that exists; rather, the being, i.e., presencing and unconcealment, of beings as a whole is silently presupposed by every "There is . . . " (true or false). Indifference to this difference is the criterion of what Heidegger calls "metaphysics": thinking which ignores ontological difference, assimilating being to what is (what exists), as if being were "itself" something that there is, the highest, most incorruptible or certain being, grounding all the rest. Metaphysics from Plato (at least) to Nietzsche (supposedly) overlooks, ignores, and finally quite forgets about the ontological difference of being in favor of a theoretical account of what is.

For Heidegger, this is not the logical aberration of the positivists but a world-historical destiny and the fate of thinking in the West. Understanding this history is indispensable for the correct formulation of the *Seinsfrage*. "We can first ask this question only by way of a discussion of Occidental-European metaphysics, specifically, in reference to the forgottenness of being that has prevailed therein from the beginning." Heidegger cannot say that this historical "oblivion of being" is a mistake; it is not an error in the sense of a falsification or distortion affecting the accuracy with which a being has been represented. Rather,

> Oblivion of being belongs to the self-veiling essence of being. It belongs so essentially to the destiny of being that the dawn of this destiny rises as the unveiling of what is present in its presencing. This means that the history of being begins with the oblivion of being, since being—together with its essence, its difference from beings—keeps to itself. The difference collapses. It remains forgotten.

"The oblivion of the difference is all the same not a lack," he says; "but rather the richest and most prodigious event: in it the history of the Western world comes to be borne out. It is the event of metaphysics.

What now *is* stands in the shadow of the already foregone destiny of being's oblivion." Heidegger calls for a step back from the metaphysical oblivion of being, an "attempt to think being without regard to its being grounded in terms of beings." He envisions this as "the task of thinking" at "the end of philosophy."[18]

Heidegger and Saussure have something in common. While both introduce an idea of original difference, i.e., a difference which does not depend on prior identities but instead reverses the traditional priority, coming before and conditioning the identity of beings, both nevertheless limit this in a way that respects the traditional interpretation of being as presence. Saussure limits original difference to the sphere of the semiological, and it is in the name of the presence or self-identical being of signs and languages that he posits the synchronic totality of *la langue*. And if Heidegger insists on the originality of ontological difference, on its irreducibility to differences of kind or respect among beings, it is for the sake of thinking more penetratingly the presence (being) of what there is. Not only do "ontic" differences among beings remain as secondary and derived as they were for Plato; neither Aristotle nor Thomas would object to Heidegger's conception of science as "a kind of cognizing for the sake of cognizing as such. . . . What is to be unveiled should become manifest, solely in view of its own self, in whatever its pure essential character and specific mode of being may be. What is to be unveiled is the sole court of appeal of its determinability, of the concepts that are suitable for interpreting it." Heidegger even produces a variation on the secondary sign: "The essential being of language is saying as showing. Its showing character is not based on signs of any kind; rather, all signs arise from a showing within whose realm and for whose purposes they can be signs."[19]

Derrida has observed "the ambiguity of the Heideggerian situation with respect to the metaphysics of presence and logocentrism. It is at once contained within and transgresses it. But it is impossible to separate the two" (*G*, 22). Elsewhere he expands on Heidegger's dilemma:

> It remains that being, which is nothing, is not a being, cannot be said, cannot say itself, except in the ontic metaphor. And the choice of one or the other group of metaphors is necessarily significant. It is within a metaphorical insistence, then, that the interpretation of the meaning of being is produced. And *if Heidegger has radically deconstructed the domination of metaphysics by the present, he has done so in order to lead us to think the presence of the present.* But the thinking of this presence can only

BARRY ALLEN

metaphorize, by means of a profound necessity from which one cannot simply decide to escape, the language that it decon-structs. (*M*, 131, my emphasis)[20]

Despite his wish to think differently from a metaphysics that has prevailed since the Greeks, Heidegger abides by the Greek determination of being as presence, with its interpretation of *a* being as a unity, self-identically this or that, somewhere sometime present. Even if this presence (being) has presuppositions which philosophy ancient and modern is in no position to accommodate, Heidegger nevertheless assumes that (with the unique exception of the *Dasein*, the entity we ourselves are), "what is" is in each case fully present and identical to itself (*Vorhandensein*).

Yet if self-identity defers to *différance* and presence to differential iteration, the very idea of an "ontological difference" between self-identical, fully present beings and their presence or being as such must seem very doubtful. While Derrida says he would not "dispense with the passage through the truth of being," not "'criticize,' 'contest,' or misconstrue its incessant necessity" (*M*, 22), elsewhere he suggests a more confrontational position: "No doubt Nietzsche called for an active forgetting of being: it would not have the metaphysical form imputed to it by Heidegger" (*M*, 136).

The thought of unlimited, original, nontotalizable differences undermines *ontic* presuppositions of Greek metaphysics Heidegger never questions. Unlimited and irreducible difference, and the deferral or *différance* this introduces into ontology, destroys the interpretation of *a* being as what is somewhere sometime present, with all of the traits classical ontology ascribes to such a presence: unity, enduring self-identity, truth. The ontological difference between *what* (self-identically, univocally, fully) is present and this presence *itself* has never come to pass; being is deferred ad infinitum; and with nothing fully present, Heidegger's question concerning the presence of the present is relieved of its reason, *aufgehoben*, de-constructed.[21] There is no task, matter, or directive for thought in Heidegger's descriptions of the "self-veiling essence of being" or "being—together with its essence, its difference from beings."

The Language of Linguistic Science

The armature of Derrida's argumentation is Saussure's principle of semiological difference and its radical un-limitation by the oppositions that have traditionally hemmed in the sign, condemning it to a secondary, derivative sort of being. One way to criticize Derrida would therefore be to criticize Saussure's principle of difference. Were this open to serious doubt, the deconstructions might deconstruct.

In a recent study of Saussure, David Holdcroft argues that there are good reasons for rejecting his principle. Holdcroft distinguishes two theses both so original to Saussure that he could and did mix them up:

> T_1 The value of a linguistic item is determined by the set of syntagmatic and associative relations that it enters into with other items in a *langue*.
>
> T_2 In a language there are only differences without positive terms.

Saussure maintains both, and sometimes seems to suggest that T_2 follows from T_1, which is not so. That is the first of three claims Holdcroft makes about these theses:

1. T_1 and T_2 are logically independent; in particular T_2 does not follow from T_1.
2. T_1 is a thesis to which post-Saussurean structural linguistics is deeply committed, while there is no such commitment to T_2.
3. T_2 is very doubtful. Not only are some syntagmatic and associative relations not entirely negative differences; some are not even differential at all. So while "structuralist and post-structuralist philosophers often cite [T_2] as one of Saussure's major insights," in doing so "they have tried to build on one of the most opaque parts of Saussure's theory, and one, moreover, which the actual practice of structural linguistics does not presuppose."[22]

Since a given signified is different from every other element in a *langue*, "it is difficult to see how it would be graspable if its characterization depended only on differences." Linguistic value would be so unsystematic, depending on so many seemingly pointless differences (*vacillation/crustacean*), that "we should be adrift in a sea of differences without any principle of relevance."[23] Holdcroft claims that only when the differences in question are specifically oppositions does difference delimit and reciprocally determine the semantic identity of a linguistic sign (Saussure's *signifié*). Not all differences are oppositional. A tarpaulin is different from beef, but *tarpaulin/beef* are not opposing terms. I learn nothing (or very little) about of the significance of *Monday* by learning that is not a pungent condiment, not a carnivore, not rasping or friable. The case is otherwise with its difference from *Wednesday* and *weekend*. Only where differences are specifically oppositional does reciprocal delimitation take place. Yet if the principle of difference is really a principle of opposition, it cannot have the generality Saussure claims; for by no means all the terms of a language are related oppositionally. There are part-whole relations (*collar/shirt*), kind/member relations (*flower/peony*), and other instances where reciprocal opposition plays no role in the determination of semantic identity.

If the principle of difference is valid only when limited to specifically oppositional difference, then it cannot be "the absolutely final law of language." Yet not only must difference be limited; it even loses what originality it may have seemed to have in semantic fields where it remains determinative. Opposition involves a pair of terms (*red/green, male/female,* etc.) situated in a common field where despite their difference they are in a more original way signs of the same. Thus for instance the opposed terms *red/green* signify differences of color, but the very possibility of these differences presupposes that there is a more primordial respect in which the different significations are the same: both signify color. Unlike what is simply different (*emulsion/fez*), oppositions delimit a unified field of sameness, a logical space whose internal relations they systematically articulate. Where two terms are opposed they are at the same time and more deeply the same, and the relation between them cannot be entirely negative: "the specification of the similarity [should] count as a positive feature."[24] Difference, as opposition, is therefore subordinate to sameness, delimited by the more primordial forms of self-identical being (being colored, being animate, etc.) which make oppositions possible.

In sum: Saussure's principle is valid only when restricted to properly opposed terms, and once so restricted the differences in question are neither entirely negative nor anywhere original. The conclusion to draw may seem to be that the principle of difference cannot have anything like the significance some of Saussure's remarks suggest. But I draw a more qualified conclusion. Holdcroft's argument brings out the tension there is in Saussure between the principle of difference and the idea of *langue* as "a grammatical system existing potentially in every brain."[25] These are irreconcilable. But it does not follow that it is the principle of difference which one must question. One might equally well maintain that verbal meaning is differential through and through and reject Saussure's linguistics, his syncrhonic system and his cerebral *méchanisme de la langue*.

Derrida clearly does not accept the limitation of difference to opposition:

> But what happens *before* the difference becomes opposition in
> the trait, or *without* its doing so? And what if there were not
> even a *becoming* here? For *becoming* has perhaps always had as
> its concept this determination of difference as opposition.[26]

Holdcroft may assume Saussure was right about at least this much· How·
ever obscure and incomplete the concept of *langue* may be, languages
are nevertheless synchronic systems somehow represented in the brain.
For what does his argument come to? Were Saussure's principle really
unlimited and original, then "we should be adrift on a sea of differences
without any principle of relevance." And what is the precise critical force
of this remark? That languages would be labyrinths lacking the sys-
tematicity presupposed by their representation in a finite list of rules,
rules that speakers internalize, enabling them to make infinite use of finite means. In other words, were difference really unlimited and original, languages simply would not exist, at least not if languages are
anything like what many philosophers and linguists since Saussure have
assumed they are.

But is this conception of a language really so certain? a proven
result of modern linguistic science? The picture of language as the im-
plementation of a synchronic formal structure or a system of rules has
attracted skepticism from the beginning of "modern" linguistics. Let me
briefly notice four other skeptics, before returning to Derrida.

1. One of the earliest and still most penetrating criticisms of Saussure came from the circle around Bakhtin in the Soviet Union in the late
1920s. In a work Bakhtin may or may not have written (published under
the name of his colleague Vološinov in 1929), Saussure is criticized for
"assuming a special kind of discontinuity between the history of language and the system of language (i.e., language in its ahistorical, synchronic dimension)." For Vološinov/Bakhtin, this entire approach is
misguided. Languages are not "systems" and the use of language is not
the deployment of what are recognizably the same units; whatever sameness there may be in linguistic signs is unimportant. "What is important
for the speaker about a linguistic form is not that it is a stable and always
self-equivalent signal, but that it is an always changeable and adaptable
sign." "The basic task of understanding does not at all amount to recognizing the linguistic form used by the speaker as the familiar, 'that very
same,' form. . . . It amounts to understanding its novelty and not to recognizing its identity." The constituent factor for the linguistic sign is
therefore "not at all its self-identity as signal but its specific variability;
and the constituent factor for understanding linguistic forms is not rec-

ognition of 'the same thing' but understanding in the proper sense of the word, i.e., orientation in the particular, given context."[27]

What Bakhtin says of semiotics applies mutatis mutandis to the semiology of Saussure: "semiotics prefers to deal with the transmission of a ready-made message by means of a ready-made code, whereas, in living speech, messages are, strictly speaking, created for the first time in the process of transmission, and ultimately there is no code." Bakhtin pointed out that the linguists' common language (language "itself," not *parole*, performance or historical practice) "is never given but in fact always ordained."[28] That is certainly true of Saussure. When the latter says that amid the disparate mass of facts involved in *langage* linguistic structure (*langue*) "stands out like a well-defined entity," it is a stipulation or a wish but not an established fact. Saussure distinguishes *langue* from *parole* in order to say that while *parole* is just patter, just people saying what they happen to, *langue* can be studied as a synchronic structure. Saussure did not discover this structure or prove that it exists; he posits its experience a priori and says that it *has* to exist (if linguistics is to be a science).

2. Wittgenstein would have no use for Saussure's distinction between *langue* and *parole*. A language game is nothing like a *langue;* playing one is not the "performance" that deploys a formal system in *parole;* any "rules" that may govern what is done are historically conditioned and socially reproduced norms of behavior, and there is nothing essentially "linguistic" about the language games, no structural features or specific functions by which we may know them all to be instances of language. Indeed, there is no such thing as language "itself." Where there is language one finds "a complicated network of similarities, overlapping and criss-crossing: sometimes overall similarities, sometimes similarities of detail." But there is nothing that is always the same, nothing that *must* be present if there is language at all. Referring to his earlier *Tractatus Logico-Philosophicus*, Wittgenstein says, "what we call 'sentence' and 'language' has not the formal unity that I had imagined, but is [a] family of structures more or less related to one another." Language is the language games, a heterogeneous ensemble of conventional practices.[29]

It has to be said, however, that Wittgenstein's thought about language games and forms of life shows no inclination to connect the collapse of synchronic formalism and the opening up of language to practice with the social, political, economic, and rhetorical differences of power which prevail there. It were as if he saw no interesting connection between the "agreement" indispensable to communication or the normativity it presupposes (section 242), and the ethically sensitive, often problematic political relationships of people bound to one another by the intersubjectivity of speech and reply, reproducing and extending prevailing yet contingent norms for the use of language.

3. Roy Harris looks into this more closely. "Saussure in the end failed to see that the 'work' plausibly attributable to any internal linguistic machinery will depend on the work already done by external machinery in society . . . a system of social control capable of maintaining a high degree of linguistic conformity."[30] The campaigns on behalf of "standard" French, "standard" English, etc. waged from the latter eighteenth century were crucial for this development. Where Quintilian and the grammarians of antiquity were educators of a small elite, in the European eighteenth century grammar too had its revolution. *Everybody* should receive the benefits of "correct" language. These efforts contributed profoundly to a "normalizing" of European language practices by militant intervention against "non-standard" forms, attacking social differences at the root of the language practices which sustain them. Harris writes:

> prescriptivist programmes of grammar for the people were in fact successful. By the time Saussure died [1913] they had contributed to linguistic standardisation on a scale Europe had not seen since the days of the Roman empire. Local dialects were everywhere in decline, their eventual demise hastened by educational syllabuses based on the national language. Regional literary traditions were dead or dying, those who strove to maintain them increasingly stigmatised as quaint rustics, out of touch with the modern world. Europe's apparently relentless progress toward national linguistic uniformity itself reinforced prescriptivism, which in turn accelerated that progress.[31]

It is hollow for contemporary linguists to proclaim their anti-prescriptivist stance; for the very possibility of their investigations, the source of those "linguistic intuitions" upon which they rely for evidence of the structures they postulate, is sullied by a prescriptivist history which worked (and continues to work) to make language practice uniform and to *induce* those congruent intuitions by social discipline. A linguistic intuition is an artifact; it is as historical as Gothic architecture, the novel, vending machines, or patriarchy. By the time the world was ready for a "structural" linguistics, European language practices had had more than a millennium to beat themselves into the shapes of the grammarian, which the "generative" grammarians then rediscovered in the brain. But the normativity we experience in language is historical, not structural; it is a matter of historically precipitated normative forms, produced and maintained by asymmetrical differences of social power, above all, those centered around pedagogic institutions and practices.

4. Donald Davidson has advanced the curious claim that "there is no such thing as a language."

> In linguistic communication nothing corresponds to a linguistic
> competence as often described; that is, . . . there is no such
> thing as a language, not if a language is anything like what
> many philosophers and linguists have supposed. There is there-
> fore no such thing to be learned, mastered, or born with. We
> must give up the idea of a clearly defined shared structure
> which language-users acquire and then apply to cases.[32]

Davidson's argument begins with the apparently marginal phenomenon of malaprops. What interests him is that "the hearer has no trouble understanding a speaker in the way the speaker intends." When Mrs. Malaprop commends a nice derangement of epitaphs, her interlocutors understand her (as she intended) to have commended a nice arrangement of epithets, even though nothing about the past use of "derangement" or "epithet" prepares them for this interpretation. Davidson regards this as evidence of an ability to interpret another speaker *despite* what one has previously heard or despite the other's flagrant violation of any rule that may have guided past interpretations. Obviously less marginal phenomena like new proper names or new words of any kind which, provided informal contextual clues, are understood on first hearing suggest the same conclusion. Our ability to understand one another's speech seems to be independent of internalized rules, generative grammar, or even a common language. "What interpreter and speaker share, to the extent that communication succeeds, is . . . not a language governed by rules or conventions known to speaker and interpreter in advance; [and] what the speaker and interpreter know in advance is not (necessarily) shared, and so is not a language governed by shared rules or conventions."[33]

As is well known, Davidson's constant point of departure in the philosophy of language is Tarski's work on the concept of truth in formal languages.[34] After Tarski it is difficult to assume that the systematic inferential patterns in which truth-value is conserved in linguistic behavior, patterns which constitute the subject matter of logic, depend on or imply anything more than patterns found in the metalanguage in which a truth-predicate is defined. What Davidson finds striking about Tarski's procedure for defining such a predicate is "not that the phrase 'is true' can be replaced, for that can be the point of definition; what is striking is that it is not replaced by anything else, semantic or otherwise." This is striking because it implies that logically distinct truths (e.g., "Snow is white" and "Grass is green") are not differentiated *ontologically* by differences in the beings whose being would make them true. If "Snow is white" and "Grass is green" are different truths, it is because of *intralinguistic* differences of inferential relationship; it is not because different beings "make" these sentences true. "Nothing," Davidson says, "no *thing*, makes sentences and theories true."[35]

In a certain respect, Saussure's principle of difference has a comparable implication, namely, that, contrary to a long tradition in Western reflection on language, verbal meaning and all its associated values (including reference and truth) are *indifferent* to the putative existence of what is not itself more verbal meaning. The effects of verbal meaning are effects of difference and do not evince the presence of anything that is emphatically not more of the same. Saussure limits the originality of differences to the specifically semiological, where he posits a totality in which differences are contained and synchronically structured. Yet as I mentioned, the principle of difference is itself a reason against this traditional subordination of signs to a fully present nonsign, even if it were the synchronic totality of *la langue*. But relieving the principle of difference of this a priori constraint undermines the distinction between language as a synchronic system and culture as historically contingent practice. The differences which give the occasional sign what value it has "are themselves *effects*."

> They have not fallen from the sky fully formed and are no
> more inscribed in a *topos noëtos* than they are prescribed in the
> grey matter of the brain. . . . differences [are]"historical" from
> the outset and in each of their aspects. (*M*, 11)

> differences . . . [are not] inscribed once and for all in a closed
> system, a static structure that a synchronic and taxonomic op-
> eration could exhaust. Differences are the effects of transfor-
> mations, and from this vantage the theme of *différance* is
> incompatible with the static, synchronic, taxonomic, ahistoric
> motifs in the concept of *structure*.[36]

To say that differences are the effects of transformations is to say that language is the transformation of language, language practice the transformation of its own past. It does not exist except where it has already existed; it "begins" with repetition, which is a way of saying that it is through and through historical, at no point made to be what it is by nature. A synchronic science of language as it has been conceived since Saussure is therefore not to be anticipated. Once difference is unlimited, once no fully present not-itself-a-sign is posited to limit the differences of signs, then all the careful distinctions (system/content, arbitrary/motivated, convention/nature, text/context) that made the idea of language "itself" (or a science thereof) seem intelligible are relieved of their reason, deconstructed.

Truth in Signs

On an unlimited interpretation of the principle of difference, reference and truth are as indifferent as any symbolic value to something that would just "be there," present, durably identical to itself, indifferent to the speech or mind that would copy it. Now while this may disappoint one who anticipates the very disclosure of what is, it obviously does not mean that truth does not exist. Derrida writes:

> the value of truth (and all those values associated with it) is never contested or destroyed in my writings, but only reinscribed in more powerful, larger, more stratified contexts . . . interpretative contexts (that is, within relations of force that are always differential—for example, socio-political-institutional—but even beyond these determinations) that are relatively stable, sometimes apparently almost unshakable.
> (L, 146)[37]

I take the point to be that for truth-value (and associated values like reference, translation, relevance, implication, objectivity, etc.) to "be determinate" in any case, depends on nothing that is indifferent to the asymmetrical relationships of power that work to settle texts in contexts. The only "constitution" of meaning, the only "determination" of reference, the only "making true" is the work of productive powers which evaluate these values and make selected judgments circulate, *passing* for true, relevant, implied, objective, etc. This *passing for true* is the only "determination" there is for truth-values. But it is a contingent practice of evaluation, and not a "transcendental" constitution, of truth. Like Davidson, though with a deeper appreciation of its implications,

Derrida can say that nothing—no *thing*—makes a sentence or theory true, not even a social thing like a practice, or a relative thing like a relationship of power.

Derrida's work may in a sense not contest or destroy truth's value. But if there is nothing more *to* the occasional truth than the fact of its passing in practice, if nothing but the historically relative stability of contextualizing practice *makes* a truth true, if this "making" is not a transcendental "act" of constitution but a historically conditioned *effect* of social power, a *making-pass* (for true, probable, objective, etc.), then a different perspective opens on truth. The "value of truth" can and must be "reinscribed" where Derrida said it belongs: "in more powerful, larger, more stratified . . . interpretative contexts"; in the institutional-social practice where it always has been anyway, even when philosophers preferred to avert their eyes from time, history, contingency, and dream of True Being. And since it was this very Being whose presence was supposed to distinguish the mimetic, vicegerent Truth of the Philosophers from falsity and mere opinion, one should conclude that there is no philosophically important difference between what "really is true" and what passes for true in the framework of discursive practice.

Derrida writes, "there is something political in the very project of attempting to fix the content of utterances."

> This is inevitable; one cannot do anything, least of all speak, without determining (in a manner that is not only theoretical but practical and performative) a context. Such experience is always political because it implies, insofar as it involves determination, a certain type of non-"natural" relationship to others . . . non-natural relations of power that by essence are mobile and founded upon complex conventional structures.

"Once this generality and this a priori structure have been recognized," he adds,

> the question can be raised, not whether a politics is implied (it always is), but which politics is implied in . . . a [given] practice of contextualization. This you can then go on to analyze, but you cannot suspect it, much less denounce it, except on the basis of another contextual determination every bit as political. In short, I do not believe that any neutrality is possible here. (*L*, 136, 147)

In these remarks Derrida seems to find his way to a point that Foucault insisted on. While language practices are inseparable from social power-relationships—while as Foucault said "it is in discourse that power and knowledge are joined together"[38]—power is not something that is necessarily wicked or irrational. It is not always on the other side of freedom, or objectivity, or truth. Yet this does oblige one to question the assumption that the only way truth might enter into the tangible circuits of social power and political control is by first becoming a mere passing-for-true which is really false, as if truth "itself" could not fail to be, if not the lamp of liberation, at least neutral among parties. To the contrary; as Foucault remarks, "truth is a thing of this world: it is produced only by virtue of multiple forms of constraint. And it induces regular effects of power."[39]

I see no reason why Derrida cannot agree with Foucault that the distribution of truth-values over statements, their routine penetration of practical reasoning through private consultation and public communications, and the effects of this (whether global or carefully focused) on how subjects envision their options and choose and act, are effects of the asymmetrical differences of power which divide us and govern our conduct. When we consider the ethical character and political implications of inquiry and knowledge, and of all the practices and interests interwoven with these, it cannot be a matter of no importance who is said to need or lack the truth and who is said to have it.

"I ask questions of philosophy," Derrida says, "and naturally this supposes a certain identification, a certain translation of myself into the body of a philosopher. But I don't feel that that's where I'm situated."[40] Not only is the feeling different; the very questions his work raises deliberately exceed the limits within which academic discipline tries to control intellectual practice, in philosophy and elsewhere:

> deconstruction (I use this word for the sake of rapid convenience, though it is a word I have never liked and one whose fortune has disagreeably surprised me) [is] not primarily a matter of philosophical contents, themes or theses, philosophemes, poems, theologemes or ideologemes, but especially and inseparably meaningful frames, institutional structures, pedagogical or rhetorical norms, the possibilities of law, of authority, of evaluation and of representation.[41]

Even if there is no time whose thought is not governed by what it does not know, there will always be a point to the effort to exceed the limits of what passes for known—the effort to think differently, instead of legitimating what is already known. To work through Derrida is to work through some of the deeper historical limitations of the present—not toward the transcendent unlimited, of course, but toward different delimitations, different questions, and priorities, and toward different practice, in philosophy, in the universities, in English, and elsewhere.

2

Derrida's
Ethical Re-Turn

Richard Kearney

A recurring concern with "otherness" has been a central feature of Derrida's writing since the early sixties. This originally took the form of an epistemological contrast between a metaphysics of "presence" and all that escapes or subverts it—what Derrida calls "alterity." Derrida's two early deconstructive commentaries on Husserl—*Introduction to the Origin of Geometry* (1962), and *Speech and Phenomena* (1967)—and subsequent collections such as *Writing and Difference* (1967), *Of Grammatology* (1967), *Dissemination* (1972), and *Margins of Philosophy* (1972), are all representative of this epistemological version of deconstruction. But a certain shift seems to occur in Derrida's writing after 1972 marked by a more pronounced emphasis on the question of ethical responsibility. It is not my intention here to try to locate this shift in terms of some event in Derrida's biography (e.g., the important break with the *Tel Quel* group in 1972), but to follow its implications in Derrida's own thinking. I should also make clear from the outset that I am not claiming that Derrida underwent some kind of Pauline conversion to a particular moral system of rights and wrongs. When I speak of "ethics" I do so not in this sense of morality, but in the general sense hinted at by Derrida himself when he talks about that "singular responsibility without which there would be no morality, law or politics."[1]

I

If I were to phrase this shift in terms of Derrida's relation to two of his most influential contempories I'd be tempted to say that his later writing supplements a Heideggerian resolve to deconstruct metaphysics with a Levinasian attention to the ethical demands of the other. The dimension of alterity is now seen as a trace of the irreducible other as well as an undecidable surplus of *Sein* over *Seiendes*. But if it can be shown that Derrida supplements Heidegger with Levinas in this way, such a turn should be construed less as a rupture than a return: a reworking of the same in other terms. And here Derrida remains faithful to the key Heideggerian trope of the *Kehre* or winding twist on a mountain path, which brings what was tacitly there to closer attention. What Derrida sees after his "turn" on the winding path of thought is, however, different from what Heidegger saw—or at least represents a different way of seeing. For where Heidegger reads the *Es Gibt* of Being as a presence in absence, an unconcealment in concealment, Derrida reads it as amongst other things, *une trace de l'autre.*

It is all a question ultimately, of who or what does the giving. And how we inquire into the manner of such giving—ethically or epistemologically. In a note to his 1986 lecture to the Hebrew University of Jerusalem, entitled "Comment ne pas parler," Derrida offers some hints. "The thinking of the gift opens the space where being and time give themselves and give rise to thinking," he writes. And he adds that questions relating to this matter are those which "expressly orient all the texts which I have published since 1972 or thereabouts."[2] The key question, it would seem, is the question of the other-who-gives; and it is surely significant that Derrida's Jerusalem lecture is published in a collection of his essays bearing the subtitle, "Inventions de l'autre." Derrida is aware of a crucial ethical dilemma underlying this whole question—is it the other-who-gives who invents me or is it I who invents the other-who-gives? "Invention of the other," as Derrida himself puts it, "is it the absolute initiative for which the other is responsible and accountable? Or is it rather the other that I imagine as a retention of my psyche, my soul, my mirror image?" ("Comment," 587).

It is not that Derrida wishes to break with a Heideggerean line of questioning. On the contrary, Derrida's note on the thinking of the gift is part of a commentary on Heidegger's famous maxim from *Zeit und Sein*—"*Es gibt Zeit. Es gibt Sein.*" What is different about Derrida's thinking here and in other texts after 1972, is that another dimension—the ethical—is added to the ontologico-epistemological concerns dominating his early writings. This ethical inflection is witnessed in a wide variety of later essays dealing with the role of alterity and responsibility in: (a) religion (*Schibboleth* [1986], "Of an Apocalyptic Tone" [1984], "Circonfession" [1991]); (b) education (the texts on GREPH and the Collège International de Philosophie in *Du Droit à la Philosophie* [1990]); (c) law ("Force of Law 'The Mystical Foundation of Authority,' " the analysis of the American Declaration of Independence in *Otobiographies* [1984]); and (d) politics ("Le Dernier mot du racism" [1983]; "Admiration de Nelson Mandela" [1986]; "No Apocalypse, Not Now" [1984]; or "Art against Apartheid" in *Critical Inquiry* [1986], where he actually claims that deconstruction can take the form of "active interventions that transform contexts"). While Derrida never abandons the Heideggerean project of deconstructing metaphysics, these later texts testify to a determination to reread the deconstructive turn in the light of an ethical re-turn—or if you prefer, to reread Heidegger in the light of Levinas.

Other commentators have already made a claim for the compatibility of deconstruction and ethics. The most cogent of such claims, in my view, is to be found in Christopher Norris's *Derrida* (1987). Here is a passage outlining his argument:

> Deconstruction has been wrongly understood by those who regard it as a species of out-and-out hermeneutic license, a justification for indulging all manner of interpretative games. . . . Derrida cannot be understood as simply going along with this anti-enlightenment drift in the discourse of post-structuralism. . . . Only by pressing the aporias (of textual readings of phenomenology, structuralism, metaphysics, etc.) to the limits of conceptual explanation can philosophy begin to perceive what lies beyond. And this—as Derrida argues—will take us into the domain of ethics, rather than epistemology. There is an ethical dimension to Derrida's writings which has yet to be made good by most of his commentators. . . . For Derrida, as for Levinas, there is an ethical injunction to challenge philosophy on terms which offer the maximum resistance to its powers of recuperative grasp. And this challenge can only be sustained through a close and reasoned engagement with the texts where philosophy stakes its claims to truth.[3]

II

The ethics of deconstruction was a subject I discussed with Derrida in a dialogue which took place in 1982.[4] When I put to him the common charge of moral nihilism he answered that "deconstruction is not an enclosure in nothingness but an openness towards the other" (*Dialogues*, 124). And in response to my related accusation that "deconstruction is so obsessed with the play of difference that it ultimately ends up indifferent to everything," Derrida strenuously rejected the caricature of deconstruction as a "gratuitous chess game with a combination of signs closed up in language as in a cave" (ibid.). He went on to insist that deconstruction seeks not to abandon ethics but to resituate and reinscribe its key concepts of the self and other; and, so doing, to "reevaluate the indispensable notion of responsibility" (ibid., 121, 125).[5]

The ethical implications of deconstruction are not, Derrida makes plain, something injected into his writing *after* some kind of sudden conversion in the early seventies. They were there from the very outset, albeit somewhat masked by the initial emphasis of Derrida's work on questions of epistemology and metaphysics. But they were there nonetheless, in however problematic a manner, and were especially evident in his early essays on the Jewish authors, Levinas and Jabes, in *Writing and Difference*. In these writings, however, Derrida is of the view that the language of ethics is intrinsically compromised by the language of ontology. An ethics of alterity and infinity, as promoted by someone like Levinas, cannot be removed, he believes, from an ontology of totality and violence. The language of ethics and the language of ontology presuppose and precondition each other. Or, as Derrida puts it, "pure nonviolence, like pure violence, is a contradictory concept."[6] This is not to say that nonviolence must always be preceded by violence, only that it cannot lay claim to some immaculately conceived origin entirely free from violence. There is no such thing as an original peace, any more than there is an original violence. There is always a "double origin," as Derrida terms it in his essay on Jabes; for peace (like war) cannot be located in a specific spatiotemporal moment, prior or posterior to another, and recuperable in terms of memory, representation, or transcendental analysis.

Derrida's deconstructive logic of both/and/neither/nor would here seem to be undermining Levinas' statement in *Totality and Infinity* (1961) that just as peace precedes war, the ethical relation precedes the language of ontology, e.g., concept, intentionality, representation, and system. Over and against Levinas, Derrida is asserting that "peace is made only in a certain silence which is determined and protected by the violence of speech" (*WD*, 148). Levinas cannot shake off the Heideggerean ghost. "No ethics in Levinas' sense," writes Derrida, "can be opened without the thought of Being" (*WD*, 127). In short, if the ethical relation presupposes language, and language is the ontological medium of comprehension (which for Levinas belongs to the "violent play of the same" hostile to the transcendence of the face), then ethics is always already implicated in violence, though never of course *pure* violence (*WD*, 116). Whence Derrida's controversial conclusion—"one never escapes the economy of war" (*WD*, 148).

While the above line of argument displays Derrida's deconstructive approach to the logocentric structure of moral dualism, it does not mean that he is any less sympathetic to Levinas' promotion of an ethics of alterity. His disagreement with Levinas, it seems to me, is on epistemological rather than ethical grounds. This appears quite obvious in our 1982 dialogue where he acknowledges that "deconstruction is, in itself, a positive response to an alterity which necessarily calls, summons or motivates it. Deconstruction is therefore vocation—a response to a call" (*Dialogues*, 118). This call is prephilosophical in that it cannot, as Derrida puts it, be "detected with the aid of a philosophical lamp" (ibid.). But it is not pre-ethical if we are to take Levinas' understanding of ethics as a "preconceptual experience of provocation by the other." Indeed, the following statement by Derrida in our dialogue might well have been penned by Levinas himself: "The other precedes philosophy and necessarily invokes and provokes the subject before any genuine questioning can begin. It is in this rapport with the other that affirmation expresses itself" (ibid.).

But if we are to believe Derrida's claim that deconstruction is not a matter of amoral indifference and negation, surely we are entitled to ask what, if anything, it *affirms*? It is here that we may usefully examine some of Derrida's statements on the role of responsibility to the other in education, politics, and religion. The deconstruction of logocentric metaphysics takes on less academic proportions when it is applied to the more engaged critiques of what Derrida terms phallogocentrism, a principle which informs many of our institutions and traditions. Citing a number of examples from psychoanalysis, feminism, and the literary avant-garde, Derrida speaks of a "mutation" which cannot be thematically objectified but which is "bringing about such a radical change in our understanding of the world that a return to the former logocentric philosophies of mastery, possession, totalization or certitude may soon be unthinkable" (*Dialogues*, 121). And though he remains skeptical of the fashionable liberal terminology of historical progress, especially with respect to liberation movements—including the women's movement— he is prepared to recognize the "enormous deconstructive import of the feminine as an uprooting of our phallogocentric culture" (ibid.). It is hard to deny some element of ethical evaluation behind such a recognition even if Derrida would surely be loathe in this context to apply the traditional moral dualism of good and evil.

III

A similar scruple to undermine the structures of logocentric sameness or totality in the name of the "other" also informs Derrida's writing about writing. Here again he launches a campaign against the traditional meta-physical dualism separating philosophy and literature, recommending instead a "crossing over of each into the other giving rise to something else, some other site" (ibid., 122). He cites the apocalyptic impact of catachresis as a deconstructive form of rhetoric which signals "another kind of writing"; one which stakes out the faults and deviations of lan-guage and which may even mark a certain "monstrous mutation" where otherness can break through the "normative precedents" of logocen-trism. Such attentiveness to disclosures of alterity is surely an ethical form of vigilance? How else are we to understand the admission that "deconstruction is always deeply concerned with the 'other' of lan-guage"; or that "the critique of logocentrism is above all else the search for the 'other' and the 'other of language' "? (ibid., 123).

It is certainly in the discussion of writing—or what we might call "poetics"—that Derrida's concern for the ethics of alterity first appears; even though, as we shall see, this concern takes more explicit form in his later writings on education, apartheid, law, and religion. Writing is ethi-cal for Derrida to the extent that a literary text is one which remains structurally open to the other. The signature of the author always re-quires the countersignature of the reader. This relay of signatures dis-closes how the authorial subject of the text is already beholden to his/her other. The author always inscribes himself in relation to the other. And this basic question of literary answerability—of reader to author and vice versa— entails the corollary question of ethical responsibility. Derrida puts this in the quasi-biblical terms of a "mutual indebtment" or "covenant" (*alliance*), whereby each of the correspondents, author and reader, inherits responsibility for the life or death of the other. The reader, for example, can live on after the death of the author, "in mem-ory of the other, bearing the mourning of the other."[7] But the text also calls for ethical vigilance in determining for us the specific singularity of each reading: a singularity which respects the alterity of the text as law, as something beyond the mere whim or fancy of interpretation (*Der-*

ridabase, 175). The literary text, Derrida admits, raises a fundamental ethical and political question insofar as it inscribes a law which says *"tu dois,"* and thus necessitates a response, a summons, a "yes" (*Derridabase,* 181–82). Whether the "yes" be that of Zarathustra, Molly Bloom, or a prophet in the desert, in each case it is a response to a voice that calls to be heard and answered. But because this law of answerability belongs to writing, it is always informed by an element of humility and humor. Or to follow the argument of Derrida's disciple of literary deconstruction, Hillis Miller, an "ethics of reading" results from the fact that deconstruction exposes the text as the site of aporetic conflict between incommensurable readings, thereby placing the reader in the situation of having to respond with an interpretation even though he/she can no longer know in advance what a "true" interpretation is.[8]

In soliciting an ethical response to otherness, the literary text enables us to question the prevailing dogmas about what is ethical (see *Derridabase,* 181–82). In this sense, literary writing puts the dominant language of moral and political institutions into question. It reminds us that all moral principles are impure in some fundamental sense, never totally adequate or absolute, never wholly certain about what is absolute good and what absolute evil.[9] And this in turn raises the question of judgment. Can we set ourselves up as final arbiters if, as an ethics of reading teaches us, every ethic of good and evil remains inherently undecidable? (see *Derridabase,* 189). Can an ethics of action sustain the ambiguity of this "non-ethical ethical opening of the ethical" which Derrida identifies with literary responsibility? (*G,* 202).

Derrida holds fast to the ethical "effects" of textual deconstruction. The traces of otherness in the text—which Derrida's analyses of "translation," "signature," "gift," "debt," and "promise" disclose—signals an operation of *différance* with inherently ethical implications. *Différance* is another word for that otherness of the text which we respond to when we say "yes"—yes to a gift which precedes our choice of meanings, just as language was first received by the first mortal before it was ever spoken or written by him. The act of writing or reading is a reminder that language is always already given, shot through with the trace of another who has already been there or promises to come. Once again, Derrida employs a quasireligious terminology, and while he states there is no necessity to equate this gift of language with a god, he does say that "god" is one of the names for this event (see *Derridabase,* 215). The reader or recipient of language is never a unique originator of language any more than the author is. There is no pure origin of language—or, by extension, of law or society. Language is a web of traces where the subject—writer or reader—is always beholden to another who has given, called, promised, demanded. In short, writing is ethical because it is a site of intertextual alliance between author and reader, because it foregrounds the disclosure of alterity.

IV

If Derrida first discloses the ethics of alterity in his deconstructive poetics of *writing,* he pursues it in his later commentaries on *law* and *religion.* Derrida comes to the question of law via the question of foundation. What, he asks, is the legitimating origin (or original legitimation) of our laws? Whether one is inquiring about the founding principle of a university, a state, or a legal constitution, the problem of legitimation is the same. And this problem can be stated as follows : the foundation of a law is always outside the law thus founded. The principle of foundation cannot found itself. Or as Derrida puts it in his deconstructive analysis of the foundation of the American Constitution in *Otobiographies,* the origin of every state is in some sense illegitimate. It arises from a *coup de force* (which is also an act of inscription or writing). The foundation of any and every law is marked by an originary contamination.

The claim that the first inscription of law is intermingled with illegitimacy can itself be seen as a certain ethic of impurity—that is, an ethic which refuses all purist claims to some founding unitary absolute. And it is just such an ethic that Derrida explores in his controversial text, "Force of Law: The 'Mystical Foundation of Authority.' "[10] It is here that Derrida offers his most strenuous response to date to the charge that deconstruction is unethical or antiethical. The incompatibility of deconstruction and justice is, he retorts, only apparent. And to support his contention he cites a number of his own texts which he argues have been informed by an ethical concern for justice. These include the various texts devoted to Levinas and the relation of violence and metaphysics; to Hegel and the philosophy of right (e.g., in *Glas*); to the origin of law in Kafka's *Vor dem Gesetz* (*Devant la loi*); and to the legitimating power of constitutions (in *Otobiographies* and "Admiration de Nelson Mandela"). And he adds, furthermore, that most of his other writings also testify to an underlying concern for justice. "It goes without saying," he writes, "that the discourses on double affirmation, the gift beyond exchange and distribution, the undecidable, the incommensurable or the incalculable, or on singularity, difference and heterogeneity are

also, through and through, at least obliquely discourses on justice"
("Force," 929).

Derrida states that the purpose of "Force of Law" is to problematize the whole question of legitimation—and, by extension, of evaluation
(ibid., 931). And his main claim is that while deconstruction appears not
to address the problem of justice, it has in fact been doing just this all
along—albeit indirectly. The reason it has been indirect is, Derrida explains, because it is impossible to speak directly about justice, to thematize and objectify it without betraying it.

But how is one to speak of an ethical authority or truth of law? If
the search for an original grounding of law is itself groundless, if indeed
the very opposition between foundation and antifoundation is to put
aside as an unhelpful metaphysical dualism, then how is one to avoid the
confusion that the origin of law is in fact "mystical"? (ibid., 943). Derrida
actually uses the term "mystical" to name the "aporia or abyss opened
up by the deconstructability of law." But while he is prepared to concede
that law is deconstructable—to the extent that it claims to be founded on
something, e.g., conventions, rules, norms, or nature itself—this is not
so of justice. Justice is beyond such claims and considerations for Derrida. Justice is deconstruction and deconstruction is justice (ibid., 945).

Why? Because justice is the experience of aporia, of the impossible, of the undecidable. Moreover, says Derrida, a desire for justice
whose structure would not be such an experience of aporia would have
no chance to be what it is, namely a "*call* for justice." So how are we to
distinguish concretely between *law* and *justice*? Law, in contrast to justice, can be accounted for in terms of a good rule applied to a particular
case (i.e., what Kant would call a "determinant judgment"). Justice, on
the other hand, is incalculable by definition for it entails moments in
which the decision between just and unjust cannot be insured by a rule
(ibid., 947). Justice involves singularity. It concerns the "other as other"
in a unique situation, irreducible to principles of duty, rights, or objective law. In fact, what Derrida calls justice is very close to what Levinas
calls ethics, as would appear evident from his claim that "to address oneself to the other in the language of the other is, it seems the condition of
all possible justice" (ibid., 949). Derrida will return to this Levinasian
connection later in the essay.

To accept such a claim is to acknowledge that "deconstruction
calls for an increase in responsibility" (ibid.). Such an increased responsibility may well involve a momentary suspension, or even transgression,
of the traditional definitions of responsibility according to the criteria of
human law or conscience. Indeed, Derrida refers to it as an impossible

responsibility to the extent that it is never fulfilled or fulfillable. "In the end," he writes, "where will deconstruction find its force, its movement or its motivation, if not in this always unsatisfied appeal beyond the given determination of what we call, in determined contexts, justice, the possibility of justice?" (ibid., 957). In short, where the responsibility demanded by justice is infinite, incalculable, heterogenous, and inimical to rules and symmetry, that of law is statutory and stabilizable, it is a matter of legality and right calculable within a system of regulated codes and presentations (ibid., 959).

At this point Derrida explicitly invokes Levinas' ethical definition of justice in support of his own deconstructive approach. Such a definition is particularly relevant because of the "heterogenous relation to others, to the faces of otherness that govern me, whose infinity I cannot thematize and whose hostage I remain" (ibid.). Commenting on a section of Levinas' *Totality and Infinity*, titled "Truth and Justice," Derrida approvingly cites the author's equation of justice and ethics— " . . . the relation to others, that is to say, justice." Moreover, he identifies the proximity of such an ethics of justice to the Hebrew definition of sanctity as "the demand of the other": a demand which is a "practically infinite right," and whose asymmetry transcends the "concept of man" with its "rules of calculated proportions" (ibid.). As soon as such rules are operative, as they must be in constitutions and institutions, justice becomes law. The difficulty about this position is, of course, that the ethical demands of justice often require us to have recourse to law. The infinite demand of the other is almost invariably translated, at some point of action or interpretation, into the legal system of anonymous exchange, impartial distribution, and equal symmetry (ibid., 961f.). Incalculable justice requires us to calculate, and Derrida admits as much (ibid., 971). But even in those legal instances where the singular case of the "other" is to be applied to the universalizable code of the "same," there remains a crucial trace of justice. This Derrida identifies with the "undecidable." He writes:

> The undecidable is not merely the oscillation or tension between two decisions, it is the experience of that which, though heterogenous, foreign to the order of the calculable and the rule, it still obliged . . . to give itself up to the impossible decision while taking account of law and rules. A decision that didn't go through the ordeal of the undecidable would not be a free decision, it would only be the programmable application or unfolding of a calculable process. It might be legal, it would not be just. (Ibid., 963)

The fact is, however, that no decision is ever totally pure, wholly present to itself. No decision is unconditionally decidable. There is never an absolute legal decision, since an element of incalculable singularity always enters in. Nor is there ever an absolutely just decision, since some element of rule determination is always operative, even if it be as a past memory or future anticipation. All decisions are to some degree impure. The undecidable and the decidable are inextricably linked to each other.

The undecidable character of justice is, therefore, that which deconstructs from within any presumption of certainty when it comes to the criteriology of a legal decision. This is not to claim that legal decisions or judgments cannot be made; it is simply to allow for that moment of suspense whenever a rule is being applied to a singular event. For such an allowance is a matter of justice—an acknowledgment of otherness in sameness, of the extralegal in the legal. Derrida states his position on the justice of deconstruction in the following post-Kantian definition of the "idea of justice" as a primordial indebtedness to the other:

> The deconstruction of all presumption of all determinant certi-
> tude of a present justice, itself operates on the basis of an infi-
> nite "idea of justice," infinite because it is irreducible,
> irreducible because owed to the other, owed to the other, be-
> fore any contract, because it has come, the other's coming as
> the singularity that is always other. (Ibid., 965)

What Derrida is suggesting in this somewhat cryptic passage is that justice is the idea of a gift without exchange, of a relation to the other that is utterly irreducible to the normal rules of circulation, gratitude, recognition, or symmetry. And that is why it appears to imply a certain kind of "madness" or "mystique." Other names, perhaps misnomers, for deconstruction. Derrida locates this ethical relation (or nonrelation) of deconstruction at a prereflective level, where decisions are made in the name of justice. But such a level must be understood as prior to the emergence of an academic theoretical discipline called "law" or "morality." "Deconstruction is mad about this kind of justice," insists Derrida with aphoristic aptness. It is "mad about the desire for justice." And he adds, "this kind of justice which isn't law, is the very movement of deconstruction at work in law and the history of law in political history and history itself, before it even presents itself as the discourse that the academy or modern culture label 'deconstructionism' " (ibid., 965).

The precedents for this idea of justice are multiple. The "type" ranges from the messianic demand for a kingdom in the Jewish-Christian-Islamic tradition, to the Kantian regulative idea and the eschato-teleology of the Hegelian-Marxist revolution. While Derrida acknowledges these diverse instances he remains reserved. Noting the ethical motivation of such ideals of justice (i.e., that which "keeps us moving"), he notes a conflict between the fact that such ideals involve a period of "waiting" and the fact that justice itself—no matter how unpresentable and undecidable— is something which cannot *wait*. Derrida appreciates the urgency of ethics. And against those who charge deconstruction with indifference and inaction he insists that "a just decision is always required immediately, right away" (ibid., 967). Justice rends time and defies dialectics. It is a finite moment of precipitous urgency, which interrupts all the cognitive deliberation which precedes it. "The instant of decision is a madness," writes Derrida, in a phrase borrowed from Kierkegaard's reflections in *Either/Or*. It acts "in the night of non-knowledge and non-rule" (ibid.). All cognitive systems of truth are thus considered secondary to the demands of decision. But where Kierkegaard saw the ultimate decision as a movement leading beyond ethics to religion, Derrida remains closer to Levinas' notion that the ethical rapport with otherness is itself an act of holy madness—or "sanctity."

It is just here at the crucial moment of decision that ethical justice parts company with legal truth. Or, as Derrida puts—rephrasing Levinas' famous claim in *Totality and Infinity* that "truth presupposes justice"—*"la justice, y a que ça de vrai"* (ibid., 969). But if Derrida does not subscribe to Kierkegaard's subordination of ethics to religion, he does not reject the interest of religion in justice. Indeed, as a sort of link between Kierkegaard and Levinas he rehearses Walter Benjamin's view that justice without law, which respects the irreducible singularity of each situation over and above the requirements of universal reason, is another word for "God" (ibid., 1023). More specifically, it is the "God" of the Judaic Scriptures who "forbids all murder" and reveals that the worth of man is the "yet to come (*à-venir*) of justice," and that "what is sacred in his life is not his life (as vitalism or biologism hold) but the justice of his life" (ibid., 1029). It is this very demand for justice which, in Derrida's view, the final solution tried to eliminate. And this demand for justice is also a "mission to name" received by Jews from God. It is the "possibility of giving, inscribing, calling and recalling the name" (ibid., 1044–45).

V

We might summarize Derrida's argument by saying that the demand to name the unnameable, to decide the undecidable, resides at the very heart of the deconstructive idea of justice. And nowhere is it more manifest than in the fact that justice demands to be done immediately and yet is never reducible to a fully present moment, to a moment of full presence. Dogmatism and ideology are the results of worshipping the law for its own sake, or revering it as adequate to each singular decision that has to be made. They are temptations also for those messianic Marxists like Benjamin who are so eager to make the mystical idea of justice immediately present that they often ignore the finite historical conditions in which justice, as an ethical responsibility, is a task which always remains to be done (ibid., 1045). The temptation is equally present in the eschatological gestures of a thinker like Heidegger, whose determination to deconstruct metaphysics at all costs runs the risk of neglecting the ethical responsibility to the singular demands for justice made in each singular historical moment (ibid., 1045). And when Derrida reproaches Benjamin and Heidegger in this manner one cannot help feeling he is also issuing a subtle warning to himself.

Justice is something which is always demanded and never accomplished. And that is why the demand that justice be done *now* and the recognition that justice is always *still to be done*, always *à-venir*, are two sides of the same undecidable coin. Taking the example of the declaration of the universal rights of man, Derrida fully endorses the political struggle for concrete historical freedoms ("nothing seems less outdated," as he puts it, "than the classical emancipatory ideal" [ibid., 971]); but he equally appreciates that such struggles in the here and now of history are never fully realized. Politicization is interminable, concludes Derrida, even if it cannot, and should not, ever be total. "For each specific advance in politicization obliges me to reconsider and so to reinterpret the very foundations of law such as they had previously been calculated or delimited" (ibid.). The endless refounding and reforming of our legal and political institutions is an indispensable process spurred on by the irremissible and inalienable demand that justice remains to be done. "There is an *avenir* for justice and there is no justice except to the degree that some event is possible which, as event, exceeds calculation, rules, programs, anticipations and so forth. Justice as the experience of absolute alterity is unpresentable, but it is the chance of the event and the condition of history" (ibid.).

Derrida is prepared to accept, however, that there is good and bad eschatology. In our 1982 dialogue, Derrida concedes that "all genuine questioning is summoned by a certain type of eschatology, though it is impossible to define this eschatology in philosophical terms" (*Dialogues*, 119). He is even prepared to admit that "the style of (deconstructive) questioning as an exodus and dissemination in the desert might produce certain prophetic resonances" (ibid.). Derrida's rather surprising allusion here to prophetic eschatology is tentative, hypothetical, and even skeptical. He is clearly not embracing a theological affirmation of revealed biblical truths. At most, he is talking about a "rhetoric" of prophetic discourse which is shared, as he puts it, by "several other contemporary thinkers" (Levinas? De Man? Bloom? Hartman? Lyotard?). This is what he calls a certain "search for hope without hope" which might be considered by some—though he does not himself endorse the claim—to assume a certain "prophetic allure" (ibid.).

What does follow from this rather portentous observation is that deconstruction, as a rhetoric of pseudoprophetic exodus, can be related to a "politics of the emigré or exile" (ibid.). This involves a defense of the homeless or nomadic subject against the absolutist ideologies which victimize and scapegoat the "alien." It is, in Levinas' ethical terms, a defense of "infinity" against "totality." Or as Derrida puts it in *De l'esprit: Heidegger et la question*: "Nazism was not born in the desert."[11]

VI

Such an ethics of exodus is historically allied with the Jewish tradition, along with a special fascination for writing, exegesis, and eschatology. All are present, obliquely or openly, in Derrida's deconstructive approach. Moreover, Derrida's allegiance to this tradition is also manifest in his recurring treatment of the theme of circumcision—a wound word always open to, addressed to, answerable to, the other. Commenting on the line from the Jewish poet Paul Celan—"*Diesem/beschneide das Wort*"—Derrida writes:

> This word to be circumcised, to be circumcised for someone,
> on someone, this word which must therefore be given, and
> given once circumcised, to be understood as an open word. As
> a wound, you say. Yes and no. Open first as a door, open to
> the stranger, the other, the neighbor, the host or whoever.
> Doubtless to someone in the shape of an absolute future who
> will come, or more precisely who would come because this

avenir, which is *à-venir,* is a coming which must not be certified
or calculated.[12]

Not surprisingly, this theme of circumcision as a Jewish mark of dedica-
tion to the irreducible other is to reappear as a central theme in Derrida's autobiographical sketch, "Circonfession." [13]

But Derrida's fascination with the ethico-eschatological implications of revelation are not confined to his own Jewish background. He
also acknowledges the influence of this theme in the Christian Scriptures, and especially the gospel of St. John, which he analyzes in detail in
his conclusion to *D'un certain ton apocalyptique adopté naguère en
philosophie.*[14] Derrida devotes much attention here to the key terms of
prophetic eschatology—*"viens"* and *"à-venir."* And he explores the
ways in which such summons by, and on behalf of, the other can take the
apocalyptic guise of a monstrous mutation in history. Eschatology is ter-
atology. A double-edged coming of pain and parousia, of monstrosity
and messianism, of otherness as host and as hostage. This anticipates
Derrida's reading of the shibboleth as a threshold guarded over by two
guardians of the Jewish law—Elijah and Kafka—a threshold at once separating us *from* the other and summoning us *to* the other, at once ampu-
tation and advent. "Just here," Derrida writes, "the monster, or Elijah,
the host or other stands before the door as before the law. Think of *Vor
dem Gesetz.* Before the Law, of Kafka; but also of all those in Judaism who
associate the door with the law" (*Schibboleth,* 103).

In most of the texts published prior to the eighties, Derrida remained highly discreet about his fidelity (or infidelity) to the Jewish ethos
of exodus. And even when, in our 1982 dialogue, he is prepared to acknowledge that the Jew-as-other serves as a figure of alterity in his
deconstruction of Greek metaphysics, it is only in terms of the following
proviso:

> the paradox is that I have never actually invoked the Jewish
> tradition in any "rooted" or direct manner. Though I was born
> a Jew, I do not live or think within a living Jewish tradition. So
> that if there is a Judaic dimension to my thinking which may
> from time to time have spoken in or through me, this has
> never assumed the form of an explicit fidelity or debt to that
> culture. (*Dialogues,* 107)

The fact is, of course, that Derrida goes on in this dialogue to discuss the
Judaic themes of prophecy, ethics, and alterity in quite a revealing fash-

ion; and in a series of texts published since 1972 this interest in the scrip-
tural ethics of otherness becomes more and more explicitly, from "The
Force of Law," *Schibboleth, De L'esprit,* and *D'un certain ton apocalyptique*
already cited, to texts such as *Feu la cendre* (1987), *Devant la Loi* (1984),
Des Tours de Babel: Sur Walter Benjamin (1985), and perhaps most significantly the quasi-"religious" texts, "Comment ne pas parler" and "Circonfession."

In "Comment ne pas parler," Derrida raises the following leading
questions about the Jewish-Arab otherness which ghosts his writing.
"What of negative theology and its ghosts in a tradition of thought which
would be neither Greek nor Christian? In other words, what of Jewish
and Arab thinking on this issue?" And he goes on: "In everything I will
say a certain absence, a desert space will perhaps enable this question to
resonate . . . a place of resonance about which there will be nothing
said, or almost nothing" ("Comment," 562–63). But Derrida is not content to let the matter rest there. He moves from this allegiance of the
unspoken to a more articulate, and one might say, confessional statement:

> In spite of this silence, or in truth because of it, I may perhaps
> be permitted to reread this lecture as the most "autobiographi-
> cal" discourse I have yet risked. . . . If one day I should tell my
> story, nothing in the narrative could even begin to speak of
> what really matters if it did not begin with this fact: I have
> never yet been able, due to lack of competence and self-
> authority, to speak of that which my birth should have given
> me most intimately: Jew and Arab. . . . In short, how not to
> speak of oneself? But also: how to do so without becoming an
> invention of the other? or inventing the other? ("Comment,"
> 562)

The text where this theme of *l'invention de l'autre* assumes most
telling form is "Circonfession"—a candidly confessional text which explores the biographical overlaps between the author's early life in North
Africa and that of St. Augustine. It also plays on the Jewish initiatory rite
of circumcision. As one might expect, such an exercise in avowal has
much to say about the role of the "other" in both religious and ethical
experience. But I will confine my remarks to just one or two passages of
this most revealing text.

The eschatological connotations of circumcision first emerge in a
discussion of the term *escare.* Derrida refers to both its Anglo-Saxon ety-

mology of "scar" and its more contemporary allusion to the explosive *éclat* of avant-garde writing. Speaking as both Jew and avant-garde author, Derrida pursues this "eschatology of circumcision" as follows: "The violence of breaking open carried out by the avant-garde, which beyond all the old usages of this password they've never forgiven me, being an eschatologist, the most advanced, the last avant-garde which counts . . . " ("Circonfession," 92). Derrida goes on to note the ancient alliance between the religious role of eschatology and Elijah—the last of the prophets and Derrida's own guide and guardian through the rite of circumcision, a rite wherein the biblical alliance is each time renewed and repeated (ibid.).

VII

But if Derrida does betray a predilection for a certain eschatological tradition, he is careful to resist the suggestion that deconstruction is another form of "negative theology" (see *Derridabase*, 78–79; "Comment," 535–95). *Différance*, he insists, is not another proper name for God (nor indeed an improper or "negative" name), for that would be to give it the role of a transcendental signifier or signified; it would be to reduce the irrepressible play of otherness to a metaphysical presence; a betrayal of the interminable dissemination of words—which responds and is responsible to the call of the other, the "*viens*" of alterity—by fixing the play of signification to a First or Last Word. This important reservation about negative theology notwithstanding, Derrida does acknowledge the possibility of theologians displacing the ontotheological fetish of God in favor of a God beyond God (see "Comment," 560–61; also *E*, 179–84). But this acknowledgment is laconically stated, not explored.

The otherness of the other, which the metaphysical names for God as First Cause or Supreme Being seek to capture, is something which eludes all memory and all anticipation. The ethics of alterity is impelled by the recognition that the other precedes primary narcissism and exceeds the project of immortality. Or to put it in another way, the otherness of the other both preexists me and postexists me. It provokes the contamination of the same by the nonsame, of presence by absence, of identity by difference. As such it remains something which cannot be philosophically defined. Something which remains, at best, a discrete religious enigma. It cannot be named, only confessed. As Derrida puts it in "Circonfession" in response to his mother's question whether he believes in God:

> my religion about which no one understands anything. . . . she
> (my mother) should know that the endurance of God in my life
> goes under other names—so much so that I'm taken quite un-
> derstandly for an atheist—the omnipresence in me of what I
> call God in my absolved language, absolutely private, being nei-
> ther an eye witness nor a voice that does other than make me
> talk in order to say nothing, nor a transcendental law, nor an
> immanent schechina": that feminine figure of a Yahweh who
> remains so strange yet so familiar, being none of these things
> but rather the secret from which I am excluded. ("Circonfes-
> sion," 146–47)

Such a God is what Derrida calls "the other in me"—or the "atheist
God"—who is "infinitely smaller and larger than me" (ibid., 201).

But one of the things which an ethics of eschatology must safeguard against is the danger of mistaking deconstruction for a new religion; or more tempting still for a new form of prophecy substituting
itself for the last (true) prophet, Elijah. "As I am some One," writes
Derrida,

> whom the One God never ceases to decircumcise, in other
> words, someone who resolutely bleeds into dispersal, *salus in*
> *sanguine* all those who can no longer sleep from it who pretend
> to be waiting for me there where I have already come, like the
> truest of false prophets, those who want to deport their obses-
> sion with Elijah, their attraction repulsion, drawn and pro-
> jected into the periphery of a phase, into the periphrases of my
> signature. (Ibid., 208)

This is Derrida at his most paradoxical—tantalizingly obscure, tellingly
elliptical, engagingly noncommittal. But one thing which does come
across in these teasing passages is a realization that the God Derrida is
addressing is not the God of metaphysics or dogmatism, but the ethical
other of dispossession, discretion, disparition. In one of his most overtly
confessional statements to date, Derrida takes up again the analogy with
his Carthaginian predecessor and addresses his "hidden god." "[Y]ou
who are not graspable under this name or that," he ejaculates,

> it is you the hidden god more than one, capable each time of
> receiving my prayer, you are the destination of my prayer, you
> know everything before me, you are the unconscious god—we
> never seem to miss each other—you are the measure they can-

> not take, and that is why they ask who it is that I still address
> from the depths of my solitude; you are a mortal god, that is
> why I write, why I write to you my god . . . to save you from
> your own immortality. (Ibid., 244)

Derrida's lowercase "god" here differs from the higher-case God
of metaphysics in being the destination of direct address, an other who
calls and receives. It is also the "god" of Talmudic repute who set aside
the Seventh Day of Creation as a space—a gap, a desert, a void—for
endless invention, a labor of inscription and reinsciption to be carried
out by mortals. This would seem to be what Derrida has in mind when he
cites Augustine's phrase in the *Confessions* (XIII, xxxv, 50) about the
"Seventh Day which has no evening and no sunset" ("Circonfession,"
254). Or when he speaks of "the violence of the void by means of which
God earths himself to death in me" (ibid., 252): a violence which Derrida
identifies with a form of writing which remains faithful to the other and
yet estranged, which respects the alien precisely by alienating us from it,
which refuses the facility of immediate possession or the certainty of decidable affirmation and negation. "All of this," he says, "turns around
nothing, around a Nothing where God reminds himself to me, its my
only memory, the condition of all my fidelities, the name of God, amidst
the ashes of Elijah, one evening of rest which never arrives" (ibid., 253).
Thus the author declares himself an alien of all languages (like Kafka or
Benjamin?) because beholden to a language (Hebrew?) he does not
speak or understand. Whence his special obsession with words, letters,
writing, with a kind of scripture which can be awaited because it has
not yet come, a language recalled as still to come, a *"mémoire à venir"*
(ibid., 267).

But while Derrida refuses to take up occupancy in the land of
Hebrew, he continues to express fidelity to what he terms the "remains
of Judaism": the hope of the last of the prophets Elijah, the remaindered
resurrection symbolized by that Sabbath without evening, that eschatology without end. Derrida's lingering commitment to Judaism is informed by an ethic of reserve and vigilance. "One has to get up early,"
he writes,

> at the dawn of the day without evening, because finally but fi-
> nally who else am I in truth, who am I if I don't live what I in-
> habit and where I take place, *Ich bleibe also Jude,* that is to say
> today in what remains of Judaism in the world, Europe and the
> other, and in this remains I am only someone to whom so little

remains that deep down, already dead like the son beside the
widow, I await the resurrection of Elijah, and to have adressed
the interminably preliminary question of knowing how they,
the Jews and others, can interpret the "circonfession," the fact
that I am here living what remains of Judaism. (Ibid., 280)

To this uncharacteristically biographical avowal Derrida appends the following note of hesitation and humility: "We are so few and so divided,
you know, I am still waiting before I make the next step and add another
word, the name from which I hope resurrection" (ibid., 280).

VIII

The above reading of Derrida's texts on writing, law, and Judaism suggest that deconstruction's obsession with alterity is compatible with an
ethics of "increased responsibility." Indeed, it might even be said that it
serves as some kind of philosophical *condition* of it. For to safeguard the
other from all logocentric strategies to objectify and reify is to guard the
other as an irreducible locus of address and response—arguably the *sine
qua non* of all ethical discourse. This is surely why Derrida is so adamant
in his claim that deconstruction is "no centralising power of mastery and
domination" but an "openness towards the other" (*Dialogues*, 125). A
claim reinforced by the key statements cited above to the effect that "the
critique of logocentrism is above all the search for the other" (ibid.,
123); and that it is an attempt to "reevaluate the indispensable notion of
'responsibility' " (ibid., 121).

The fact that the term "responsibility" is used here in quotation
marks is itself a token of Derrida's resolve to reevaluate the operative
concepts of ethics. And presupposed by the reevaluation of "responsibility" is, logically, the reevaluation of the players who summon and respond—i.e., the ethical subject and the ethical other. This is why Derrida
challenges all metaphysical attempts to reduce the subject and its other
to categories of "mastery, possession, totalization or certitude" (ibid.,
121). It is also why he discerns in writing—and especially avant-garde
writing—the possibility of suspending our natural attitude to "self" and
"other" and reinscribing them in other ways. Deconstruction, in this respect, might be seen as a more elaborate and interrogative mode of writing, a way of rendering the traditional question of reference more
complex and problematic. It even asks, as Derrida admits, "whether our
term 'reference' is entirely adequate for designating the 'other.' "

RICHARD KEARNEY

This should not be taken to mean, as many critics of Derrida have suggested, that deconstruction is now confined to a prison-house of language with no reference to anything outside it. The very question of inside and outside is put in question by deconstruction. But this does not entail, as might first appear, an abandonment of responsibility to the otherness of the other. On the contrary, it demands it. "The other," writes Derrida, "which is beyond language and which summons language—is perhaps not a referent in the normal sense which linguists have attached to this term" (ibid., 123). But he insists that to distance oneself thus from the habitual structures of reference—thereby complicating our common logocentric assumptions about it—"does not amount to saying that there is nothing beyond language" (ibid., 124). The ethics of responsibility to the other demands that there *is*. Hence the retort to those who charge Derrida with nihilism—"deconstruction is not an enclosure in nothingness but an openness towards the other" (ibid.).

Since, moreover, it takes two to play the ethical game of responsibility, deconstruction is committed to a reinscription of not only the "other" but also the "subject." Over and against all the suspicions that deconstruction has obliterated the reality of the human subject, Derrida resolutely replies that far from seeking to "destroy the subject," he seeks only to "resituate" it in terms more vigilant and responsive to the other (ibid., 125). So that whether it be a question of the "other" who summons or the "subject" who responds, the reserve of quotation marks signals an ethical reservation—the reservation that neither "subject" nor "other" be mistaken for referential objects or transcendental signifieds which could be reduced to a closed logocentric system. The fact that "subject" and "other" are reevaluated in the name of an ethics of eschatology means that the responsibility they bear to one another is without end. Here we are concerned with an almost impossible responsibility, without the slightest hint of closure or reprieve.

We began this discussion of the ethics of deconstruction by situating Derrida in relation to two of his most influential contemporaries—Heidegger and Levinas. This influence is clearly not a question of either/or but rather—as one would expect from deconstruction—of both/and/neither/nor. That is to say, Heideggerian destruction and Levinasian ethics are and remain two aspects of Derrida's thinking which mutually contaminate and "supplement" each other. The working hypothesis of our reading here has been, however, that while Derrida tends to lean toward a more Heideggerean position in the texts up to 1972—as in the famous critique of Levinas in "Violence and Metaphysics"—he appears to favor a more Levinasian position in the post-1972 texts. I repeat that I

am not claiming that he chooses *between* Heidegger and Levinas; only
that the mutual contamination of both seems, in the later texts, to ap-
proximate more to the language of ethics than to that of ontology, however "destructive."

Already in our 1982 dialogue, Derrida was marking a definite difference from Heidegger; as when he states that his rapport with Heideg
ger is also a "non rapport" evident in their differing "understanding of
language" (*Dialogues,* 110). The contrast here is quite unambiguous.
Whereas Heidegger hailed Greek and German as the two exclusive languages of Being, Derrida insists that the language of Western culture—
as indeed of all cultures—is inhabited by its "other." The deconstruction of Western logocentrism is thus propelled from within by the fact
that "Europe has always registered the impact of heterogenous, non-
European influences" (ibid., 116). And it is because it is thus ghosted by,
and answerable to its "other," that it is constantly compelled to put itself
into question, to interrogate its own Eurocentric claim to master and
possess the universe of meaning. In short, the impulse of Western metaphysics to deconstruct itself is ultimately a force of ethical responsibility
to its "other." And Derrida's claim that the Jewish tradition—and to
some extent that of Christian mysticism (e.g., St. John, the early Augustine, Eckhart, or Cusa)—perdure as heterogenous elements "threatening and unsettling the assured 'identities' of Western philosophy," is
another way of acknowledging this responsibility. The contamination of
the Greek *Logos* by its other is something reviled by Heidegger but cham-
pioned by Derrida. "The surreptitious deconstruction of the Greek
Logos is at work from the very origin of our Western culture," argues
Derrida. "Already the translation of Greek concepts into other languages—Latin, Arabic, German, French, English, etc.—or indeed the
translation of Hebraic or Arabic ideas and structures into metaphysical
terms, produces 'fissures' in the presumed 'solidity' of Greek philosophy
by introducing alien and conflicting elements" (ibid., 117).

Derrida is here manifestly at odds with Heidegger and in tune
with an ethics of alterity à la Levinas. But such a statement is not the kind
of thing to be found in Derrida's writings up to the eighties. Indeed, as
he concedes in the 1982 dialogue, the "ethical" or "Judaic" element of
Levinas' thought remained for his early texts "a discreet rather than decisive reference" (ibid., 108; see also *Derridabase,* 279–87). That said, it is
undeniable that it comes more and more to the fore after the "ethical return" of such thinking in the seventies and eighties; and it even takes the
form of a critical confrontation with Heidegger in *De l'esprit* (1987).
Here Derrida points out that Heidegger's recourse to the Graeco-

Germanic concept of *Geist* during the fatal 1933–35 period—and most ominously in the 1933 *Rektoratsrede* where he celebrates Hitler—bespeaks an ethical and political blindness. Moreover, the conspicuous omission of any reference to the Hebrew word for spirit, *ruah*, lends further credence to the suspicion that Heidegger wanted no outside influences to contaminate what he saw as the "real" language of Being. Derrida's suggestion is that Heidegger's philosophical "forgetting" of *ruah* cannot be totally divorced from the historical repression of the Jews during the Third Reich. And here, it seems, Derrida is adverting to the intimate implication of ethics in questions of textual discourse. The simple fact is that all questions of language are about a rapport, or nonrapport, with the "other." Or as he puts it in *Schibboleth,* another contemporaneous text much concerned with matters of the *ruah,* the inalienable task of naming is to convoke the other, "to speak of the other, and to the other, to speak" (22).

This is one of the central motifs of Paul Celan's poetry analyzed in this text. And it is not lost on Derrida. He is aware that it was this Jewish poet who visited Heidegger in his mountain retreat in Todtnauberg after the war, to hear a word of apology for the great error. Heidegger did not utter the "hoped for" word; and Celan registered his disappointment in a poem entitled *Todtnauberg.* But if Celan did not go as far as Adorno in declaring a moratorium on poetry after Auschwitz, he did leave his meeting with Heidegger more persuaded than ever that no poetics of dwelling can be divorced from an ethics of responsibility. On the basis of the above passages—even though Derrida never makes a clear statement on the matter—it would appear reasonable to conclude that Celan's persuasion is not far removed from Derrida's own. Indeed, one could even make the claim that deconstruction is one particular effort, successful or otherwise, to combine a poetics of language with an ethical openness to the other.

As soon as we speak, or listen, we are indebted to the other, bespoken to the other, summoned by the other, responsible for the other. This is, I believe, one of the morals of the story of deconstruction— language is ethics. Not ethics as a system of directives or dogmas, to be sure, but as an obsession with the irreducible other. How else are we to make sense of Derrida's increasing concern with the ethical effects of language, not only in Judaism, law, and avant-garde writing, but also in such everyday controversies as educational reform, apartheid, and the nuclear threat. So that no matter how self-regarding, oblique, and obscure Derrida becomes, one is never allowed to forget that he has never forgotten the other. Perhaps that is what he means when he insists that "deconstruction is justice."

3

The French Derrideans: Politicizing Deconstruction or Deconstructing the Political?

Nancy Fraser

In the summer of 1980, a conference entitled "The Ends of Man: Spin-offs of the Work of Jacques Derrida" ("Les fins de l'homme: A partir du travail de Jacques Derrida") was held at Cérisy, France. Participants included many French philosophers in and around the Derridean circle as well as a number of American literary critics. Readers of the proceedings of this event are likely to find that the most interesting—and, as it subsequently turned out, the most fruitful—portion of the meeting was the "Political Seminar."[1] Here, at last, were raised explicitly all the questions that have long been bugging those who have followed the career of Derrida's writings and their peculiar reception in the United States: Does deconstruction have any political implications? Does it have any political significance beyond the byzantine and incestuous struggles it has provoked in American academic lit crit departments? Is it possible—and desirable—to articulate a deconstructive politics? Why, despite the revolutionary rhetoric of his writings circa 1968[2] and despite the widespread assumption that he is "of the left," has Derrida so consistently, deliberately, and dexterously avoided the topic of politics?

Why, for example, has he danced so nimbly around the tenacious efforts of interviewers to establish where he stands vis-à-vis Marxism?[3] Why has he continued "to defer indefinitely" the encounter of deconstruction with "the text of Marx" that he has on occasion promised? Or, is there *already* a politics implicit in his work? If so, what is it and is it a tenable one? What problems does Derrida's very complex relationship with Heidegger pose for those wishing to politicize deconstruction? What sort of politics is possible at "the end of metaphysics" or "in the wake of deconstruction"? What sort of political thought remains possible once one has deconstructed all the traditional bases of political reflection? Is it possible to rethink the political from a Derridean standpoint? What might such an effort look like?

Participants in the "Political Seminar" at Cérisy proposed a number of mutually incompatible answers to these questions. Not surprisingly, the chief upshot of the sessions was the proliferation of further questions and a recognition that an ongoing, systematic inquiry was needed if these were ever to be satisfactorily resolved. A few months later the Center for Philosophical Research on the Political was launched at the École Normale Supérieure in Paris. Under its auspices, as organized by Strasbourg philosophers Jean-Luc Nancy and Philippe Lacoue-Labarthe, a group composed mainly of philosophers, including but not limited to many of the Cérisy participants, has since been pursuing the inquiry.[4] The center holds about six meetings a year to hear and discuss papers both by people whom I shall call "members" (people who attend regularly, have been associated with or influenced by Derrida, and have not necessarily done previous work directly oriented to specifically political questions) and by people whom I shall call "nonmembers" (people who do not attend regularly, have not been especially identified with deconstruction, and whose work has long been explicitly concerned with politics—for example, Claude Lefort, former Althusserians Étienne Balibar and Jacques Ranciére, and *Esprit* editor Paul Thibaud). Papers presented during the first year of the center's existence, along with the text of its inaugural, founding statement, have been collected and published under the title *Rejouer le politique*.[5] The second year's papers have appeared in another volume, *Le retrait du politique*.[6]

The central trajectory of the center's work, especially as defined by the members' papers that appear in these volumes, is an interesting and original one. It is a trajectory that will probably surprise many American readers both pro- and anti-deconstruction, for it is deeply marked with Heideggerian and Arendtian motifs and is profoundly suspicious of the sorts of projects for politicizing deconstruction or articulating a deconstructive politics that have appeared in the United States.[7] In order to understand this unexpected line of thought, to see why and how it has taken the form it has, and eventually to assess its merits, it is necessary to look first at the discussions of the Cérisy "Political Seminar."

Two of the Cérisy presentations, though extremely well conceived and well written and though marked by a number of original and provocative themes, could be said to have been predictable. Each of these sought to isolate what its author considered the most fundamental "gesture" of Derridean deconstruction and to determine its political significance. Each treated that gesture as the basis for a politics of deconstruction and tried to elaborate it into a substantive, programmatic political orientation. It will come as no surprise to readers of Derrida that the two papers in question fastened upon different gestures and thus presented different—indeed, opposing—deconstructive politics.

What we might call the "left gesture" and hence the left version of deconstructive politics was presented by literary critic Gayatri Chakravorty Spivak.[8] Although she conceded that "Derrida no longer invokes this project" (511), Spivak nevertheless oriented her paper to the apocalyptic closing of his 1968 essay "The Ends of Man." The project of deconstruction, she quoted approvingly, is that of "a radical shake-up [*ébranlement*], [which] can come only from the outside [and which] takes place [*se joue*] in the violent relationship—be it 'linguistic' . . . or ethnological, economic, political, or military—between *all* of the West and its other."[9] The aim, in other words, is to pave the way for revolution, to destabilize the West by forcing it to confront the other that it excludes. For Spivak, this other is "women, . . . the non-Western world, . . . the victims of capitalism" (513). But, she argued, "*all* the relations between East and West are today written in terms of the possibility of the production, maximally, of absolute surplus value and, minimally, of relative surplus value; and this is not only in the 'pure' sense of an effect in excess of a text" (511). In her view, it was Derrida himself who showed that "the working body, although it be a text, is certainly not one text among others" and that "the economy is not one domain among others" (511). Thus, concluded Spivak, the discourse of deconstruction cannot continue to exclude that of political economy. To persist in reducing the latter to "the status of [a] precritical method duped by its own axiomatic" is to be duped oneself in turn (507). It is to fall back "into a precritical, ideological space" (513), to reproduce the very gesture of marginalization-exclusion that Derrida himself has repeatedly condemned ever since his 1967 *Speech and Phenomena* (508). It is to establish a "binary opposition" by means of "a certain ethico-political decision" establishing "centralized norms by means of strategic exclusions" (506). This ignores the "most important 'political' lesson" to be learned from Derrida: theory is a practice; one must be careful "not to exclude the other term of a polarity or the margins of a center"; one must "put in question the normative character of the institutions and disciplines in and by which we live" (506).

Thus for the sake of the project of a "radical shake-up of the West from the outside," Spivak urged deconstruction to deconstruct its own exclusion of political economy. She claimed that a subtle reading of Marx would reveal a deconstructor *avant la lettre*. Contemporary Derrideans should follow Marx's example and "confront the false other of philosophy, make a performative or revolutionary contingency erupt into [it, make] felt the heterogeneity of being and knowledge and of being and doing." They should de-center their own discourse, "open it onto an 'outside' constituted by ethical-political contingencies" (514).

The discussion that followed Spivak's Cérisy presentation did not directly confront or challenge the political orientation she proposed. Instead, participants noted that there were metaphysical elements in Marxism themselves in need of deconstruction: the presupposition of a "quasidivine" labor power producing more than it consumes; the elaboration of that labor power as the "source or origin of surplus value for the sake of assigning a proper terminus (a *'propre'*) to the movement, really produced by nothing, of production of surplus value"; the concepts of disappropriation, mediation, and appropriation.[10] But subsequent developments in the "Political Seminar" soon revealed that many of the participants did not share Spivak's commitment to a politicized deconstruction in the service of Marxism, however nonclassical.

If Spivak's version of deconstructive politics was anchored in the apocalyptic closing gesture of "The Ends of Man," the next presentation proposed an alternative politics based on the explicit rejection of that gesture. French philosopher Jacob Rogozinski titled his paper "Deconstruct the Revolution."[11] He argued that, *pace* Spivak, the "inaugural gesture" of deconstruction, the one that opens its field of operation, is the *rejection* of the radical cut or break (*coupure*). To her citation from "The Ends of Man," Rogozinski counterposed the following passage from *Positions*: "I do not believe in decisive ruptures, in an unequivocal 'epistemological break,' as it is called today. Breaks are always, and fatally, reinscribed in an old cloth that must continually, interminably be undone."[12] There is, then, no transgression that is unrecuperable, that cannot be reinstalled within the closure it tries to exceed. Indeed, it is the impossibility of a break that makes deconstruction necessary. For

Derrida, claimed Rogozinski, the idea of such a break is a mere ruse of the system, a wily strategy by means of which it recuperates protest. Hence, an even wilier counterstrategy is called for. Deconstruction can only be a "double-game, a double writing." It must substitute for the violent, eruptive temporality of the break (and of Spivak's Marxism) a temporality of its own: one of patient, enduring, interminable work, Penelopean or Sisyphean labor, "an acute vigilance and perhaps a silent distress" (518).

Hence, argued Rogozinski, a politics of deconstruction can be inaugurated only by a rejection of revolution. It must deconstruct revolution as the metaphysical project of an impossible radical break. It must expose the latter's "arche-teleological structure" which projects an origin and an end, promising an "end of man" (communism, the proletariat) as the total reappropriation of his *propre* and as the return of the *parousia* of his presence. It must show that Marxism, qua project of revolution, is "the last avatar of political metaphysics" (520).

But, continued Rogozinski, a deconstructive politics that was content simply to deconstruct the metaphysics of the *propre* in political philosophy would not be adequate. It would fail to see that in political philosophy *before* Marx, this metaphysics functioned as a guard against the tyranny and terror that was its "inadmissable other." For in order to define the conditions of legitimate authority, the tradition always conjured up the figure of the gravest danger, the most extreme decay of *Mitsein*. And it elected to link the latter in every case to a disturbance of the *propre*. The demand for the *propre*, then, was always the antistrophe in a chorus bewailing the menace of tyranny. This tradition reached its apogee in Hegel, where the gesture of *Aufhebung*—qua absolute reappropriation of absolute loss—became the guard protecting against terror. In the sections of the *Phenomenology* that treat the French Revolution, the *Aufhebung* was the mechanism for overcoming the unthinkable horror of a death *sans phrase*; it overcame the meaningless, uncompensated death that issued from the revolutionary assertion of the absolute, abstract freedom of unmediated self-consciousness. In place of this "death worse than death," the *Aufhebung*, qua recovery of the *propre*, substituted a "beautiful death under the yoke of the Law" (521–22).

It follows, *pace* Spivak, that it is Hegel, and not Marx, who is the deconstructor *avant la lettre*. For Hegel, claimed Rogozinski, conceives terror as the foreclosure of *différance*, as the actualized presence of the absolute. In opposition to terror, Hegelian political philosophy is established "in the shelter of *différance*." It exiles the absolute to another world outside history and time, refrains from attempting to realize it here and now, defers it to eternity. It maintains differentiations within civil society as well as the differentiation between civil society and the state. Thus it takes account of *différance* by accepting and reinscribing differences at the heart of social space. Hegelian politics, then, preserves a nondialectical, *unaufheb*able cleavage (522–23).

But this puts it in diametric opposition to Marxism, which seeks dialectically to overcome or abrogate *différance* in its "utopia of the totally transparent, self-reconciled *'une-société'* " (523). Marxian politics thus attacks "the stronghold of discretion protecting the reserve of the absolute" and unleashes revolutionary terror. If the *propre* is metaphysics' guard against terror, its "inadmissable other," then Marxism is "the lowering of that guard [and] hence (unhappily) the least metaphysical of projects" (523). Quoting Adorno, Rogozinski concluded that deconstruction must side with Hegel against Marx; it ought not simply deconstruct metaphysics but should be "in solidarity with metaphysics in the moment of its fall" (523).

Rogozinski ended his paper by formulating what he saw as deconstruction's present dilemma: on the one hand, it inaugurates itself by rejecting the radical break and contents itself with the sort of patient, faithful, disinterested endurance that corresponds to a politics of resistance. But, on the other hand, it does so in the name of another, more radical rupture; invoking the apocalyptic tone par excellence, "it sets its sights on the *'outre-clôture'* [and] surrenders to the fascination of the beyond, seek[ing] the 'Orient of its text,' the other space beyond the frontiers delimiting Western metaphysics" (523). Deconstruction contains, thus, two different calls to *différance,* two different intonations and intensities. One calls us to a politics of resistance that preserves *différance* as a guard against terror. The other calls us to a "wholly other politics," one of revolution more radical than has ever been conceived, one that celebrates *différance* as "absolute danger" and "the monstrosity of the future" (524). Deconstruction slides incessantly—strategically, it would claim—between a politics of revolution and a politics of resistance. It says that the alternatives are undecidable and lingers on the threshold, refusing to choose. But, concluded Rogozinski: "Now you have no choice: you must choose. The impossible choice of your death presses you more and more. You are required to choose, and quickly, between a 'beautiful death' under the yoke of the Law, and that other monstrous death that is worse than death" (525).

The discussion following this remarkable tour de force was lively and contentious.[13] If the seminar participants were unwilling to accept Spivak's reading of Marx, they did not like Rogozinski's any better. Many speakers objected to his hypostatization of *the one* Marxism and *the one* project of revolution; they appealed to the variety of Marxian and revolutionary theories, parties, and political tendencies. But the most interesting response was that of Derrida himself, who delivered some of his most straightforward and revealing remarks to date on the topic of politics. Derrida claimed to agree with the broad lines of the argument but to disagree with Rogozinski's conclusions. He said that he had deliberately not produced a discourse against revolution or Marxism, in order to avoid contributing to the "anti-Marxist concert" of the 1968 period. He did not, and *does* not, want to weaken "what Marxism and the proletariat can constitute as a force in France" (527). Despite his distrust of the idea of revolution qua *metaphysical* concept, he does not "devalue what [this idea] could contribute . . . as a force of 'regroupment' [*rassemblement*]" (527).

So, for the sake of the traditional leftist aim of not splitting the left, Derrida claimed to have adopted a "complex," "encumbered" strategy. He had refrained from a frontal attack while marking a series of "virtual differences or divergences" from the revolutionary project. This strategy was marked in his writings, he said, by "a sort of withdrawal or retreat [*retrait*], a silence on Marxism—a blank signifying . . . that Marxism was not attacked like such and such other theoretical comfort. . . . This blank was not neutral. . . . It was a perceptible political gesture" (527). But having defended this strategy as appropriate to the political context in 1968, Derrida did not protest when Jean-Luc Nancy replied that it had now become necessary to substitute a reading of Marx for this "blank" (528).

Whether such a reading is actually produced—and if it is, what it looks like—remains to be seen. But what is evident even now is Derrida's determination to avoid or reject the Spivak-Rogozinski alternative. His own Cérisy paper was a refusal of the alternative between an apocalyptic and an antiapocalyptic discourse.[14] And this refusal seemed in tune with the general sentiment in the "Political Seminar." Indeed, the refusal to choose between the two political orientations proposed there was later to become in effect the "inaugurating gesture" of the Center for Philosophical Research on the Political. For in an implicit repetition of a philosophical move at least as old as Kant, the members of the center have refused to defend one side of the antinomy against the other and have instead retreated to a deeper level of analysis which interrogates the conditions of possibility shared by both.

This move was already foreshadowed at Cérisy in a presentation by Jean-Luc Nancy, made outside the framework of the "Political Seminar." In "The Free Voice of Man," Nancy explored the important and difficult problem of the status of the various quasi-ethical imperatives or obligations—the *il faut*'s—in Derrida's writings: *il faut déconstruire la philosophie; il faut penser l'écriture; il faut entendre doublement*; and so on.[15] More important than his solution, it seems to me, was Nancy's way of posing the issue. He began by invoking Heidegger's response in "The Letter on Humanism" to the question, When are you going to produce an ethics? Nancy noted that Heidegger rebuffed the suggestion, arguing that an ethics, like a logic or a physics, made sense only within the confines of the metaphysical tradition and that the task of thought at the end of metaphysics was to think the "unthought" of that tradition—to think, in this case, the prior, enabling background, itself nonethical, upon which the domain of the ethical is instituted. Nancy argued that Derrida would have to make a similar response to the demand to produce an ethics, especially, he claimed, were such a demand to understand ethics as the translation into practice of a philosophical theory. For Nancy endorsed what he took to be Heidegger's view of the matter: namely, that ethics is metaphysical insofar as it has been conceived in the Western tradition as *the practical effectuation of the philosophical*, that is, as the effectuation in practice of theoretical knowledge and thus as presupposing the prior establishment of the domain of the philosophical. Nancy inferred that deconstruction "does its duty" (*fait son devoir*) when it rebuffs the demand for an ethics and instead deconstructs that demand, showing where it comes from and interrogating the "essence" (in Heidegger's sense of the "*transcendentale*") of the ethical.

Although the Center for Philosophical Research on the Political has never explicitly addressed the question of the relation between ethics and politics, it has in fact proceeded as if the two were analogous. It has subjected the political to a line of interrogation paralleling that which Nancy proposed for the ethical. This has been tantamount to refusing Spivak's and Rogozinski's demands that it produce a politics of deconstruction—the practice of the theory—while offering instead to deconstruct the political.

The outlines of this program were already visible in two other presentations at the Cérisy "Political Seminar." Christopher Fynsk broached the problem of the political by noting a certain doubleness in Derrida's work.[16] On the one hand, there is the *retrait* of or from politics in his writings; Derrida avoids any direct engagement with political questions and resists demands for an explicit, immediate politicization of his work. But on the other hand, and at the same time, he claims that his practice *is* political and that philosophical activity in general is a political practice. Fynsk sought to explain this apparent contradiction by noting that it has become a truism of the modern age that politics is the horizon of every practice, that every act is necessarily inscribed within the domain of the political, presupposing political institutions and producing political effects. But, he argued, this "self-evident" omnipresence of the political makes it difficult to assign any determinate meaning to the term "politics." When everything is political, the sense and specificity of the political recedes, giving rise to still another inflection of the expression *"le retrait du politique"*: the retreat or withdrawal of the political. Henceforth, this expression will evoke Hannah Arendt's diagnosis of modernity as the age in which the sphere of the political is engulfed by the socioeconomic, in which the public space for normative deliberation about common ends is overrun by administrative decision-making, interest brokering, and obsession with the (putatively prepolitical) problems of "national housekeeping"—a diagnosis, incidentally, in which Marxism appears as the culmination of the sad trend.[17]

The theme of the *retrait du politique* was later to become a leitmotif of the center's work. It was further elaborated at Cérisy by Philippe Lacoue-Labarthe.[18] He cited Derrida's remark in "The Ends of Man" that there is an "essential belonging-to-one-another [*co-appartenance*] of the political and the philosophical." This remark, claimed Lacoue-Labarthe, posed the question of "the bond indissociably uniting the philosophical and the political" (494). Paraphrasing Heidegger's claims about technology,[19] he argued that "the unconditional [or total] domination of the political in the modern age represents the completion of a philosophical program. In the [self-evident omnipresence of the] political today, the philosophical reigns" (494). This was to echo Nancy's view, itself inspired by Heidegger, that the tendency in contemporary culture to see everything as political presupposes a prior determination of the political as the practical effectuation of the philosophical. Given this analysis, Lacoue-Labarthe defended Derrida's retreat (*retrait*) from politics as the necessary response to the withdrawal (*retrait*) of the political. Those who would oppose the reign of the philosophical, he claimed, cannot avoid such a retreat (494).

But, Lacoue-Labarthe went on to argue, this retreat from the political cannot be a simple gesture. It is not as if one can turn away from the political and move on to something else. On the contrary, today there is not and cannot be something other than the political. To retreat from the political, then, is not to move into a *retraite* (a nonpolitical refuge or haven) (495); it is rather to step back from "our passionate obsession with the political" in order to interrogate it. It is to refuse the

"intimidation" of the political, especially as exercised by Marxism (495).
One resists the pressure to produce a deconstructive politics and instead
questions the *obviousness* of the political. One interrogates the "essence
of the political" (497).

The discussion following Fynsk's and Lacoue-Labarthe's Cérisy
presentations turned on a number of issues that have continued to be
subjects of controversy among the center's members.[20] One of these was
the question of the adequacy of the Heideggerian assumption of a basic
unity or homogeneity of Western metaphysics that permits one to speak
of "*the philosophical*" in the singular. Another was the question, raised by
American literary critic David Carroll, of the applicability of the notion
of "the total domination of the political" outside France—in the United
States, for example. More generally, French philosopher Sara Kofman
questioned the appropriateness of supposing a quasi-Heideggerian
framework. Why appeal to Heidegger, she asked, in order to think the
political implications of deconstruction, given the enormous differences
separating the respective political practices of Heidegger and Derrida?
Lacoue-Labarthe's response underlined a distinction that was to become
canonical for the center: one can recognize, he claimed, that there may
be a stratum of thought common to Heidegger and Derrida vis-à-vis *the
political* (*le politique*) without ignoring the differences between them at
the level of politics (*la politique*). On the other hand, distinguishing between *le politique* and *la politique* in this way does not obviate the necessity of asking if and how the two are related. There must come a point,
claimed Lacoue-Labarthe—as there surely did, alas, for Heidegger—at
which one's *politics* encroaches upon one's conception of *the political*.

Nearly all the major themes of the center's work were already
broached in the Cérisy presentations of Nancy, Fynsk, and Lacoue-
Labarthe: the theme of the *retrait du politique* (with its double signification of, first, the disengagement from and resistance to the insistent
demands of, for instance, Spivak and Rogozinski for a politics of deconstruction, and second, the receding of the specificity of the political in
the contemporary truism that "everything is political"); the theme of the
essence of the political (the program of interrogating the constitution and
institution of the political in Western culture); the theme of the *essential
belonging-to-one-another of the political and the philosophical* (the way in
which the constitution and institution of the political is related to that of
the philosophical); and the theme of the distinction between *le politique*
and *la politique*. Together, these themes comprise a decision to replace
the project of politicizing deconstruction with the project of deconstructing the political.

That project and its salient themes were elaborated more systematically in the "Ouverture" or inaugural lecture delivered by Nancy and Lacoue-Labarthe at the first meeting of the Center for Philosophical Research on the Political on 8 December 1980.[21] This remarkable document is worth explicating at some length. The authors begin by explaining their choice of a name for the center. They claim that In calling the workspace they wish to create the "Center for Philosophical Research on the Political," they intend to suggest a double aim: first, they envision a *philosophical* interrogation of the political, one that excludes other possible approaches; but second, this philosophical interrogation is not one that supposes that philosophy is itself privileged or unproblematic—on the contrary, it problematizes philosophy, by interrogating the latter's relation to the political (12–13).

The justification for the first of these aims runs as follows: empirical investigation of the political—investigation aimed at establishing a political science or a political theory or at discovering or inventing a new concept of the political—is excluded because it can no longer be "decisive." Such investigation itself issues from and is determined by a preestablished philosophical field—one that is old, past, closed. Discourses claiming to be independent of the philosophical, whether by treating the political itself as an autonomous positive domain or by subordinating it to some other autonomous positive domain (for instance, the economic or the psychoanalytic), are not in fact independent. Rather, they have philosophical presuppositions—and not for reasons that are merely accidental. These discourses *necessarily* bear the marks of the "essential belonging-to-one-another" of the philosophical and the political in the Western tradition (13–14).

It is this "essential belonging-to-one-another" that justifies as well the second prong of the center's double aim. In Western culture ever since the contemporaneous institution of philosophy and the Greek polis, there has always been a reciprocal implication of the political and the philosophical such that neither is anterior or exterior to the other. Indeed, this reciprocal implication is part and parcel of what Nancy and Lacoue-Labarthe take to be our current predicament (14–15). We live, say the authors of the "Ouverture" in the age of the "total domination of the political." It is the age of the completion or fulfillment ("*l'accomplissement*"), of the philosophical *in* the political, in a sense precisely analogous to that in which Heidegger claimed that metaphysics was completed, or fulfilled, *in* modern technology.[22] We necessarily act within the "closure of the political" (15). Sartre was right, though not in the way he thought, when he claimed that Marxism was the unsurpassable horizon of our time. This is true when it is construed as meaning that socialism ("really existing socialism") is the most complete realization of the drive to impose philosophy on existence. *Philosophy* is what is being completed and effectuated in the discourse analyzed by Rogozinski: the great "enlightening," progressive, secular-eschatological discourse of revolution as humanity's self-reappropriation and self-actualization (though it does *not* follow that one should therefore endorse the counterdiscourse of the *nouveaux philosophes* [16]).

In Nancy and Lacoue-Labarthe's view, to recognize our confinement in the closure of the political is to realize that despite real possibilities of revolt here and there (in truth, less here than there), History-with-a-capital-*H* is finished. We can no longer accept theories offering global political solutions to inhumanity, for we have seen, Nancy and Lacoue-Labarthe claim, that the project of social transparence, of the utopian homogenization of the "social bond," leads to totalitarianism. Indeed, if the definition of totalitarianism is the universalization of one domain of reference to the point where it usurps and excludes all others, then the epoch of the completion of the philosophical in the political is the totalitarian age par excellence (16–17).

But, say the authors, the project of interrogating the philosophical essence of the political is not equivalent to simply denouncing, from the outside, as it were, by means of a simple *political* critique, the various metaphysical programs for founding the political or for programming existence philosophically. Rather, the work of the center must take into account the fact that such denunciations—which are now commonplace—are themselves internal to and determined by the development of philosophy. They are part of an epochal process akin to what Nietzsche called "European nihilism" and to what Heidegger called "the overcoming of metaphysics": a process wherein philosophy is undermining its own foundation, delegitimating its own authority, *de*instituting itself.[23] Deconstruction is itself an immanent component of this process (17–18).

Nancy and Lacoue-Labarthe infer that recognition of the closure of the political and of the self-deinstitution of philosophy requires us to think the *re-trait du politique* in two senses: first, as a *withdrawal* on our part from the blinding self-evidence of the political, which marks our confinement in its closure; and second, as a *retracing* of the political from the standpoint of its essence. Moreover, we are required to distinguish rigorously between the political (*le politique*) and politics (*la politique*) (18).

That last distinction complicates the character of the center's work. On the one hand, say the authors, to deconstruct the political and

the essential belonging-to-one-another of the political and the philosophical is *not* to take a *political position*; it is rather to question the very
position of *the political*. The task, in other words, is *not to institute a new
politics* but, rather, to *think the institution of the political* in Western
thought (15). But, on the other hand, they claim that the work of the
center is not and cannot be a retreat to apoliticism (18). There is and can
be no nonpolitical *outre-clôture* to which one could safely emigrate; besides, it is unavoidable that the center's work will produce political effects (20). So to interrogate the essence of the political cannot be to
discard or sublimate political or class struggles. Such struggles are the
givens of the age and there is no way around them (24). It follows, for
Lacoue-Labarthe and Nancy, that the *retrait du politique* must itself be a
political gesture, albeit a somewhat unusual one. It permits one to "exceed something of the political"—but not by a *sortie* outside the political
(18–19). It is a kind of *engagement*—but one that does not consist in
pledging oneself to one or another politics (19).

The authors of the "Ouverture" go on to argue that the "engaged" character of the center's work requires it to reexamine a variety
of received political notions. For example, it can no longer accept the
traditional left maxim, invoked by Derrida at Cérisy, that enjoins silence
on certain matters in order to avoid harming the left. To keep such silence today, they claim, is to court a far greater risk: namely, the very
extinction of every left (20). Thus, the center must address itself to Marxism. In doing this, it need not start from scratch but may critically appropriate some important recent work by nondeconstructionist thinkers,
for example, Claude Lefort's work on the "lacuna of the political" in
Marx. Marx's neglect of the political, along with his early project of ne-
gating the state as a separate instance in society, which in the East has
meant the incursion of the state into all social instances, should be re-
thought from the standpoint of the center's problematic. It should be
related to the way in which the question of the specificity of the political
has repeatedly surfaced in such diverse Marxian currents as Council
Communism, Gramscism, Althusserianism, and Maoism. The center
should also address the question of the temporary form of the political
that becomes necessary in the revolutionary transition to communism
(the dictatorship of the proletariat—a form that is encrusted in the socialist countries). Nor should the center ignore the question of the ultimate form of the political given the project of overcoming the split
between civil society and the state, that is, the complete engulfment of
the political by the social (20–21).[24]

In addition to work on Marx and Marxism, Nancy and Lacoue-

Labarthe propose a line of inquiry oriented to thinkers like Heidegger
and Bataille, who have produced discourses "at the extreme limit or border of the political." These discourses sought, unsuccessfully, to exceed
the political by avoiding the presupposition of the *subject*, a presupposition that has always marked more properly metaphysical political discourses, paradigmatically that of Hegel. Heidegger and Bataille
attempted to locate an *outre-sujet* of the political (22–23); they failed,
however, and ended up inadvertently reintroducing quasisubjectivities,
thereby confirming that "behind the self-evidence of the political is dis-
simulated the self-evidence of the subject" (23). From this, the authors
of the "Ouverture" infer that the center must rethink the state, power,
and political struggles without assuming the "arche-teleological domination of the subject" (24)

In order not to presuppose the subject, it will be necessary, they
claim, to problematize the very notion of the "social bond," for that notion has always been thought as a relationship among previously constituted subjects. Consequently, it too can be seen as a "limit-question" of
the political, one that must repeatedly surface as such in the tradition.
Thus, argue Lacoue-Labarthe and Nancy, the center should interrogate
the diverse forms in which the problematic of "the other" repeatedly
arises in political philosophy: the questions of "forms of sympathy," conflict and *Mitsein* (24–25). A reading of Freud, for example, may demonstrate how the motifs of sociality and alterity make the question of the
"social bond" a limit question for psychoanalysis, one that it can neither
avoid nor resolve. On their reading of Freud, the birth or fabrication of
the subject arises from its bond to the paradigm of subjectivity represented "in the form of the Father" (25–26). But, they suggest, this bond
is achieved only with the concomitant withdrawal of what is neither subject nor object, "the mother." Despite the danger that such a formula
may give rise to a host of *Schwärmerei,* one could say, claim the authors of
the "Ouverture," that "behind the political (if it must be identified with
the Father), [lies] 'the mother' " (26).

It is here, say Lacoue-Labarthe and Nancy, that the work of the
center rejoins the Derridean source of its inspiration. In trying to think a
process in which something recedes as the political is installed, they ask,
What nondialectical negativity, what nonunity and nontotality withdraws
or recedes or is divided or subtracted in the fabrication of the "social
bond"? (26). For the essence of the political cannot be an originary social
organism or harmony or communion, any more than it can be a partition
of functions and differences. Nor can it be anarchy. It must, rather, be
"the an-anarchy of the *arché* itself" (27). In other words, the question of

the *retrait du politique* rejoins the general problematic of the opening of the *trace* as elaborated by Derrida (27).

Thus in their "Ouverture," Nancy and Lacoue-Labarthe sketch a program for rethinking the political from the standpoint of deconstruction. It is a program that, in its purity and rigor, is far more faithful to the spirit of Derrida's work than the latter's own comparatively simplistic leftist remarks at Cérisy. But it also—indeed, *therefore*—reveals all the more starkly the limitations of deconstruction as an outlook seeking to confront the political.

Consider again the way in which the center's project emerged: In the rhetoric and politics of Gayatri Spivak, the Derrideans found themselves face-to-face with the authentic political expression of Derridean *apocalyptism:* revolution as a celebration of the "monstrousness" of the "wholly other." But this in the end is only a pose, one that does not do justice to the depths of the historical experience from which deconstruction emerged. Rogozinski was right to detect a "silent distress" beneath Derridean bravado. It is the existential distress of a specific cultural experience: the experience of nihilism in the immediate wake of the historical *dépassement* of Marxism. Rogozinski's own politics of resistance, however inadequate to the complexities of contemporary social reality, remains the authentic expression of the deep, *tragic* current underlying deconstruction's compulsive playfulness. When sounded against that tragic strain, Derrida's political line about not splitting the left rings false. Hence, Nancy and Lacoue-Labarthe have little difficulty in showing that it travesties the rigorous ethos of deconstruction—an ethos that they seek to maintain, even as Derrida threatens to abandon it.

The standpoint of Nancy and Lacoue-Labarthe, then, is founded on the collapse of three political orientations, three versions of *la politique:* Spivak's, Rogozinski's, and Derrida's. The authors of the "Ouverture" reject each of the three—and rightly, in my view—as inadequate. But it is telling that, in doing so, they do not debate their opponents on the latters' own—*political*—terms. Rather, they refuse the very genre of political debate and in this way, too, maintain the ethos of deconstruction. For there is one sort of difference that deconstruction cannot tolerate: namely, difference as dispute, as good, old-fashioned, political fight. And so, Nancy and Lacoue-Labarthe are utterly—one might say, terribly—faithful to deconstruction in refusing to engage in political debate.[25]

But this leaves them poised between the horns of a dilemma. On the one hand, they long, with all the poignancy evoked by Rogozinski, for a post-Marxian politics, a genuine "engagement." But, on the other hand, the supposed historical unavailability at present of a viable political stance, of *une politique,* aborts that longing and drives them back to *le politique,* to the philosophical interrogation of the political.

It seems, then, that the "Ouverture" of Lacoue-Labarthe and Nancy is the scene of a dialectic of aborted desire, a scene replete with tensions that threaten to shatter it. But if this is so, then it is likely that their project, like deconstruction itself, is only a temporary way station on the exodus from Marxism now being traveled by the French intelligentsia. It is not and cannot be a permanent resting place. Indeed, the subsequent career of the Center for Philosophical Research on the Political tends to bear this out.

The fragility of the center's project could be surmised from the fact that during the first year of its existence, only two of the papers presented directly pursued the program laid out in the "Ouverture." Not surprisingly, these were written by Nancy and Lacoue-Labarthe, respectively. In "The Juri-Diction of the Hegelian Monarch," Nancy provided a deconstructive reading of *The Philosophy of Right* that showed how the problem of the social bond was a limit question for a thought about the political that presupposed the self-evidence of the subject.[26] In "Transcendence Ends in Politics," Lacoue-Labarthe investigated both the "essential belonging-to-one-another" of the political and the philosophical, and also the relation between *le politique* and *la politique* in Heidegger's Nazi-era writings.[27]

The second year of the center's existence brought some attempts on the part of members at criticism of the "Ouverture" program. Denis Kambouchner questioned the exclusion of empirical work and argued that Nancy and Lacoue-Labarthe were in danger of succumbing to idealism.[28] Philippe Soulez adduced some Lacanian considerations against the formula: "Behind the political [qua Father, lies] 'the mother.' "[29] But it was the intervention of nonmember Claude Lefort that provoked the most unambiguous expression of the fragility of the program of sublimating the desire for *la politique* in an interrogation of *le politique.*

The subject of Lefort's paper was the differences between democracy and totalitarianism.[30] It elicited, in response, the most interesting section of yet another text by Lacoue-Labarthe and Nancy.[31] At the closing session of the center's second year, the principal organizers sought to take stock of the previous two years' work and to see how things stood in relation to the questions posed in the "Ouverture." After reprising a number of that document's salient themes and replying to the charge of idealism, they try to locate their own conception of totalitarianism in relation to Lefort's. Nancy and Lacoue-Labarthe distinguish two senses of "totalitarianism." First, there is their own very general sense suggested in the notion of "the total domination of the political." This sense concerns the universalization of the political to the point of usurping and excluding every other domain of reference. It finds symptomatic expression in the contemporary truism that "everything is political." This generalized sense of "totalitarianism" is not empirical, they claim, although it does permit the thematization of certain salient "facts" of the age: the Arendtian paradox of the disappearance of the specificity of the political in its very domination; the confounding of the political with other instances, such as the socioeconomic, the technological, the cultural, and the psychological; and the consequent banalization of the political. The result of the rise of totalitarianism in this sense, they say, is that nowhere can even the slightest specifically political question be posed; nowhere can the question of a new politics have the slightest chance of emerging—none of which, however, prevents "politics as usual" from being carried on (188–89).

Nancy and Lacoue-Labarthe distinguish this first sense of totalitarianism from a second, narrower one. The latter emerges from the political-scientific analyses—by, for example, Arendt and Lefort—of notable cases like nazism, fascism, Stalinism, and Soviet-type societies. Here, totalitarianism is a response to the "crisis of democracy." Following the erosion of authority, traditions, and religion, modern democracy rests on a desubstantialized and disincarnated form of power. Thus, it institutes a version of the political that is bereft of metaphysical foundations, devoid of transcendence. The result is a "delocalization" of the political: the dismemberment of the political body "which is no longer one except in the pure dispersion of suffrage," and the consequent surrender of political affairs to the play of interests. Responding, then, to this democratic "impasse," totalitarianism in the narrow sense is the attempt at a mad, frenzied resubstantialization and reincarnation of the political body. It remolds the political by force so as willfully to impose transcendence and unity (189–90).

Nancy and Lacoue-Labarthe claim that their adherence to the first, generalized sense of totalitarianism does not lead them to reject this second, more specific sense. The latter, too, must continue to be investigated "in all its (apparent) heterogeneity" with the former (190). But, they go on to argue, such investigation should be informed by certain questions suggested by the generalized sense of totalitarianism: Isn't the "reincarnation" notion applicable, above all, to a first (albeit still-extant), pure, radically brutal historical face of totalitarianism? And hasn't there since been installed, in the "democratic" societies, under the general domination of systems governed by technical and performative criteria, a second, inconspicuous, insidious, "soft" form of totalitarianism?[32] Isn't this "soft totalitarianism" a response, *internal to democracy*, to the "democratic crisis"—one that, unlike "hard totalitarianism," does not assume the guise of a rebuke (*redressement*)? Isn't it the case, then, that despite the crying differences, a certain ready-made and widely circulating opposition between totalitarianism and democracy is rather too simple? Granted, "we don't have camps, and our police, whatever their 'technological advancedness,' are not omnipresent political police. But his doesn't mean, however, that the democracy we have is that described by Tocqueville. And if the democracy of Tocqueville contained the germ of classical totalitarianism, there is no guarantee that ours is not in the process of secreting something else, a brand new form [*une forme inédite*] of totalitarianism" (191).

With explicit reference to the work of Hannah Arendt, Nancy and Lacoue-Labarthe link the withdrawal of the political in "soft totalitarianism" to the rise of the "economic-socio-techno-cultural complex," a complex that is no longer simply the state. They claim that this complex is characterized by (1) the triumph of the *animal laborans;* (2) the colonization of the public space by a *gesellschaftlich* sociality, such that common life is governed by considerations pertaining to subsistence and not by genuinely public or political ends; and (3) the loss of authority as a distinct element of power, a loss concomitant with the loss of liberty. They argue that these characteristics of soft totalitarianism demonstrate the insufficiency of simple critiques of classical totalitarianism. If classical totalitarianism proceeds from the "incorporation and presentation of transcendence," then soft totalitarianism proceeds from the *dissolution* of transcendence, a dissolution that pervades and thus homogenizes every sphere of life, eliminating alterity (191–92).

The *retrait du politique,* therefore, is the withdrawal of the transcendence or alterity of the political vis-à-vis other social instances. But, say Lacoue-Labarthe and Nancy, it does not follow that the task is to achieve a new political transcendence. That, indeed, is the program of classical totalitarianism. The task is rather to interrogate the way in which the *retrait* requires us to displace and reelaborate the concept of political transcendence, to think a "wholly transformed" transcendence or alterity of the political (192–93).

Reinstalling a (nontotalitarian) alterity of the political today, they claim, would require the following: (1) the overcoming of the present dissociation of *power* (material constraint) from *authority* (transcendence); (2) the repair of the presently disrupted relation of the community to what Arendt called "immortality" (a this-worldly immortality in which the community preserves the words and deeds of mortals through remembrance); and (3) the restoration of the community's capacity to represent its communality to itself in the political sphere (193–94).

Nancy and Lacoue-Labarthe go on to interweave these quasi-Arendtian observations with more properly Heideggerian motifs. The *retrait du politique*, they claim, is not a wholly privative phenomenon. Rather it is a withdrawal that releases or delivers something else: it makes something appear—namely, the possibility, indeed the necessity of re-tracing the political anew. Furthermore, it is probably the case that what receded or withdrew is something that had never occurred in the first place; it is doubtful that the polis described by Arendt ever existed. But Nancy and Lacoue-Labarthe deny that the task is to make it occur now, or to pull the political out of its withdrawal, or even to achieve a new founding of the political. They want, instead, to pose what they take to be a more fundamental question: To what is the *retrait du politique* linked? Is it linked to the withdrawal of the unity, totality, and effective manifestation of the community? (194–95).

Thus, Nancy and Lacoue-Labarthe paraphrase Heidegger in claiming that from or in the withdrawal of the political, the political "it-self" arises as a question and as an exigency. What is released is the opening of a question: On the basis of what, against what, is the closure of the political traced? The answer is not simply: on the basis of, or against, the nonpolitical (an answer popularized by Pierre Clastres's defense of anarchism, *Society Against the State*).[33] It is rather: on the basis of, or against, the "essence of the political," the essence which is withdrawn in the total completion of the political in the "techno-social" (195–96).

Provisionally, several things may be said, claim Nancy and Lacoue-Labarthe about the "essence of the political." This essence is masked by various metaphysical programs that purport to ground the political domain on a transcendent foundation. Chief among these in the modern period is the attempt to found the political on a preconstituted, preindividuated, autonomous subjectivity. It is no wonder, then, that those seeking to avoid foundationalism often substitute the notion of human finitude for that of autonomous subjectivity. But that substitution is by itself insufficient for the center's purposes: it is not guaranteed to lead beyond the politics of liberal democracy. Moreover, since finitude devolves upon immersion in an always already given, contingent sociohistorical matrix, it fails to problematize, but rather takes for granted, the existence of the social bond. In other words, it forecloses those questions that Nancy and Lacoue-Labarthe earlier took as crucial to their project: the questions circulating around the shadowy, enigmatic figure of "the mother," namely the questions of the social constitution of identity, of the constitution of social identity, and of a prepolitical, "originary" or sociality (196–97).

Nancy and Lacoue-Labarthe claim that these themes lead back to the problem of the specificity of the political—to the "philosophical fact" that at least since Aristotle, the being together of human beings, of the *zoon politikon,* is not based on the factual given of needs and the vital necessities of life. It is based rather on that other given: the sharing in ethical or evaluative speech. It is the excess of this second given over the first, of "living well" over mere "life" or social "living together," that defines the *zoon politikon.*[34] And it is the question of a "good" over and above every organization of needs and regulation of forces that remains in *retrait* today and thereby opens the question of the political (13).

This most recent statement of Nancy and Lacoue-Labarthe's program is notable for the sharp relief into which it throws the dilemma I noted earlier. On the one hand, the authors seek to resist the pressure to produce a politics, and they strive instead to maintain a pure, rigorous, deconstructive, quasi-transcendental interrogation of the political. But, on the other hand, they entertain the not-so-secret hope that the thought engendered by means of this approach will yield insights that will be relevant to *la politique.* Hence, there is an incessant sliding back and forth between two heterogeneous levels of analysis, a constant venturing toward the taking of a political position and a drawing back to metapolitical philosophical reflection.

This oscillation is clearly visible in the treatment of totalitarianism. The thesis about "hard" and "soft" totalitarianism is patently a *political position,* a venture into *la politique.* For totalitarianism is without doubt a *politically contested notion.* And Nancy and Lacoue-Labarthe concede as much when they counterpose their conception to that of Lefort, arguing that the latter is not adequate to think the character of contemporary Western societies. Here, they are supposing a *specific interpretation of social reality,* a view that is not merely deconstructive and philosophical, but *empirical, normative,* and *critical.* They are confronting the *political* problem of the character and meaning of contemporary scientific-technological culture. And this necessarily brings them into dialogue—indeed, into conflict—with competing *political* positions and interpretations. On the one hand, they must contest Lefort and other theorists of Soviet-type societies. But also, and on the other hand, whether they admit it or not, they must contest competing theories of Western political culture—most prominently, perhaps, those of Habermas and Foucault, not to mention Marx and Weber. Only if they are willing to enter the fray against such alternatives can they possibly make good their claims about "the total domination of the political" and "soft totalitarianism."

But just when such straightforwardly empirical and political argumentation is called for, just when *la politique* is about to be broached in earnest, Nancy and Lacoue-Labarthe remove themselves from the scene of conflict and draw back into quasi-Heideggerian speculation. They reflect on the "essence of the political," the "delivery of the question of the political," "finitude," the "social bond," an "originary sociality," "the mother," and a "wholly transformed alterity." The problem is not that such speculation is in itself useless or irrelevant. It is rather that it functions for Nancy and Lacoue-Labarthe as a means of avoiding the step into politics to which the logic of their own hopes and thought would otherwise drive them.

This is evident in a somewhat different way in their treatment of the Arendtian themes of the receding of the specificity of the political in the rise of the "economic-socio-techno-cultural complex"; the triumph of the *animal laborans;* the colonization of the public space by *gesellschaftlich* sociality; the loss of authority, of this-worldly immortality, of the transcendence or alterity of the political vis-à-vis "life," needs, and the prepolitical in general. With the introduction of such themes, Nancy and Lacoue-Labarthe verge once again upon politics proper. Indeed, they urge these themes against the politics of Lefort, whom they take to be insufficiently critical of contemporary "democratic" societies. But just when one would expect them to continue in this Arendtian vein, to call for a new or renewed transcendence or alterity of the political, to bring into being now the "politicity" of a polis that may never have existed— just at this point, they draw back once again and explicitly deny that any such *normative political* tasks and conclusions follow. Instead, they conclude that one must think the *retrait,* the essence, the tracing of the closure, and the rest.

Similarly, when Nancy and Lacoue-Labarthe invoke Aristotle at the close of their text, they stop just short of embracing any normative political conclusions. They appeal to the excess of "living well" over mere life, of the sharing in ethical or evaluative speech over mere need and necessity. They claim that it is the question of a "good" over and above every organization of needs and regulation of forces that opens the question of the *retrait* of the political today. But it is significant that they do not proceed from these remarks to call for an institution or restitution of noninstrumental, normative, political deliberation about "the good life." It is significant that, instead, they note parenthetically that this "good" beyond every organization of needs and regulation of forces is one that they "charge with no moral weight" (198).

What these discussions of totalitarianism, Arendt, and Aristotle show, in my view, is the fragile, slippery character of the tightrope on which Nancy and Lacoue-Labarthe are walking. They are engaged in a sort of balancing act, one which probably cannot be maintained with much fruitfulness for very long. It is likely that one of two things will happen. Either they will try to maintain the rigorous exclusion of politics, and especially of empirical and normative considerations—in which case the political import of their philosophical work will diminish. Or they will cross the line and enter upon concrete political reflection—in which case their work will become increasingly empirical and normative and therefore increasingly *contested*. In either case, one avenue appears to be excluded, the one to which Nancy and Lacoue-Labarthe apparently hope to keep—namely, the middle way of a philosophical interrogation of the political that somehow ends up producing profound, new, politically relevant insights without dirtying any hands in political struggle.

This impasse is quite intractable. But one ought not, on that account, underestimate the importance of the questions Nancy and Lacoue-Labarthe are asking. When they probe the meaning, character, and boundaries of the domain of the political as instituted in Western civilization, the historical transformations that domain has undergone since its Greek beginnings, and its specifically modern (and, we might add, postmodern) features, they broach issues that are central to contemporary political reflection. This is evident in the way their project links up with two more specific sets of empirically and normatively anchored questions.

First, and most explicitly, Nancy and Lacoue-Labarthe broach a series of issues concerning the relation between the political and economic dimensions of contemporary societies. These issues have arisen as a result of the concurrent development of welfare state capitalism in the West and authoritarian state socialism in the East (where they reached a new pitch of articulateness and insistence in Poland, in Solidarity's struggle for an "autonomous civil society"). From the Western perspective, these issues can be decisively formulated: When, in the late modern period, even capitalist economic production is socialized to the point of defying the label "private enterprise"; when, therefore, justice requires that the domain of the political be *quantitatively* enlarged so as to include the previously excluded "social question," and, when, *pace* Arendt, politics must, as a result, become political economy, what *qualitative* transformations of the political are needed to prevent its being overrun by instrumental reason and reduced to administration? What transformations can stem the homogenizing and antidemocratic tendencies that accompany the blurring of the division between civil society and the state (both in its communist form of rule by a centralized state planning apparatus and in its capitalist form of rule by a combined corporate and state-bureaucratic managerial elite)? How can both participatory democracy and the qualitative diversity of human experience be fostered in the face of these developments? What new, still uninvented, postliberal and post-Marxian models of democratic, decentralized, socialist, or mixed political economies can do justice both to the specificity of the political and to its connectedness with the socioeconomic?[35]

Second, but far more obliquely, the center's problematic links up with a range of issues concerning the relationship between the political and the familiar or domestic dimensions of contemporary societies. When they problematize the contemporary truism that "everything is political" and suggest instead that "behind the political (if it must be identified with the Father), lies the 'mother,' " Nancy and Lacoue-Labarthe at once gesture at and recoil from questions now being posed by Western feminists. Indeed, the contrast between their silence here and their volubility concerning Marxism has the significance of a symptom, since the current wave of feminist scholarship is without doubt the most advanced post-Marxian interrogation of the political now in progress[36]—an interrogation, one should note, that remains engaged while problematizing extant concepts and institutions of the political, and which avoids the snares of transcendentalism by incorporating empirical and normative elements into its philosophical critique.

Like it or not, then, Nancy and Lacoue-Labarthe are de facto engaged in a covert dialogue with a movement that is questioning the relationship between the political and the familial. When this is acknowledged, a number of issues cry out for explicit consideration: If, as Arendt contended, the institution of the political in the West depended upon, indeed was the flip side of, the institution of the familial; and if the familial, as a sphere of inequality and exploitation, can no longer be immune from critique and transformation, then how must and ought the political sphere change as well? For example, if, as Arendt argued, modern political culture, including Marxism, has been deformed by its obsession with the production of food and objects to the neglect of symbolic action; and if, *pace* Arendt, this is nowhere more evident than in the undervaluation and privatization of women's childrearing work (which—as the cultivation of persons—is symbolic action par excellence), then how might an equitable reorganization of childrearing, one that put it at the center of public concern, help to revitalize and transform the political? Finally, if women's traditional domestic activities, including the emotional servicing of men and children, have contributed to the development of enclaves (at least) of distinctive women's cultures with distinctive women's values, and if these values, which include nurturance, caring, affectivity, and nonviolence, have been denigrated and occluded in a sexist and androcentric political culture that privileges autonomy, sovereignty, and instrumental reason, then how might the political be transformed if women's cultures were liberated from domesticity and permitted to infuse public life?

Together, these two sets of questions form the outer horizon of Nancy and Lacoue-Labarthe's work. That this is so is, for me, a large part of the interest and importance of that work. But it is also an indication of its limitations. For to begin to answer these questions in earnest is of necessity to abandon transcendental and deconstructive discourse for inquiry of a different sort. It remains for the Center for Philosophical Research on the Political to join the ranks of those seeking to rise to this challenge.

Postscript

The preceding account was written in the fall of 1982.

On 16 November 1984, Philippe Lacoue-Labarthe and Jean-Luc Nancy announced that they were indefinitely suspending the activities of the Center for Philosophical Research on the Political. In a memorandum sent to members, they claimed that the center had ceased to be a place where one could advance the project of interrogating "the essence of the political." That project required that all questions concerning the political be kept open and that all certitudes be bracketed, but this was no longer the case at the center. On the contrary, during the previous two years, a certain facile, taken-for-granted consensus had settled in and closed off the opening in which radical questioning had, for a time, been possible. This consensus bore on three principal concerns. First, "totalitarianism," originally the sign of a series of questions about the similarities and differences among a variety of historical and contemporary societies, had congealed into a "simple and vehement designation of *the sole* political danger . . . henceforth incarnated by regimes of Marxist provenance." Second, Marxism, too, had ceased to be a question and had become—simply—past, outmoded, obsolete, an unfortunate nineteenth-century ideology to which one now opposed conceptions of a somehow still relevant eighteenth century—conceptions of liberty (as opposed to equality) and of right (as opposed to politics). Finally, the political itself had acquired the one-dimensional signification of a danger and an impasse, so that it was no longer possible to consider the character and organization of collective identity and sovereignty—which meant that "the ethical or the aesthetic, even the religious" had come to be privileged over the political. The result was the surrender of the very object of the center's interrogation and, simultaneously, the triumph of apoliticism. But this was, in reality, capitulation to a determinate political position, namely, the "economic neoliberalism" and "political neoconformism" now sweeping France, a born-again liberalism arising from what it proclaims to be the ashes of Marxism.

This, of course, is only one side of the story. Lacking the other side(s), one might well hesitate to offer an analysis. Nonetheless, I cannot resist pointing out that the demise of the center recapitulates its constitutive dilemma.

In their memorandum, Nancy and Lacoue-Labarthe note that in dissolving the center they are responding to a political exigency. Indeed, they have taken what, from one point of view, appears to be a straightforwardly political stand: they are opposing anti-Marxist neoliberalism. But from another point of view, the situation is more complicated. The dominant thrust of their dissolution memorandum is not to marshal *political* arguments against the neoliberals; it is, rather, to accuse them of violating the transcendental pact, of breaking faith with the interrogation of the essence of the political. The problem, in other words, is less that their opponents have bad politics than that they have politics—which is a fair guess as to how the neoliberal tendency won hegemony in the center in the first place.

Moreover, there is a sense in which the neoliberal position represents one—if not *the*—legitimate working out of at least some of Nancy and Lacoue-Labarthe's own views. What they now excoriate as "apoliticism," for example, is a not wholly unfaithful elaboration of their own theme of "the total domination of the political." After all, that theme was always inherently ambiguous. It compounded Heidegger's already overblown suspicion of technology and Arendt's already too categorical suspicion of "the social" into an even more global and undifferentiated suspicion of the political, thereby seeming to surrender the possibility of *political* opposition to administration and instrumental reason. No wonder, then, that some members concluded that henceforth such opposition must be waged under the banner of "the ethical or the aesthetic, even the religious."

A similar argument could doubtless be made with respect to anti-Marxism. In fact, of the three issues discussed in the dissolution memorandum, only one—namely, totalitarianism—is altogether unambiguous. For only with respect to that issue do Nancy and Lacoue-Labarthe assert themselves unequivocally. First, they reject a use of the term "totalitarianism" that would put them in lockstep with NATO, and *that* is a political stand. Second, they insist on conceptual distinctions adequate to the empirical complexity of contemporary social reality, East *and* West, and *that* is a post-transcendental methodological stand. "Totalitarianism," then, remains the site of the most advanced strand of their thought, the strand that could, in principle, lead beyond the current impasse and transform their problematic.

Two years ago I argued that the Center for Philosophical Research on the Political would be but "a temporary way station on the exodus from Marxism now being traveled by the French intelligentsia [and not] a permanent resting place." Now the precise character of the journey—its possible and actual destinations—is more evident. One route runs through the Center for Philosophical Research on the Political to "apolitical neoliberalism." Another, barely visible, would require French post-Marxists to develop links with German Critical Theory and Anglo-American socialist feminism. Given the larger currents of contemporary French culture, including widespread disillusionment with the Mittérand government, the pressures to take the first route are enormous. That Nancy and Lacoue Labarthe nonetheless refuse it is certainly to their credit. Still, one hopes they will soon venture forth from their transcendental safe house.

4

The Violence
of the Masquerade:
Law Dressed Up
as Justice

Drucilla Cornell

From our childhood, most of us are familiar with the myth, "The Emperor's New Clothes." Deconstruction, both by its friends and its foes in legal circles, is understood to rip away law's pretension to be other than politics. Deconstruction, in other words, supposedly exposes the nakedness of power struggles and indeed, of violence masqueraded as the rule of law. The enemies of deconstruction challenge this exposure as itself an act of violence which leaves in its stead only the "right" of force and, as a result, levels the moral differences between legal systems and blurs the all-to-real distinctions between different kinds of violent acts. At first glance, the title of Jacques Derrida's essay, "Force of Law: The 'Mystical Foundation of Authority,' "[1] seems to confirm this interpretation. It also, in turn, informs Dominick LaCapra's subtle and thoughtful commentary,[2] which evidences his concern that deconstruction may—in our obviously violent world—succumb to the allure of violence, rather than help us to demystify its seductive power. But is Derrida *legitimately* charged with this interpretation of his text? And if he is, what is the process of *legitimation* that determines that this

78

interpretation is justified? More importantly—what is the implicit position on the significance of right as established, legal norms that deconstruction is accused of "going on strike" against? This last question becomes extremely important because it is precisely the "on strike" posture not only *before* established legal norms, but also seemingly before the very idea of legal norms, that troubles LaCapra. Undoubtedly, Derrida's engagement with Walter Benjamin's text, "Critique of Violence,"[3] has been interpreted as further evidence of the inherent danger in upholding the position that law is always deconstructable. It is this position that law is always deconstructable that makes *possible* the "on strike" posture toward any legal system.[4] Walter Benjamin's text has often—and to my mind mistakenly—been interpreted to erase human responsibility for violence, because the distinction between mythic violence—the violence that founds or constitutes law (right)—and the divine violence that is its "antithesis" (because it destroys rather than founds, expiates rather than upholds), is ultimately undecidable for Benjamin. Lawmaking or founding violence is then distinguished, at least in a preliminary manner, from law-preserving or -conserving *force*. We will see the significance of this further distinction shortly. If this undecidability was the end of the matter, if we simply turned to God's judgment, there would be no *critique* of violence. Of course, there is one interpretation, already presented, which states that Benjamin—and then Derrida—does erase the very basis on which the critique of violence proceeds.[5] But this interpretation fails to take notice of the opening reminder of Benjamin's text, to which Derrida returns us again and again, and which structures the unfolding of his own text. To quote Benjamin:

> The task of a critique of violence can be summarized as that of expounding its relation to law and justice. For a cause, however effective becomes violent, in the precise sense of the word, only when it bears on moral issues. The sphere of these issues is defined by the concepts of law and justice.[6]

Derrida's text proceeds precisely through the configuration of the concepts of justice and law in which the critique of violence, understood as "judgement, evaluation, examination that provides itself with the means to judge violence,"[7] must take place. Critique, in this sense, is hardly the simple glorification of violence per se, since Benjamin and Derrida carefully distinguish between different kinds of violence. Indeed, they both question the traditional positivist and naturalist justifications for violence as legitimate enforcement for the maintenance of an established legal system or as a necessary means to achieve a just end. In other words, both thinkers are concerned with *rationalizations of bloodless* bureaucratic violence that LaCapra rightfully associates with some of the horrors of the twentieth century.[8] Benjamin's own text speaks more to the analysis of different kinds of violence, and more specifically to law and the force of law as law-conserving violence, than to justice. But Derrida explicitly begins his text with the "Possibility of Justice" as presented in the title of the conference.[9] It is only once we accept the uncrossable divide between law and justice that deconstruction both exposes and protects *in the very deconstruction of the identification of law as justice,* that we can apprehend the full significance of Derrida's seemingly surprising statement that "deconstruction is justice."[10] What is missed in the interpretation I have described is that the undecidability which can be used to expose any legal system's process of the self-legitimation of authority as myth, leaves us—the "us" here being specifically those who enact and enforce the law—with an *inescapable responsibility* for violence, precisely because violence cannot be fully rationalized and therefore justified in advance. The "feigning [of] presence"[11] inherent in the founding violence of the state, using Derrida's phrase, disguises the retrospective act of justification and thus *seemingly,* but only seemingly, erases responsibility by justification. To quote Derrida:

> Here we "touch" without touching this extraordinary paradox:
> the inaccessible transcendence of the law before which and
> prior to which "man" stands fast only appears infinitely tran-
> scendent and thus theological to the extent that, so near him,
> it depends only on him, on the performative act by which he
> institutes it: the law is transcendent, violent and non-violent,
> because it depends only on who is before it—and so prior to
> it—, on who produces it, founds it, authorizes it in an absolute
> performative whose presence always escapes him. The law is
> transcendent and theological, and so always to come, always
> promised, because it is immanent, finite and so already past.
>   Only the yet-to-come [*avenir*] will produce intelligibility or
> interpretability of this law.[12]

Law never catches up with its projected justification. Therefore, there can be no insurance of a metalanguage in relation to the "performativity of institutional language or its dominant interpretation."[13] In other words, might can never justify right precisely because the establishment of right can never be fully rationalized. It does not mean the reverse, as LaCapra seems to fear it might, if taken to its logical conclusion. For LaCapra, in spite of his clear recognition that Derrida explicitly rejects the idea that might makes right in some parts of text, there is still the danger that undecidability can possibly lead to this conception of law. To quote LaCapra:

> A second movement at least seems to identify the undecidable with force or even violence and to give to violence the power to generate or create justice and law. Justice and law, which of course cannot be conflated, nonetheless seem to originate in force or violence. The extreme misreading of this movement would be the conclusion that might makes right—a conclusion explicitly rejected at one point in Derrida's essay but perhaps insufficiently guarded against at others.[14]

But to understand why deconstruction does not reduce itself to the most recent and sophisticated brand of legal positivism, which of course does assert that might does indeed make right, it is useful to contrast deconstruction *as* the force of justice against law with Stanley Fish's insistent identification of law with justice.[15] Fish understands that as a philosophical matter law can never catch up with its justifications, but that as a practical reality its functional machinery renders its philosophical inadequacy before its own claims irrelevant. Indeed, the system sets the limit of relevance. The machine, in other words, functions to erase the mystical foundations of its own authority. My critical disagreement with Fish, a disagreement behind which I am bringing the force of deconstruction, is that the legal machine he celebrates as a marvel, I abhor as a monster.

In the case of law, there is a reason to be afraid of ghosts. But to see why I think the practical erasure of the mystical foundation of authority by the legal system must be told as a horror story, let me turn to an actual case that embodies the two myths of legality and legal culture that Fish consistently returns us to. For Fish, contemporary American legal interpretation, both in constitutional law, as well as in other areas, functions primarily through two myths of justification for decision.[16] The first is "the intent of the founding fathers," or some other conception of an original foundation. The second is "the plain meaning of the words," whether of the relevant statutes, precedent, or of the Constitution itself. In terms of deconstruction, the second can be interpreted as the myth of full readability. These myths, as Fish well recognizes, conserve law as a self-legitimating machine by returning legal interpretation to a supposed origin that repeats itself as a self-enclosed hermeneutic circle. This, in turn, allows the identification of justice with law and with the perpetuation of the "current" legal system.[17]

To "see" the violence inherent in being before the law in the many senses of that phrase which Derrida plays on, let us imagine the scene in Georgia that sets the stage for *Bowers v. Hardwick*,[18] Two men are peacefully making love, little knowing that they were before the law and soon to be proclaimed guilty of sodomy as a criminal offense. Fish's glee is in showing the impotence—and I am using that world deliberately— of the philosophical challenge to the political critique of the legal mechanism that justifies perpetuation of the system itself as a system. The law just keeps coming. Remember the childhood ghost story, "Bloody Bones," to help you envision the scene. The law is on the first step. The philosopher desperately tries to check the law, but to no avail, by appealing to "outside" norms of justice. The law is on the second step. Now the feminist critic tries to dismantle the law machine which is operating against her. Again, the law simply wipes off the criticism of its masquerade (here, heterosexual bias) as irrelevant. The law is on the third step. It draws closer to its victims. Fish admires precisely this *force of law,* the so-called potency to keep coming in spite of its critics and its philosophical bankruptcy, a bankruptcy not only acknowledged but continually exposed by Fish himself. Once it is wound up, there is no stopping the law, and what winds it up is its own functions as elaborated in the myths of legal culture. Thus, although law may be a human construct insofar as we are all captured by its mandates, its constructibility, and thus its potential deconstructibility, it has no "consequences."[19]

In *Bowers v. Hardwick* we do indeed see the force of law as it makes itself felt, in spite of the criticisms of the opinion by "the philosophers." Justice White concludes and upholds as a matter of law that the state of Georgia has the right to make homosexual sodomy a criminal offense.[20] Some commentators, defending the opinion, have relied precisely on the myth of the intent of the founding fathers. The argument is that there is no evidence that the intent of the founding fathers was to provide a right of privacy or any other kind of right for homosexuals.

The arguments against the philosophical justification of this position repeated by Fish are obvious. The concept of intent is problematic when speaking of living writers, for all the reasons discussed in writing on legal interpretation. But in the case of interpreting dead writers who have been *silent* on the issue, the subtle complexities of interpreting through intent, are no longer subtle, but are manifestly ludicrous. The process of interpreting intent *always* involves construction once there is a written text that supposedly introduces the intent. But, *here*, there is only silence, an absence of voice, simply because the *founding* fathers never addressed homosexuality. That this silence means that there is no right of homosexuality and they thought it so self-evident as never to speak of it, is clearly only one interpretation and one that can never be clarified except in the infinite regress of construction. Since the process involved in interpreting from silence clearly entails construction, the judges own values are involved. In this case we do not even need to go further into the complexities of readability and unreadability of a text, because we are literally left with silence, no word on homosexuality.

But in Justice White's opinion we are, indeed, returned to the problem of the readability or the unreadability of the text of the Constitution and of the precedent that supposedly just "states" its meaning. Justice White rejects the Eleventh Circuit's[21] holding that the Georgia statute violated the respondent's fundamental right "because his homosexual right is a private and intimate association that is beyond the reach of state regulation by reason of the Ninth Amendment and the Due Process Clause of the Fourteenth Amendment."[22] The Eleventh Circuit relied on the line of precedent from *Griswold*[23] through *Roe*[24] and *Carey*[25] to read the right of privacy to include "homosexual activity." Justice White rejects this reading. He does so, as we will see, by narrowly construing the right supposedly implicated in this case, and then by reading the language of the holding of each case in a "literalist" manner, implicitly relying on "the plain meaning of the words." Do we find any language in these cases about homosexuality? Justice White cannot find any such language. Since he cannot find any such language, Justice White concludes that "the plain meaning of the words" did not mandate this extension of the right of privacy to "homosexual activity." To quote Justice White:

> Accepting the decisions in these cases and the above description of them, we think it evident that none of the rights announced in those cases bears any resemblance to the claimed constitutional right of homosexuals to engage in acts of sodomy that is asserted in this case. No connection between family, marriage, or procreation on the one hand and homosexual activity on the other has been demonstrated, either by the Court of Appeals or by respondent.[26]

We do not need to develop a sophisticated philosophical critique to point to the flaw in Justice White's "literalist" interpretation of the cases. We can simply rely on one of the oldest and most established "principles" of constitutional interpretation. That principle is that cases should be narrowly decided. If one accepts that that principle was operative in the cases associated with the establishment of the "right of privacy,"[27] then the reason none of these cases "spoke" to homosexuality was that the question of homosexuality wasn't before them. Judges under this principle are to decide cases, not advance norms or speculate about all possible extensions of the right. When and how the right is to be extended is dependent on the concrete facts of each case. In spite of what he says he is doing, Justice White, like the commentators already mentioned, is interpreting from a silence, and a silence that inheres in the principle that constitutional cases in particular should be construed narrowly. (Need I add here that if one is a homosexual, the right to engage in homosexual activity might have everything to do with "family, marriage, and procreation,"[28] even though Justice White argues the contrary position? As a result, his very interpretation of the "privacy" cases—as being about "family, marriage, and procreation"—could be used against him. Can White's blindness to this obvious reality be separated from his own acceptance of an implied heterosexuality as legitimate and, indeed, as the only right way to live?)

Justice White's opinion does not simply rest on his reading of the cases, but also rests on an implicit conception of the readability of the Constitution. For Justice White, the Constitution is fully readable. Once again, he does not find anything in the Constitution itself that mentions the right to homosexuality. Therefore, Justice White interprets the Eleventh Circuit as creating such a right out of thin air, rather than on a reading of the Constitution and of precedent that understands what is *fundamental* and necessary to privacy as a right "established" by the Constitution. For Justice White to simply create a "new" fundamental right would be the most dangerous kind of activism, particularly in the case of homosexuality. And why is this the case for Justice White? As Justice White explains:

> Proscriptions against that conduct have ancient roots. See generally, Survey on the Constitutional Right to Privacy in the Context of Homo-sexual Activity, 40 U. Miami L. Rev. 521, 525 (1986). Sodomy was a criminal offense at common law and was forbidden by the laws of the original 13 states when they ratified the Bill of Rights. In 1868 , when the Fourteenth Amendment was ratified, all but 5 of the 37 states had criminal sodomy laws. In fact, until 1961, all 50 states outlawed sodomy, and today, 24 States and the District of Columbia continue to provide criminal penalties for sodomy performed in

private and between consenting adults. See Survey U. Miami L. Rev. *supra* at 524, n.9. Against this background to claim that a right to engage in such conduct is "deeply rooted in this Nation's history and tradition" or "implicit in the concept of ordered liberty" is, at best, facetious.[29]

For White, not only is the danger of activism always to be guarded against, but it must be specifically forsaken in a case such as this one. Again, the *justification* for his position turns on his implicit conception of the readability of the Constitution. To quote Justice White, "[t]he Court is most vulnerable and comes nearest to illegitimacy when it deals with judge-made constitutional law having little or no cognizable roots in the language or design of the Constitution."[30]

I have critiqued the charge of judicial activism elsewhere as a fundamental misunderstanding of the inevitable role of normative construction in legal interpretation[31] once we understand that interpretation is also evaluation. Fish has his own version of this critique.[32] The point I want to make here is that for Fish, the power of law to enforce its own premises as the truth of the system erases the significance of its philosophical interlocutors, rendering their protest impotent. The concrete result in this case is that the criminal sanctions against gay men are given constitutional legitimation in that it is now proclaimed to be legally acceptable for states to outlaw homosexual love and sexual engagement.

Is this a classic example of the conserving violence of law? The answer, I believe, is unquestionably, yes. But more importantly, given the analysis of Justice White, it demonstrates a profound point about the relationship, emphasized by Derrida, between conserving violence and the violence of foundation. To quote Derrida, and I quote in full, because I believe this quotation is crucial to my own response to LaCapra's concern that Derrida yields to the temptation of violence:

> For beyond Benjamin's explicit purpose, I shall propose the interpretation according to which the very violence of the foundation or position of law (*Rechtsetzende Gewalt*) must envelop the violence of conservation (*Rechtserhaltende Gewalt*) and cannot break with it. It belongs to the structure of fundamental violence that it calls for the repetition of itself and founds what ought to be conserved, conservable, promised to heritage and tradition, to be shared. A foundation is a promise. Every position [*Setzung*] permits and promises [*permet et pro-met*], it position *en mettant et en promettant*. And even if a promise is not kept in fact, iterability inscribes the promise as the guard in the

most irruptive instant of foundation. Thus it inscribes the possibility of repetition at the heart of the originary. . . . Position
is already iterability, a call for self-conserving repetition. Conservation in its turn refounds, so that it can conserve what it
claims to found. Thus there can be no rigorous opposition between positioning and conservation, only what I will call (and
Benjamin does not name it) a *différantielle* contamination between the two, with all the paradoxes that this may lead to.[33]

The call for self-conserving repetition is the basis for Justice
White's opinion, and more specifically, for his rejection of "reading
into" the Constitution, *in spite of his interpretation of precedent,* a fundamental liberty to engage in "homosexual sodomy." As White further explains:

Striving to assure itself and the public that announcing rights
not readily identifiable in the Constitution's text involves much
more than the imposition of the Justices' own choice of values
on the States and the Federal Government, the Court has
sought to identify the nature of the rights qualifying for heightened judicial protection.[34]

To summarize again, the result for White is that "fundamental
liberties" should be limited to those that are "deeply rooted in the Nation's history and tradition."[35] For Justice White, as we have also seen,
the evidence that the right to engage "in homosexual sodomy" is not a
fundamental liberty is the "fact" that at the time the Fourteenth Amendment was passed, all but five of the thirty-seven states in the union had
criminal sodomy laws, and that most states continue to have such laws. In
his dissent, Blackmun vehemently rejects the appeal to the *fact* of the
existence of antisodomy criminal statutes as a basis for the continuing
prohibition of the denial of a right, characterized by Blackmun not as the
right to engage in homosexual sodomy but as the right "to be let
alone."[36]
Quoting Justice Holmes, Blackmun reminds us that:

It is revolting to have no better reason for a rule of law than
that it was laid down in the time of Henry IV. It is still more
revolting if the grounds upon which it was laid down have van-
ished long since, and the rule simply persists from blind imita-
tion of the past.[37]

Derrida gives us insight into how the traditional positivist conception of law, in spite of Justice Holmes' remark and Justice Blackmun's concern, consists precisely in this self-conserving repetition. For Fish, as we have seen, it is the practical power of the legal system to preserve itself through the conflation of repetition with justification that makes it a legal system. Of course, Fish recognizes that repetition as iterability also allows for evolution. But evolution is the only possibility when *justification* is identified as the functioning of the system itself. Law, for Fish—in spite of his remarks to the contrary—is not deconstructible and, therefore, is also not radically transformable. As a system it becomes its own "positive" social reality in which the status of its own myths cannot be challenged.

It is, however, precisely the status, as myth of its originary foundation and the "plain meaning of the words"—or in more technical language, the readability of the text—that Derrida challenges in the name of justice. We are now returned to LaCapra's concern about the potentially dangerous equalizing force in Derrida's own argument. LaCapra reinterprets what he reads as one of Derrida's riskier statements. Let me first quote Derrida's statement: "Since the origin of authority, the foundation or ground, the position of law can't by definition rest on anything but themselves, they are themselves a violence without ground."[38] LaCapra reformulates Derrida's statement in the hope of making it less subject to abuse. To quote LaCapra: "Since the origin of authority, the foundation or ground, the position of the law can't by definition rest on anything but themselves, the question of their ultimate foundation or ground is literally pointless."[39]

My disagreement with LaCapra's restatement is as follows: it is not that the question of the ultimate ground or foundation of law is pointless for Derrida; instead it is the question of the ultimate ground or correctly stated lack of such that *must* be asked, if we are to heed the call of justice. That no justificatory discourse *can* or *should* insure the role of a metalanguage in relation to its dominant interpretation, *means* that the conserving promise of law can never be fully actualized in a hermeneutical circle that successfully turns back in on itself, and therefore grounds itself.

Of course, there are, at least at first glance, two kinds of violence at issue here; the violence of the foundation or the establishment of a legal system, and then the law-conserving or jurispathetic violence of an actual legal system. But Derrida demonstrates in his engagement with Benjamin's text just how these two kinds of violence are contaminated. To concretize the significance this contamination, we are again returned to *Bowers v. Hardwick*. The erasure of the status of the intent of the founding fathers and the plain meaning of the words as legal myths is the basis for the *justification* of the jurispathetic or law-conserving violence of the decision. The exposure of the mystical foundation of authority, which is another way of writing that the performativity of institutive language cannot be fully incorporated by the system once it is established (and thus cannot become fully self-justifying), does show that the establishment of law is violence in the sense of an *imposition* without a *present* justification. But this exposure should not be understood as succumbing to the lure of violence. Instead, the tautology upon which Justice White's opinion rests: "the law is and therefore it is justified to be, because it is," is exposed as tautology rather than justification. The point, then, of questioning the origin of authority is precisely to undermine the conflation of justification with an appeal to the origin, a conflation made possible because of the erasure of the mystical foundation of authority. LaCapra's reformulation may be "riskier" than Derrida's own because it can potentially turn us away from the operational force of the legal myths that seemingly create a self-justifying system. The result, as we have seen, is the violence of Justice White's opinion in which description is identified as prescription, criminal persecution of homosexuals defended as the necessity of the rule of law.

But does the deconstructionist intervention lead us to the conclusion that LaCapra fears it might, that conclusion being that all legal systems, because they are based on a mystical foundation of authority, have "something rotten"[40] at the core and are therefore "equal."[41] In one sense, LaCapra is right to worry about the equalizing force of deconstruction. The equality between legal systems is indeed that all such systems are deconstructible. But it is precisely this equality that allows for legal transformation, including legal transformation in the name of the traditional emancipatory ideals. Derrida reminds us that there is "nothing . . . less outdated" than those ideals.[42] As we have seen in *Bowers*, achieving them remains an aspiration, but an aspiration that is not just impotent idealism against the ever-functioning, nondeconstructible machine. As we have seen, Derrida is in disagreement with Fish about deconstructibility of law. For Fish, since law, or any other social context, defines the parameters of discourse, the transformative challenges to the system are rendered impotent because they can only challenge the system from within it. "There is" no other "place" for them to be but within the system.[43] But for Derrida "there is" no system that can catch up with itself and therefore establish itself as the only reality. To think that any social system, legal or otherwise can "fill" social reality is just another myth, the myth of full presence. In Fish, it is practically insignificant that law is a social construct, because social construct or not we can not deconstruct the machine. In Derridean deconstruction the opposite conclusion is reached. As Derrida explains, returning us to the excess of the performative language that *establishes* a legal system:

> Even if the success of the performatives that found law or right (for example, and this is more than an example, of a state as guarantor of a right) presupposes earlier conditions and conventions (for example in the national or international arena), the same "mystical" limit will reappear at the supposed origin of their dominant interpretation.
> The structure I am describing here is a structure in which law [*droit*] is essentially deconstructible, whether because it is founded, constructed on interpretable and transformable textual strata, (and that is the history of law [*droit*], its possible and necessary transformation, sometimes its amelioration), or because its ultimate foundation is by definition unfounded. The fact that law is deconstructible is not bad news. We may even see in this a stroke of luck for politics, for all historical progress.[44]

The deconstructibility of law, then, as Derrida understands it, is a theoretical conception that *does* have practical consequences; the practical consequences are precisely that law cannot *inevitably* shut out its challengers and prevent transformation, at least not on the basis that the law itself demands that it do so. It should not come as a surprise, then, that the Eleventh Circuit, the court that found that the Georgia statute violated the respondent's fundamental rights, rested on the Ninth Amendment as well as on the Fourteenth Amendment of the Constitution. The Ninth Amendment can and, to my mind, should be interpreted to attempt fidelity to the deconstructibility of even the "best" constitution, so as to allow for historical change in the name of justice.[45] The Ninth Amendment can also be understood from within the problematic of what *constitutes* the intent of the "founding fathers." The intent of the Constitution can only be *to be just* if it is to meet its aspiration to democratic justification. The Bill of Rights clearly attempts to spell out the conditions of justice as they were understood at the time of the passage of the Constitution. But the Ninth Amendment also recognizes the limit of *any description* of the conditions of justice, including those embodied in the Bill of Rights. An obvious example is the call of homosexuals for justice, for their "fundamental liberty." The Ninth Amendment should be, and indeed was, used by the Eleventh Circuit to guard against the tautology upon which Justice White's opinion rests.[46] Silence, in other words, is to be constructed as the "not yet thought," not the "self-evident that need not be spoken."

But does this interpretation of the Ninth Amendment mean that there is no legitimacy to the conservation of law? Can a legal system completely escape its promise of conservation that inheres in its myth of origin? Certainly Derrida does not think so. Indeed, for Derrida, a legal system could not aspire to justice if it did not make this promise to conservation of principle and the rule of law. But it would also not aspire to justice unless it understood this promise as a promise to justice. Again we are returned to the recognition, at least in my interpretation of the Ninth Amendment, of this paradox.

It is precisely this paradox, which for Derrida is inescapable, that makes justice an aporia, rather than a projected ideal.[47] To try exactly to define what justice *is* would once again collapse prescription into description and fail to heed the humility before justice inherent in my interpretation of the Ninth Amendment. Such an attempt shuts off the call of justice, rather than heeding it, and leads to the travesty of justice, so eloquently described by Justice Holmes.[48] But, of course, a legal system if it is *to be* just must also promise universality, the fair application of the rules. As a result, we have what for Derrida is the first aporia of justice, *epoche* and rule. This aporia stems from the responsibility of the judge not only to state the law but to *judge* it.

> In short, for a decision to be just and responsible, it must, in its proper moment if there is one, be both regulated and without regulation: it must conserve the law and also destroy it or suspend it enough to have to reinvent it in each case, rejustify it, it least reinvent it in the reaffirmation and the new and free confirmation of its principle.[49]

Justice White failed to meet his responsibility precisely because he replaced description with judgment, and indeed, a description of state laws a hundred years past, and in very different social and political circumstances.

But if justice *is* (note the constative language) only as aporia, if no descriptive set of current conditions for justice can be identified *as* justice, does that mean that all legal systems are equal in their embodiment of the emancipatory ideals? Is that what the "equality" that all legal systems are deconstructible boils down to? And worse yet, if that is the conclusion, does that not mean that we have an excuse to skirt our responsibility as political and ethical participants in our legal culture? Derrida explicitly disagrees with that conclusion. "That justice exceeds law and calculation, that the unpresentable exceeds the determinable cannot and should not serve as an alibi for staying out of juridico-political battles, within an institution or a state or between one institution or state or others."[50]

But let me state this positioning vis-à-vis the deconstructibility of law even more strongly. The deconstructibility of law is what allows for the possibility of transformation, not just the evolution of the legal system. This very openness to transformation, which in my interpretation of the Ninth Amendment should be understood as institutional humility before the call to justice, can itself be *translated* as a standard by which to judge "competing" legal systems. It can also be *translated* into a standard by which we can judge the justices themselves as to how they have exercised their responsibility. Compare for example, Justice White's majority opinion with Justice Blackmun's dissent.[51] Thus, we can respond to La-Capra's concern that all legal systems not be conceived as equally "rotten." All judges are not equal in the exercise of their responsibility to justice, even if justice can not be determined as a set of established norms. (Nor does the deconstructibility of law absolutely forbid competing judgments about the immanent norms of competing systems, in terms of their ability *to correct injustice* as a matter of right, but that is a different question.) Indeed, what is "rotten" in a legal system is precisely the erasure of its own mystical foundation of authority so that the system can dress itself up as justice. Thus, Derrida can rightly argue that deconstruction

> hyperbolically raises the stakes of exacting justice; it is sensitivity to a sort of essential disproportion that must inscribe excess and inadequation in itself and that strives to denounce not only theoretical limits but also concrete injustices, with the most palpable effects, in the good conscience that dogmatically stops before any inherited determination of justice.[52]

It is this "rottenness" in our own legal system as it is evidenced in Justice White's opinion that causes me to refer to the legal system as Fish describes it as a monster.

But for LaCapra, there is also another issue, separate if connected to the potential equalization of legal systems due to their inherent "rottenness." That danger is a danger of an irresponsible turn to violence, because there can be no projected standards by which to judge *in advance* the acceptability of violent acts. For LaCapra, this danger inheres in the complete disassociation of cognition and action that he reads as inherent in Benjamin's text, and perhaps in Derrida's engagement with Benjamin. As LaCapra reminds us in a potential disagreement with Derrida's formulation of this disassociation·

> As Derrida himself elsewhere emphasizes, the performative is never pure or autonomous; it always comes to some degree bound up with other functions of language. And justificatory discourse—however uncertain its grounds and deprived of the superordinate and masterful status of metalanguage—is never entirely absent from a revolutionary situation or *a coup de force*.[53]

But Derrida certainly is not arguing that justificatory language has nothing to do with revolutionary situations. His argument is instead that the justificatory language of *revolutionary* violence depends on what has yet to be established, and of course, as a result might yet come into being. If it did not depend on what was yet to come it would not be *revolutionary* violence. To quote Derrida:

> A "successful" revolution, the "successful foundation of a State (in somewhat the same sense that one speaks of a " 'felicitous' performative speech act") will produce *après coup* what it was destined in advance to produce, namely, proper interpretative models to read in return, to give sense, necessity and above all legitimacy to the violence that has produced, among others, the interpretative model in question, that is, the discourse of its self-legitimation. . . . There are cases in which it is not known for generations if the performative of the violent founding of a state is "felicitous" or not.[54]

That separation of cognition and action by time means that no acts of violence can truly be justified at the time they take place, if by truly justified one means cognitive assurance of the rightness of action. I believe that this interpretation of Derrida's engagement with Benjamin is the reading that does full justice to the seriousness with which both authors take the command "thou shall not kill."[55] Thus, we can only be just to Benjamin's text and to Derrida's reading if we understand the responsibility imposed upon us by Benjamin's infamous statement about divine violence. "For it is never reason that decides on the justification of means and the justness of ends, but fate-imposed violence in the former and God on the latter."[56] Since there can be no cognitive assurance in advance of action, we are left with our responsibility for what we do. We can not escape responsibility by appealing to established conventions. Revolutionary violence cannot be rationalized by an appeal to what "is" for what "is" is exactly what is to be overturned. In this sense, each one of us is put on the line in a revolutionary situation. Of course, the inability to know whether or not the situation actually demands violence, also means there can be no justification for not acting. This kind of undecidability is truly frightening. But it may not be more frightening than the justifications for violence whether it be the death penalty or the war machine, put forward by the state. LaCapra worries precisely about the day to dayness of extreme violence in the modern/postmodern state.[57] But so does Benjamin in his discussion of the police.[58] The need to have some standards to curtail violence, particularly this kind of highly rationalized violence, should not be confused with a justification for revolutionary violence. The problem is not that there are not reasons given for violence. It is not even that these reasons should better be understood as rationalizations. It is rather that revolutionary violence cannot be rationalized, because all forms of rationalization would necessarily take the form of an appeal to what has already been established. Of course, revolutionary movements project ideals from within their present discourse. But if they are *revolutionary* movements they also reject the limits of that discourse. Can they do so? Have they done so? Judgment awaits these movements in the future. Perhaps we can better understand Benjamin's refusal of human rationalizations for violence by appealing to Monique Wittig's myth, *Les Guérillères*.[59] In *Les Guérillères*, we are truly comforted with a revolutionary situation, the overthrow of patriarchy with its corresponding enforcement of heterosexuality. In the myth, the Amazons take up arms. Is this mythic violence governed by fate? Is the goal the establishment of a new state? Would this new state not be the reversal of patriarchy and therefore its reinstatement? Or does this "war" signify divine violence, the violence that truly expiates? The text presents those questions as myth, but also as possibility "presented" in literary form.

How could the women in the myth know in advance, particularly if one shares the feminist premise that all culture has been shaped by the inequality of the gender divide as defined by patriarchy? If one projects an ideal even supposed by feminine norms, are these norms not contaminated by the patriarchical order with which the women are at "war." Rather than a decision about the resolution of this dilemma, Wittig's myth symbolizes the process of questioning that must inform a revolutionary situation, which calls into question all the traditional justifications for what is. I am relying on this myth, which challenges one of the deepest cultural structures, because I believe it allows us to experience the impossibility of deciding in advance whether the symbolized war against patriarchy can be determined *in advance*, either as mythic or divine, or as justified or unjustified.

Yet, I agree with LaCapra that we need "limited forms of control."[60] But these limited forms of control are just that, limited forms. Should we ever risk the challenge to these limited forms? Would LaCapra say never? If so, my own response to him can only be a quote from Brecht: "Never say never." And why? Because it would not be just to do so.

Derrida's text leaves us with the infinite responsibility undecidability imposes on us. Undecidability in no way alleviates responsibility. The opposite is the case. We cannot be excused from our own role in history because we could not know so as to be reassured that we were right in advance.

5

Politics beyond Humanism:
Mandela and
the Struggle
against Apartheid

Robert Bernasconi

W hat, if anything, is at stake in the course of a deconstruction? One can imagine this question being raised as an objection by someone already convinced that deconstruction represents the forces of arbitrariness and nihilism in contemporary thought. The question could also be posed more positively, as I intend to pose it here, in the context of the ever-growing interest in the politics of deconstruction. It is tempting to include Derrida himself among those whose interest in the politics of deconstruction has been on the increase, but it would be a mistake to think that this concern is only recent. One could, for example, turn to the opening pages of the 1968 essay "The Ends of Man," which not only assert the political import of philosophy, but also express solidarity with those in the United States fighting against their country's official policy in Vietnam and elsewhere.[1] One could also describe as political the introduction to the second part of *Of Grammatology*, where it is shown that Lévi-Strauss's critique of ethnocentrism betrays itself by its own ethnocentric gestures.[2] Nor need one stop there. One of deconstruction's most profoundly "political" interventions has lain in disturbing the confidence with which the boundaries between disciplines and areas are maintained. In consequence, the usual restrictions placed on a term like "the political" have been disturbed.

Nevertheless, a distinction needs to be drawn between the politics of deconstruction and Derrida's own politics. There is an obvious sense in which Derrida's judgments about American foreign policy might be held to be entirely irrelevant to an assessment of the politics of deconstruction. Much of the suspicion directed at the politics of deconstruction arises from the fact that deconstruction tends to be presented as a formal method, which as such can be applied to a variety of purposes, including disreputable ones. Derrida himself, particularly early on, tended to describe deconstruction in formalistic terms, for example, in *Positions*[3] or in the final pages of "The Ends of Man."[4] Indeed, it is by showing the rigor of this formalism that one best answers the familiar attack on the alleged arbitrariness of deconstruction.[5] But there is still an openness to deconstruction rendered all the more suspicious to traditionalists because of its own suspicion of ethics. The problem is that so long as deconstruction is portrayed as a formal method it would appear to lack an ethical-political direction independent of that given it by its practitioners. At very least, the argument would run, deconstruction's formalism amounts to a neutrality which can be put to the service of any political cause, including that of whitewashing. And this is precisely the tenor of the accusations that have arisen in the wake of the recent revelations about Paul de Man's journalism during the Second World War and the continuing exposure of Heiddeger's Nazism. Even though the two cases would appear to be very different, opponents of deconstruction allege that Derrida's treatment of both figures betrays the sinister capacity of deconstruction to neutralize offensive phrases and to withhold from passing decisive critical judgments.

Richard Bernstein in a recent essay has provided a partial response to the complaint that the ethical-political is peripheral to Derrida. Bernstein has such little sympathy for Derrida's attempt to question the possibility of "warranting" ethical-political positions that he concludes without hesitation that Derrida never satisfactorily answers the question of how we can warrant such "positions."[6] Nevertheless, this does not mean to Bernstein that deconstruction is thereby restricted to the level of a formalist philosophy. Bernstein recognizes what he calls "Derrida's ethical-political horizon" as a point of departure for virtually everything he has written (*JSP*, 108). Bernstein locates this horizon in Derrida's exposure of the search for an *arche* as an attempt to repress and master our anxiety in the face of the uncanny (*JSP*, 95–96).[7] He of-

fers the following sentence from "Violence and Metaphysics," Derrida's
early essay on Levinas, as possibly providing the "justification" of Derrida's "fundamental thought": "The best liberation from violence is a
certain putting into question, which makes the search for an *archia* tremble."[8] Surprisingly, Bernstein does not reflect either on the transformation that "warranting" would need to undergo within such a perspective,
or on the way notions like position-taking and critique would also have to
come under scrutiny. Not that there are any ready answers to such questions, questions which Derrida in his most recent essays continues to explore, often still in dialogue with Levinas. That is why, while sharing
Bernstein's conviction that there is a strong ethical component to deconstruction, as I put it elsewhere, I find "the ethical enactment above all in
the way deconstruction ultimately refuses to adopt the standpoint of critique, renouncing the passing of judgments on its own behalf in its own
voice."[9] I shall not here rehearse these issues which I have explored elsewhere in connection with Derrida's reading of Levinas. I shall instead
take the ethical-political dimension of Derrida's "protest against metaphysics" (*JSP*, 97) beyond the level of metaphorics, where Bernstein situ-
ates it, by examining two of Derrida's more politically charged texts, the
early essay "The Ends of Man" and the more recent "The Laws of Reflection: Nelson Mandela, in Admiration."[10]

There are reasons which might tell against using "The Ends of
Man." It is almost twenty-five years old and was a text that Derrida at
first did not make available in French, suggesting perhaps some hesitation on his part about it. On the other hand, as one of his most frequently cited essays, not only for its elaboration—which I shall again
rehearse in a moment—of the twin strategies of deconstruction, but also
for establishing Derrida's reputation as a critic of Heidegger, it has set
the tone for the Anglo-American discussion of Derrida and is thus in
some respects responsible for the way the question of the politics of
deconstruction has been posed within the English-language discussion.
The fact that, so far as I am aware, nobody has bothered to relate the
discussion of Heidegger to the final discussion of strategy, let alone to
the political dimension of the essay, is symptomatic of the way Derrida's
texts are often pillaged for quotations rather than read in their entirety.
It should have been clear all along that had Derrida identified Heidegger
as a metaphysician, as he allegedly did, he would himself have repeated a
metaphysical gesture, a gesture forgetful of the very need to interweave
the strategies set out at the end of the essay. This is not the occasion to
offer a detailed reading which would attempt to show how the various
parts of the essay hang together, but some pointers can be offered.[11]

One should not ignore Derrida's explanation of how, in advance of attending the conference in New York at which the paper was delivered, he had secured permission from the organizers to express "a certain point of solidarity" with those opposing the Vietnam war. The significance of that gesture today lies in large measure in the admission that accompanied it that he was well aware of the limited value of such declarations. This in turn led Derrida to a more general reflection on the way in which, at least under certain circumstances, political opposition is circumscribed in advance: "That a declaration of opposition to some official policy is authorized, and authorized by the authorities, also means, precisely to that extent, that the declaration does not upset the given order, is not *bothersome*" (*M*, 134/114). Derrida's observations about the effect of opposition can easily be verified. Direct opposition often serves to confirm what it seeks to put in question by agreeing to operate within circumscribed limits which leave the system intact. This tends to be the case with opposition parties in a democracy, as is most clear in the United Kingdom where the official opposition in Parliament is referred to as "Her Majesty's Loyal Opposition." Such systems often channel the expression of dissent in such a way that whole groups of people are excluded. Opposition parties awaiting their turn at government often seem to have little interest in overturning institutions, whatever historical injustices they may enshrine. More dramatically, acts of violence against a regime may serve the regime in question, for example, by rallying support for the status quo, even to the point where a regime might solicit or even fabricate such violence.

The connection between the political preamble of "The Ends of Man" and the remainder of the essay lies primarily in the sense in which deconstruction attempts to address the paradox according to which one often seems only to affirm what one sets out to deny. The familiar deconstructive strategies arise from reflection on this paradox. They acknowledge that to address a hierarchically determined oppositional system, it is not sufficient simply to reverse the priorities. The task is to neutralize or displace the opposition itself. If speech is privileged over writing as a mark of presence over absence, simply to reverse the order so that writing is understood as in some way prior to speech leaves the conceptual scheme in place. Only by locating within the scheme a reliance on that which cannot be defined in terms of the scheme, does one both engage with and at the same time transcend the scheme. In the case of the opposition between speech and writing this leads Derrida to acknowledge an arche-writing which is neither speech nor writing but undecidable between the two. The two stages of reversal and displacement need not

always be separated, but they must both be operative. Although it is clear
that to reverse the priority without displacing the opposition is simply to
oppose without addressing the schema itself, to attempt a neutralization
without reversing threatens to leave the dominant system intact. What
complicates this familiar picture is the fact that what is at issue in deconstruction is the governing system of Western metaphysics itself. Derrida
sometimes equates that system with the *logos* or reason, although, as we
shall see, he means by that not just a certain logic, the logic of opposition, but a series of distinctions each with its privileged term. Derrida in
another place refers to a "a Hegelian law" according to which one cannot speak out against reason except by being for it. This means that the
revolution against reason can be made only from within it and so is limited in scope to "what is called, precisely in the language of a department
of *internal* affairs, a disturbance" (*ED*, 59/36). Derrida elsewhere acknowledges this as an "indestructible and unforeseeable resource of the
Greek logos," a "power of envelopment," one which does not exclude
radical change, but which imposes "the necessity of lodging oneself
within traditional conceptuality in order to destroy it" (*ED*, 165/
111–12). In consequence, one must have recourse to stratagems and
strategies (*ED*, 59/36), the strategies that are outlines at the close of
"The Ends of Man" and which are inspired by the ambiguous regard in
which Derrida holds the idea of the end of philosophy.

One reason why the idea of the end of philosophy does not survive Derrida's scrutiny is that it creates an opposition between the inside
and outside of philosophy, and so maintains the very logic which is at
issue. Nevertheless, Derrida does appear to accept the basic diagnosis
that gives rise to what he prefers to describe as "the closure of philosophy." Derrida relates deconstruction to a history of metaphysics which is
in large measure borrowed from Heidegger and which questions, as Heidegger also does, the familiar conception of history. Derrida's subsequent caution in such essays as "Sending" about the totalizing tendency
of such a history cannot be understood as being directed "against" Heidegger without recognizing that they are also "against" a certain earlier
incarnation of Derrida, one which Derrida would surely be the first to
recognize that he cannot simply discard.[12] "The Ends of Man" itself offers an illustration of this when Derrida unquestioningly accepts Heidegger's identification in the "Letter on Humanism" of humanism with
metaphysics.[13] What Derrida does attempt, over and beyond Heidegger,
is to explore the difficulty of entertaining their association without laps-
ing immediately into the very metaphysical humanism whose circum-
scription is supposed to be possible only once it has lost its hold.

Hence Derrida's interest lies, in the first instance, in observing the necessity which makes "the Hegelian, Husserlian, and Heideggerian critiques or *de-limitations* of metaphysical humanism appear to belong to the very sphere of that which they criticize or de-limit" (*M*, 142/119). It amounts to showing the consequence of reading the texts of these authors simply within an oppositional framework. To understand them as having simply denounced humanism and metaphysics is, Derrida suggests, to remain at the level of an anthropologistic reading, a "first reading" (*M*, 141/119). He tries to provide an indication of how they might be read in such a way as to avoid this immediate collapse back into the realm which is to be left behind. The impression is given that this is to be accomplished by appealing to the ambiguity of the end of metaphysics, and thus of humanism, but the details are not altogether clear. With reference to Hegel, for example, Derrida briefly notes that phenomenology is not in an external relation to anthropology; it is the *relève*, the *Aufhebung*, the sublation, of anthropology so that it is *no longer* but it is *still* a science of man (*M*, 143/121). This ambiguity takes place in the *Phenomenology of Spirit* as the unity of the two ends of man, the unity of the death of man and of the completion or accomplishment of man (*M*, 144/121). Yet, Derrida insists that this ambiguity of Hegel's thinking of the end of man, in terms of the unity of man as a teleology of the *we*, is already prescribed in advance in metaphysics (*M*, 144/121). Indeed, against all those who imagine that it might be easy to leave metaphysical humanism behind, Derrida judges that it is still difficult to think of the end of man without introducing the dialectics of truth and negativity, as his brief reference to Husserl quickly illustrates.

Derrida's discussion of Heidegger is richer and more complex than his discussion of Hegel and Husserl, and it is the appropriate place of concentration for understanding how he negotiates these difficulties. Derrida shows how the equivocality of Hegel's gesture is repeated by Heidegger both insofar as Dasein is not man and yet is nothing other than man (*M*, 151/127), and insofar as the end is both telos and death (*M*, 161/134). Derrida again appears to focus his attention on showing how Heidegger also fails to change ground. So, for example, in reference to the unity of man, Derrida writes that "We can see then that Dasein, though *not* man, is nevertheless *nothing other* than man. It is, as we shall see, a repetition of the essence of man permitting a return to what is on this side of the metaphysical concepts of *humanitas*" (*M*, 151/127). Derrida also points to Heidegger's privileging of speech over writing (*M*, 159n/132n), to his use of the ontic metaphor of proximity which traps his discourse in the opposition of the near and the far (*M*, 152/127), and to his appeal to the "we," as evidence of a reliance on the teleological language of metaphysics (*M*, 149/124–25). But even if this is the dominant focus of Derrida's reading, it is not its exclusive focus, as he makes clear at the outset when he indicates that he is not going to enclose Heidegger's text in a closure that Heidegger had delimited better than anyone (*M*, 147/123).

"The Ends of Man" offers a reading of Heidegger which predominantly conforms to what Derrida at the end of the essay calls the first strategy. The first strategy by which the West is made to tremble is described as an "attempt at an exit and a deconstruction without changing terrain by repeating what is implicit in the founding concepts and the original problematic, by using against the edifice the instruments or stones available in the house, that is, equally, in language" (*M*, 162/135). Derrida is careful not to limit Heidegger to this strategy. Heidegger's rereading of the question of Being only "*resembles*, at least, a coming into consciousness, without break, displacement, or change of terrain" (*M*, 151/126. My italics). "The style of the first deconstruction is *mostly* that of the Heideggerian question" (*M*, 163/135. My italics). These qualifications are necessary because Derrida also acknowledges the presence of the second strategy "in texts of the Heideggerian type." Derrida characterizes the second strategy as that of changing terrain in a discontinuous fashion by brutally placing oneself outside. It fails because "the simple practice of language reinstates the new terrain on the oldest ground" (*M*, 162–63/135). In other words, the second strategy is of itself no more successful at shifting ground than the first. Hence Derrida's reliance on "a new writing" which would weave and interlace the two motifs of deconstruction, so that one would "speak several languages and produce several texts at once" (*M*, 163/135). Only in this way, by what Derrida calls a "strategic bet" (*M*, 162/134), can one overcome the univocality imposed by the logic of opposition.

One difficulty facing readers of "The Ends of Man" has been that of seeing where the second strategy interrupts and disturbs the first strategy, with its concentration on the opposition of near and far (*M*, 158–59/132). However, a series of additions to the 1968 text for the republication of the essay in 1972 highlight the places where the governing scheme is disturbed. It would be going too far to say that the second strategy was added to the first at this late stage, but it was certainly accentuated by Derrida's revisions. So, for example, in the first version of the essay Derrida had already insisted that the "phenomenological metaphor," on which a word like *Lichtung* relies, refers to the space of presence and the presence of space within the opposition of the near and the far. In the second version he added a sentence which transformed the meaning of the paragraph by referring the near and the far not to the opposition of space and time, but to the opening of *Lichtung* which precedes it: "The near and the far are thought here, consequently, before the opposition of space and time, according to the opening of a spacing which belongs neither to time nor to space, and which dislocates while producing it, any presence of the present" (*M*, 159–60/132–33). The gesture is that of the first strategy, insofar as the move is that of making explicit what stands prior to the opposition, but the necessity by which Heidegger remains trapped in the metaphorics of language in which the deconstruction is being carried out (*M*, 157/131), does not prove decisive. And this is because the second strategy is also at play, as is evident in the discussion of proximity.

Without exploring the details of Derrida's account, which would make it necessary to debate with him the details of Heidegger's texts, we may note that Derrida is insistent that the use of the ontic metaphor to say proximity does not reduce that proximity to an ontic proximity (*M*, 157/131). Similarly with "the proper," and the family of words *eigen*, *eigentlich*, *Ereignis* and so on. Derrida tells us that the proper "is not to be taken in a metaphysical sense" (*M*, 160/133), even though the co-propriety of Being and man is thought as inseparability, as it had been in metaphysics. "The propriety, the co-propriety of Being and man, is proximity as inseparability. It is as inseparability, furthermore, that the relations of being (substance or *res*) with its essential predicate were conceived in metaphysics" ("EM," 54). In 1972 the second of these sentences was changed to read, "But it is an inseparability, furthermore, that the relations of being (substance or *res*) with its essential predicate were conceived in metaphysics *afterward*."[14] The *ensuite* seems to be called upon to function like the more familiar *après coup*. It introduces a paradoxical relation between the within and the outside without holding them to the status of an opposition. This ambiguity is addressed again a few lines later: "But this trembling—which can only come from a certain outside—was already requisite within the very structure that it solicits." And then he adds for the republication of the essay in *Margins of Philosophy*, "Its margin was marked in its own body" (*M*, 161/133–34).

Derrida's contribution is to identify and separate the strategies at work in Heidegger's texts so that those texts can be found to address the questions posed by the Hegelian law. Although Derrida never departs from his recognition of the power of the *logos* to change transgressions into "false exits" (*M*, 162/135), at the close of "The Ends of Man" the emphasis is on the repented claim that "a radical trembling can only come from the *outside*" (*M*, 162/134), even if it cannot be simple "outside." The logic of opposition is displaced by the logic of alterity: "This trembling is played out in the violent relationship of the West to its other, whether a 'linguistic' relationship (where very quickly the question of the limits of everything leading back to the question of the meaning of Being arises), or ethnological, economic, political, military, relationships, etc." (*M*, 162/134–35). In this context Derrida has relatively little to say about this "other," except to make some precautions to combat the tendency whereby the West would already have circumscribed its other in advance, as, for example, the very designation—in English—of the West as "Western" does for the Orient, making it into the "East."

Nevertheless, the extension of the realm where this logic operates beyond the linguistic to, for example, the ethnological, the economic, the political, and the military is significant. Not least because it would make clear that the ethical-political direction of deconstruction is not simply based on a metaphorics, a proposition which deconstruction would have already challenged in advance. There is an historical characterization of the metaphysical tradition which guides deconstruction at every stage. Metaphysics, in the broadest sense, is not only humanist. It is also, for example, racist, colonialist, imperialist, and phallocentric.[15] The nature of this historical conjunction, the sense in which humanism might bear some responsibility, for example, for providing the conditions under which racism flourished, is a possibility that should not be dismissed, simply because humanism, once it had become a philanthropic idea rather than primarily an educational one, has also proved a vital resource in combatting racism.[16] My insistence on history at this point may seem eccentric, particularly in comparison with the way Derrida has often been appropriated in the United States, but it should not be forgotten that in "The Ends of Man" Derrida singles out for praise Heidegger's brief (and somewhat incomplete) historical observations in the "Letter on Humanism":

> Any questioning of humanism that does not first catch up with
> the archeological radicalness of the questions sketched by Hei-
> degger, and does not make use of the information he provides
> concerning the genesis of the concept and the value man (the
> renewal of the Greek *paideia* in Roman culture, the Christianiz-
> ing of the Latin *humanitas,* the rebirth of Hellenism in the
> fourteenth and eighteenth centuries, etc.), any metahumanist
> position that does not place itself within the opening of these
> questions remains historically regional, periodic, and periph-

eral, juridically secondary and dependent, whatever interest
and necessity it might retain as such. (*M*, 153/128)

By the same token, any deconstruction which is not guided by a
radical historical questioning will fail to engage what is at issue, however
faithfully it follows the methodological procedures associated with
deconstruction.

As "The Ends of Man" develops, the discussion of politics becomes less thematic. In consequence, it does not address directly the
question whether oppositional thought can be neutralized in the "political" arena in such a way as to allow for the possibility of a radically new
schema. Is displacement of the logic of opposition by a logic of alterity
both effective and necessary also in politics? Twenty years after "The
Ends of Man" essay Derrida confronted humanism's opposition to
apartheid. The dangers inherent in this gesture cannot be underestimated. The most popular, and perhaps also in the present context the
most powerful, argument against apartheid, and indeed against all forms
of racism, probably lies in the appeal to the concept of "man" as established by metaphysical humanism. Black and white are subsumed under
the more general concept of humanity so that discrimination on the basis
of color is said to be contrary to human rights. Quite simply, why do
anything to disturb the operation of this easily grasped critique of a de-
spicable political system?

"Racism's Last Word," a text written for the catalogue of a 1983
exhibition entitled "Art against Apartheid," can serve as a transition
between "The Ends of Man" and the 1986 essay on Mandela, which contains Derrida's most developed presentation of these issues. In "Racism's Last Word" Derrida recognizes that the fight against apartheid has
been for the most part waged in terms of the humanitarian values of "the
West." The South African government shares with its opponents the
same language and the same fundamental convictions. It can therefore
be opposed on its own terms and its manifest hypocrisy readily exposed.
One could give examples: the Republic of South Africa proclaims equality before the law at the same time as denying it to a majority of its citizens. Derrida, however, is more interested in extending the case. The
hypocrisy is not confined to Pretoria. The "contradiction" is not limited
to South Africa. It is "internal to the West and to the assertion of its
rights."[17] The whole of Western history is indicated. The 1973 declaration of the General Assembly of the United Nations may have proclaimed that *apartheid* is a "crime against humanity," but the fact that
many of the signatories of that resolution are not doing all that is re-

quired—"that is the least one can say"—to force the South African regime to abolish apartheid, represents a "contradiction" (*Ps*, 358/*RWD*,
334). Any improvements that might be taking place in the situation of
blacks in South Africa, insofar as they are motivated primarily by economic considerations, do nothing to alter the fact that in apartheid "the
customary discourse on man, humanism and human rights, has encoun-
tered its effective and as yet unthought limit, the limit of the whole system in which it acquires meaning" (*Ps*, 361/*RWD*, 337).

Derrida begins "Racism's Last Word" in the optative mood:
"APARTHEID—may that remain the name from now on, the unique
appellation for the ultimate racism in the world, the last of many" (*Ps*,
353/*RWD*, 330). It is a sentence which is readily misunderstood. In
"But, beyond . . . ," an Open Letter to Ann McClintock and Rob
Nixon, Derrida emphasizes that this prescriptive utterance should not
be confused with a descriptive one (*RWD*, 357). Furthermore, it seems
that the whole text (and particularly the first section) is largely a commentary on this one sentence. It is not an historical sentence; nor a judicial one. It is "an appeal. . . . I asked for a promise" (*RWD*, 358).
Nevertheless, it soon becomes clear that a historical framework of some
kind is presupposed. "Apartheid is famous, in sum, for manifesting the
lowest extreme of racism [*la dernière extrémité du racisme*], its end and the
narrow-minded self-sufficiency of its intention, its eschatology, the death
rattle of what is already an interminable agony, something like the setting in the West of racism—but also, and this will have to be specified
below, racism as a Western thing" (*Ps*, 355/*RWD*, 331–32). One might
ask what authorizes this declaration that the lowest racism is also the last,
if it is not simply a reliance on the fact that *dernier* means both "last" and
"lowest"? Derrida is not simply saying that he does not see either in the
past or the present any other racist states as extreme as that to be found
in South Africa in 1983. The statement seems to presuppose the kind of
metanarrative of which Derrida himself is usually highly suspicious. Indeed, Derrida would appear to be drawing on the same ambiguity that he
found in Heidegger in "The Ends of Man." According to Heidegger in
"The End of Philosophy and the Task of Thinking," the end of metaphysics is neither its coming to a halt nor its perfection, but its completion (*Vollendung*).[18] And yet Derrida is not wrong to see a similar
equivocality in Heidegger's conception to that he had found in Hegel.
The play of telos and death everywhere marks Heidegger's account of
the history of metaphysics (*M*, 161/134). Derrida carries this over into
his account of racism: the lowest racism is also the ultimate racism.
Apartheid is both a culmination and a death of racism. That at least is the

most plausible explanation of why Derrida appears to conceive of the end of apartheid to which the organizers of the exhibition looked—"The day will come . . . " (cited in *RWD*, 329)—to be also the end of racism.

If Derrida's conception of the last racism is not to be preposterous, an absurd pipe-dream, it must find its underpinning in the framework of the closure, rather than an end, of racism.[19] But why indulge in a rhetoric which is the most confusing the less one knows of Derrida's other texts, particularly when the stakes are so high and the chances of Derrida reaching a new audience not inconsiderable? Why introduce deconstruction here at all? Whatever answer one might want to give to those questions, knowledge of Derrida's other writings not only help make sense of some of Derrida's more surprising claims. They also transform the sense of what appear to be familiar assertions, such as that racism is a Western thing (*Ps*, 355/*RWD*, 332). It is true that Derrida makes this claim with astonishing ease, as if it was familiar. And in a sense it is. Africans struggling against racism have long maintained that racism is a Western problem. Racism is not part of the African heritage. This was the view of the ANC Youth League Manifesto of 1944. The blacks are obliged to view the problems of Africa through the perspective of race only because of the whites.[20] But the assertion that racism is a Western thing is of a somewhat different order from the assertion that "apartheid was a European 'creation,' " or even the further claim that state racism has "no meaning and would have had no chance outside a European 'discourse' on the concept of race," (*Ps*, 357/*RWD*, 333). By saying that racism is a Western thing, Derrida wants us to understand that it is a Western metaphysical thing. Only by associating racism with Western metaphysics in this way can Derrida look to the end of its history ("the end of a history"—*Ps*, 354/*RWD*, 330) to mark also the last racism in the required sense.

Once it is recognized that Derrida is drawing on Heidegger in this way, his strategy in "Racism's Last Word" becomes much clearer. It must be remembered that in "The Ends of Man" Derrida had insisted on the unity of metaphysics and humanism as already propounded by Heidegger in the "Letter on Humanism." Together with the recognition that racism is something Western, the stage is set for recognizing a complicity between humanism and racism. This is the background from which Derrida doubts that humanism will of itself be a sufficient resource to combat racism. It explains the extraordinary gap between Derrida's observations and the conclusion he apparently draws from it. More is at issue than the contradiction between the humanist values espoused by the South African system and the operation of that system.

ROBERT   BERNASCONI

More is at issue than the contradiction between the sentiments expressed by the United Nations and their failure to act in a decisive way in
accord with those sentiments. Humanism is insufficient to overcome racism for the same reason that Western metaphysics cannot be made to
tremble from within, but only from the outside. Even if the specific sense
of the following sentences is not entirely clear, perhaps particularly without visiting the exhibition, the necessity underlying them (which is the
same as that explicated in "The Ends of Man") is apparent: "In this collective and international exhibition . . . , pictorial, sculptural idioms will
be crossing, but they will be attempting to speak the other's language
without renouncing their own. And in order to effect this translation,
their common reference henceforth makes an appeal to a language that
cannot be found, a language at once very old, older than Europe, but for
that reason to be invented once more" (Ps, 356–57/RWD, 333). That is
to say, Derrida seeks in the exhibition what recourse to humanist values
lacks—an alterity which supplements a projected history of the West in
which apartheid is situated.

The essay on Mandela develops this sense of why the resources of
the West might be insufficient to the task of combatting apartheid. That
is why Derrida asks at the outset about Mandela's admiration for Magna
Carta, the Petition of Rights, the Bill of Rights, and British political institutions, which would seem to associate him inextricably with a European, even an Anglo-American, history: "He admires the law, he says it
clearly, but is this law, which gives orders to constitutions and declarations, essentially a thing of the West?" (Ps, 455–56/NM, 16). If it is, then
Mandela's appeal to that tradition as part of the struggle against apartheid, would have to be understood as "a sort of specular opposition, a
domestic war that the West carried on with itself, in its own name" (Ps,
456/NM, 16). This would mean that Mandela could be characterized as
the rightful inheritor of the tradition inaugurated by Magna Carta,
someone who, employing the terms of that tradition, opposed apartheid's illegitimate assumption of its language. Mandela would have identified an internal contradiction within the system in a debate which
would have no need to appeal to "a radical otherness or a true dissym-
metry" (Ps, 456/NM, 16). On this interpretation, Mandela's position
would be like the humanist attack on apartheid, and indeed Derrida observes that Mandela frequently employs the language of "human dig-
nity" and calls upon what is worthy of the name "human" (Ps, 456/NM,
17). When Derrida turns to the Freedom Charter of 1955 with its faith-
fulness to the principles of parliamentary democracy of the Anglo-
American type, he finds that it operates by "a simple specular inver-

sion." However, if this is all there is, it would mean that "the struggle of the black community (or non-'white' communities) would be undertaken in the name of an imported law and model, which were betrayed, in the first place, by the first to import them" (*Ps*, 460/*NM*, 22). The struggle against apartheid would be a question of showing the white population that they had not been true to their own principles. The principles of the struggle would be entirely Western.

The alternative that Derrida considers in the course of his essay is the possibility that Mandela "respects the *logic* of the legacy enough to turn it upon occasion against those who claim to be its guardians, enough to reveal, despite and against the usurpers, what has never yet been seen in the inheritance" (*Ps*, 456/*NM*, 17). Does Mandela conserve and reproduce? Or does he "by the unheard-of *act* of a reflection" give birth to "what had never seen the light of day"? Derrida's answer is in terms of the law as that which does not simply reproduce the visible and open the eyes of the white population to it. The law is invisible and lacks an objective representation. Its task is to produce the visible, to transport the invisible into the visible (*Ps*, 461/*NM*, 23).

So long as Mandela appeals to the tradition inaugurated by Magna Carta, he is, in the words of "The Ends of Man," "using against the edifice the instruments or stones available in the house" (*M*, 162/135). Presumably it is for this reason that Derrida says that this first reason is reason itself (*Ps*, 461/*NM*, 23): the *logos*. However, Derrida also locates in Mandela a second strategy which, like that in "The Ends of Man," attempts to change terrain in a discontinuous and irruptive fashion (*M*, 162/135). Derrida finds it in Mandela's appeal to African society "before 'the arrival of the white man' " (*Ps*, 461/*NM*, 23). Mandela not only admires Western democracy. He is fascinated by the structure and organization of early African societies, where "the seeds of a revolutionary democracy in which none will be held in slavery or servitude, and in which poverty, want, and insecurity shall be no more." Derrida calls this "the supplementary paradox" that "the *effective* accomplishment, the filling out of the democratic form, the *real* determination of the formality, *will only have taken place* in the past of this non-Western society" (*Ps*, 462/*NM*, 25). In this way, the revolutionary democracy, of which Western democracy is only an incomplete, a formal, and thus a potential image, is "already virtually accomplished" in African, non-Western democracy (*Ps*, 462/*NM*, 25).

Derrida is not only thereby transferring the issue from that of an internal dispute within Western culture to one in which the West relates to its other. He understands this relation in terms of "virtuality" and thus in terms of the logic of supplementarity developed in *Of Grammatology* (*G*, 263–66/185–87). Derrida had explored there how for Rousseau pity was innate not as a given in the sense of a real presence, but as a reserve. In the same way, the African democratic model, virtual in the society of the ancestors, was not revealed in the sense of being developed for reflection until after the violent eruption of the "white man" (*Ps*, 461/*NM*, 22–23).

The logic of supplementarity becomes crucial later in the essay when Derrida understands Mandela's work as a lawyer as setting himself *"against the code in the code"* in the sense of making visible just what the code in action rendered unreadable (*Ps*, 469/*NM*, 34). So, for example, when Mandela defies the law by practicing as an attorney without the special authorization required of nonwhites, he is said to "repair, supplement, reconstruct, add on to a deontology where the whites were finally showing themselves deficient" (*Ps*, 470/*NM*, 35). In other words, Derrida interprets this not simply as a gesture of opposition, whereby Mandela would confine himself to showing what he himself calls "scorn for the law"—like that of the South African regime (*Ps*, 470/*NM*, 35–36)—which would be no more than a simple specular inversion. Derrida interprets it as a "supplementary inversion." According to Derrida, Mandela scorns the law out of respect for the law, "a superior law," a "law of laws" (*Ps*, 464/*NM*, 27), "a law beyond legality" (*Ps*, 469/*NM*, 34).

In his attempt to find such a law in Mandela, Derrida again recalls Rousseau, although in a way which seems to me to be not unproblematic. Derrida writes, "And sometimes we think we hear Rousseau's accent in these confessions, hearing a voice which never ceases to appeal to *the voice of conscience*, to the immediate and unfailing sentiment of justice, to this law of laws that speaks in us before us, because it is inscribed within our hearts" (*Ps*, 464/*NM*, 27). Of course, as Derrida surely knows, Rousseau's law of the heart is far from an immediate and unfailing sentiment. The point of the reference to Rousseau is that it enables Derrida to identify the superior law as conscience. Derrida writes, "Conscience and conscience of the law, these two make only one" (*Ps*, 465/*NM*, 28). This sounds better in French than in English. More importantly, it does not reflect Mandela's usage. Mandela invariably distinguishes between law and conscience. Conscience is higher than the law. If Mandela emphasizes that he is a man of the law, it is not in order to point to a higher law, but to highlight the fact that in "this conflict between the law and our conscience" which confronts the African people, he is more than this. He is a man of "public morality and conscience" (*SL*, 153). Derrida turns Mandela's language around, so that conscience becomes, in Derrida's phrase, the law of laws. Only once in the texts under discussion does Mandela speak in a sufficiently ambiguous way to allow such an interpretation. Mandela says, "I was made, by the law, a criminal, not because of what I had done, but because of what I stood for, because of what I thought, because of my conscience" (SL, 157). "By the law": Derrida perhaps reads "by my conscience," whereas it is more likely that Mandela means the law administered by the white court he is addressing, the law which has brought itself into contempt (cf. SL, 156). It is true that Mandela recognizes discriminating laws as unjust and he thereby appeals to a higher concept of justice, but it is one internal to the system and so cannot occupy the place Derrida would give it. Mandela writes: "I regarded it as a duty . . . to cry out against this discrimination, which is essentially unjust and opposed to the whole basis of the attitude towards justice which is part of the tradition of legal training in this country" (SL, 151). The question then, as Derrida structures it, would have to be whether "conscience" can reveal what, as Derrida puts it, has "never yet been seen in the inheritance" (Ps, 456/NM, 17). But "conscience" in what sense?

The conscience which sets Mandela against the law is not the private voice which addresses him as an isolated individual. Mandela knows such a voice and it emerges, for example, in a letter he wrote from prison to his wife Winnie on hearing of the death of her sister: "Yet there have been moments when that love and happiness, that trust and hope, have turned into pure agony, when conscience and a sense of guilt have ravaged every part of my being, when I have wondered whether any kind of commitment can ever be sufficient excuse for abandoning a young and inexperienced woman in a pitiless desert, literally throwing her into the hands of highwaymen."[21] The conscience which puts Mandela in conflict with the law is one he associates with " public morality." If it is customary to set conscience against public morality, this is because conscience has come to be identified with the private judgment which sets one apart from the many. Mandela, by contrast, is sustained by a conscience he identifies with "the overwhelming majority of mankind" who share a hatred of racial discrimination (SL, 159). He associates conscience with the many—"mankind" (SL, 138), "all men of good will" (SL, 39), or "the African people" (SL, 153).

But who are "the people"? This question introduces perhaps the most important point at which Rousseau mediates and perhaps distorts Derrida's reading of Mandela, not least because it enables the question of the identity of the people to be understood in terms of their formation. Or, in the language of Western political philosophy, their foundation. Derrida refers Mandela's discussion of "the will of the people" to Rousseau's general will, and says, as if by way of justification, "Mandela often reminds us of Rousseau even if he never quotes him" (*Ps*, 458/*NM*, 19). Unfortunately, the echo of Rousseau that Derrida hears is partly the consequence of an error in the French translation of the Freedom Charter. Mandela's phrase "the will of the people" (*SL*, 50) was translated into French as "*la volunté du peuple tout entier*" (*Ps*, 458–59). The error was compounded when Derrida's text was returned to English and the phrase became "the will of the entire nation" (*NM*, 20). The imagined echo of Rousseau led Derrida to introduce a reference to social contract theory, as if this was the only way in which the identity of a people could be understood. Derrida writes, "The total unity of a nation [*L'unité totale du peuple*] is not identified for the first time except by a contract—formal or not, written or not—which institutes some fundamental law" (*Ps*, 459/*NM*, 20). This no doubt encourages Derrida to introduce Rousseau's "general will" and the question of the "virtual identity" of a people that it poses (*Ps*, 458–59/*NM*, 20), a question Derrida pursues in other contexts also.[22]

It is true that unity is an issue for Mandela, although not in the form of a "total unity," if that would mean adopting the measures proposed by Rousseau to secure the general will, such as preventing all associations, all "political society," from being formed.[23] Furthermore, social contract theory identifies the problem of politics as that of overcoming an original individualism. This individualism is foreign to Mandela. Indeed, it would also have been foreign to the Greeks, who had a different conception again, defining human being in terms of the *polis*. Derrida, by assuming that the people need foundation like a Roman city or a modern state, threatens to silence the other and to engulf Mandela within a metaphysical problematic. As a corrective, but no more than that because the contrast is too easily drawn and the terms in need of a more careful scrutiny, one can refer to the characterization to be found in the Manifesto of the ANC Youth League, to which Mandela contributed. Two very different outlooks are contrasted there. On the one hand, there is the perspective of the white population, which is that of private lives and private deaths, personal power and fame, and above all a division of the universe into "a host of individual little entities which cannot help being in constant conflict" (*SL*, 12). On the other hand, there is the perspective of the African, who is said to regard the universe as "one composite whole . . . whose individual parts exist merely as interdependent aspects of one whole realizing their fullest life in the corporate life where communal contentment is the absolute measure of values" (*SL*,

12). Whereas the Europeans are described as having a philosophy which divides, the African philosophy of life is said to drive toward harmony and unity, understood—and it is important to insist on this, because the character of this unity is precisely the issue—in terms of "social responsibility." When Mandela emphasizes unity, it is in the first instance with reference to the unity of the African people amongst themselves (SL, 101). Tribalism was one of the contributing causes of white domination (SL, 23–24) and it remains a "mortal foe of African nationalism" (SL, 27). Not that this nationalism should be seen as an offshoot of Western nationalism. The ANC Youth League Manifesto understands such nationalism, in terms which Derrida would perhaps read as following the logic of supplementarity, "as a higher development of a process which was already in progress when the white man arrived" (SL, 27), although it is no doubt given another meaning by the white man. It is a nationalism prior to nations and one which displaces the claims of the Republic of South Africa to be able to establish its legitimacy by tracing its formation back to an original beginning. In situating himself in relation to the history of the struggle against the white invaders by drawing on a tradition that predates their arrival, Mandela appeals to resources that lie outside the West's definition of itself, resources the West has ignored.[24]

Mandela's idea of the unity of the people does not depend on the eradication of differences, even when the unity of the people takes the form of "the solidarity of all democratic forces regardless of race, party affiliation, religious belief and ideological conviction" (SL, 60). To this extent, Mandela already departs from that kind of humanism that reduces people simply to the status of "men." Furthermore, Mandela characterizes this solidarity in terms of "black unity," a unity defined not by the commonality of a single interest, except for an interest in overcoming apartheid and its effects. Mandela does not understand "blacks" to refer simply to Africans, but seems most often to employ the word to refer to "all those who are not whites."[25] Sometimes, as in "Mandela's Call," a message written after the Soweto uprising of 1976, Mandela includes some whites under the label "black": "The first condition for victory is black unity. Every effort to divide the blacks, to woo and pit one black group against another, must be vigorously repulsed. Our people— African, Coloured, Indian and democratic whites—must be united into a single massive and solid wall of resistance, of united mass action" (SL, 191). "Black unity" as the unity of "our people," where "we" are identified by reference to color only in virtue of "our" opposition to white racism, points to a "we" that does not yet exist, the "we" that is anticipated by the Freedom Charter.

When the Freedom Charter appeals to the will of the people against the government—"No government can justly claim authority unless it is based on the will of the people" (*SL*, 50)—the issue is not that of the exclusion of one part, albeit a large part, of the people from the identity of the nation. The issue is not that the Republic operates with a partial and thus defective concept of the people. It is simply that the government was conducting business without reference to the people, that is to say, the peoples of South Africa. The immediate reference of the Freedom Charter was not to social contract theory, but to the United National Universal Declaration of Human Rights of 1948 (Article 21.3), as Mandela himself acknowledged in his trial statement of 1964 (*SL*, 164). And the Universal Declaration of Human Rights, though in general more "Western" than universal, need not in this instance be regarded as an appeal to so-called Western values specifically. It is an appeal to conscience in Mandela's sense. This is because the principle involved is one that Mandela appeals to as universally acknowledged as sacred, at least throughout the civilized world from which South Africa by that token had excluded itself (*SL*, 137).

Who then are "the people"? The signatories of the Freedom Charter are defined, in a phrase that would appear to be a conscious rewriting of the American Declaration of Independence, as "we, the people of South Africa, black and white, together—equals, countrymen and brothers" (*SL*, 51). This new definition of the people of South Africa looks beyond the fact that there is not yet equality or fellowship across the races. A similar language to that of the Freedom Charter can be found in some of Mandela's own texts, such as "Verwoerd's Tribalism." Commenting on the claim of the Freedom Charter that "South Africa belongs to all who live in it, black and white" (*SL*, 50), he writes "At present, South Africa does not 'belong' except in a moral sense to all" (*SL*, 78). The "all" is constituted only with reference to a future, a we, that does not yet exist.

Derrida, who appears to have had access only to a very limited selection of Mandela's writings,[26] poses the question of virtual identity in a slightly different contest. He appeals to the "prescriptive value" of certain statements from the Freedom Charter which posit the people in the future: "The people shall govern!" "All national groups shall have equal rights!" "All shall be equal before the law!" (*SL*, 51–52; cf. *Ps*, 459/*NM*, 21). The analysis of the relation between descriptive and prescriptive statements offered by Derrida in this context is richer than the simple contrast he draws in response to McClintock and Nixon. Derrida understands the Freedom Charter as exhibiting a similar problem to that

he identified with reference to the American Declaration of Independence or the founding of the South African Republic. What is at issue is
an "extraordinary performative" whereby what is constituted must nevertheless be presupposed. This is what allows Derrida to introduce the
problematics of the social contract (*Ps*, 458–60/*NM*, 19–21). The Freedom Charter not only concerns the people of South Africa in the form of
prescriptions for the future directed at a people that does not yet exist.
The Charter is already signed by this people which is still to come and yet
speaks from a present in which "our people," the Africans, find themselves "robbed of their birthright to land, liberty and justice by a form of
government founded on injustice and inequality" (*SL*, 50). The curious
temporality of the Freedom Charter is characterized by Derrida in the
following terms: "The Charter speaks in the present, a present supposed
to be founded on the *description* of a historical fact, which, in turn,
should be recognized in the future. It also speaks in the future, a future
which has a *prescriptive* value" (*Ps*, 459/*NM*, 21).

However acute Derrida's analysis, there is a concern that he applied his account to every act of foundation, every act of giving birth by a
kind of fiction which records the unity of a nation as "what will have
been there" (*Ps*, 457/*NM*, 18). He alleges that the authors of the Freedom Charter are setting one fiction against another (*Ps*, 459/*NM*, 20).
The difference in the case of South Africa was only a certain excessive-
ness whereby "the violence was too great, *visibly too great*." "The white
community was *too* much in the minority, the disproportionality of
wealth *too* flagrant" in such a way that the violence of the origin repeats
itself indefinitely (*Ps*, 457/*NM*, 18). But does one not concede too much
if one applies the paradoxes of social contract theory even to the foundation of white South Africa? Certainly Derrida does not forget what was
already in place but summarily excluded. He does not allow "the *official*
lie of a white migration that preceded black migration" to go un-
remarked (*Ps*, 357/*RWD*, 333). Nor does he ignore that what is at issue is
a gradual process from a *coup de force* to "foundation" (*Ps*, 458/*NM*, 20),
such that the foundation of South Africa and the foundation of apartheid are by no means simple events of the kind projected by political
theorists. Nevertheless, what separates the Republic of South Africa
from the South Africa of the Freedom Charter is that the initiators of the
former neither sought nor anticipated the unanimity of a first convention where the entire people would indeed speak with one voice, which
was something social contract theorists needed in order to establish the
state's legitimacy from their individualist starting-point (*CS*, 359/52).[27]
If Derrida does not make more of this difference it is perhaps because it

would still be insufficient in order to establish that the state racism of apartheid is "the unique and last in the world" with all the connotations given to this phrase in "Racism's Last Word" (*Ps*, 458/NM, 18). Derrida reaffirms in the essay on Mandela that this can only be accomplished insofar as he draws on what might still be called a philosophy of history, one that arises only at the end, or rather the closure, of metaphysics and humanism, "the closure of an epoch, for example that of the Christian West" (*Ps*, 471/NM, 37).

Mandela also has his philosophy of history. Indeed it is by appealing to a conception of history that Mandela comes increasingly to avoid the prescriptive language of ethical imperatives of the kind found, for example, in his Presidential Address to the ANC Conference: "You must protect and defend your trade unions. . . . You must never surrender" (*SL*, 40). Subsequently, the prescriptive language tends to be couched in terms of necessity—the impossibility of acquiescing. "Men are not capable of doing nothing, saying nothing, of not reacting to injustice, of not protesting against oppression, of not striving for the good of society and the good life in the way they see it" (*SL*, 156). Here it is less a prescription than a necessity determined by conscience. Thinking ahead to the time when he will be released from prison, Mandela says he will "still be moved, as men are always moved by their consciences" (*SL*, 159). The struggle that is Mandela's life was not one he chose: "No man in his right sense would voluntarily choose such a life in preference to the one of normal family life which exists in every civilized community" (*SL*, 157). But South Africa is not a civilized community and there is in consequence no such choice. No choice but to struggle. It is perhaps in this sense that Mandela's references to history should be understood. Although occasionally the reference is backward looking, as when he says that "History shows that penalties do not deter men when their conscience is aroused," even then the point is made to express a conviction about the future, that penalties will not deter his people or his colleagues (*SL*, 158). History confirms him in the conviction that injustice will not triumph. Mandela told the court in 1962 that "no power on earth can stop an oppressed people determined to win their freedom. History punishes those who resort to reason and force to suppress the claims and legitimate aspirations of the majority of the country's citizens" (*SL*, 144). From prison he wrote that "victory is certain" (*SL*, 191) and he echoes the sentiment of Castro's famous defense, "History will absolve me," when he concludes that "I have no doubt that posterity will pronounce that I was innocent" (*SL*, 160). There is therefore for Mandela also an inevitability at work and one has to ask what sustains his sense of it. Does it arise from his belief in humanity or from a conviction that justice always prevails? Or does it have its source in Mandela's unusual sense of "public morality," which is sustained not by a sense of humanity as a whole, but by a conception of "black unity" as the unity of the opponents of apartheid irrespective of their color?

Derrida has gone far beyond the task of explicating the presuppositions which would legitimate Mandela's language or the task of clarifying the argument of the ANC as in his analysis of the Freedom Charter. The question is inevitably raised as to whether one does indeed read Mandela—whether this is admiration—when one imposes on him a question which is not his, such as that of the closure, when one reads him in terms of a logic of supplementarity developed in the course of a reading of Rousseau, and when one transforms his appeal to the will of the people into a reference to Rousseau's general will. What is the law of reflection operating here when Derrida finds Rousseau, "his" Rousseau, in Mandela? There is something troubling about Derrida's reading of Mandela, which goes far beyond questions of textual fidelity. There is a suspicion that Derrida domesticates Mandela, reduces him to an already established discourse and schema, and refuses to allow him to speak as an other, in spite of the fact that the reading of Mandela is introduced as a questioning of whether the West has sufficient resources within it to combat apartheid. It is not simply that Derrida blindly imposes a formalistic structure on Mandela drawn from the problematic of the end of Western metaphysics. The point is rather whether Derrida should not, for all his admiration for Mandela, also find him threatening. And should not Mandela himself also make "us" tremble, particularly if "we" are white "Westerners"? Is there not an ethnocentrism at work in Derrida's assimilation of Mandela to Rousseau, and in the importation of the law of laws (the *nomos*) at the very point where Derrida looks for a trembling that, as "The Ends of Man" insisted, could only come from the outside? Or is Derrida bound by a logic whereby this outside can only be found within, albeit on the margins, precisely because it is the other of the West? Does not Derrida enclose Mandela a little too quickly? Is not the logic of the closure pursued at the cost of a heterogeneity whose necessity Derrida himself acknowledges? These questions will have to remain unanswered until the opportunity arises to explore further the nature of alterity, a question which would again return us to Levinas. In any event, they are, to paraphrase "Violence and Metaphysics," Derrida's own questions.

Meanwhile, there is the question as to what the specific contribution of "Racism's Last Word" and "The Laws of Reflection" might be to the debate about racism. It has already been noted that "Racism's Last Word" is an occasional essay for an art exhibition against apartheid. Nor should it be forgotten that the essay on Mandela appeared initially in a volume especially dedicated to him, where it stood out from the others precisely for the penetration and depth of its engagement with Mandela.[28] Both essays were therefore originally addressed not to or even at racists, but to audiences that were already committed to the overthrow of racism. One should not ignore the context of these essays when reading them now and be disappointed because they fail to accomplish what they never attempted. For the same reason one should not approach what are basically occasional essays expecting them to open new horizons for deconstruction. Nevertheless, I shall attempt to explore briefly four points raised by a reading of the essays. First, there is the question of the strategies used to address racism and the way that these are themselves sometimes labeled racist. Secondly, there is the related question of the positive role of humanism in combatting racism, about which Derrida says little in these essays. Thirdly, there are the dangers and resources attending an attempt at deconstruction within the realm of racial difference. Fourthly, there is the possibility of introducing a conceptuality which Derrida appears to be in the course of developing and which might address the issue, but which in the essays under scrutiny is not yet brought to bear.

As to the first, one might think, for example, of the complaint that positive discrimination as conceived in the United States is itself racist, or even of the way white politicians will often insist, somewhat paradoxically, that black leaders should use a language free of racial designation. Both the current attack on positive discrimination and the widespread accusations leveled against black community politics seem to start from the assumption that centuries of white racism has not left an economic, institutional, educational, and communal legacy that needs to be redressed. Afrocentrism is not ethnocentric in the same sense that Eurocentrism is. Judged contextually, Afrocentrism in America is provoked by the suppression of African culture by a dominant culture that has been imposed on Americans of African descent from the moment the slaves were captured and transported. Similarly, Mandela did not deny that blacks were capable of racism against whites, or in certain contexts against each other (*SL*, 133), but he was adamant that "the non-European liberation movement" was not racialist (*SL*, 45). This was not just a statement of the reality and goals of the movement. It reflected in the political realm the same strategic necessity that, within the terms prepared by Western philosophy, deconstruction articulates with particular clarity. There must be a moment of opposition in which the terms of the governing hierarchy are reversed, but, to anticipate the third of these four points, this moment is not simply one of opposition, which always runs the risk of leaving the governing structural schema intact. In the deconstructive strategy the reversal of hierarchy is a prelude to a displacement of the schema.

Secondly, one should not be misled into thinking that, because of the charges he levels against humanism, Derrida renounces humanism altogether in the struggle against racism. This is made clear elsewhere, for example in *Of Spirit,* in the context of a return to the question of Heidegger's "anthropocentric or even humanist teleology" as a schema which Heidegger "can no doubt modify, displace, shift—but not destroy."[29] Derrida acknowledges, "I do not mean to criticize this humanist teleology. It is no doubt more urgent to recall that, in spite of all denegations or all the avoidances one could wish, it has remained *up till now* (in Heidegger's time and situation, but this has not radically changed today) the price to be paid in the ethico-political denunciation of biologism, racism, naturalism etc." (*E,* 87/56). If Derrida does not dwell on this in the essays on racism, it is because their focus is to show the ultimate inadequacy of humanism to combat racism, even a certain complicity between them, that could also be exposed by historical investigations of humanism of the kind that Derrida called for in "The Ends of Man." But in contrast to the apparent search for a state of purity free from metaphysics that seems to inspire some of Derrida's followers to search out and dismiss all "incidents" of metaphysics and the use of metaphysical concepts, Derrida himself seems to acknowledge the need to use whatever resources are available.

Thirdly, there are the dangers attendant on the application of deconstruction to the fight against racism. I have already noted that the use of what from a certain perspective may look like racist or humanist gestures, does not within a deconstructive strategy amount to a commitment to racism or humanism, precisely because they are being worked in order to produce a shift away from the schema whereby humanism opposes racism and yet at the same time threatens to uphold it. The strategy is dangerous. One might, for example, reinforce racist stereotypes in the course of trying to alter the valuation placed on them prior to their neutralization. Nevertheless, Derrida has consistently insisted on the contrary danger of moving too quickly to neutralization and so leaving the previous scheme in place (*P,* 57/41). As Derrida recognized in an interview with Christie McDonald on the question of sexual difference, taking account of the prevailing conditions often requires the preservation of metaphysical presuppositions, even if they are to be questioned later.[30] Perhaps any effective intervention against racism is liable to repeat to some extent the very gestures it seeks to oppose and so itself might be labeled racist. But within deconstructive politics, opposition is never *simply* opposition. It already points beyond it, as perhaps Mandela did with a concept of "black unity" that anticipates the constitution of the South African people as a community of equals at the same time as it heightens the opposition by uniting the groups opposed to the upholders of white supremacy.

Finally, although I have suggested that Derrida's focus on the "law" in his essay on Mandela appears to be faithful neither to Mandela's usage nor to the task at hand. There are other routes that might have been taken and which might have been more effective. For example, Derrida might have focused on the notion of "people," both the people and a people, both our people and their people, both people and peoples. Such a reading would work under the shadow of the Heideggerian *Volk* but would not be confined to that orbit. One wonders too that the Heideggerian *Geschlecht* was not also brought to bear. The multivocity of the German word *Geschlecht* has been the subject of a number of essays and papers over the years which belong—and this may be fitting—to a larger indeterminate project. As Derrida reminded us at the outset, *Geschlecht* means sex, race, family, generation, lineage, species, genre/genus.[31] In that first essay, Derrida focused on sexual difference in Heidegger. In "*Geschlecht II:* Heidegger's Hand," *Geschlecht* becomes another word for humanity. He quotes Heidegger as saying "our language calls humanity . . . *Geschlecht.*"[32] The suggestion is not that this word stands outside metaphysical humanism and that recourse to it magically quiets the suspicious surrounding the word "man" and the values of humanism. This is clear from the discussion of Fichte's use of the word early in the essay where *Geschlecht* is not determined by birth, native soil, or race (*DP*, 162). Rather, the issue is again that of "man, man's humanity, and of humanism" (*DP*, 163) at the time of the end of humanism, the time of the ends of man. But this remains at best a promise.

It would seem then that the specific danger threatening deconstruction in the political realm lies less in the formalism of its strategies, than in its heightened awareness of the complexity of intervention in the political arena, which might seem exaggerated to the point of being debilitating. What saves deconstructive politics from formalism and neutrality is also what saves it from inaction and silence. Deconstruction is not just inventive, it is called by the other. Or rather, and the qualification is decisive, it is called by the other of metaphysical humanism. Once

it is recognized that metaphysical humanism is not only to be understood
as logocentric, but also as, for example, Eurocentric, phallocentric, colonialist, and racist, then there is at least a preliminary answer, beyond
Bernstein's appeal to a metaphorics, to the question of what directs Derrida's ethical-political intervention. At the same time, it is this very characterization of the other *in advance,* which threatens that in one way or
another there will be an assimilation of the other to the same, such as was
observed when Derrida read Mandela in terms of Rousseau. That is to
say, even though this particular assimilation of Mandela may not have
been inevitable, Mandela's own need to employ the language of the
West, at the same time as he drew from outside, it has the force of a
strategic necessity. So long as the historical analysis of the West on which
deconstruction depends remains persuasive, deconstruction will have a
role in the political arena. That is because it has the capacity to elucidate
the strategies in terms of which one might respond to the situation that
analysis describes. And so long as that analysis holds, there is no clear
end to deconstruction in sight, any more than there is a clear end to
racism outside of a promise: an inevitable end inevitably deferred. But
Derrida's own questioning of the West's exclusionary account of its own
history, joined with other analyses, other ways of questioning, including
a questioning by voices that come from what within this schema are the
voices of the outside, suggests that it does at least make sense to add the
proviso "so long as the analysis holds."[33]

6

Predication as Originary Violence: A Phenomenological Critique of Derrida's View of Intentionality

Dallas Willard

W hat happens to *intentionality* in the thought of Jacques Derrida? When he is finished—when the terminological chain of *différance* has been finely interwoven with and marked off from that of "presence"—what has been made of that common state of affairs in which an "act" of consciousness and/or language "selects" *its* object? What then are its components to be, and how are they related? For example, when I recall the first automobile I owned, or plan what I will work on during my next sabbatical leave, or savor the colors in a sunset sky? How does Derrida analyze that peculiar type of *affinity* between particular events of consciousness and specifically correlated events (of the various possible types) which we often express by the prepositions "of" and "about"? What is the basic nature, according to him, of that *ofness* or *aboutness* which is characteristic of acts of consciousness? Especially, how does *différance* enter into it?

The fabled king Midas of Phrygia turned everything he touched, including his food, into gold. There is a long-standing tradition in Western thought according to which whatever objects present themselves *to* consciousness are the *products* of some more fundamental type of "touching" between the mind and—something else. Our first thesis here is that Derrida falls squarely within this "Midas" tradition in the interpretation of intentionality: a tradition which very few philosophers in the modern period—possibly only Husserl, though the most common reading does not even exempt him—have managed to escape. It seems clear that intentionality for Derrida really is a kind of *making:* a making that is always a remaking, thus moving all "objects"—the individual as well as the universal—into the realm of the *ideal* as he understands it, and simultaneously doing "violence" to that *from which* this "ideal" object of consciousness is produced, as well as to the produced object itself. Our second thesis will be that his view is descriptively false to the facts of consciousness, and driven by metaphysical prejudices—perhaps, ultimately, historical prejudices—which he not only never rationally supports, but which are in fact rationally insupportable—perhaps by his own insistence.

Beginning with Bergson

The Midas tradition extends into obscure antiquity. Locke and Kant are the most obvious members of it from within the "modern" period of philosophy; and they, of course, are highly instructive to study in clarifying its dynamics. But here we shall begin with Bergson, who, in truth, left so very little for Derrida to say. Emmanuel Levinas has recently tried to remind us of the extent to which Bergson preempted the later critiques of technological rationalism and "logocentrism" with his own form of "life" philosophy and his analysis of the relationship between concepts, language, history, and *durée*.[1] But Bergson remained a basically hopeful philosopher. Perhaps there *should* be no serene philosophers in a world where, increasingly, only sour resentment and despair seemed appropriate—especially toward the intellect, which had proven astonishingly inept at realizing the hopes of the Enlightenment for humankind. Thus Bergson's name and spirit practically disappeared, though his substance continued to be of great historical effect in the work of people who might be embarrassed to be associated with him.

Now we find Bergson saying that:

> What I see and hear of the outer world is purely and simply
> a selection made by my senses to serve as a light to my con-
> duct. . . . My senses and my consciousness, therefore, give me

no more than a practical simplification of reality. In the vision they furnish me of myself and things, the differences that are useless to man are obliterated, the resemblances that are useful to him are emphasized; ways are traced out for me in advance, along which my activity is to travel. These ways are the ways which all mankind has trod before me. Things have been classified with a view to the use I can derive from them. And it is this classification I perceive, far more clearly than the color and shape of things. . . . The individuality of things escapes us. . . . In short, we do not see the actual things themselves; in most cases we confine ourselves to reading the labels affixed to them. . . . The word . . . intervenes between it [the things] and ourselves. . . .

Not only external objects, but even our own mental states, are screened from us in their inmost, their personal aspects, in the original life they possess. . . . We catch only the impersonal aspect of our feelings, that aspect which speech has set down once for all because it is almost the same, in the same conditions, for all men. Thus, even in our own individual, individuality escapes our ken. . . . [W]e live in a zone midway between things and ourselves, externally to things, externally also to ourselves.[2]

Of course Bergson did concede that metaphysical "intuition" and the experience of art allow us, upon occasion, to get to *the individual,* and thus, with reference to the self, to "grasp something that has nothing in common with language, certain rhythms of life and breath that are closer to man that his inmost feelings, being the living law—varying with each individual—of his enthusiasm and despair, his hopes and regrets."[3] Although they all decry the "objective" mode of knowledge, there still is some kind of "knowledge"—for Bergson as well as for the existentialists and for Derrida himself—which accesses what cannot be accessed "objectively" or "logocentrically."

Sartre and the Touch

Sartre at one point gave great promise of escaping the Midas model, with some help from Husserl. In his brilliant little note, "Une idée fondamentale de la 'Phénoménologie' de Husserl, l'intentionnalité," which appeared in *La nouvelle revue française* for January of 1939, he deftly skewered the idealisms of Brunschvicg, Lalande, and Meyerson by describing how, for them,

> the mental spider draws things into its web, covers them with a pale spittle, and slowly swallows them, turning them into its own substance. What is a table, a stone, or a house? It is a certain assemblage of "contents of consciousness," an arrangement of those contents. An alimentary philosophy! How evidently true! Is not the table the actual content of my perceptions? And is not my perception the present state of my consciousness? . . . In vain did the more simple and uncultivated among us search for something solid, something which, at last, was not mental. Everywhere we were met only by a flabby mixture in which we discerned—ourselves!

By contrast, Sartre notes,

> Husserl never ceased to assert that the thing cannot be dissolved into consciousness. You see, possibly, this tree here. But you see it there at the roadside, just there where it is.—Amidst the dust. Alone and withered in the heat. Twenty leagues from the Mediterranian coast. It could not enter into your consciousness, for it is not of the same nature as your consciousness.[4]

But, alas! Hopes are only to be dashed. By the time we get to *Being and Nothingness*, if not earlier, the table, stone, tree, etc., which was saved from being "mental," now proves to be something that, through its necessary "world," is internally related to, and so could not exist without, the "*pour-soi*," "*Dasein*," or "Nothingness"—and now we must also say that "*différance*"—that alone can explain the possibility of a *world*—of a structure of identities and differences opened up by interwoven "nots" or "lacks." (See "Part Two" of *Being and Nothingness*.)[5] This is, today, a familiar story, and needs no elaboration. The only consolation it offers us is that tables and trees are, at least, not parts of *someone's* mind. But, under such headings as the "noematic," the "non-real," or the "ideal," their *substance* has nevertheless been transformed by "the Midas touch" of consciousness, generously interpreted, into something that, whether "mental" or not, would not exist without "the mental spider"—now, however, a spider conceived in social/historical/linguistic terms and inscribed front and back with names such as Hegel, Marx, Nietzsche, Saussure, Freud, Lévi-Strauss, etc.

DALLAS   WILLARD

Exempting Husserl

When we turn to Derrida's writings, two significant points become very clear. One is that the overall view of the "world" of science and common sense objects expressed by Bergson and Sartre, according to which it is a *product* of human reality, is the one accepted by Derrida. Admittedly, his *presentation* of this view significantly differs at certain points from that of his predecessors—including Heidegger, to whom he no doubt is closest. But the cognitive substance of what he says remains much the same as the views of Bergson and Sartre. We will come back to this claim below, to give it a basis in the Derridean texts.

The other point is that Derrida certainly believes that the view of the world and of the objects of science outlined above, according to which they are fundamentally "products" of *Dasein,* is also the view of Husserl. I shall not try to support this claim here, because I think any careful reading of Derrida's *Edmund Husserl's "Origin of Geometry": An Introduction* and *Speech and Phenomena* will amply show it to be true. He believes this, I think, because he accepts the interpretation of Husserl according to which the objects of consciousness are noemata.[6] And I strongly agree that Husserl can be exempted from the tradition of the Midas touch *only if* he *does not* hold that objects of consciousness are, in general, noemata.

But in my opinion he did *not* hold that noemata are *the* objects of consciousness—and also did not equate the ideal with the unreal, as Derrida constantly assumes. To the contrary, for him the usual objects of consciousness, whether real or ideal, are not noemata—though noemata can, of course, be taken as objects of consciousness in special acts directed, precisely, upon them—and those "usual" objects would continue to exist and to be what they are if all consciousness disappeared from the universe. Such objects, that is, as stars and galaxies, worms and algae, trees and stones, colors and shapes, concepts and numbers. Not some "metaphysical correlate" of them, but these themselves as they may now be given to a veridical consciousness. And, for Husserl, even such objects as *would* disappear with consciousness, e.g., acts of consciousness themselves, would not disappear because they ceased to be "present," but because they make up consciousness.

Derrida's views are parasitical upon Husserl's texts. His interpretations of Husserl's views enter essentially into, and (in a rhetorical manner) provide substantial force for, his own presentations. So it will be appropriate to refer to a few passages from *Ideas I*[7] in support of my claims about Husserl's views, though I cannot hope here to set aside what has by now become an entrenched interpretation of them. In truth, he is not misread in the manner indicated for lack of his explicit statements to the contrary. Subsection 43 of *Ideas I* is headed, "Light on a Fundamental Error." The fundamental error in question is that of "supposing that perception (and, each in their own way, every other type of thing intuition) fails to arrive at the thing itself" because of the appearances necessary to see it—except in the case of God, who allegedly cognizes them "without mediation through 'appearances.'" The idea is that appearances *prevent* us from seeing what appears. Indeed, the spatial thing can only be given to us in connection with appearances, which it always exceeds or transcends. But "the spatial thing which we see is, despite all its transcedence, perceived, given *in person* to consciousness. An image or sign is *not* given in its place."[8]

The standard reading of Husserl today—even among many who agree that *the* object is for him not the noema—is that the transcendent and possibly real object is only a something referred to by means of the corresponding noemata or appearances, which of course are mind/language/history dependent insofar as they are temporal events. But Husserl holds there to be an unbridgeable difference of essence between consciousness *via* meanings or symbols, and perception. In the former case "we intuit something *in* consciousness as imaging or signitively pointing to something else. Having the one within our field of intuition, we are not directed upon it, but, through the medium of a founded apprehending, upon the other: the imaged, the designated. But there is none of this in the perception, as little as in plain and simple recollection or phantasy." The tree, table, etc. is directly present to us, no matter how complicated the act in which *it* is given.

Moreover, what *is* intuited in the usual perception does not *mean*, is not of or about, something else, as the appearance or noema most certainly is. This writing pad is not *of* something, as its appearances as well as acts of perceiving it are, each in their own way, *of it*. Both the intentional experience ("act") and the corresponding noema ("appearance") have a content and, based therein, a reference to an object, the object being the same for both (see end of subsection 129 of *Ideas I*). But for Husserl the object itself has, in the usual case, neither content nor object in that same sense, and hence is neither act nor noema (appearance). So the ("usual") object is not a noema.

Finally, all objects, even when they are experienced, come to consciousness *as* being there prior to their being known, and not as being *produced* or as being *dependent upon* the acts or appearances in which they come to consciousness (see subsections 45 and 52). He is especially em-

phatic about the absurdity of holding ideal objects (essences) to be produced by psychical acts (subsection 22). Any alleged dependence of our
usual objects upon mental activities is not something *findable*, but can
only be derived from metaphysical prejudice. Appearances (whether
called noemata or not) are radically different kinds of things from trees
and tables. You only have to attend to their details to see. To suppose
that we might not be able to tell when we are contemplating a table and
when we are contemplating the appearance of a table is to make an as-
tounding, gratuitous concession from which there is no recovery in philosophical work. For what could possibly be more obvious than that a
table is not an appearance of a table—once you attend to what an appearance of a table is?

One of Husserl's discussions concerns the claim "that when we
think we perceive, e.g., the property of white, we really only perceive, or
otherwise present to ourselves, a resemblance between the apparent object and other objects." In a manner characteristic of his whole approach he responds that here

> in the face of all *Evidenz* an object evidently different from our
> intentional object has been substituted for it. The thing com-
> prised in my intuition's intention, the thing I think that I am
> grasping perceptually or imaging in phantasy stands by and
> large above all dispute. I may be deceived as to the existence of
> the object of perception, but not as to the fact that I do per-
> ceive it as determined in this or that way, that my percept's tar-
> get is not some totally different object, a pine tree, e.g., instead
> of a cockroach. This *Evidenz in characterizing description (or in
> identification and distinction of intentional objects),* has, no doubt,
> its understandable limits, but it is true and genuine *Evidenz.*[9]

My hope is that considerations such as these will strongly suggest,
at least, that Husserl is not in the Midas touch tradition of epistemology.
Or, in any case, that the line of interpretation that puts him there by
treating *his* noemata as the objects of the usual acts of consciousness is
mistaken. And surely there is no other ground in his writings for associating him with that tradition.

Derrida's Position

By contrast, a very simple line of reasoning locates Derrida squarely in
the Midas tradition:

1. The everyday objects of consciousness and discourse (or the objects of the usual consciousness and discourse) have their being as "presence," in his special sense of the term.
2. Presence involves a certain self-containedness and discreteness that alone makes reidentification and identity possible. But this "presence" results only from ab-straction: a pulling-away-from, an ex-traction from the logocentrically ineffable and yet essential union with what, at the level of ordinary discourse, is different from, outside of, that which has presence.
3. This "ex-traction" to create "beings" (with lower case "b"), things "present" (the usual sorts of objects), is the work of *naming* and *predication*. That is, of language. These two linguistic functions constitute a "violence" to the "deeper" unification of beings where the *arche-writing* of *différance* without identity reigns. It thus gives rise to trees, tables, persons (subjects), as well as to numbers and colors and virtues, etc. Without it they would lack presence and would not exist.
4. Naming and predication are functions of language, and hence of "transcendental historicity," not of individual minds—which, as *beings*, are themselves only results (in some sense) of naming and predicating.
5. But while language and historicity are "more" than individual human beings, they do not produce *beings* apart from individual human beings.

Hence: Ordinary objects, *beings*, things "present," are after all the outcome of individual minds ("inhabited" by or "inhabiting" language and historicity, to be sure) touching (being touched by) originary unity or process and transforming "something" of "it" into trees, tables, persons, etc. Without such minds there would be no world of beings. This is our first thesis, stated above.

Derrida's System

To explain the reasoning back of this thesis we look more closely at Derrida's system. He has a *system* of thought. Not that he denies this. Indeed, he affirms it—with his standard qualifiers.[10] And what he says about the limits of "system," as one link in the logocentric conceptual chain, is a part of his system. But what must be emphasized is that he *does* tell us *how things essentially stand*. His writings are full of synthetic a priori statements—e.g., that "It is impossible for any identity to be closed in upon itself, on the inside of its proper interiority, or on its coincidence with itself. The irreducibility of spacing is the irreducibility of the other" (*P*, 94). Or: "There cannot be a unique sign for a unique thing."[11] His claim that in certain areas we cannot, strictly, state essence is a part of his report on, precisely, how things essentially stand. This is not changed at all by his further claim that the "telling" of how things essentially stand must be done by putting stress on the logocentric framework and causing it to "tremble" by showing its constitutive contrasts—especially the one between presence and absence—require that the opposing terms inhabit each other through the dynamism of *différance* and "trace." In this regard he is only one more in a long line of nineteenth- and twentieth-century philosophers who have held that the "real philosophical stuff" can only be *shown* and cannot be *said*.

Derrida's system is basically tripartite. It is strongly Kantian. Another close parallel would be with critical realism as practiced in Anglo-American philosophy of this century. In each case, the world of objects of science and common sense—including the individual self—is treated as a result of some deeper level of "interaction" between factors of what there is. The three dimensions of the "system" are:

1. The realm of identifiable (reidentifiable) objects or *b*eings, including the self, the *B*eing of which is, according to Derrida, *presence*. For these, to be is to be present or have presence, which is achievable only through the violence of predication. "There is no presence," he says, "before and outside semiological *différance*" (*P*, 28).[12]
2. The realm of *différance*, of a deferring and differing, of a movement that is neither active nor passive, that does not involve or presuppose, and yet somehow makes place for, identities capable of presence, objects of the everyday sort (*M*, 9–11). This is the realm of the "infrastructure"—of the tain of the mirror which has no resemblance to the objects mirrored but makes it possible for them to be reflected—of which, according to Derrida, there is no name, essence, or science (*G*, 49, 93).[13]
3. The interaction between the realm of beings and the realm of *différance*, as "the process of scission and division which would produce or constitute different things or differences" (*M*, 9).

Naming and Predication as "Violence"

Here we are especially interested in the status of the world of ordinary objects or beings. They originate, as we have indicated, through a certain *violence*. "The structure of violence is complex," Derrida holds, and its possibility—writing—is no less so. . . . To name, to give names that it will on occasion be forbidden to pronounce, such is the originary violence of language which consists in inscribing within a difference, in classifying, in suspending the vocative absolute. To think the unique *within* the system, to inscribe it there, such is the gesture of the arche-writing: arche-violence, loss of the proper, of absolute proximity, of self-presence, in truth the loss of what has never taken place, of the self-presence which has never been given but only dreamed of and always already split, repeated, incapable of appearing to itself except in its own disappearance. (*G*, 112; cf. *WD*, 147–49)

Proper names, indeed, never function except as "a designation of appurtenance and a linguistico-social classification" (*G*, 111). What is really at work in names is a system of classification, expressed in predicates, through which things are designated in terms of their other, subjected to "the violence of difference, of classification, and of the system of appelations" (*G*, 110). Within the organized meanings of a language, nothing ever *just* is what is *called*. What is made present in the predicate or name is treated as *just this*. The mastery that comes from this *making* something to be present founds "a sort of infinite assurance. The power of repetition that the *eidos* and *ousia* made available seems to acquire an absolute independence. Ideality and substantiality relate to themselves in the element of the *res cogitans*, by a movement of pure auto-affection. Consciousness is the experience of pure auto-affection" (*G*, 97–98).

Whatever is an object of linguistic meaning will, therefore, always be characteristically different from whatever is not an object—specifically, it will always have the presence which makes it a being. And yet, *as* classified, it also bears the essential traces of its other within it—as the letter "a" is marked by its place in the system of the alphabet, its relationships with the other letters. Thus, even "The thing itself is a sign" (*G*, 49). That is, it always points to the absent which is present within it through the relationships implicit in its classification or kind. Thus: "From the moment that there is meaning there is nothing but signs. *We think only in signs*" (*G*, 50). The signified which transcends the system of signifiers is an illusion. "Writing" he says, is "the impossibility of a chain arresting itself on a signified that would not relaunch this signified, in that the signified is already in the position of the signifying substitution" (*P*, 82; cf. *WD*, 25).

Two Crucial Clarifications

Yet the being that is given or taken as present is not, for Derrida, an illusion. In his interview with Kearney he responds vigorously to the oft-repeated claim that he denies the existence of the subject, the person—and by implication of other "substances":

> I have never said that the subject should be dispensed with. Only that it should be deconstructed. To deconstruct the subject does not mean to deny its existence. There are subjects, "operations" or "effects" of subjectivity. This is an incontrovertible fact. To acknowledge this does not mean, however, that the subject is what it *says* it is. The subject is not some extra-linguistic substance or identity, some pure *cogito* of self-presence; it is always inscribed in language. My work does not, therefore, destroy the subject; it simply tries to resituate it.[14]

This is a highly important statement for interpreting Derrida's views. The beings (whose Being is presence) really do exist—though Derrida, like Heidegger, never provides a clarification of what it is, in general, for something to be: of the difference between being and not-being. (The distinction between the being and its Being—the ontico-ontological difference—gets all the attention and the difference between being and not-being gets lost.) Trees and tables, colors and numbers, *are,* even though without the violence which enables them, forces them, to have "presence" they *would* not exist.

This clarification goes hand in hand with another important statement to Kearney. Derrida emphatically rejects the view "that deconstruction is a suspension of reference," along with those critiques which see his "work as a declaration that there is nothing beyond language, that we are imprisoned in language."[15] It is, he says, "the exact opposite. The critique of logocentrism is above all else the search for the 'other' and the 'other of language.'" He refers to those who (referring to him) treat "Post-Structuralism" as the view "that there is nothing beyond language, that we are submerged in words—and other stupidities of that sort." True,

> deconstruction tries to show that the question of reference is much more complex and problematic than traditional theories supposed. . . . [And] the other, which is beyond language and which summons language, is perhaps not a "referent" in the normal [?] sense which linguists have attached to this term. But

> to distance oneself thus . . . does not amount to saying there is
> *nothing* beyond language.[16]

These highly significant correctives to popular misunderstanding must
be kept in mind. However, one must also be clear about what it is *in
Derrida's texts* that gives rise to such misunderstandings. It *is* his view that
the usual sorts of objects, including and especially linguistic signs themselves (*WD*, 50), have a Being tied to the kind of identity (reidentifiability,
hence freedom from context, hence *ideality*) which they possess. That is,
a Being which is presence. To be is, for them, to have presence. And
presence does not belong to anything apart from significations or concepts, which do not exist outside of language. (Here as usual add-in all of
the deconstructive points about "inside/outside.") On the other hand,
différance, trace, mark, etc., do not exist or have an essence (*G*, 167; *M*,
121–25)—when "exist" is used to indicate the Being of what has presence. What is "outside" of language does not "exist"—even if in some
sense (which Derrida can hardly be said to have made comprehensible) it
"has Being." Accordingly, it is hardly appropriate, though it is understandable, for him to refer to "stupidities of that sort." The problem is
not stupidity, and Derrida should accept this share of responsibility for
the misunderstanding. Clearly, for him, the world of objects *with* presence would not exist but for language and its gathering and dissemination significations; for presence, the self-identity that gives logocentrism
its power and allows us to subject beings to standard logic, mathematics,
and the like, is a function of language—even of "writing" in the *usual*
sense of that term. What that "other" is that transcends, lies outside of,
language (again, in the *usual* sense) can hardly be regarded as obvious.

The Midas Touch Remains

Let us now grant to Derrida that language and meanings are not the
inventions, are not *produced* or brought into being, by individual subjects. The beings of our world are formed by a historical reality. Can
Derrida, given this, escape the charge of subjectivism, of being in the
"Midas touch" tradition of epistemology? I don't see how. Language
and historicity do not obtain and have effects in their own right. Derrida
more than most wants to reject action from a heavenly "safe place." If
individuals are at the disposal of language and history, owe their beingly
Being to it, it is also true that language and history certainly have power

only through their insertion into individuals (or through insertion of individuals into them). The being and action of significations is not indifferent to that of persons. While language and history are indifferent to any arbitrary individual subject, they are totally dependent upon the existence and activities of language users. Concepts and signs do not have a being apart from individual humans: one from where, irrespective of individuals, they might gather the logocentrically reindentifiable object into that degree of presence (never *complete* or unadulterated with absence, of course) which allows it to be (have presence)—which allows there to be oak trees in North America, for instance.

Language and significations require the existence of historically developing communities of communication. It is for *the individuals* that make up such communities, not for language or history apart from them, that there is a world and that there are oak trees in North America. Language is existentially dependent upon the individual subjects, though not on any one of them in particular. This is not lessened by the fact that the subjects must be qualified in a certain fashion that has developed historically. And it does not really help, I think, to point out that to raise the question about individual subject and language in this way is to fall back into the oppositional structures of logocentrism (or of "metaphysics" or even "philosophy," in Derrida's special sense). However you interpret it, the fact remains that language is powerless to structure objects except through the actions of individuals. Contact with individual minds "results" in beings. No contact, no beings. Of course the minds are beings too—but then nothing is ever *just* what it is for Derrida.

The Intentional Nexus
in Deconstruction

These remarks bring to light the fact that Derrida really has no account at all of *how* language (conceptual systems) and the self relate to each other and to the objects present to or through them. In this he is like the antipsychologistic logicians of the early and mid-twentieth century, who divorced the science of logic from mental events so far that they could no longer explain how logic could serve in the critique of actual thought and discourse.[17] Derrida wants to avoid both empiricism and Platonism. He tries to do this by introducing sense (concepts, essences, significations) which provide a moving structure without reference to an absolute beginning or end. But this is where the properly phenomenological critique of his views begins to take hold. For the fact is that he simply has no account of how sense history enters into the individual mind or minds at a given time to yield the correlative world of beings—including subjects. His investigations are, apparently, not even intended to operate at that level of analysis. The result is that in fleeing from origins, transcendental signifieds, and the like, he leaves us with no positive analysis of intention ality: of the grounds (in the act and in the object) of the intentional grasp of the object by the act. And even if it were shown that a logocentric account of this nexus *cannot* be wholly correct, it does not follow that no account is available or required.

Instead of doing the canonical phenomenological labor of examining particular cases where an act of a certain type is directed upon its object, he contents himself with general argumentations derived from selected associations of certain terms. The basic term examined is, of course, "representation." This term, he states, can be understood "in the sense of representation, as repetition or reproduction of presentation, as the *Vergegenwärtigung* which modifies a *Präsentation* or *Gegenwärtigung.* And it can be understood as what takes the place of, what occupies the place of, another *Vorstellung* (*Repräsentation, Repräsentant, Stellvertreter*).[18] Thus the specific phenomenon of intentionality (ofness, aboutness) is ignored in favor of what Derrida will call *différance*, in the form of repetition (being the "same" as, though not merely "identical" with) and replacement.

But now a few questions must be asked. First, do we not know that the affinity which my present perception has with this computer screen, its intentional bearing upon it, is not a matter of the latter (or the former) being a repetition of and/or replacement for the former (or the latter)? Isn't it just nonsense to suppose that any part of my perception or that perception as a whole repeats or replaces the screen? Can any of Derrida's points about *différence* change this? Secondly, how would it assist my act to be about the screen if part of it did repeat or replace the screen or conversely? After all, "repeating" and "replacing" often occur in contexts where they do not involve the repeated or replaced standing in the intentional nexus with what repeats or replaces it. Just as, contrary to the suggestion of many, similarity is too general a trait to use as an analysis of "ofness" or representation, so with *différance.*

One sees evidence in many of Derrida's statements that he has simply lost the sense of basic semantical and intentionalistic terms. For example, one of his more well-known theses is that "even within so-called phonetic writing, the 'graphic' signifier refers to the phoneme through a web of many dimensions which binds it, like all signifiers, to other written and oral signifiers, within a 'total' system open, let us say, to all possible investments of sense" (*G,* 45). Now in fact the graphic signifer does not *refer* to the phoneme at all. It is not of or about or intentionally directed upon it. It has some sort of relationship to it, and perhaps what Derrida says about *différance* casts some light upon that relationship. But to speak of "reference" here is simply to deprive the word of any utility for semantic analysis. A similar point is to be made for the claim that the signified always becomes a sign because an absence always inhabits its presence. The *différance* structures of Derrida are found just about everywhere, so far as I can tell. But intentionality, the affinity of a given act or sign with its specific object, is a specific type of union which, on the whole, appears to be pretty rare in the universe. We have to consider the possibility that, distracted by his ingenious and fruitful insights into *différance,* Derrida has yet to discover or discuss intentionality. A general point about sameness (namely, that where present it is never simply "identity," but always "deconstructs" to exhibit "otherness," always necessarily involves difference, when examined with care—and what else was it that F. H. Bradley and many others like him taught us?) cannot be turned into a philosophical account of practically everything, even if it does suggest intriguing things about Western culture and history.

Voice and Consciousness

Derrida's discussion of voice and consciousness—an indispensable cornerstone of his entire system—shows the same phenomenological flaws as noted above. "Why," he asks, "is the epoch of the *phōnē* also the epoch of being in the form of presence, that is, of ideality?" (*SP,* 74). His answer is that voice "is a medium that does not impair the presence and self-presence of the acts that aim at" the (always ideal) signified (*SP,* 75–76). "The ideality of the object, which is only its being-for a nonempirical consciousness, can only be expressed in an element whose phenomenality does not have a worldly form. . . . My words are 'alive' because they seem not to leave me: not to fall outside me, outside by breath, at a visible distance" (*SP,* 76).

> The "apparent transcendence" of the voice thus results from
> the fact that the signified, which is always ideal by essence, the
> "expressed" *Bedeutung,* is immediately present in the act of ex-

pression. This immediate presence results from the fact that the phenomenological "body" of the signifier seems to fade away at the very moment it is produced; it seems already to belong to the element of ideality. It phenomenologically reduces itself, transforming the worldly opacity of its body into pure diaphaneity. (*SP,* 77)

Thus, "the signifier, animated by my breath and by the meaning-intention . . . is in absolute proximity to me. The living act . . . seems not to separate itself from itself, from its own self-presence" (*SP,* 77). Thus it becomes paradigmatic of beings (with small "b"). "The subject can hear or speak to himself and be affected by the signifier he produces, without passing through an external detour, the world, the sphere of what is not 'his own.' Every other form of auto-affection must . . . pass through what is outside the sphere of 'ownness'" (*SP,* 78). This leads Derrida to hold that "*de jure* and by virtue of its structure, no consciousness is possible without the voice. The voice is the being which is present to itself in the form of universality, as con-sciousness; the voice *is* consciousness" (*SP,* 79–80).

Now we must note, to being with, that Derrida here does not trouble himself to describe in detail a specific case of the experience of voice or speech. He begins *von oben,* with the general claim that an *object* is ideal and so can only be expressed—we are never told why—by "an element" also exerpted from the context of real or worldly existence. His next claim is that my speech, my spoken words, seem not to leave me and take on separate existence, but to fade away, allowing the signified to be (to seem?) immediately present in the act of expression, thus giving the act the type of undivided self-identity and ideality that characterizes beings: allowing the *immediate* presence of the signified in the act of expression.

But let us look at some facts. Speech, my words, in soliloquy or in colloquy, are sounds experienced as *located* in my specific parts of my body. When I *say* there is great danger of war in the Middle East, the words used are experienced as sounds *moving* in and from my chest and throat. (Try it and see. *That* is the simple phenomenological test.) When things are in good working order, speaking may be relatively effortless, but it is never a case of unmediated auto-affection, as anyone learning to speak a new language (to *make* the unaccustomed sounds with their bodily parts) or suffering from a good case of laryngitis can easily testify.

The crucial difference between spoken and written symbolism has nothing to do with "proximity," but with the fact that speech consists of events, while writing consists in continuants or substances which are the results of events. Spoken words do not become "diaphanous." In the manner of *events* they simply cease to exist after an appropriate temporal elongation, which is very different from becoming diaphanous. But they no more have a special proximity to the act of expression than, for example, the movements of the fingers in the sign language of the deaf, which utilizes space and not sound.

Once these matters are clear from the descriptive analysis of actual speaking, we will then understand that to say that no consciousness is possible without speech is to say something obviously false. Consciousness *constantly* and *mainly* occurs without corresponding speech. Hence, consciousness is not essentially linguistic. This, as a matter of historical fact, is a point upon which all of the great philosophers through the centuries (Plato, Descartes, Kant, etc.), up to and including Husserl, agreed—perhaps because simple description of the details of specific events in our conscious life will show it to be so. (How to explain the twentieth-century reversal on this point is another matter.) And if to claim that voice is consciousness, that no consciousness is possible without speech, is *not* to say something obviously false, it is to use the word "voice" in a way that has nothing to do with actual speech or language. As, for example, when voice is said to *be* consciousness—where, so far as I can tell, speech or "voice" is (falsely) assigned the absolute self-presence often said to be the essence of consciousness. Here, instead of an honest reference to language, a cosmic principle of the most obscure nature (*différance*, "writing") is invoked.

So it emerges, in my opinion, that Derrida does not really have a view of the specific phenomenon of intentionality or meaning. However intriguing in other respects, his reflections on *différance* cast no light on how language (name, predicate) works through individual minds to accomplish presence and thereby the corresponding "objects." They also provide no understanding of wherein consists that peculiar affinity or selectivity of the act (or sign), bearing upon its object or referent, that we call "intentionality." It is not so much that his account is wrong as that it really is no account at all of these matters.

7

Is Derrida a Transcendental Philosopher?

Richard Rorty

For years a quarrel has been simmering among Derrida's American admirers. On the one side there are the people who admire Derrida for having invented a new, splendidly ironic way of writing about the philosophical tradition. On the other side are those who admire him for having given us rigorous arguments for surprising philosophical conclusions. The former emphasize the playful, distancing, oblique way in which Derrida handles traditional philosophical figures and topics. The second emphasize what they take to be his results, his philosophical discoveries. Roughly speaking, the first are content to admire his manner, whereas the second want to say that the important thing is his matter—the truths that he has set forth.

Geoffrey Hartman's *Saving the Text* set the tone for the first way of appropriating Derrida. At the same time that I was picking up this tone from Hartman, and imitating it, Jonathan Culler was criticizing Hartman for light-mindedness. The term "Derridadaism," Culler said, was "a witty gesture by which Geoffrey Hartman blots out Derridean argument."[1] I weighed in on Hartman's side, claiming that Culler was too heavy-handed in his treatment of Derrida, too anxious to treat him as having demonstrated theorems which literary critics might now proceed to apply.[2] I thought it too much to ask of "deconstruction" that it be, in

Culler's words, *both* "rigorous argument within philosophy and displacement of philosophical categories and philosophical attempts at masters."[3] Something, I claimed, had to go. I suggested we jettison the
"rigorous argument" part.

This suggestion was contested by Christopher Norris.[4] Norris was
concerned to show that Derrida has arguments, good solid arguments,
and is not just playing around. Like Culler, he was also concerned to
block my attempt to assimilate deconstruction to pragmatism. Whereas a
pragmatist view of truth, Culler said, treats conventionally accepted
norms as foundations, deconstruction goes on to point out that "norms
are produced by acts of exclusion." "Objectivity," Culler quite justly
pointed out, "is constituted by excluding the views of those who do not
count as sane and rational men: women, children, poets, prophets, mad-
men."[5] Culler was the first to make the suggestion, later taken up and
developed in considerable detail by others,[6] that pragmatism (or at least
my version of it) and deconstruction differ in that the one tends toward
political conservatism and the other toward political radicalism.

In his recent book on Derrida, Norris repeats this suggestion, and
reaffirms that to read Derrida in Hartman's and my way is

> to ignore the awkward fact that Derrida has devoted the bulk
> of his writings to a patient working-through (albeit on his own,
> very different terms) of precisely those problems that have oc-
> cupied philosophers in the "mainstream" tradition, from Kant
> to Husserl and Frege. And this because those problems are in-
> dubitably *there*, installed within philosophy and reaching be-
> yond it into every department of modern institutionalized
> knowledge.[7]

The quarrel about whether Derrida has arguments thus gets
linked to a quarrel about whether he is a private writer—writing for the
delight of us insiders who share his background, who find the same
rather esoteric things as funny or beautiful or moving as he does—or
rather a writer with a public mission, someone who gives us weapons
with which to subvert "institutionalized knowledge" and thus social institutions. I have urged that Derrida be treated as the first sort of writer,[8]
whereas most of his American admirers have treated him as, at least in
part, the second. Lumping both quarrels together, one can say that there
is a quarrel between those of us who read Derrida on Plato, Hegel, and
Heidegger in the same way as we read Bloom or Cavell on Emerson or
Freud—in order to see these authors transfigured, beaten into fascinat-

ing new shapes—and those who read Derrida to get ammunition, and a strategy, for the struggle to bring about social change.

Norris thinks that Derrida should be read as a transcendental philosopher in the Kantian tradition—somebody who digs out hitherto unsuspected presuppositions. "Derrida," he says, "is broaching something like a Kantian transcendental deduction, an argument to demonstrate ('perversely' enough) that *a priori* notions of logical truth are *a priori* ruled out of court by rigorous reflection on the powers and limits of textual critique."[9] By contrast, my view of Derrida is that he nudges us into a world in which "rigorous reflection on the powers and limits . . . " has as little place as do "*a priori* notions of logical truth." This world has as little room for transcendental deductions, or for rigor, as for self-authenticating moments of immediate presence to consciousness.

On my view, the only thing that can displace an intellectual world is another intellectual world—a new alternative, rather than an argument against an old alternative. The idea that there is some neutral ground on which to mount an argument against something as big as "logocentrism" strikes me as one more logocentric hallucination. I do not think that demonstrations of "internal incoherence" or of "presuppositional relationships" ever do much to disabuse us of bad old ideas or institutions. Disabusing gets done, instead, by offering us sparkling new ideas, or utopian visions of glorious new institutions. The result of genuinely original thought, on my view, is not so much to refute or subvert our previous beliefs as to help us forget them by giving us a substitute for them. I take refutation to be a mark of originality, and I value Derrida's originality too much to praise him in those terms. So I find little use, in reading or discussing him, for the notion of "rigorous argumentation."

Culler and Norris have now been joined, on their side of the quarrel I have been describing, by Rodolphe Gasché. Gasché's *The Tain of the Mirror* is by far the most ambitious and detailed attempt to treat Derrida as a rigorous transcendental philosopher. Gasché says that

> [i]n this book I hope that I have found a middle ground between the structural plurality of Derrida's philosophy—a plurality that makes it impossible to elevate any final essence of his book into its true meaning—and the strict criteria to which any interpretation of his work must yield, if it is to be about that work and not merely a private fantasy. These criteria, at center stage in this book, are, as I shall show, philosophical and not literary in nature.[10]

Just as in the case of Culler I doubted that one could displace philosophical concepts while still having rigorous philosophical arguments, so in Gasché's case I doubt that one can eschew the project of stating Derrida's "true meaning" while still judging him by "strict criteria." I do not think that one should try to pay good old logocentric compliments to enemies of logocentrism.

In what follows, I shall try to spell out why the compliments Gasché offers Derrida seem to me misapplied. To my mind, "private fantasy" is, if not entirely adequate, at least a somewhat better compliment. Many responsibilities begin in dreams, and many transfigurations of the tradition begin in private fantasies. Think, for example, of Plato's or St. Paul's private fantasies—fantasies so original and utopian that they became the common sense of later times. Someday, for all I know, there may be some social changes (perhaps even changes for the better) which retrospection will see as having originated in Derrida's fantasies. But the *arguments* which Derrida can be read as offering on behalf of his fantasies seem to me no better than the ones Plato offered for his. Anybody who reads through Plato in search of rigorous arguments is in for a disappointment. I think that the same goes for Derrida.

I can begin quarreling with Gasché by taking up his distinction between philosophy and literature. On my view, "philosophy" is either a term defined by choosing a list of writers (e.g., Parmenides, Plato, Aristotle, Kant, Hegel, Heidegger) and then specifying what they all have in common, or else just the name of an academic department. The first sense of the term is hard to apply to a writer who, like Derrida, is trying to extricate himself from the tradition defined by such a list. But the second sense of the term is not much help either, for in this sense "philosophy" is just an omnium gatherum of disparate activities united by nothing more than a complicated tangle of genealogical connections— connections so tenuous that one can no longer detect even a family resemblance between the activities.[11] Only if one buys in on the logocentric idea that there just *must* be an autonomous discipline which adjudicates ultimate questions would "philosophy" have a third sense, one appropriate for Gasché's purposes. It is only by reference to some such idea that it makes sense to worry, as he does, about the lines between philosophy and literature.

For my purposes, the important place to draw a line is not between philosophy and nonphilosophy but rather between topics which we know how to argue about and those we do not. It is the line between the attempt to be objective—to get a consensus on what we should believe—and a willingness to abandon consensus in the hope of transfiguration. Gasché, by contrast, thinks that we can separate the philosophical books (or, at least the important philosophical books of recent centuries) from other books by a fairly straightforward test. The former are the books in which we find a specifically *transcendental* project—a project of answering some question of the form "what are the conditions of the possibility of . . . ?"—of, for example, experience, self-consciousness, language or philosophy itself.

I have to admit that asking and answering that question is, indeed, the mark of a distinct genre. But unlike Gasché I think that it is a thoroughly self-deceptive question. The habit of posing it—asking for noncausal, nonempirical, nonhistorical conditions—is the distinctive feature of a tradition which stretches from the *Critique of Pure Reason* through Hegel's *Science of Logic* to *Being and Time* (and, if Gasché is right about the early Derrida's intentions, through *Of Grammatology*). The trouble with the question is that is looks like a "scientific" one, as if we knew how to debate the relative merits of alternative answers, just as we know how to debate alternative answers to questions about the conditions for the *actuality* of various things (e.g., political changes, quasars, psychoses). But it is not. Since that for which the conditions of possibility are sought is always *everything* that any previous philosopher has envisaged—the whole range of what has been discussed up to now—anybody is at liberty to identify any ingenious gimmick that he dreams up as a "condition of possibility."

The sort of gimmick in question is exemplified by Kantian "transcendental synthesis," Hegelian "self-diremption of the concept," Heideggerian *Sorge,* and (on Gasché's interpretation) Derridean *différance.* These suggestions about transcendental conditions are so many leaps into the darkness which surrounds the totality of everything previously illuminated. In the nature of the case, there can be no preexistent logical space, no "strict criteria" for choosing among these alternatives. If there were, the question about "conditions of possibility" would automatically become merely "positive" and not properly "transcendental" or "reflective."[12] Once again, I would want to insist that you cannot have it both ways. You cannot see these leaps in the dark as the magnificent poetic acts they are and still talk about "philosophical rigor." Rigor just does not come into it.

The insusceptibility to argument is what makes "the philosophy of reflection"—the tradition of transcendental inquiry within which Gasché wishes to embed Derrida—the *bête noire* of philosophers who take public discussability as the essence of rationality. Habermas's polemic against the late Heidegger and against Derrida has the same motives as Carnap's attack on the early Heidegger.[13] Like Carnap, Habermas thinks that philosophy ought to be argumentative. He thinks that Heidegger, and Derrida are merely oracular. My own view is that we should avoid slogans like "philosophy ought to be argumentative" (or any other slogan that begins "philosophy ought to be . . . ") and recognize that the writers usually identified as "philosophers" include both argumentative problem-solvers like Aristotle and Russell and oracular world-disclosers like Plato and Hegel—both people good at rendering public accounts and people good at leaping in the dark.

But this conciliatory ecumenicism still leaves me hostile to those who, like Gasché, think that one can synthesize world-disclosing and problem-solving into a single activity called "reflection." In particular, I object to the idea that one can be "rigorous" if one's procedure consists in inventing new words for what one is pleased to call "conditions of possibility" rather than playing sentences using old words off against each other. The latter activity is what I take to constitute argumentation. Poetic world-disclosers like Hegel, Heidegger, and Derrida have to pay a price, and part of that price is the inappropriateness to their work of notions like "argumentation" and "rigor."[14]

Habermas differs with me and agrees with Gasché in thinking that philosophy ought to be argumentative, but he agrees with me and differs from Gasché in refusing to see the transitions in Hegel's *Logic,* or the successive "discoveries" of new "conditions of possibility" which fill the pages of *Being and Time,* as *arguments.* Habermas and I are both in sympathy with Ernst Tugendhat's nominalist, Wittgensteinian rejection of the idea that one can be nonpropositional and still be argumentative. Tugendhat sees the attempt of a German tradition stemming from Hegel to work at a subpropositional level, while nevertheless claiming the "cognitive status" which people like Carnap want to deny them, as doomed to failure.[15] By contrast, Gasché explicitly rejects Tugendhat's "theoretical ascetism," his self-confinement to "linguistic and propositional truth."[16] Gasché thinks that such confinement will forbid one to do something which needs to be done, and which Derrida may in fact have accomplished.

Whereas Gasché thinks that words like *"différance"* and "iterability" signify "infrastructures"—structures which it is Derrida's great achievement to have unearthed—I see these notions as merely abbreviations for the familiar Peircean-Wittgensteinian, anti-Cartesian thesis that meaning is a function of context, and that there is no theoretical barrier to an endless sequence of recontextualizations. I think the problems with taking this Derridean jargon as seriously as Gasché does are the same as those which arise if one takes the jargon of *Being and Time* as a serious answer to questions of the form "How is the ontic possible? What are its *ontological* conditions?" If one thinks of writers like Hegel, Heidegger, and Derrida as digging down to successively deeper levels of noncausal conditions—as scientists dig down to ever deeper levels of causal conditions (molecules behind tables, atoms behind molecules, quarks behind atoms . . .)—then the hapless and tedious metaphilosophical question "How can we tell when we have hit bottom?" is bound to arise. More important, so will the question "Within what language are we to lay out arguments demonstrating (or even just making plausible) that we have *correctly* identified these conditions?"

The latter question causes no great embarrassment for physicists, since they can say in advance what they want to get out of their theorizing. But it *should* embarrass people concerned with the question of what *philosophical* vocabulary to use, rather than with the question of what vocabulary will help us accomplish some specific purpose (e.g., splitting the atom, curing cancer, persuading the populace). For either the language in which the arguments are given is itself an antecedently given one or it is a disposable ladder-language, one which can be forgotten once it has been *aufgehoben*. The former alternative is impossible of one's aim is to cast doubt on *all* final vocabularies previously available—an ambition common to Hegel, Heidegger, and Derrida. Seizing the latter horn of the dilemma, however, requires admitting that the arguments which one uses must themselves be thrown away once they have achieved their purpose. But that would mean, on the normal understanding of the term, that these were not *arguments,* but rather suggestions about how to speak differently. Argumentation requires that the same vocabulary be used in premises and conclusions—that both be part of the same language game. Hegelian *Aufhebung* is something quite different. It is what happens when we play elements of an old vocabulary off against each other in order to make us impatient for a new vocabulary. But that activity is quite different from playing old beliefs against other old beliefs in an attempt to see which survives. An existing language game will provide "standard rules" for the latter activity, but *nothing* could provide such rules for the former. Yet Gasché tells us that "Derrida's work is genuinely philosophical inquiry that takes the standard rules of philosophy very seriously."[17]

On my view, it is precisely *Aufhebung* that Derrida is so good at. But one could only think of this practice as *argumentative* if one had a conception of argument as subpropositional—one which allowed the unit of argumentation to be the word rather than the sentence. That is, indeed, a conception of argumentation which, notoriously, we find in Hegel's *Logic*—the text to which Gasché traces back "the philosophy of reflection." Hegel tried to give a sense to the idea that there are inferential relations among individual concepts which are not reducible to inferential relations among sentences which use the words signifying those concepts—that there is a "movement of the concept" for the philosopher to follow, not reducible to the reweaving of a web of belief by playing beliefs off against each other. Hegel thought that he followed this movement as he went from "Being" at the beginning of the *Logic* to "the Absolute Idea" at its end.

Nominalists like myself—those for whom language is a tool rather than a medium, and for whom a concept is just the regular use of a mark or noise—cannot make sense of Hegel's claim that a concept like "Being" breaks apart, sunders itself, turns into its opposite, etc., nor of Gasché's Derridean claim that "concepts and discursive totalities are already cracked and fissured by necessary contradictions and heterogeneities."[18] The best we nominalists can do with such claims is to construe them as saying that one can always make an old language game look bad by thinking up a better one—replace an old tool with a new one by using an old word in a new way (e.g., as the "privileged" rather than the "derivative" term of a contrast), or by replacing it with a new word. But this need for replacement is *ours,* not the concept's. *It* does not go to pieces; rather, *we* set it aside and replace it with something else.

Gasché is quite right in saying that to follow Wittgenstein and Tugendhat in this nominalism will reduce what he wants to call "philosophical reflection" to "a fluidization or liquefaction (*Verflüssigung*) of all oppositions and particularities by means of objective irony."[19] Such liquefaction is what I am calling *Aufhebung* and praising Derrida for having done spectacularly well. We nominalists think that all that philosophers of the world-disclosing (as opposed to the problem-solving) sort can do is to fluidize old vocabularies. We cannot make sense of the notion of discovering a "condition of the possibility of language"—nor, indeed, of the notion of "language" as something homogeneous enough to have "conditions." If, with Wittgenstein, Tugendhat, Quine, and Davidson, one ceases to see language as a medium, one will reject a fortiori Gasché's claim that "[language] must, in philosophical terms, be thought of as a totalizing medium."[20] That is only how a certain antinominalistic philosophical tradition—"the philosophy of reflection"—must think of it.

If one does think of it that way, to be sure, then one will have to worry about whether one has got hold of a true or a false totality. One will worry about whether one has burrowed, deeply enough (whether, for example, Derridean infrastructures, though doubtless deeper than mere Heideggerian *Existentiale*, may not conceal still deeper and more mysterious entities which underlie *them*). But if, with Wittgenstein, one starts to think of vocabularies as tools, then totality is no longer a problem. One will be content to use lots of different vocabularies for one's different purposes, without worrying much about their relation to one another. (In particular, one will be more willing to accept a private-public split: using one set of words in one's dealings with others, and another when engaged in self-creation.) The idea of an overview of the entire realm of possibility (one made possible by having penetrated to the conditionless conditions of that realm) seems, from this Wittgensteinian angle, crazy. For we nominalists think that the realm of possibility expands whenever somebody thinks up a new vocabulary, and thereby discloses (or invents—the difference is beside any relevant point) a new set of possible worlds.

Nominalists see language as just human beings using marks and noises to get what they want. One of the things we want to do with language is to get food, another is to get sex, another is to understand the origin of the universe. Another is to enhance our sense of human solidarity, and still another may be to create oneself by developing one's own private, autonomous, philosophical language. It is possible that a single vocabulary might serve two or more of these aims, but there is no reason to think that there is any great big metavocabulary which will somehow get at the least common denominator of all the various uses of all the various marks and noises which we use for all these various purposes. So there is no reason to lump these uses together into something big called "Language," and then to look for its "condition of possibility," any more than to lump all our beliefs about the spatiotemporal world together into something called "experience" and then look, as Kant did, for *its* "condition of possibility." Nor is there any reason to lump all attempts to formulate great big new vocabularies, made by people with many different purposes (e.g., Plato, St. Paul, Newton, Marx, Freud, Heidegger), into something called "the discourse of philosophy" and then to look for conditions of the possibility of that discourse.

How does one go about deciding whether to read Derrida my way or Gasché's way? How does one decide whether he is really a much-misunderstood transcendental "philosopher of reflection," a latter-day Hegel, or really a much-misunderstood nominalist, a sort of French Wittgenstein?[21] Not easily. Derrida makes noises of both sorts. Sometimes he warns us against the attempt to hypostatize something called "language." Thus, early in *Of Grammatology* he says "This inflation of the sign 'language' is the inflation of the sign itself, absolute inflation, inflation itself" (p. 6). But, also, he immediately goes on to talk in a grandiloquent, Hegel-Heidegger, "destiny of Europe" tone about how "a historico-metaphysical epoch *must* finally determine as language the totality of its problematic horizon."[22]

Derrida himself, I have to admit, used to use words like "rigorous" a lot. There is a lot in his early work which chimes with Gasché's interpretation.[23] But as he moves along from the early criticisms of Husserl through *Glas* to texts like the "envois" section of *The Post Card*, the tone has changed. I should like to think of Derrida as moving away from the academic, "standard rules of philosophy" manner of his early work to a manner more like the later Wittgenstein's. Indeed, I should like to see his early work as something of a false start, in the same way that *Being and Time* is, in the light of Heidegger's later work, a false start, and as Wittgenstein thought his *Tractatus* to have been a false start.

But perhaps it is just too soon for a judgment to be rendered on whether Gasché or I am looking at Derrida from the right angle, or whether we both may not be somewhat squinty-eyed. For Derrida is, to put it mildly, still going strong. Still, it may be a service to those coming to Derrida for the first time to have a choice between opposed readings at their disposal.

8

On Not Circumventing the Quasi-Transcendental: The Case of Rorty and Derrida

John D. Caputo

Rorty: On Not Suspending the Natural Attitude

Rorty has given up the traditional idea of "philosophical knowledge," the idea that there is some sort or entity or principle or condition which philosophers can come up with, so long as they argue carefully, which "explains" or "grounds" what the rest of us are doing. Rorty has given up the Kantian idea that there is a "philosophical tribunal"[1] whose job it is to adjudicate conflicting claims about science or morals or art, in virtue of something which philosophers know and which nobody else knows, not unless they become philosophers, too. He rejects the idea that philosophers, in virtue of some method or capacity, can cut through appearances and get to what is "really" going on, can penetrate beneath the surface or rise above the lower world the rest of us live in. He rejects the idea that it is the office of some "nonempirical super science" (*CIS*, 4) called philosophy to establish entities like the Form of the Good, the *prima causa*, the monad, absolute *Geist*, the Will to Power, Being (as opposed to beings)—or generally anything we feel an irresistible urge to capitalize—whose role it would be to keep order either in the sciences or in the everyday world we live in.

J O H N   D .   C A P U T O

Put in Husserlian terms, Rorty sees absolutely no reason whatever to suspend the natural attitude which, as far as he is concerned, can
take care of itself and does not stand in need of transcendental aid.[2]
Some natural attitudes are better than others, but it is the business of the
natural attitude itself to put its own house in order, without foreign intervention. There is no need to acquire, and no way to establish, the
transcendental conditions of possibility which back up the empirical
world, which ground and found it, which adjudicate its disputes and provide an overarching hook upon which the empirical ego can grasp whenever things get too stormy in the empirical world below.

Rorty rejects the idea that philosophers can come up with an idea
of human nature which would pick out something quintessentially human which would not be a function of socialization, which would see to it
that socialization does not go all the way down (*CIS*, 185). He rejects the
idea that philosophers have found a way to come up with anything quintessential, with any essence at all, human or natural. He rejects the idea
that the physical sciences can come to the rescue, now that religion and
philosophy have faltered, and cut through the world of familiar objects,
like Eddington's table, to the mathematical properties of Physical Reality
itself. The urge to capitalize in the physical sciences is just as unjustified
as it is in metaphysics and religion.[3] He shows a steadfastly nominalist
and historicist (*CIS*, xvi, 74) skepticism about essence, reality, overarching principles, ahistorical conditions of possibility, and whatever else is
dreamt of in our philosophies.

Rorty has no knock down arguments against these entities and
principles; he does not think you can drive your opponents up an argumentative wall (*CIS*, 53). He does not want to be drawn into the fray, get
caught arguing the inverse side of metaphysics (which *is* philosophy, Heidegger says), defending an inverted metaphysics, which is metaphysics all
the same. Rorty is just incredulous toward such constructs: he greets
them with a blink, a yawn, and particularly a smile. On this point, at least,
he fits Lyotard's famous definition of postmodernism as "incredulity towards metanarratives," toward *grands récits*, big stories.[4] When it comes
to big stories, Rorty is a big skeptic; he is very incredulous about the sorts
of things that philosophers have allowed themselves to believe, and he
has set about, very adroitly, finding a way of not letting himself be drawn
into these beliefs. His idea is to back himself out of the vocabularies of
the classical theories, to ease himself out of their language games, by
simply "redescribing" the situations which the philosophers think are so
troubled as to drive them to seek a uniquely philosophical solution.

The effect of a good redescription on Rorty's terms will be therapeutic, to make the problem go away by seeing that, on this alternate description, there is no problem, that things can get along just fine without the philosophical intervention, that the natural attitude can take care of itself, that nobody in the natural attitude is feeling the pain that the philosophers are trying to cure. All you really need to see on Rorty's terms is that the vocabulary with which we describe the world or one another can always be revised, that any person or object or event can always be recontextualized, that any description can be replaced by redescription which will not suffer from the disadvantages of the prior description. Of course, the new vocabulary will generate new disadvantages of its own. But as Nietzsche might have said, final vocabularies are something to be overcome. All this Nietzschean-Rortian insight requires is a certain ironic distance from our current "final" vocabulary which sees that it is not final at all but "contingent" (CIS, 73).

What lies behind all this is the philosophical cramp that language is a "medium," either of representation, as in the realist correspondence theory of truth, or of expression, as in the more romanticized idealist theories that language is the way Spirit, Thought, History, or Being comes into words and so comes to be as Spirit, Thought, History, or Being. Rorty's notion is to kick this habit of thinking that language is a medium, that it is anything at all, anything *philosophical*, i.e., like a medium, and to realize that it is just a tool by means of which we make our way around the world.[5] Apart from the various natural languages which are the object of study in linguistics and in the various language departments, there just is no philosophical thing called language (CIS, 14–15).

The skill and the adroitness, the grace and the good humor, the originality, insightfulness, and wide-ranging literateness with which he has set about the delicate operation of articulating and defending this version of neo-pragmatism is pretty much what we mean nowadays by "Rorty." The name of the thinker, Heidegger says, stands for a matter to be thought. But what does "Rorty" stand for? How shall we *classify* it? (The problem of classification is a central question raised by Rorty.) What is its genre? Does "Rorty" stand for a "philosophy"? If you like. So long as you do not get in heat over that. So long as all you mean by "philosophy" is a kind of writing,[6] a frank and literate line of reflection which expresses itself about a wide range of human affairs, without pretense to expert knowledge (*episteme*), with an eye toward uncomplicating some of the muddles that philosophers, scientists, theologians, and artists have created for the rest of us, toward untying a few knots, and letting the natural attitude take care of itself. The whole idea is to give the natural attitude some room to breathe and to allow it to straighten out its own affairs. To refer to it as "philosophy" at this point is mostly aimed at offering relief to desperate catalogue librarians, and it is based upon little more than checking the footnotes to see what books are being cited. But it does not have much more punch than that (*CIS*, 135–36).

One might object that the "very idea" of the "natural attitude" is a *philosophical* idea. Nobody who actually *lives in* the natural attitude ever thought of it. The "very idea" of a natural attitude arises only from a transcendental standpoint, only by distinguishing the natural attitude from the transcendental attitude, so that the very identification *of* the natural attitude already presupposes the *epoché*, viz., that you have stepped outside of the natural attitude.[7] So Rorty has, as I said, a delicate operation (cf. *CIS* 7–8) on his hands, which it seems to me must always involve two stages. First, he must defend the natural attitude against its metaphysical detractors and transcendental *conquistadores,* those who think the natural attitude cannot conduct its own affairs, that it requires transcendental monitoring and colonizing by a more "advanced," high-order consciousness. Secondly, he must eventually talk philosophers out of making this distinction at all, so that eventually even talk about the "natural attitude" would disappear, even as Nietzsche hoped that the apparent world too would disappear, and even as Heidegger said we should leave metaphysics to itself and cease all overcoming of metaphysics.[8]

The idea is to just knock off philosophizing in the traditional way, to kick the traditional philosophical habit, the way one would quit smoking. This of course drives "professional philosophers" mad, i.e., people who get tenure and promotion, sabbatical leaves and cushy grants, people who in general make a profitable living from "philosophy." They do not want Rorty's line to get back to their academic deans or to the NEH. The delicious thing about Rorty's line is how nicely it cuts across the once well-entrenched divide between analytic and continental philosophy, how he overruns both their camps, and leaves a lot of very unhappy philosophical campers shaking their fists in anger at him. Analytic philosophers: because he has, unforgivably, made philosophy interesting and significant to a larger public; because he has broken ranks with a narrow in-group in the prestige universities who have made a career of patting each other on the back and recommending one another for prestige appointments while no one else reads or cares about their precious little papers. Continental philosophers: because he has invaded their turf, laid hands on their favorite thinkers, explained them in a way that can be understood, and stolen some of their best lines—like "the end of philosophy" or "overcoming metaphysics."

Professional politics aside, it is truly interesting how Rorty's line converges with the more radical developments in continental thought in the last twenty years. His work intersects in interesting ways with Nietzsche and the late Heidegger; with the work of "postmodernists" like Derrida, Lyotard, and Foucault; it bears on the exchanges between Gadamer, Lyotard, and Habermas. Rorty's ability to spot this convergence and to translate it into his own terms has made him, like it or not, the most widely read "philosopher" writing in English. Of course this convergence has been reached by tunneling toward the same center from entirely different directions: Rorty from a skeptical antimetaphysical tradition which has been shaving down metaphysical pretensions ever since Ockham unsheathed his razor; the postmodernists from the high-flying speculations of Hegelian dialectics, Husserl's transcendental phenomenology, and Heidegger's History of Being. But they have joined rails in a middle which Rorty was the first to spot.

Rorty's "Derrida"

Rorty shows a particular appreciation for the work of Derrida. In Rorty's terms, Derrida is a master of "self-creation," a genius of "autonomy," i.e., of creating idiosyncratic, virtually *unclassifiable* texts which hold our interest, which repay endless rereading, and which leave us wondering at how he does it. Derrida has succeeded in making himself different, has come to grips with the anxiety of influence with great aplomb by writing in a magnificently assimilative but creative manner, sounding now like Husserl, now like Rousseau, now like Heidegger—or Freud, or Lacan, or Blanchot, or Hegel, or Levinas (this could get to be a long list)—but always sounding different. Derrida has mastered the art of being idiosyncratic, of repeating the people he happens to have read but with a difference, a difference which is immensely creative, highly associative, ingeniously complicated (*CIS,* 126ff.; cf. xiv). Derrida composes fantastic "texts," rich, lush, overfull texts which overlap with other texts, which allude to philosophers, psychoanalysts, poets, and novelists in a way which sends his readers scurrying to the library to track down the disseminative excess of allusion, citation, creative misrepresentation, miming, playing; texts full of multilingual puns and tremendously funny jokes. Derrida is not a master of thought, which is the highest compliment grave old Heidegger could pay anyone, but a master of writing, of texts, of invention, an impressario who stages breathtaking productions, a genius at being brilliant, a philosophical virtuoso the likes of which we have not seen since Nietzsche and Kierkegaard.

Derrida has made himself into a work of art, has created a text out of the uncontrollably dense, complex of people he has met (like Proust: *CIS*, 100), books he has read, cities and even campuses he has visited, talks he has given. Derrida is utterly scandalous in this regard. He incorporates the most extraordinarily "contingent" things into his "philosophical" texts: the landscape at Cornell University, which is woven into a discussion of the philosophical problem of the "abyss," i.e., of nonfoundationalism; or the spelling of his own name which leads him to associate the "da" in Derrida with "*Da-sein*" (Heidegger) and Freud's *fort-da*. He writes a book—*The Post Card*—which is paradigmatic for Rorty of Derrida the writer—which consists of a series of love letters which are filled with private allusions, including an account of his visit to Oxford and a trip with Jonathan Culler to the Bodleian Library. The "book" itself includes a series of fantastic, entertaining, outrageous, obscene speculations on a postcard which he found in the Library bookstore—and which could still be found there as late as a visit I made to Oxford in 1988—in which a diminutive Plato appears to be standing behind (whence the obscenity) a much larger, seated Socrates, who is writing. Derrida's delight in this seeming reversal of the most honored filial relation in Western philosophy knows no limit, and the "book" he writes on the "subject" is only to be compared with the "aesthetic writings" of Kierkegaard for wit and imaginativeness.[9]

Unless you consider *Glas*,[10] which I would say is his masterpiece and is even more complex, more unreadably readable and idiosyncratic than *The Post Card*, and which is more germane for considering Rorty's relationship to Derrida, although Rorty tries to duck *Glas* (*CIS*, 126). *Glas* requires a companion volume entitled (what else?) *Glassary* in order to track down the allusions to Hegel, in the left column, and Genet, in the right column. "Philosophically" (I can hear the good reader gasp), it turns on a series of interrelated philosophical problems.

The problem of the author: which Derrida addresses by means of a "theory" and practice of "auto-graphy," which means that a writer is always signing his or her own name. In the left column, Hegel is *aigle*, the soaring eagle of *sa, savoir absolute*, his/her, *s(ignifi)a(nt)*, *Ça* (the unconscious), and whatever else you can come up with. *Sa*, the soaring eagle of speculative knowledge which swoops down on every unsuspecting particular, lifts it up (*relever*) into the universal and carries it back in its grasping (*begreifen*) conceptual claws to its cold mountain top of absolute knowledge. On the right side, in a parallel column, Genet who cannot stop signing *genêt,* the mountain flower, who keeps spreading flowers all over the place, Genet whose fags wear flowers in the most embarrassing places. On the left, a column made stiff and hard by the rigor of the absolute *Begriff;* on the right, cut flowers, headcuts of criminals cut from newspapers hanging on the prison wall, guillotines, castrations, all of this cut and stitched together into the text of *Glas,* with the glue of *Glas,* which likes to slide these slippery (*glissant*) signifiers the one inside the other, maybe even *a tergo,* with the aid of a little vasoline.

The problem of the family: on the left, the life of Jesus in Hegel's *Early Theological Writings,* i.e., his *"Jugend"-Schriften,* the child-writings which are the father of the mature man/Hegel, according to any good teleological genealogy (e.g., Bourgeois's). Hegel is always telling the story of the "speculative family" in which the Father generates his Son who must be broken up and spread out as Spirit. That involves a holy family composed of a man with only an actual mother but a father being in itself; and the bourgeois family, a good Prussian patriarchal family, whose son leaves the inwardness of hearth and home for the outwardness of commercial life, in order finally to be reconciled by the *Staat;* and a number of very improper fag families in the "other" column.

The problem of woman: Antigone, the sister who defies the public law of the father, of the state, of day, in name of the inwardness of the family, mourning, the night. While in the right hand column Genet is telling the story of transvestites, men/women, and of outlaw families, unfamilies of fags and homicidal rapists who make "unnatural" love and who bear the most delicately beautiful names, religious names like nuns who have left the world, names like Our Lady of the Flowers, First Communion, etc.

The problem of the proper name: when they are arraigned before the judge, and called by their "proper," legal names, the names that have been attached to them by the law for the purpose of surveillance, their bourgeois names, then they know they are already dead men.

The problem of the system: a rich thematics of "fragments" and remnants which means to say, like Johannes Climacus, that the system can never close over, that there are always remainders and fragments, always outlaws, always the inassimilable, indigestible, ungraspable. *Individuum ineffabile est.* There is something always already incalculable in the infinite Hegelian calculus. And this "calculus" contains an almost perfectly private allusion, except that Derrida gave it away. In 1987, while lecturing on *Glas,* Derrida told his audience that the thematics of "calculus" in *Glas* was also making allusion to his mother (the woman, who is daughter/mother/sister, is important in *Glas*) who was suffering from gallstones (*calculs*) at the time. That was a little joke, for Mom, who would appreciate being immortalized, or at least mentioned, in what would get to be a very famous book. A little like having a book dedicated to her, but inside the margins, and more importantly *privately,* until Derrida let his joke out in public.

I could go on—which is of course the whole idea. One could always go on, enjoying more and more of this inexhaustibly complex text, more and more *jouissance,* so long as you get these jokes. But you "get the idea." Which is *not* the idea, just what Derrida does not want, that you sum it up and "grasp" its logocentric "point" with your eagle claws, consume it and then move on. The quasi-idea is to linger and languish in the gooey glue of *Glas.* Now that is the Derrida whom Rorty admires, Derrida on his best day, the Derrida who is making himself beautiful and different by one of the most fascinating exercises in "autonomy" of this century, be weaving a rich full text out of his most private life, even out of the contingencies of his own name.

Still, there is a side of Derrida that Rorty does not admire, and that is the side where Derrida gets serious, when he is no longer a comic writer but starts trotting out new metaphysical creatures of his own devising, "quasi-entities" whose hiddenness reminds us of the hidden God in negative theology.[11] As you might expect, you can only get to know these quasi-entities if you are a philosopher and have the credentials to make the right arguments. That is the side of Derrida which argues for philosophical ideas like *différance, archi-écriture,* supplement, undecidability, etc. For a while, in his early writings, Derrida even adopted an unmistakeably apocalyptic tone about these quasi-entities, announcing the end of the age of the book and the beginning of writing. While Derrida has shaken that particularly bad habit, he still talks like "metaphysics" is an inescapable, encompassing something or other which has a hold on us which is deeper than we can say. That makes Rorty squirm in his seat because Rorty thinks that deconstruction on its best day should help us circumvent metaphysics, not mystify it all the more.[12]

The central claim that is made on behalf of *différance* which Rorty goes after is that it is a transcendental "condition of possibility" for speech and writing in the empirical sense. That brings Derrida squarely back to a version of transcendental philosophy, a variation on Kant and Husserl, which has an explanation for everything that is going on in the natural attitude. That puts Derrida and deconstruction in the superior position of knowing, in virtue of a philosophical theory, what is going on in language and what sorts of traps those folks down there in the life world—e.g., literary critics—keep walking into. The clearest instance of this adaptation of Derrida is that of Paul de Man, who thinks that Derrida gives him the wherewithal to straighten out the "naive" literary critics who still think that language refers to the world.[13] According to de Man, naive literary critics "resist theory," i.e., "literary theory" just because "theory"—i.e., Derrida's theory of *différance*—problematizes this naive belief in the worldliness of literary language by discovering the purely literary quality of language whose virtue is that, unlike scientific language, it refers to nothing other than itself. That Diltheyan split (between natural and literary language) gives de Man his elegiac tone, always mourning the loss of the world, which picks up on the nostalgic, negative-theological, apocalytic side of Derrida, which is the worst side of Derrida, the side that has forgotten that he is a comic writer. Derrida's job is to make fun of philosophy, to make it look bad by making it look funny. The worst thing he can do is to get drawn into the game of which he makes such stupendous fun.

But that is just not true, according to Christopher Norris and Rodolphe Gasché, whose readings of Derrida Rorty strongly opposes.[14] Norris says that it is a big mistake for Rorty and others to think that Derrida is just making fun of philosophy, that Derrida just throws philosophy into confusion by showing that every time it thinks it has come upon reference all it really finds is difference, that philosophical arguments always get washed out by their literariness, that philosophy is just writing and has no gifts or expertise of its own, that philosophy is always deluded to think that it has an argument over and beyond rhetorical force. Norris thinks that Derrida has rigor—he stands erect, like the left hand column of *Glas*. Derrida gives rigorous and close readings of philosophers, and his deconstructive analysis of Husserl is an exemplary piece of close argumentation, which shows how Husserl needs what he has excluded. What Derrida does, Norris says "amount[s] to a form of Kantian transcendental deduction. . . . [It] pose[s] the question: what must be the necessary *presuppositions* about language if language is to make any kind of coherent or intelligible sense?"[15] Derrida has "earned" his eagle's wings as a philosopher; he can soar with the best of them. He does deconstruction in a philosophical way which reminds us, as Norris says in *Derrida*, of the Enlightenment tradition of making arguments and doing critiques.[16] Derrida is not against philosophy but against a false idea of philosophy which is fed by logocentric delusions, like thinking that it has God's point of view. The Western philosophical tradition is all we have, and you have to work within it; you can't go beyond philosophy, no more than Foucault could write a history of madness from the standpoint of the mad.[17] You can't have God's point of view, or the madman's;

all you have is human reason. But Derrida's aim is to be relentlessly critical of what calls itself reason, particularly when the university starts
building nuclear bombs in the name of reason, which would see to it
there *is* nothing rather than something. You work from within, including
from within professional philosophical expertise, and you try to make a
difference.

But Rorty thinks it really would be odd for Derrida to end up like
that, delivered over to the hands of Gasché and Norris. If *différance* picks
out the transcendental conditions of possibility of speaking and writing
in the empirical sense, then that

> would require us to envisage all such inventions before their
> occurrence. The idea that we do have such a metavocabulary at
> our disposal, one which gives us a "logical space" in which to
> "place" anything which anybody will ever say, seems just one
> more version of the dream of "presence" from which ironists
> since Hegel have been trying to wake us. (*CIS*, 125)

Rorty is right, in my view, not to challenge the "accuracy" (*CIS*, 123) of
Norris's and Gasche's treatment of Derrida. Their commentaries, in my
view, play the strategically useful role of emphasizing (perhaps overem-
phasizing, and generating an accuracy problem of their own) Derrida's
more serious transcendental side (since Derrida's wilder side is well
known).[18] Rorty's portrait just waves off every serious moment in Derrida as a kind of philosophical hangover, and it reads works like *The Post
Card* too one-sidedly. But Rorty thinks that, if it is accurate, the Norris-
Gasché line accurately portrays Derrida at his worst. Setting accuracy
aside, the question is whether it is not just incoherent of Derrida to make
a transcendental move, whether that is not just one more unfortunate
relapse into the metaphysical dream of presence, just as Rorty says. How
can Derrida possibly think that with his notion of *différance* he has at-
tained some logical space within which he can place anything that anybody is ever going to say?

Derrida: A Kind of Transcendental Philosopher

In my view, Derrida is indeed committed to something like what Norris
and Gasché attribute to him. Derrida does indeed have a certain "philo-

sophical idea" about language. You might even say he has a (kind of) "theory"—that is a strong word which Derrida is not comfortable with: it implies mastery and a totalizing overview. He has a theory about what is going on in language and other sign-making or meaning-making or more generally effect-producing quasisystems or "economies," as he might call them (like painting and architecture).

To put things in too simple a way, I would say there are two phases to this quasitheory. The first phase is the part that Derrida has borrowed from Saussure. Derrida thinks these economies produce their effects by a kind of "spacing," by producing marks or traces which make nominal unities called "words" or concepts or meaning—or beauty, rhythm, symmetry or asymmetry, or whatever you *need*—not merely and not primarily in virtue of the intrinsic "substance" of the "signifier" but in terms of the "differential" relationship—the "space"—between the signifiers. It does not matter whether you speak or write, whether you use "give" or "*geben*," what does matter is that the "difference," the space between "give" and "live," *geben* and *leben*, be discernible. Derrida calls this spacing "*archi-écriture*" or "*différance*," which are not quasi-entities but, to put it the way Rorty would prefer, just an odd sort of vocabulary Derrida adopted as a contingent result of the books he was told to read, or that he got interested in, when he went to school in Paris. Specifically it was something he was getting from Saussure, mediated through the Copenhagen school of structural linguistics.

Derrida does have an idea of what language "must be" be if it is, as Norris says, to make "any kind of coherent or intelligible sense." So Derrida is a transcendental philosopher—*almost*. He is very close to the edge of transcendental philosophy; he hovers around its margins, is in between the columns of *Glas*, in their interplay, working the levers between the columns. But that transcendental side, played up by Gasché and Norris, is only the *half* of it, and this brings us to the second phase of his "theory." For Derrida is also supplying the presuppositions for thinking that whatever sense language does make will also be *unmade*, that the things we *do* with words will come *undone*. You might say, from Rorty's standpoint, he is asserting that, and explaining why, final vocabularies are *never* final, that and why final vocabularies are always contingent and revisable, and that you need different vocabularies for different things. That is why Gasché is circumspect enough to call this a *quasi-transcendental* philosophy, borrowing a (pretty funny) move in *Glas* (although the joke dies under Gasché's knife) in which Derrida, commenting on the analysis of *Antigone* in Hegel's *Phenomenology of Spirit*, addresses the question of something which a system cannot assimilate (a constant issue in *Glas*): "And what if what cannot be assimilated, the absolute indigestible, played a fundamental role in the system, an abyssal role, rather, playing. . . . The left-hand column text breaks here, is followed by 12 pages of inserted text drawn from Hegel's letters to and about his sister, and then continues: " . . . a quasi-transcendental role . . . " (*Glas*, 171–82a/151–62a).

The "quasi-transcendental" entity in this text is the sister, not just Antigone but the "figure" (*Gestalt*) of the sister in the *Phenomenology*, a little fragment of this vast book to which no attention has been paid but which for Derrida is both necessary and impossible in the system, which makes the system both possible and impossible, that is, plays a "quasi-transcendental role." So the second step in Derrida's "quasitheory" is to see to it that it is a theory which says that you cannot have a theory in a strong sense, without the "quasi." Derrida is arguing that linguistic systems are differential; that they produce nominal and conceptual unities as effects of the differential play (or spacing) that is opened up between the marks or traces; that this differential spacing is, as Hjelmslev showed, indifferent to the distinction between phonic and graphic marks; and finally that this notion of meaning as an effect of differential spacing displaces the primacy of intentional subjects expressing their thoughts by means of external signs.

But what Derrida added to all this, the twist he put on it—which is analogous to what Gödel does to mathematical systems—was to radicalize that argument, to push it further. He shows that Husserl's and Hjelmslev's attempt to enclose or regulate such a differential play by a purely formal system, to close the circle of its play, to formalize it, was misbegotten on the very grounds of a differential play. For it belongs to the very idea of differential play that the play is of itself self-differentiating, disseminating, and that any such formal rules as one could devise would be themselves "effects" of the play not the "basis" of it, subsets of the play of signifiers, not rules which govern it.[19] In Rorty's terms, any rules you would devise about what future final vocabularies would look like would themselves be contingent features of the final vocabulary you currently favor, without predictive power for what future vocabularies will look like. In Derrida's terms, it is always too late to assert our superiority over, our transcendental mastery of, language, for we are always already speaking and drawing on its resources. We have said yes to language before we say yes to anything else. Yes, yes.[20]

But of course it is also true that anything Derrida himself would say about the differential play would be in the same predicament, an effect of the play, not the play itself (rather the way that anything Rorty would say about the contingency of final vocabularies would still be contingent). It is always already too late for Derrida too. That is why he devised the strategy of inventing words like *différance*, with the purely graphic alteration, which is not a word or a concept—at least not the first three or four times he used it, as Rorty rightly points out,[21] after which it is too late again. But at least the first couple of times he uses you see what he is up to, what he is pointing to. Once it sediments and becomes part of the established vocabulary of "deconstruction," he has to move on and try it another way. In his earlier works Derrida tended to spell all this out; in his later works he takes it for granted. In *Glas*, which is his major work, he is just putting it to work.

So what does that do to Derrida? Does that make deconstruction a practice with a philosophical theory behind it to back it up (which is what the title of one of Norris's first books suggests),[22] which is just what philosophy has always been doing and about which Rorty has well-known complaints? Well, yes and no. Almost.

Yes, inasmuch as Derrida did not just drop out of a tree one day and start talking funny. He was led to what he had to say by Saussure, Husserl, Heidegger, Nietzsche, and Freud (among others), and he works it out case by case with painful detail. That is, Derrida has reasons for saying what he is saying and every once in a while he will lay them out— as in his argument with Searle who it seems to me (*pace* Rorty, *CIS*, 132–43) to this day does not get what Derrida is up to. If you make Derrida abandon this side, then the whole thing is just crazy, and Derrida is just running off at the mouth, albeit in a most entertaining way. Now that is what Rorty seems to want, that is, that Derrida would write in this entertaining way but for no good reason, or for his own amusement and that of those with a similar sense of humor. He is just having fun. He is making himself beautiful and carving out a sphere of autonomy for himself in a particularly brilliant way. So where's the problem? Derrida: that's not philosophy, that's entertainment.[23]

Now that may be Rorty, but it's not Derrida. (But can it even really even be Rorty? I will come back to this point at the end.)

So if Derrida is a philosopher who gives reasons if you disagree with him or make fun of him, it is true that Derrida is also *not* a philosopher, not a transcendental philosopher, and that is the side that Rorty likes. For what Derrida comes up with when he starts talking like a philosopher is that you cannot come up with anything like a philosophical theory, or with distinctions between theory and practice, or the *Geisteswissenschaften* and *Naturwissenschaften,* or analytic and synthetic, at least not for long. For sooner or later the differential play in what your theory is trying to stick together will make it come undone. Sooner or later, someone will give you a close reading; they will descend upon you and disclose that your *arche/principium/*emperor-prince has no clothes, that the distinctions you are making have sprung a leak, that you need and use what you are excluding, that your metaphorics contradicts your thematics, that you can't make the distinction between metaphorical and literal stick, and so on. And that goes for deconstruction too were deconstruction ever to be so foolish as to state itself baldly as a theory.

The upshot of this is that Derrida is both inside and outside philosophy, on the margins of philosophy, that he is a "certain kind" of philosopher. He has reasons for thinking that what philosophy calls reason does not hold water, that is, is without reason or has become unreasonable. The reasons (plural) for not believing in Reason (capitalized, singular) are better than the reasons for believing in it.

But his whole idea is to stay inside/outside philosophy and the university, to be adept at its games, to move with ease within its habits of thought and institutional corridors, and to disrupt its tendencies to start congratulating itself for being the home of Reason, the house of Being, the capital of everything that is Capitalized, including capital (money), or the place where the revolt against capital will be fomented, or the defender of bourgeois liberalism, or the guardian of truth, or any of the other unguarded things we say on behalf of academic learning or the university at commencement exercises. That is why Rorty is badly mistaken to think that "there is no moral to these fantasies, nor any public (pedagogic or political) use to be made of them" (*CIS*, 125; cf. 68, 83). Derrida stays close to philosophers and the university, moves with ease among their arguments, cultivates their language, reads them with a punishing closeness, gains their confidence, finds what is closest to their heart and then pulls the string, the loose thread in the text. After meeting all the standards of the philosophers, he breaks free and produces a scandalous writing which writes differently.

Now it is precisely this marginality, this nonpositionality of being inside/outside, which constitutes the "transcendental" motif in Derrida, the moment of what is called in *Glas* the transcendental ex-position (out of place). Antigone's place is both necessary and impossible. It is necessary because it provides the transition from natural to spiritual desire. That is, the relation of brother and sister is both sexual—they form a couple, a single pair of members of the opposite sex—and not sexual, without desire, and so it is the mediating *rélève* between the two. Yet this is impossible, for it contradicts everything that Hegel says about the battle for recognition; this is a mediation and reconciliation of what has never done battle. The sister has transcendental status for Derrida because she is a possibility which the system must exclude even as she is needed as a stop or a station in the progress of absolute knowledge, an interruption to be assimilated, on the way to the reconciliation of divine and human law. You can't have absolute knowledge without the sister, but once you do, you do not have the system any longer. It makes the system possible and impossible. The sister is inside and outside the system The very thing that is excluded is what makes the system possible and must be included (*Glas*, 170a–71a/150a–51a).

That is what Derrida is always doing with philosophical texts, showing how the very thing that makes them possible also makes them impossible, which is something he can predict will happen inasmuch as any assembly of signifiers is always already set adrift by *différance*. That is his almost transcendental, quasi-transcendental role. Almost. A broken, split transcendental. But notice that is *not* what he does in the other column with Genet, a text which he just lets play. Genet is already set adrift, already in play; Hegel has to be reminded of the play; but Derrida, who is neither Hegel nor Genet, is the inter-play, is the space and the spacing between them, as their columnizer.

Rorty is pushing Derrida into the Genet column, and Norris is pushing him into the Hegel (Kant) column, while Derrida himself is doing a double writing. Rorty's "Derrida at his best" transgresses philosophy, strays outside its borders into a scandalous, comic, different discourse, which has dropped the pretention of being transcendental. Rorty's "Derrida at his worst" remains inside philosophy, has reasons for his distrust of Reason and sounds for all the world like a philosopher. Norris on the other hand does not take enough precautions to keep Derrida out of the Hegel column. His transcendental Derrida is too strong, too erect, too stiff.

A Critique of Pure Autonomy

But this is an odd sort of transcendental, even for a quasi-transcendental, because it is a transcendental without a subject. It is a kind of anonymous transcendental, an impersonal field, populated by neither an empirical nor a transcendental subject, by no subject at all, but only by the play of differences. The standard transcendental is a subjective condition which makes the unity of objects possible, but the field of *différance* is a different transcendental, which makes any kind of unity, subjective or objective, im/possible.

Rorty, on the other hand, despite his account of the "contingency of the self" (*CIS*, 23ff.) and of its utter "socialization," operates within the most classical assumption of individual, subjective autonomy. His redescription of Derrida in terms of "autonomy" is the part that falls the widest of its mark. It is not a redescription but a contradiction of Derrida. The whole point of Derrida's analysis of discourse in terms of *différance*, i.e., of differentially related signifiers, is to underline the notion that languages are not "invented" by "subjects" (and I would think that the same thing is true of any adequate conception of a "language game"). The very idea of thinking of language in terms of a language game or of a play of signifiers is to get over the idea of a game invented and played by the players, which is the familiar, common-sensical, classical, subjectivistic, and "metaphysical" model of language, one which in other respects Rorty seems intent on abandoning.[24] The idea is rather to think of language as a game which plays the players, which exceeds and overtakes, which precedes and antedates, the interiority of a private subjectivity. On both the Derridean and Wittgensteinian models, a language is not something a private, interior self devises in order to enter the world and communicate its inner thoughts. Rather it is a game into which one is entered from the start by being thrown into the world, a game which plays the "I," which brings the "I" about, and marks it forever with the contingencies of its birth and upbringing. Language is not a matter of an "I" which expresses its "inner thought" by outer marks. It is rather a behavior which is acquired by picking up the conventions of making marks in the ways adopted by those who "bring me up," by means of which "I" am slowly brought up or drawn into the higher order operations of thinking and imagining, and get to be a certain sort of "I." The "I" thus is not the interior, anterior inventor of the language, but one of things produced by it, an "effect" of the game. So the extent to which I will be able to acquire these higher order operations is very much a contingent function of the subtlety, complexity, and nuances of the "vocabulary" (and the grammar) with which I am presented by my birth and education, of the degree to which the differential play to which I am exposed is differentiated enough, of the subtlety of the strategies that have been devised in the game I am taught to play.

On such a model it would be quite perverse and wrongheaded to think in terms of the "autonomy" of the subject, of the "freedom" to engage in "self-creation." The point of this model is exactly the opposite, to stress the impersonal, structural, community-wide, historical, and unconscious forces which rule over—but not with formalizable rules—or hold sway in the language game to which I belong. Such quasistructures prevent "self-creation" in any strong sense; indeed they make the "self" the "creation" (or effect) of the linguistic play. If anything enjoys "autonomy" here, it is not the self but the game which seems to carry the selves along by its own momentum, which is the "text" in the Derridean sense. For Derrida autonomy is a more likely predicate of a text, of writing, that orphan, which having lost its voice and its father to speak on its behalf, is "on its own," cut off from its father/author and its reference to the world.

That is why Derrida would never want to describe *Glas* or *The Post Card* in terms of a virtuoso performance of autonomy or self-creation, in terms of anything done by Jacques Derrida, the one who "signs" this text on the outside. He did not "invent" the linguistic chains which are strung together in *Glas,* the historical, etymological, graphic, and phonic associations out of which it is woven. He is not responsible for the connection between *glas* and *classicus,* for its connection with bells and tolling, for the emblematic character of *glas* for language itself as a system of "classifying," for the Hegelian impulse to let the classifying universal assimilate the classified particular. He found them—and he confounds them; he points to them and he exploits them; he lets them loose. He shows us how we are all a little lost in them, that no one can keep his head above water in the midst of them, that we are all always already swept up by them. That is why he says we sign our names, not only on the outside of the text, outside the margins or on the covers—which would signify mastery, superiority, domination of the text, as if we really were the authors and knew what we are doing—but also, always and inevitably, *inside* the text. We cannot help ourselves, we too are drawn into the text, sucked up by its tendencies and metaphorics, caught in its complexities and weblike traps. Autography flatly contradicts autonomy.

Derrida does not "deconstruct" something by means of his facile and inventive capacity for redescription or recontextualization. Rather, the language games are consistently undoing themselves and Derrida is like the first reporter on the scene of an earthquake, sending field reports back from the scene, reporting on the fissures and gaps that are breaking out all around him, even as he reports new formations that are gathering before his eyes.

Far from being a paradigmatic exercise in autonomy, the point of *Glas* is to confess the loss of autonomy, the loss of the self, of the author, of the subject, of self-creation. Rorty objects to *Glas* because it is not "readable" (*CIS,* 126). That is only partly true. Derrida would never want something purely unreadable, purely Joycean (nor would Joyce). But it is true up to a point, true that it is unreadable, which is its point,

the stylus tip that Derrida wants us to be pricked by: to experience unreadability, undecipherability, the loss not only of authorial but also of
readerly authority, just the way Johannes Climacus does. Derrida wants
us to get a little lost, to lose our autonomy. In *Glas,* that is not so much a
theory he has but a performance that is being staged.

    This is also why Derrida is quite insistently and consistently con-
cerned, not with autonomy, but with heteronomy. What strikes him
about language is not the ability of the subject to keep its head in the
midst of the play—autonomy—but the dispersal of the subject into the
play, the loss of the autonomy of the subject, and the loss of the identity
of the object, in an anonymous transcendental field. That is first of all an
epistemological and metaphysical point which bears against Rorty's analysis. For, ironically enough, Rorty is still clinging to a seventeenth- and
eighteenth-century metaphysics of the subject. His nominalism turns on
a freely inventive name-making subject who invents "vocabularies," not
an impersonal field whose quasistructural laws produce certain temporary nominal unities calls "words" and "concepts." Rorty shows no interest in another nominalism, one which sees names as the effects of
impersonal, structural forces, of an anonymous quasi-transcendental
field, which is "other" than the subject, and hence heteronmous. *Ça.*

    But this talk of heteronomy also has an ethico-political point
which Rorty either misses or dismisses, i.e., the turn to the other, the
openness to the other. The politics which goes along with Rortyian autonomy is bourgeois liberalism, while the politics which goes along with
Derrida is suspicious of the bourgeoisie and is turned toward the
marginalized and excluded, the oppressed and the victimized. Derrida is
radically suspicious of ethnocentrism and Eurocentrism, while Rorty is
unfortunately prone to think that the North Atlantic nations play the
only politically worthy game in town (cf. *CIS,* 93), a role analogous to
Hegel's Prussia, except that we happened on it by chance instead of aiming the labor of the Spirit at it teleologically. Derrida is radically suspicious of saying "we" and Rorty loves to say "we liberals," which is, it
seems to me—on his terms—not only an empty but a dangerous pat on
the back. Derrida is radically suspicious of the power plays which tend to
shape the prevailing language games and the vested interests which keep
them in place—while Rorty thinks they can be flipped with a flick of his
Wittgensteinian bic.[25]

    I frankly think that Rorty knows better than this and he has been
trying to respond to this sort of criticism which, on a more radically
postmodern version of liberalism, one ought to have no truck with. But
Rorty is having a hard time shaking this criticism because his theory of

the autonomous subject ("I") is too strong, and his suspicion of the "we" is too weak, for his postmodernism. He ought to give up this talk of autonomy as one more piece of seventeenth-century metaphysics and of the contingencies of Indo-European grammar, which he doesn't need and which causes more trouble that its worth. Rorty argues with clarity and persuasiveness that the the self is contingent, that it is shaped all the way down by socialization—yet he still talks about liberal subjects and autonomous self-creators. He would do much better to drop the idea of autonomy, to celebrate more forthrightly the plurality of possible non-Western and non-European language games, to suspect more deeply the vested interests which have their way in the Great American Way, to analyze more carefully the sociopolitical factors which are deeply embedded within any socialization process and which make changing vocabularies harder than it looks. He needs to give more play to the notion of an other whom we cannot bring into our conversation,[26] who doesn't belong to NATO, and who cannot keep up with the fast clip of Rorty's highly sophisticated Euro-American conversation.

That is not Marxism, which I agree is now dead in the water—although not before leaving a lot of others dead, too—but it retains Marxism's distrust of vested power interests. Nor is it bourgeois liberalism, because it is much more self-suspicious and much less self-congratulatory than that, more concerned with the thousands of lives—American Indian lives, black American lives, Latin American lives, black South African lives: one could go on—that have likewise been sacrificed to the interests of maintaining "our" economy and the vested economic and political interests of the United States. But it retains liberalism's interest in giving people some space, in trying to reduce their suffering, in defending the weak against the strong. Call it is a kind of radicalized, postmodern liberalism or call it a non-Marxist left. Either way it is what I think Rorty—"at his best"—is or should be after. That is why Derrida seems to me to have gotten further down the road on this point than Rorty. Derrida does not think you can "circumvent" metaphysics and change vocabularies at the drop of a hat. Derrida thinks you are always already stuck in the prevailing system and that the *status quo* must be the *terminus a quo* for any changes you have in mind. He advocates not circumvention but intervention, alterations here and there, wherever possible, wherever you happen to be, making some space, creating an opening, carefully inserting a little monkey wrench here or there just when the prevailing powers are about to have their way one more time and grind somebody up. Derrida does not think in terms of my autonomy to recreate and redescribe myself, of self-creating subjects, but of local action aimed at reducing the subjection of "others" to "us." He is inclined to problematize the "we," to see us as part of the problem, and to worry over the other, the heteronomous. He is less inclined to want to bring others into our conversation, to bring them up to North Atlantic speed, than to let others be and give them some space. Derrida is after a kind of praxis of the other, answering the call of the other, and he thinks of this as a matter of intervening strategically within well-entrenched systems of power on behalf of those whom "we" are oppressing. This is neither a Marxist Apocalypse nor liberal subjects coming up with a new description of themselves with the ease with which American advertisers can redescribe carcinogens as "better things for better living."

Put in a way to appeal to a pragmatist, Derrida gets a lot more done with the language of heteronomy than Rorty does with the language of autonomy. In particular, he gets a lot more done of what Rorty himself wants to do. On this point of autonomy, Rorty's redescription of Derrida is a regrettable regression.

The Uncircumventability of the Quasi-Transcendental

What I am arguing then comes down to this. Rorty *needs* a quasi-transcendental theory of the sort one finds in Derrida, even though he does not feel that need himself. It comes to down to classifying: "Rorty" too is a kind of transcendental philosopher. I say this for two reasons.

First, Rorty needs a quasi-transcendental theory in order to avoid the illusions, both epistemological and political, of a free autonomous subject. He needs to bracket the naive empiricist idea of a free subject and see that it is the "effect" of an anonymous, quasi-transcendental field. He needs to put that particular residue of the old metaphysics of the subject, which Heidegger calls "subjectism" (*Subjektität*), to the knife of a quasi-transcendental critique, one which avoids, however, the Kantian and Husserlian mistake of reproducing the empirical subject on a higher, transcendental notch. That is what Derrida's *différance* does and what a "language-game" theory, adequately conceived, seems to do. That is what I argued in the previous section.

Secondly, Rorty needs a quasi-transcendental theory to account for what he himself does quite successfully, in particular in those areas of genuine convergence between himself and Derrida. For if, as I have argued, Rorty is not right in redescribing Derrida in terms of the "autonomy" of a subject freely inventing his own vocabulary, then his account of Derrida in terms of the "contingency" (Derrida's "chance") of our vocabularies, in terms of Derrida's deployment of private allusion, of the search for an arbitrary, idiosyncratic, unclassifiable text is right on the money, if I may be so capitalistic.

So what I want to ask now, by way of a conclusion, is this: what is the status of "Rorty," of his "theory" of the "contingency" of any "final vocabulary"? "Rorty," I claim, is extremely close to "Derrida"; "Rorty" is trying to occupy pretty much the same marginal space that Derrida is trying to straddle—without falling off. Rorty too is, or should become, a quasi-transcendental philosopher who cannot go cold turkey on philosophy, who illustrates just what Derrida means about being inside/outside philosophy, even when the whole idea is to just leave metaphysics to itself and forget about it. Rorty too has a "theory" about final vocabularies that is *almost* a philosophical one, a quasiphilosophical one. He rejects the idea that language is some sort of I-know-not-what medium which mediates between us and the world, either by representing the world accurately or bringing the world to expression. We should cut out that sort of unnecessary quasi-entity–building, which simply reproduces all the old problems—Is the medium good or bad? faithful or distortive? transparent or opaque? etc.—and just content ourselves with the fact that vocabularies, as Davidson and Wittgenstein show, are tools we use which vary with the purpose and are either efficient or inefficient (*CIS*, 11–12), which is why anybody's final vocabulary is always revisable.

Now that is to entertain a philosophical theory about language, one which uses Wittgenstein and Davidson pretty much the way Derrida uses Saussure and Hjelmslev—a pragmatic, language-game theory, albeit one which flies along at a much lower altitude than those metaphysical theories about language which soar with the eagles. But it remains a philosophical theory, not in the weak sense of a pacifier for overwrought librarians, but in a stronger sense, one which requires a little bit of expertise of a distinctly philosophical sort. For after all, nobody "down there" in the natural attitude thinks that language is a "tool."[27] The folks in the natural attitude think that hammers and pens are tools, but not language. They think that some people are good with words and others not, some things can be expressed and others—the usual example is "love"—not. But above all people in the natural attitude have what Rorty calls "common sense" (*CIS*, 74). It is in this critique of common sense that Rorty gets—understandably—a little bit transcendentally uppity. That is not a criticism; it is just part of the philosopher's trade, something I am arguing that Rorty needs because he is still implicated in a certain kind of philosophizing in a stronger sense than he is willing to let on. The folks in the natural attitude "know" that their language tells it like it is, that other people may use "different words" but these others must mean the same thing as "us," because our words pick out "chunks" (*CIS*, 5) of the world which are really there, whether you dress them up in English or French, classical Greek or Sanskrit. The world is sitting out there in itself begging to be named and there really is only one way to do that, even though some people are better at it than others.

In other words, people in the natural attitude do *not* appreciate the "contingency" of their vocabularies. They *identify* with their vocabulary and do not preserve the *ironic distance* which is required by Rorty (and Derrida), the distance between ourselves and the vocabulary of which we are currently enamored, between our current vocabulary and any possible alternative. They lack a higher-order reflectiveness about language which disengages a speaker and user of a vocabulary *from* the vocabulary he or she uses. They are unable to make that much of an *epoché*, unable to effect that much of a quasi-transcendental distancing or disengaging from the contingent vocabulary they employ. After all, to recognize a contingent vocabulary *as contingent* is already to have risen "above" it or gotten "beneath" it just this far, that one no longer *lives naively* in it. So Rorty is reproducing many key features of the transcendental reduction: disengagement, reflective distancing, the breach of naivete, thematizing of the natural attitude as such.

By putting any final vocabulary into relief, Rorty has raised himself up a notch (*relever*) and worked himself into a transcendental position. Almost. Not quite. For it is only a certain kind of transcendental, a quasi-transcendental, a broken or split transcendental, a transcendental ex-position. He certainly does not want, and has not embraced, "a metavocabulary" which "gives us a 'logical space' in which to 'place anything which anybody will every say' " (*CIS*, 125). On the contrary he has given us reasons to give up the search for such a space. His notion of the "contingency" of any "final vocabulary," which turns on the notion that language is a "tool," plays a distinctly quasi-transcendental role. It explains, in Wittgensteinian and Davidsonian terms, how we do things with words, even as it predicts that we will never have any final terms or unrevisable final vocabularies at our disposal. That is very much what Derrida thinks and what Derrida means when he speaks of "conditions of possibility and impossibility," viz., quasi-transcendental conditions. That is, Rorty and Derrida have reasons to believe that we will *never* (that's pretty transcendental talk) attain a metavocabulary within which we can place everything anybody will ever say, which will enable us to envisage what people are going to say before they say it (which is very *un*transcendental).

Let me illustrate this point with an example. In his early writings on Husserl, Derrida tried to defend the linguistic string "Green is or" against Husserl, who rejected it on the grounds that it was not only material nonsense but formal nonsense as well. On Husserl's theory, the sentence "The English language is dead" is false but meaningful. "The English language is green" is "countersensical" (*Widersinn*) but in good form, for its logical form is such that it could, with the proper substitutions, be rendered both meaningful and true. But "Green is or" for Husserl is just a plain *Unsinn*, not only semantically but logico-grammatically incoherent; it makes no sense at all, true or false, sensical nor countersensical. Derrida responded to Husserl's analysis by showing that you could *always* recontextualize "Green is or" and make it both meaningful and true—e.g., by making it the response to a request for a string of English words, or by color-coding disjunctives, or by changing its inflection, or by a homophonic play, or by a literally indefinite number of other available means.[28]

"You can always recontextualize"—that is the transcendental move: it breaks the naivete of common sense and the natural attitude by calling upon the resources of a language-game theory, or a theory of *différance*. But the notion that what you can always do is *recontextualize* a word or a sentence is the *anti*transcendental move, the one which shows the slipperiness of language, the unavailability of a final vocabulary, the sheer contingency and literally endless reconfigurability of the vocabularies we use and of the beliefs we entertain. That's the move with the historicist and nominalist drift, the one which preserves an ironic, quasi-transcendental distance.

So I would say, do not gently into that dark night which Rorty describes, the one in which something like transcendental philosophy will have passed from the scene. If you do, do not expect to find either Rorty or Derrida there. They will be both back at the university—although it is not clear what department they are in—writing more books which the catalogue librarians, driven to the edge of despair, will finally, *faut de mieux*, classify (*classicus, glas*) as philosophy.

Would it not be wonderful to write a book that no one could *classify*, for which no librarian, philosopher, encyclopedist, hermeneut, speech-act theorist, communications rationalist, curriculum specialist, realist, or idealist could find the *glas*? Would that not be a magnificent idea? Would it be a transcendental ideal?

Well, almost.

9

The World
Turned
Upside Down

John R. Searle

I

"Deconstruction" is the name of a currently influential movement in American literary criticism. The underlying theory was developed not by literary critics but by a French professor of philosophy, Jacques Derrida, and many of his ideas are in turn owing to Nietzsche and Heidegger. In *On Deconstruction,* Jonathan Culler writes as a disciple of Derrida, and his primary aim is to expound his master's philosophy and show how it "bears on the most important issues of literary theory."[1]

What exactly is deconstruction, and why has it become so influential in American literary criticism while largely ignored by American philosophers? I think if you asked most practicing deconstructionists for a definition they would not only be unable to provide one, but would regard the very request as a manifestation of that "logocentrism" which it is one of the aims of deconstruction to, well, deconstruct. By "logocentrism" they mean roughly the concern with truth, rationality, logic, and "the word" that marks the Western philosophical tradition. I think the best way to get at it, which would be endorsed by many of its practitioners, is to see it, at least initially, as a set of methods for dealing with texts, a set of textual strategies aimed in large part at subverting logocentric tendencies. One of the several merits of Culler's book is that he provides a catalog of these strategies and a characterization of their common aims: "To deconstruct a discourse is to show how it undermines the philosophy it asserts, or the hierarchical oppositions on which it relies, by identifying in the text the rhetorical operations that produce the supposed ground of argument, the key concept or premise" (86).

There are numerous such strategies but at least three stand out. First, and most important, the deconstructionist is on the lookout for any of the traditional binary oppositions in Western intellectual history, e.g., speech/writing, male/female, truth/fiction, literal/metaphorical, signified/signifier, reality/appearance. In such oppositions, the deconstructionist claims that the first or left-hand term is given a superior status over the right-hand term, which is regarded "as a complication, a negation, a manifestation, or a disruption of the first" (93). These hierarchical oppositions allegedly lie at the very heart of logocentrism with its obsessive interest in rationality, logic, and the search for truth.

The deconstructionist wants to undermine these oppositions, and so undermine logocentrism, by first reversing hierarchy, by trying to show that the right-hand term is really the prior term and that the left-hand term is just a special case of the right-hand term; the right-hand term is the condition of possibility of the left-hand term. This move gives some very curious results. It turns out that speech is really a form of writing, understanding a form of misunderstanding, and that what we think of as meaningful language is just a free play of signifiers or an endless process of grafting texts onto texts.

But this move is only a part of a two-step procedure ("*un double geste, une double science, une double écriture*"—Derrida, *Marges,* 392), and the aim of the second step is "a general *displacement* of the system" (86); the aim is to resituate, undo, or displace the entire system of values expressed by the classical opposition. This also gives curious results since it now turns out that speech and writing are both forms of "archi-writing," "man and woman are both variants of archi-woman" (171), etc. "Archi-writing" reforms the "vulgar concept of writing" into a new concept which now includes both speech and writing. Whether or not there is a "vulgar concept of woman" needing similar reform is not explicitly stated, but one may reasonably assume that Culler thinks that such is the case.

A second strategy is to look for certain key words in the text that, so to speak, give the game away. Certain key words "figure in oppositions that are essential to a text's argument, but they also function in ways that subvert those oppositions" (213). The examples Culler gives are "parergon" in Kant, "pharmakon" in Plato, "supplement" in Rousseau, and "hymen" in Mallarmé: "These terms are the points at which the strains of an attempt to sustain or impose logocentric conclusions make themselves felt in a text, moments of uncanny opacity that can lead to rewarding commentary" (213). One example of such rewarding commentary is Derrida's discovery that Rousseau uses "supplement" in discussing both his sexual experience and his theory of writing: he says both that writing is a supplement (to speech) and that masturbation is a supplement (to sex). Derrida concludes, "within the chain of supplements, it was difficult to separate writing from onanism" (*Of Grammatology,* 165).

A third strategy is to pay close attention to marginal features of the text such as the sort of metaphors that occur in it, because such marginal features "are clues to what is truly important" (146).

II

Deconstruction, as Culler describes it, may not sound very promising, but the test of a method of textual analysis lies in its results, so let us now turn to some of the examples where Culler and Derrida show us how deconstruction is supposed to work. Culler's paradigm example, the one he presents to show how the various characterizations and operations of deconstruction "might converge in practice" (86), is what he describes as Nietzsche's deconstruction of causality.

> Suppose one feels a pain. This causes one to look for a cause
> and spying, perhaps, a pin, one posits a link and reverses the
> perceptual or phenomenal order, *pain . . . pin,* to produce a
> causal sequence, *pin . . . pain.* "The fragment of the outside
> world of which we become conscious comes after the effect
> that has been produced on us and is projected *a posteriori* as its
> 'cause.' " (86)

So far this does not sound very deconstructive of anything. Culler thinks otherwise, and to get an idea of the deconstructionist style of argument it is worth quoting his commentary at some length:

> Let us be as explicit as possible about what this simple example
> implies. . . . The experience of pain, it is claimed, *causes* us to
> discover the pin [his italics] and *thus causes the production of a*

cause [my italics]. To deconstruct causality one must operate
with the notion of cause and apply it to causation itself. (87)

Thus one is "asserting the indispensability of causation while denying it
any rigorous justification" (88). Furthermore,

> the deconstruction reverses the hierarchical opposition of the
> causal scheme. The distinction between cause and effect makes
> the cause an origin, logically and temporally prior. The effect is
> derived, secondary, dependent upon the cause. Without ex-
> ploring the reasons for or the implications of this hierarchiza-
> tion, let us note that, working within the opposition, the
> deconstruction upsets the hierarchy by producing an exchange
> of properties. *If the effect is what causes the cause to become a cause,*
> *then the effect, not the cause, should be treated as the origin.* By
> showing that the argument which elevates cause can be used to
> favor effect, one uncovers and undoes the rhetorical operation
> responsible for the hierarchization and one produces a signifi-
> cant displacement. (88; my italics).

I believe that far from demonstrating the power of deconstruction, Culler's discussion of this example is a tissue of confusions. Here
are several of the most glaring mistakes.

1. There is nothing whatever in the example to support the view
that the effect "causes the production of a cause" or that the effect
"causes the cause to become a cause." The experience of pain causes us
to look for its cause and thus indirectly causes the discovery of the cause.
The idea that it *produces* the cause is exactly counter to what the example
actually shows.

2. The word "origin" is being used in two quite distinct senses. If
"origin" means causal origin then the pin is the causal origin of the pain.
If "origin" means epistemic origin, how we go about finding out, then
the experience of pain is the origin of our discovery of its cause. But it is
a simple confusion to conclude from this that there is some unitary sense
of "origin" in which "the effect and not the cause should be treated as
the origin."

3. There isn't any logical hierarchy between cause and effect in
the first place since the two are correlative terms: one is defined in terms
of the other. The *Oxford English Dictionary*, for example, defines "cause"
as "that which produces an effect" and it defines "effect" as "something
caused or produced."

4. Contrary to what Culler claims, nothing in the example shows that causation lacks any "rigorous justification," or that any "significant displacement" has come about. Our common-sense prejudices about causation deserve careful scrutiny and criticism, but nothing in Culler's discussion forces any change in our most naive views about causation.

It would no doubt be unfair to condemn deconstruction on the basis of this one example, even if it is Culler's paradigm example of the virtues of the deconstructive method. So let us now turn our attention to Derrida's favorite example of deconstruction, the deconstruction of the opposition between speech and writing to show that writing is really prior, that speech is really a form of writing. Now at first sight it seems that this is rather a side issue in philosophy; even in the philosophy of language, most authors do not devote much attention to the differences and similarities between written and spoken language. Derrida, however, thinks that the matter is of crucial importance. He thinks that the "privileging" of oral speech at the expense of writing, and the "repression" of writing, is nothing less than "the fundamental operation of the epoch," the epoch that begins with Plato and runs right through to the logocentrism of contemporary philosophy. He thinks, in short, that logocentrism is founded on phonocentrism. A fairly typical passage, which I quote at some length to give a sense of Derrida's prose, is the following:

> The privilege of the *phonè* does not depend upon a choice that
> might have been avoided. It corresponds to a moment of the
> system (let us say, of the "life" of "history" or of "being-as-
> self-relationship"). The system of "hearing/understanding-
> oneself-speak," [*s'entendre parler*] through the phonic sub-
> stance—which *presents itself* as a non-exterior, non-worldly and
> therefore non-empirical or non-contingent signifier—*has neces-*
> *sarily dominated the history of the world during an entire epoch* [my
> italics], and has even produced the idea of the world, the idea
> of world-origin, arising from the difference between the
> worldly and the non-worldly, the outside and the inside, ideal-
> ity and non-ideality, universal and non-universal, transcenden-
> tal and empirical, etc. (*Of Grammatology*, quoted by Culler, 107)

On the face of it, this claim is bizarre. This distinction between speech and writing is simply not very important to Plato, Aristotle, Aquinas, Descartes, Kant, Spinoza, Leibniz, Hume, etc. And of these listed, the only one about whom Derrida offers any evidence of the privileging of the spoken is Plato, who, in *Phaedrus,* made a few remarks about the impossibility of subjecting written texts to interrogation. Plato points out, correctly, that you can ask questions of a speaking person in a way that you cannot of a written text.[2] Notice that all these philosophers address themselves to issues such as universal and particular, transcendental and empirical, etc. For these philosophers these issues neither arise from the distinction between the oral and the written nor depend on the "privileged" status of the oral. Husserl, one of Derrida's targets, is unusual, though not unique, in thinking that meaning is present in spoken language in a way that is vastly superior to written texts.

On Derrida's account, however, it is essential not only to Husserl, but to philosophy, and indeed to "the history of the world during an entire epoch," including the present, that speech should be mistakenly privileged over writing. If Derrida's claim were to be taken at its face value, I believe that a contrary argument could be given equal or even greater plausibility. From the medieval development of Aristotle's logic through Leibniz's *Characteristica Universalis* through Frege and Russell and up to the present development of symbolic logic, it could be argued that exactly the reverse is the case; that by emphasizing logic and rationality, philosophers have tended to emphasize written language as the more perspicuous vehicle of logical relations. Indeed, as far as the present era in philosophy is concerned, it wasn't until the 1950s that serious claims were made on behalf of the ordinary spoken vernacular languages, against the written ideal symbolic languages of mathematical logic. When Derrida makes sweeping claims about "the history of the world during an entire epoch," the effect is not so much apocalyptic as simply misinformed.

However, the breathtaking implausibility of Derrida's claim suggests that something much deeper is going on, and that we must now investigate. Derrida's strategy in his effort to show that writing is really primary, that speech is really a form of writing, is to identify the features which "the classical concept of writing" attributes to writing and then show that these are features of speech as well. Thus for Derrida both written words and spoken words are repeatable or, as he prefers to say, "iterable"; both are institutional, both can be misunderstood, and perhaps most importantly, both rely on a system of differences.

This last feature is crucial to the argument. Derrida's ideas are developed from the work of the Swiss linguist Ferdinand de Saussure, who wrote, "Phonemes are characterized not, as one might think, by their own positive quality but simply by the fact that they are distinct. Phonemes are above all else opposing relative and negative entities."[3]

Saussure summarizes this point by saying, "in language there are only differences."[4] Thus, for example, the function of "*b*" in the English word "bat" depends not on its acoustic properties alone, but rather on the way in which they form part of a class which is different from the classes of acoustic properties of other elements; this difference enables us to distinguish "bat" from "pat," "bed" from "red," etc. Language consists of a system of elements whose essential functioning depends on the differences between the elements of the system.

This is an important point. But notice how Derrida transforms it:

> The play of differences supposes, in effect, syntheses and refer-
> rals which forbid at any moment, or in any sense, that a simple
> element be *present* in and of itself, referring only to itself.
> Whether in the order of spoken or written discourse, no ele-
> ment can function as a sign without referring to another ele-
> ment which itself is not simply present. *This interweaving results
> in each "element"—phoneme or grapheme—being constituted on the
> basis of the trace within it of the other elements of the chain or system*
> [my italics]. This interweaving, this textile, is the *text* produced
> only in the transformation of another text. Nothing, neither
> among the elements nor within the system, is anywhere ever
> simply present or absent. There are only, everywhere, differ-
> ences and traces of traces. (*Positions*, 26)

But this involves an important shift from Saussure's insight. The correct claim that the elements of the language only function as elements because of the differences they have from one another is converted into the false claim that the elements "consist of" (Culler) or are "constituted on" (Derrida) the *traces* of these other elements. "There are only, everywhere, differences and traces of traces." But the second thesis is not equivalent to the first, nor does it follow from it. From the fact that the elements function the way they do because of their relations to other elements, it simply does not follow that "nothing, neither among the elements nor within the system, is anywhere ever simply present or ab-sent. There are only, everywhere, differences and traces of traces."

Indeed, as with Culler's "deconstruction" of causation, the argument shows exactly the reverse of what Derrida claims. Consider an example. I understand the sentence "the cat is on the mat" the way I do because I know how it would relate to an indefinite—indeed infinite—set of other sentences, "the dog is on the mat," "the cat is on the couch," etc. But I understand the differences between the two sentences "the cat is on the mat" and "the dog is on the mat" in precisely the way I do because the word "cat" is present in the first while absent from the second, and the word "dog" is present in the second, while absent from the first. The system of differences does nothing whatever to undermine the distinction between presence and absence; on the contrary the system of differences is precisely a system of presences and absences.

This obliteration of elements in favor of traces is one of the key moves, or perhaps the key move in Derrida's philosophy of language and, arguably, in the whole metaphysics of deconstruction. For the next step is to claim that language is just a set of "institutional traces." And once this move is made, Derrida can conveniently redefine writing in such a way that all language, whether spoken or written, is writing: the instituted trace is "the possibility common to all systems of signification" (*Of Grammatology*, 46). The proof that speech is really writing then becomes trivially easy since writing has become redefined to encompass them both. This emerges in the following passage, which again I quote at some length as an illustration of the style as well as the "substance":

> Phonologism does not brook any objections as long as one conserves the colloquial concepts of speech and writing which form the solid fabric of its argumentation. Colloquial and quotidian conceptions, inhabited besides—uncontradictorily enough—by an old history, limited by frontiers that are hardly visible yet all the more rigorous by that very fact.
> I would wish rather to suggest that the alleged derivativeness of writing, however real and massive, was possible only on one condition: that the "original," "natural," etc., language had never existed, never been intact and untouched by writing, *that it had itself always been a writing* [my italics]. An archewriting whose necessity and new concept I wish to indicate and outline here; and which I continue to call writing only because it essentially communicates with the vulgar concept of writing. The latter could not have imposed itself historically except with the dissimulation of the arche-writing, by the desire for a speech displacing its other and its double and working to reduce its difference. If I persist in calling that difference writing, it is because, within the work of historical repression, writing was, by its situation, destined to signify the most formidable difference. It threatened the desire for the living speech from the closest proximity, it *breached* living speech from within and from the very beginning. And as we shall begin to see, difference cannot be thought without the *trace*. (*Of Grammatology*, 56–57)

JOHN R. SEARLE

Furthermore, once the apparatus of talking about traces and differences has been treated as definitive of writing, of textuality, this apparatus is applied pretty much all over—to experience, to the distinction
between presence and absence, to the distinction between reality and
representation. Once writing is defined in terms of difference and traces
and these have been found to be pervasive, it is not a very startling discovery that everything is really writing: "there never has been anything
but writing; there never been anything but supplements, substitu-
tive significations which could only come forth in a chain of differential
references, the 'real' supervening, and being added only while taking on
meaning from a trace and from an invocation of the supplement, etc."
(*Of Grammatology*, 159). And again: "*il n'y a pas de hors texte*" (158).

With this in mind, we can now give a general assessment of the
deconstruction of the distinction between speech and writing.

1. Derrida's eccentric reading of the history of Western philosophy, a reading according to which philosophers are supposed to be
roundly condemning writing, while privileging spoken language, is not
grounded on an actual reading of the texts of the leading figures in the
philosophical tradition. Derrida only discusses three major figures in any
detail: Plato, Rousseau, and Husserl. Rather it seems motivated by his
conviction that everything in logocentrism hinges on this issue. If he can
treat the features of a suitably redefined notion of writing as definitive of
the issues that philosophy has been concerned with—as definitive of
truth, reality, etc.—then he thinks he can deconstruct these notions.

2. The proof that speech is really writing, and that writing is prior
to speech, is based on a redefinition. By such methods one can prove
anything. One can prove that the rich are really poor, the true is really
false, etc. The only interest that such an effort might have is in the reasons given for the redefinition.

3. Derrida's redefinition of writing to "reform" the "vulgar concept" is not based on any actual empirical study of the similarities and
differences of the two forms. Nothing of the sort. He makes nothing of
the fact that speech is spoken and writing is written, for example, or of
the fact that, in consequence, written texts tend to persist throughout
time in a way that is not characteristic of spoken utterances. Rather, the
redefinition is based on a misrepresentation of the way the system of
differences functions, and the misrepresentation is not innocent. It is
designed to enable the apparatus of writing, so characterized, to be applied quite generally—to experience, to reality, etc.

Michel Foucault once characterized Derrida's prose style to me as
"*obscurantisme terroriste.*" The text is written so obscurely that you can't

figure out exactly what the thesis is (hence *"obscurantisme"*) and then
when one criticizes it, the author says, *"Vous m'avez mal compris; vous êtes
idiot"* (hence *"terroriste"*).

III

What are the results of deconstruction supposed to be? Characteristically the deconstructionist does not attempt to *prove* or *refute*, to *establish*
or *confirm*, and he is certainly not *seeking the truth.*[5] On the contrary, this
whole family of concepts is part of the logocentrism he wants to overcome; rather he seeks to *undermine*, or *call in question*, or *overcome*, or
breach, or *disclose complicities.* And the target is not just a set of philosophical and literary texts, but the Western conception of rationality and the
set of presuppositions that underlie our conceptions of language, science, and common sense, such as the distinction between reality and
appearance, and between truth and fiction. According to Culler, "The
effect of deconstructive analyses, as numerous readers can attest, is
knowledge and feelings of mastery" (255).

The trouble with this claim is that it requires us to have some
way of distinguishing genuine knowledge from its counterfeits, and
justified feelings of mastery from mere enthusiasms generated by a lot
of pretentious verbosity. And the examples that Culler and Derrida
provide are, to say the least, not very convincing. In Culler's book, we
get the following examples of knowledge and mastery: speech is a form
of writing (passim), presence is a certain type of absence (106), the
marginal is in fact central (140), the literal is metaphorical (148), truth
is a kind of fiction (181), reading is a form of misreading (176), sanity is
a kind of neurosis (160), and man is a form of woman (171). Some
readers may feel that such a list generates not so much feelings of mastery as of monotony. There is in deconstructive writing a constant
straining of the prose to attain something that sounds profound by
giving it the air of a paradox, e.g., "truths are fictions whose fictionality has been forgotten" (181).

And there is much much more. Anatomists will no doubt be interested to learn that "what we think of as the innermost spaces and places
of the body—vagina, stomach, intestine—are in fact pockets of externality folded in" (198). And logicians will no doubt be interested to learn
that logocentrism is really the same as phallocentrism. According to Derrida, the term "phallogocentrism" asserts this complicity: "It is one and

the same system: the erection of a paternal logos . . . and of the phallus as 'privileged signifier' " (Derrida; quoted by Culler, 172).

IV

I have so far been writing as if we could take Culler's account as an adequate reflection of Derrida's views, but in fact I think Culler makes Derrida look both better and worse than he really is, better in that a lot of the more dreadful aspects of Derrida's philosophy are left out or simply glossed over. Culler, for example, says little about Derrida's deconstruction of the idea that texts represent, at least sometimes, the real world, that is, about Derrida's claim that there is nothing outside the text (*il n'y a pas de hors texte*), an idea that, as I have noted, is connected to his idea that speech is really writing.

But Derrida also emerges as much more superficial than he is. He emerges as the instigator of various gimmicks for dealing with texts, and Culler doesn't seem to understand the really deep problems that led Derrida into this. Culler seems unaware that Derrida is responding to certain specific theses in Husserl and is using weapons derived in large part from Heidegger to do it (Culler's bibliography contains no references to Husserl and only one to Heidegger). I believe that Derrida's work, at least those portions I have read, is not just a series of muddles and gimmicks. There is in fact a large issue being addressed and a large mistake being made. The philosophical tradition that goes from Descartes to Husserl, and indeed a large part of the philosophical tradition that goes back to Plato, involves a search for foundations: metaphysically certain foundations of knowledge, foundations of language and meaning, foundations of mathematics, foundations of morality, etc. Husserl, for example, sought such foundations by examining the content of his conscious experiences while suspending or "bracketing" the assumption that they referred to an external world. By doing so he hoped to isolate and describe pure and indubitable structures of experience.

Now, in the twentieth century, mostly under the influence of Wittgenstein and Heidegger, we have come to believe that this general search for these sorts of foundations is misguided. There aren't in the way classical metaphysicians supposed any foundations for ethics or knowledge. For example, we can't in the traditional sense found language and knowledge on "sense data" because our sense data are already infused with our linguistic and social practices. Derrida correctly sees that there aren't any such foundations, but he then makes the mistake that marks him as a classical metaphysician. The real mistake of the classical metaphysician was not the belief that there were metaphysical foundations, but rather the belief that somehow or other such foundations were necessary, the belief that unless there are foundations something is lost or threatened or undermined or put in question.

It is this belief which Derrida shares with the tradition he seeks to deconstruct. Derrida sees that the Husserlian project of a transcendental grounding for science, language, and common sense is a failure. But what he fails to see is that this doesn't threaten science, language, or common sense in the least. As Wittgenstein says, it leaves everything exactly as it is. The only "foundation," for example, that language has or needs is that people are biologically, psychologically, and socially constituted so that they succeed in using it to state truths, to give and obey orders, to express their feelings and attitudes, to thank, apologize, warn, congratulate, etc.

One sometimes gets the impression that deconstruction is a kind of game that anyone can play. One could, for example, invent a deconstruction of deconstructionism as follows: In the hierarchical opposition, deconstruction/logocentrism (phono-phallo-logocentrism), the privileged term "deconstruction" is in fact subordinate to the devalued term "logocentrism," for, in order to establish the hierarchical superiority of deconstruction, the deconstructionist is forced to attempt to represent its superiority, its axiological primacy, by argument and persuasion, by appealing to the logocentric values he tries to devalue. But his efforts to do this are doomed to failure because of the internal inconsistency in the concept of deconstructionism itself, because of its very self-referential dependence on the authority of a prior logic. By an aporetical *Aufhebung*, deconstruction deconstructs itself.

V

One last question: Granted that deconstruction has rather obvious and manifest intellectual weaknesses, granted that it should be fairly obvious to the careful reader that the emperor has no clothes, why has it proved so influential among literary theorists? Let us make the question sharper: we live in something of a golden age in the philosophy of language.[6] It is not only the age of the great dead giants, Frege, Russell, and Wittgenstein, but also the age of Chomsky and Quine, of Austin, Tarski,

Grice, Dummett, Davidson, Putnam, Kripke, Strawson, Montague, and a dozen other first-rate writers. It is the age of generative grammar and speech-act theory, of truth-conditional semantics and possible-world semantics.

No doubt all of these theories are, in their various ways, mistaken, defective, and provisional, but for clarity, rigor, precision, theoretical comprehensiveness, and above all, intellectual content, they are written at a level that is vastly superior to that at which deconstructive philosophy is written. How then are we to account for the popularity and influence of deconstructionism among literary theorists? Why indeed do its very intellectual weaknesses seem to be a source of popularity? To understand the phenomenon fully, one would have to know much more than I do about the culture of English departments and other modern language departments in American universities. But I have observed that there are certain features of the deconstructionist ideology that fit in very well with the presuppositions behind much current literary theorizing.

When I have lectured to audiences of literary critics, I have found two pervasive philosophical presuppositions in the discussions of literary theory, both oddly enough derived from logical positivism. First there is the assumption that unless a distinction can be made rigorous and precise it isn't really a distinction at all. Many literary theorists fail to see, for example, that it is not an objection to a theory of fiction that it does not sharply divide the metaphorical from the nonmetaphorical. On the contrary, it is the condition of the adequacy of a precise theory of an indeterminate phenomenon that it should precisely characterize that phenomenon as indeterminate; and a distinction is no less a distinction for allowing for a family of related, marginal, diverging cases.

People who try to hold the assumption that genuine distinctions must be made rigid are ripe for Derrida's attempt to undermine all such distinctions. Culler, by the way, shares this assumption. For example, he claims that the fact that an expression can be both *used* and *mentioned* in the same sentence somehow weakens the distinction that philosophers and logicians make between the *use* and *mention* of expressions (119–20). In the same vein, he supposes that the fact that a single utterance might express a conscious speech act of one type and an unconscious one of another type is a serious problem for the theory of speech acts (124). He also mistakenly supposes that the theory of speech acts seeks some sort of precise dividing line between what is and what is not a promise (135). But in fact it is a consequence of the theory that in real life there can be all sorts of marginal cases within each family of speech acts.

Second, and equally positivistic, is the insistence that concepts that apply to language and literature, if they are to be truly valid, must admit of some mechanical procedure of verification. Thus, for example, if one attempts to characterize the role of intention in language, many literary critics immediately demand some mechanical criterion for ascertaining the presence and content of intentions. But, of course, there are no such criteria. How do we tell what a person's intentions are? The answer is, in all sorts of ways, and we may even get it wrong in the apparently most favorable cases. But such facts as these—that there is no mechanical decision procedure for identifying an author's intentions, or for determining whether or not a work is a work of fiction or whether an expression is used metaphorically—in no way undermines the concepts of intention, fiction, or metaphor. Our use of these concepts and our distinctions between the intentional and the unintentional, the literal and the metaphorical, and between fictional and nonfictional discourse is grounded in a complex network of linguistic and social practices. In general these practices neither require nor admit of rigorous internal boundary lines and simple mechanical methods of ascertaining the presence or absence of a phenomenon. Again the crude positivism of these assumptions I am criticizing is of a piece with Derrida's assumption that without foundations we are left with nothing but the free play of signifiers.

And there are even cruder appeals of the deconstructivist philosophy. It is apparently very congenial for some people who are professionally concerned with fictional texts to be told that all texts are really fictional anyway, and that claims that fiction differs significantly from science and philosophy can be deconstructed as a logocentric prejudice, and it seems positively exhilarating to be told that what we call "reality" is just more textuality. Furthermore, the lives of such people are made much easier than they had previously supposed, because now they don't have to worry about an author's intentions, about precisely what a text means, or about distinctions within a text between the metaphorical and the literal, or about the distinction between texts and the world because everything is just a free play of signifiers. The upper limit, and I believe the reductio ad absurdum, of this "sense of mastery" conveyed by deconstruction, is in Geoffrey Hartman's claim that the prime creative task has now passed from the literary artist to the critic.

10

Reply to Mackey

John R. Searle

In my review reprinted as the preceding essay in this collection, I made
several objections to Culler's book *On Deconstruction,* and to at least
certain aspects of Derrida's philosophy, from which Culler's views are
derived. If I am right, these objections are devastating. In his defense
of deconstruction Professor Mackey does not, for the most part, attempt
to answer my objections; rather, he changes the subject; he distracts attention from the manifest weaknesses of deconstruction by presenting a
series of claims to the effect that I have misrepresented and misunderstood Culler and Derrida.[1] I fully anticipated that this objection would
be made, and so I gave copious verbatim quotes from both authors; and
where I summarized their views, I gave extensive page references. Mackey points out correctly that the summaries are not verbatim quotes, but
he claims incorrectly that both they and my choice of quotations are mis-
representations. His strongest example is this: I quote Culler as holding
the view that "Truths are fictions whose fictionality has been forgotten."
Mackey claims that Culler is not asserting this view, since the clause occurs following an "if." But consider the whole context:

> Deconstruction's *demonstration* [my italics] that these hierar-
> chies are undone by the workings of the texts that propose
> them alters the standing of literary language. If serious lan-
> guage is a special case of the nonserious, if truths are fictions
> whose fictionality has been forgotten, then literature is not a
> deviant, parasitical instance of language. On the contrary,

other discourses can be seen as cases of a generalized literature, or archi-literature. (181)

This passage is part of Culler's attempt to develop the "consequences for
literary theory and criticism of the deconstructive practice *we have been
expounding*" (180; my italics). I believe it is quite obvious from the context that Culler is asserting (among other things) that the deconstructive
practice he has been expounding has "demonstrated" that "truths are
fictions whose fictionality has been forgotten."

Sometimes Mackey's arguments seem to border on sophistry. For
example, I summarize Culler as holding the view that all readings are
misreadings. Mackey counters, "Culler speaks of *the claim that all readings are misreadings.*" But here is the actual sentence in Culler's book:
"The claim that all readings are misreadings *can also be justified* by the
most familiar aspects of critical and interpretive practice" (176; my italics). And in the very same paragraph, Culler goes on: "every reading can
be shown to be partial. . . . The history of readings is a history of misreadings." Indeed this thesis occurs in several places in Culler's book,
e.g. "The best a reader can achieve is a strong misreading" (79–80).

Mackey says that my attributing to Culler the view that understanding is a special case of misunderstanding is similarly a misinterpre-
tation. Once again let us look at the actual sentence in Culler: "We can
thus say, in a formulation more valid than its converse, that understanding is a special case of misunderstanding, a particular deviation or determination of misunderstanding" (176). I claim that Culler holds the view
that the literal is metaphorical. Mackey cites the actual sentence: "The
literal is the opposite of the figurative, but *the literal expression is also a
metaphor whose figurality has been forgotten*" (my italics). Mackey thinks that
"the appearance of absurdity" in Culler's views is an "invention" resulting from my summaries. In fact the verbatim quotations are no less and
no more absurd than the summaries I gave. If Mackey thinks it makes a
difference, then he can simply substitute the verbatim sentences for the
summaries. For example, where I had "sanity is a kind of neurosis" put
in "it has even become something of a commonplace that 'sanity' is only
a particular determination of neurosis" (160). The first was my summary; the second was Culler's actual wording. Mackey finds the first absurd. What does he think of the second?

I believe that a careful reading of Culler's book will show that he
is committed, implicitly or explicitly, to every view I attribute to him. But
suppose we try to accept for the sake of argument Mackey's implication

that Culler himself doesn't really believe the unplausible views I attributed to him. He doesn't really think that "speech is a form of writing; presence is a certain type of absence, the marginal is in fact central, the literal is metaphorical, truth is a kind of fiction, reading is a form of misreading, understanding is a form of misunderstanding, and man is a form of a woman" (77). Then, the book would lose much, if not all, of its point, since the whole point of the book, as Culler states repeatedly, is to expound deconstructive strategies and show their value for literacy criticism. Now the first and most important strategy, according to Culler, is the deconstruction of the traditional hierarchical oppositions between truth and fiction, between the serious and the nonserious, between understanding and misunderstanding, sanity and neurosis, man and woman, . . . etc. And in every case the first step in the deconstruction is to show that the left-hand term is really a specialized case of the right-hand term. I summarize the results of these efforts. Mackey would have us believe that Culler is not even making the efforts.

Actually, the effect of Mackey's complaint is to remind us of a point that I should have made more strongly in my review. Deconstructive prose tends to be systematically evasive. Several of the examples that Mackey gives are typical of this evasiveness. Crucial words are put in quotation marks so as to suggest an ambivalence in the author's stance toward them. Thus, e.g., " 'sanity' is only a particular determination of neuroses." Or central theses are imbedded in subordinate clauses and not stated directly, as in "if truths are fictions whose fictionality has been forgotten. . . . "[2] In this way the deconstructionist can make unplausible assertions while appearing not to; and this is part of what Culler calls the deconstructionist's "nimbleness," his moving "in and out of philosophic seriousness" (155).

Mackey's letter also serves to remind us of some other gimmicks used by deconstructionist writers. In addition to systematic evasiveness, they also commonly use the "heads-I-win-tails-you-lose" form of argument. For example, I claim that the speech/writing distinction is not very important in the history of Western philosophy, and I submit as evidence the fact that Plato, Aristotle, Aquinas, Descartes, Kant, Spinoza, Leibniz, Hume, etc. have very little to say about it. I also point out that "philosophers have tended to emphasize written language as the more perspicuous vehicle of logical relations." Now, the first of these points is taken by Mackey as evidence that these philosophers have repressed writing; and the second as evidence for the philosophers' "continued dependence (nevertheless) on the writing whose difference (or differance) they had tried to repress." Notice the form of Mackey's argument here. The lack of evidence for Derrida's thesis is itself taken as a form of evidence, since it proves that the authors in question are trying to repress the phenomenon Derrida has uncovered, their urge to repress writing. And the fact that they are manifestly not repressing writing, the fact that written language is, e.g., the basis of modern mathematical logic, is taken as showing only that their valiant efforts at repression have failed. By such methods of reasoning one can "prove" absolutely anything. And as Mackey states, Derrida uses these sorts of methods over and over.

In addition to the devices of systematic evasiveness, and the heads-I-win-tails-you-lose form of argument, there is a third strategy exemplified in Mackey's letter, and that is the straw-man argument. In my review I pointed out that the Saussurean claim that language is a system of differences does nothing whatever to undermine the distinction between presence and absence, because the system of differences is precisely a system of presences and absences. "I understand the difference between the two sentences 'the cat is on the mat' and 'the dog is on the mat' in precisely the way I do because the word 'cat' is present in the first while absent from the second, and the word 'dog' is present in the second while absent from the first." Mackey counters that what Derrida is really talking about is "their presence in and of themselves—their exclusive self-reference." This is an example of the obscurantism that pervades deconstructive prose. What is it for words to be present "in and of themselves" except for them to be present? The explanation Mackey gives in terms of "exclusive self-reference" is worse than no help at all. In the two sentences given as examples, the expression "the cat" is used to refer to a cat, and the expression "the dog" is used to refer to a dog. The topic of self-reference is one that logicians and philosophers have been discussing now for over three-quarters of a century; and no one to my knowledge has ever supposed that examples of this sort were self-referential. Derrida's apparently startling claim that words are never "simply present," when stripped of its obscurity, is now converted into the triviality that they are not normally "self-referential"; a thesis no one ever denied.

The single most unplausible claim that Mackey makes is that "the deconstructionist is almost obsessively occupied with truth." If he means to imply that they seek the truth, then a purely textual analysis of the works that I have cited would show that that is simply not the case. Authors who are concerned with discovering the truth are concerned with evidence and reasons, with consistency and inconsistency, with logical consequences, explanatory adequacy, verification and testability. But all of this is part of the apparatus of the very "logo-centricism" that deconstruction seeks to undermine.

Mackey thinks that it is "a familiar fact" that "what we think of as the innermost spaces and places of body—vagina, stomach, intestine, are all in fact pockets of externality folded in." But this is not a "familiar fact" at all. The claim is just anatomically unintelligent. And such bad anatomy offers no support one way or the other for theories about literary formalism. He also claims that it is "unthinkable" that Culler and Derrida should be "bereft of (the) commonplace" that the Greeks of antiquity only read aloud. Unthinkable or not, they certainly give no indication of knowing that the relation of reading to speaking in antiquity was quite different from that of the modern era. And in any case it is hardly a "commonplace," indeed, the precise extent to which it is true is in dispute in the two works I cited (75).

At bottom, Mackey's real objection to my discussion of deconstruction is that I am not sympathetic to it. But there are reasons for my lack of sympathy. I believe that any one who reads deconstructive texts with an open mind is likely to be struck by the same phenomena that initially surprised me: the low level of philosophical argumentation, the deliberate obscurantism of the prose, the wildly exaggerated claims, and the constant striving to give the appearance of profundity by making claims that seem paradoxical, but under analysis often turn out to be silly or trivial. In my review, I gave examples of all these phenomena. There is an atmosphere of bluff and fakery that pervades much (not all, of course) deconstructive writing. What becomes even more surprising is that the authors seem to think it is all right to engage in these practices, because they hold a theory to the effect that pretensions to objective truth and rationality in science, philosophy, and common sense can be deconstructed as logocentric subterfuges. To put it crudely, they think that since everything is phony anyway, the phoniness of deconstruction is somehow acceptable, indeed commendable, since it lies right on the surface ready for further deconstruction. Thus, the general weaknesses of the deconstructive enterprise become self-justifying. With such an approach I am indeed not sympathetic.

11

The Metaphysics
of Presence:
Critique of a Critique

M. C. Dillon

errida announces the closure of the epoch of metaphysics and
develops Heidegger's project of *Destruktion* into his own method-
ology of deconstruction with the strategy of revealing to this epoch its own end. Heidegger and Derrida have in common three
beliefs which I share. The first is that the ontology which informed twentieth-century continental philosophy is an ontology centered on the
transcendental subject. The second is that this ontology began to formulate itself at the time of the ancient Greeks. And the third is that the
failure of this ontology is becoming apparent. But, whereas Heidegger
sought "to destroy the traditional content of ancient ontology" in order
to retrieve "those primordial experiences in which we achieved our first
ways of determining the nature of Being,"[1] Derrida challenges the core
notion of phenomenology, the notion that there is a retrievable domain
of primordial experience upon which an authentic understanding of Being could be founded.

Derrida's challenge derives from the deconstructive revelation
that phenomenology presupposes the very metaphysics of presence that
founded the ontology of the transcendental subject. The ground of phenomenology is the phenomenon, and the phenomenon is conceived as
presence to a subject. De-center the transcendental subject, or replace it

with historical Dasein, and presence remains. Or, as Gasché has argued,[2] reflexivity remains: presence to itself is but another name for transcendental subjectivity. In either case—whether one fastens upon the phenomenon presenting itself, or upon the presence to itself necessary for this phenomenal presentation—the grounding term is presence. And since the vocabulary of *Anwesenheit,* of presence and presencing, is still operative in Heidegger's latest writings, Derrida's deconstruction of presence purports to show that, despite his glimpses beyond, Heidegger's thinking remains within the closure of the metaphysics of presence.

Among the many themes in Derrida's deconstruction of the notion of presence, two are foundational inasmuch as they function to ground the validity of higher stories in his narrative. One is the critique of the temporality of presence, the critique that focuses on the aporetic nature of the now. The other, which involves what Derrida sometimes characterizes as the spatial aspect of presence, turns on that aspect of presence which might be described in Husserlian terms as original intuition or the self-manifestation of the phenomenon.[3] These two themes are correlates, since it is in the now that the phenomenon makes itself evident, but, following Derrida's practice, I will take them up separately before bringing them together.

The Aporetic Nature of the Now

Derrida's critique of the temporality of presence is presented in his essay, "*Ouisa* and *Gramme:* Note on a Note from *Being and Time.*"[4] The crux of his argument is the conundrum about time posed in *Physics IV* where Aristotle ponders (1) whether time belongs to beings or nonbeings, and (2) what the nature of time might be. As I read Derrida's interpretation of this text, the conundrum or aporia takes the form of a dilemma which arises from the difficulty of answering the two questions.

The first question presupposes an understanding of what it is to be, what a being is. In Derrida's reading, being, for Aristotle, has "already, secretly . . . been determined as present, and beingness (*ousia*) as presence" ("OG," 51). But the presence of the present is eternal, that which does not change, permanent presence.[5] This understanding of "beingness or *ousia*" as eternal presence is identified by Derrida as "a fundamentally Greek gesture" taken up by Hegel. I would identify it as the quintessential Eleatic thought: that which truly is does not change because it excludes what is not.[6]

The second question turns on the relation of time to the now (*nun*): is time composed of the now or not? The problem here is that the now is defined in two mutually exclusive ways. (1) "The now is given simultaneously as that which is no longer and as that which is not yet" ("OG," 39). The now is here defined as temporal flux, the evanescent boundary between past and future; it is defined by negation: not past and not future (?) The second definition of the now identifies it with the eternal present: the now names the presence which is always present, hence never changes, hence is eternal.

If time *is* (i.e., is a being), and if the being that time *is* is composed of the now, then the following dilemma surfaces. If the now is temporal (i.e., in flux, changing), it cannot *be*. But if the now *is,* it cannot be temporal. The horns of the dilemma are mutually exclusive, and neither alternative is philosophically acceptable. Time is flux, change, passage, but it *is* not (i.e., is not real); or time is real, but does not change. To grasp both horns of the dilemma is to adopt the Eleatic posture that only the eternal and immutable is real and that the appearance of flux, change, passage is an illusion. But this is to raise contradiction to the level of principle by a fundamental equivocation: time is equivocally the reality of eternal presence and the unreality of the present now which *is not.*

The magnitude of the dilemma makes resolution a matter of philosophical urgency. On this issue rests the foundation of Western thinking: the interdependence of being and time. If the contradiction is left to stand, our metaphysical foundations tremble and our culture falls.

In Derrida's deconstruction of our philosophical history, Aristotle waffles on the issue and fails to resolve the dilemma.[7] And so does every other thinker of consequence, notably Kant, Hegel, and Heidegger. Derrida's close scrutiny of selected texts shows that each of the thinkers mentioned builds his philosophy on the fundamental equivocation of the being of time and the temporality of being.[8]

How is this equivocation or contradiction or aporia to be resolved? The problem centers on the notion of *ousia,* and the solution is set forth in terms of the *gramme*—whence the title of his essay. The problem: presence is conceived by means of the now, but the now is conceived both as the evanescent passage which *is not* and the unchanging presence which eternally *is.* The solution: combine the passing moment with the unchanging now in the *gramme* or line which signifies both (1) the unreal or arbitrary atomic element in the line's infinite divisibility, and (2) the real eternity in the line's circular unchanging continuous unity. The circular clock face, with its perimeter divided into minutes or seconds or microseconds or nanoseconds, etc. (i.e., quantified, made commensurate with number in accordance with an arbitrarily adopted— unnatural, unreal—measure), is the analogue of time, the signifier of time and its being for our era.

The circular line as the ana-logue, which constitutes the significa- tion or meaning of time for our era, also appropriates the two remaining essential moments of the being of time as presence: presence as presence to itself and presence as spatialization.

Although it embodies a conceptual difficulty—the parts of the line are simultaneous but the parts of time are successive—the linear depiction of time constitutes the necessary form of sensibility: accord- ing to Derrida, the tradition from Aristotle to Kant and beyond corre- lates the linear depiction of time with the presence to itself that is the transcendental condition for the possibility of experience. As I under- stand it, the argument seems to be that the coherence of experience presupposes the continuity of temporal synthesis which must be thought as the line which converts successive now moments to copresence or simultaneity.[9]

The Spatialization of Presence

The original aporia is resolved, not by eliminating the conundrum, but by compounding it with another. The being and nonbeing of time, time as the real eternal now or the unreal passing now, come together in the *gramme*, the circular line, but this spatialization of time essentially de- pends upon the coincidence of incompossibles: the succession proper to time and the simultaneity proper to space ("OG," 55).

To explain. In the context of the metaphysics of presence, succes- sion and simultaneity are defined in mutually exclusive terms. The im- possibility of copresence of nows is the succession of nows which essentially defines time. And the necessity of that copresence or simulta- neity essentially defines space. Thus, space and time cannot be thought together. But it is necessary to think them together: space and time must coincide for the metaphysics of presence because, for something to be, it must present itself in space *and* time. What Derrida calls the "pivot of essence," the fulcrum from which metaphysics acquires its leverage, is "the small key that opens and closes the history of metaphysics." That "small key" is "the small word *hama*."

> In Greek *hama* means "together," "all at once," both together, *"at the same time."* This locution is first neither spatial nor temporal. The duplicity of the *simul* to which it refers does not yet reassemble, within itself, either points or nows, places or phrases. It says the complicity, the common origin of time and space, appearing together as the condition for all appearing of Being. ("OG," 56)

Here is the conundrum. The metaphysics of presence must define time (succession) and space (simultaneity) as mutually exclusive (i.e., as a binary opposition), yet must think them together as the condition for presence or appearing of Being.

At this point in his discourse, Derrida's argument becomes more than usually obscure. He claims that the thinking of the impossibility of the coexistence (of space and time, simultaneity and succession) requires the thought of their coexistence.[10] This is the thought expressed in the *hama*. The thought is not as obscure as Derrida's formulation would make it. The key idea is that it is mistaken to start by defining space and time in ways that render them mutually exclusive. If space and time cannot be thought separately, then to think them at all is to think them as coexistent. Hence, the thought that would conceive space and time as incompossible, to the extent that it *thinks space and time,* must think them as coexistent.[11]

The *gramme* of the circular line accomplishes the spatialization of time that cannot consistently be thought in the context of the metaphysics of presence—as it accomplishes the representation of time's essential divisibility and indivisibility, its passage through the unreal now and its permanence in the eternal now. But, as demonstrated, the spatialization of time which is necessary in order to think presence (i.e., to think of things presenting themselves in the present moment) cannot be thought in the metaphysics of presence. Again, phenomenal presencing or the self-manifestation of beings, which Derrida regards as the foundation of Western ontology ("beingness," *ousia*), itself rests upon a spatialization of time which Derrida contends is unthinkable because it embodies a double contradiction: (1) it must conceive time as both unreal and passing and as real and eternal, and (2) it must conceive space (composed of simultaneous now-points) and time (composed of successive now-points) as together (*hama*) despite the fact that their essences are defined as mutually exclusive (succession is the impossibility of simultaneity).

Implications of the Deconstruction of Presence

The epoch of Western metaphysics is defined by the line representing time as an unending circle delimited by now-points.

> The *gramme* is *comprehended* by metaphysics between the point and the circle . . . ; and all the critiques of the spatialization of time, from Aristotle to Bergson, remain within the limits of this comprehension. *Time,* then, would be but the name of the limits within which the *gramme* is thus comprehended. . . . *Nothing other has ever been* thought by the name of *time.* ("OG," 60)

Derrida goes on to imply that this circularity is the circularity of the Hegelian system *and* the circularity of Heideggerian hermeneutics.[12] He asserts that there is a "formal necessity" that dictates this conception of time "from the moment when the sign 'time' . . . begins to function in a discourse" ("OG," 60–61). And he argues that this conception of time drives all the binary oppositions that, in turn, have driven the history of metaphysics: act/potency, real/unreal, authentic/inauthentic, etc.[13]

The indictment is radical and, if upheld, devastating to Western culture. Our language and our thinking are through a "formal necessity" driven by a conception of time whose basic contradiction is recapitulated in the system of binary oppositions—among them good and evil—around which we structure our lives. If the metaphysics of presence trembles and falls under this critique, the magnitude of our need to see beyond Derrida's foreclosure can be measured by the pathetic errance of our history: it may be oppositional thinking that produces war and oppression. Where would Derrida lead us, in what direction does his writing point?

Différance and Ontological Difference

Derrida's original contributions are, as he says, nonoriginary. The antecedents of his key nonconcept, *différance,* are diverse, but two stand out: Saussure and Heidegger. Saussure's diacritical theory of language as a system of "differences without positive terms"[14] is a key source,[15] but it is Heidegger's ontological difference that is most relevant in the present discourse.

As we have seen, Derrida argues that, in *Being and Time,* Heidegger is still operating within the parameters of the metaphysics of presence. The binary opposition of authenticity and fallenness derives from the basic contradiction underlying the enigma of time. Authenticity is associated with Being or the eternity of the circle, and inauthenticity with the now-moment into which we fall in our fascination with the beings which present themselves in the moment. The correlation is only tacitly implied, but, as I interpret the key texts ("OG," 63–67, "D," 22–27), it is evident that, for Derrida, the ontological difference, in naming the difference between Being and beings, straddles the contradiction underlying the vulgar[16] conception of time: the originary difference, the ontological difference, is the difference between Being and beings, that is, the difference between the eternal present and the present now-moment.

Derrida argues that the two senses of time are assimilated to one another in *Being and Time,* but in later texts are distinguished. In "The Anaximander Fragment"[17] Heidegger speaks of an *"ungegenwärtig Anwesende,"* which leads Derrida to infer that he is distinguishing "a more original thought of Being as presence (*Anwesenheit*)" from *"Gegenwärtigkeit* (presence in the temporal sense of nowness)." Derrida suggests that *Gegenwärtigkeit* should be understood as "only a restriction" or "narrowing determination" of *Anwesenheit.*[18]

Derrida concludes *"Ousia* and *Gramme"* by interpreting the later Heidegger as working toward a de-limitation of Being along the lines of two texts. One text appeals "to a less narrow determination of presence from a more narrow determination of it, thereby going back from the present toward a more original thought of Being as presence (*Anwesenheit*)." The other text questions this thought and attempts "to think it as a closure, as *the* Greco-Western-philosophical closure." This latter text points beyond metaphysics—"making thought tremble by means of a *Wesen* that would not yet even be *Anwesen"* ("OG," 65).

The third, and most complex, of Derrida's concluding points concerns "the relationship between the two texts, between presence in general (*Anwesenheit*) and that which exceeds it before or beyond Greece." This relationship—between the metaphysics of presence and what exceeds it—cannot be thought within the context of metaphysics. "In order to exceed metaphysics it is necessary that a trace be inscribed within the text of metaphysics, a trace that continues to signal not in the direction of another presence, or another form of presence, but in the direction of an entirely other *text.*"[19]

> The mode of inscription of such a trace in the text of metaphysics is so unthinkable that it must be described as an era-

sure of the trace itself. The trace is produced as its own
erasure. And it belongs to the trace to erase itself, to elude
that which might maintain it in presence. ("OG," 65)

Here Derrida argues by analogy. As the difference between Being and
beings is forgotten/erased/covered over (and that forgetfulness also forgotten) in the reduction of Being to a being, the highest being, so is that
which underlies the ontological difference (différance)[20] covered over. It
belongs to this forgotten trace to be forgotten. Presence is the trace of
the erasure of this trace (i.e., presence is the trace of the erasure of the
trace of différance).[21] Presence is the trace that covers over and obscures,
rendering us oblivious to the trace of différance. When we think Being as
presence, we obscure différance.

Condensing Derrida's argument to its essentials, we get something like the following. In Being and Time, Heidegger names the difference between Being and beings as the ontological difference. In later
work, this ontological difference becomes articulated as the difference
between presence and the present ("OG," 66–67). This thinking, however, remains within the closure of metaphysics,[22] and hence trembles
with the deconstruction of the concept of presence (i.e., the deconstruction of the concept of time and its "together" with space). Nonetheless,
Heidegger's later thinking glimpses beyond to what subtends the difference between the trace of presence and what it obscures. What presence
obscures is différance.

Differing and Deferring

This leaves the question before us as to how différance signals beyond the
metaphysics of presence, that is, how it comes to terms with the enigmas
of time and its "together" with space. Derrida's answer is couched in
terms of the two correlates of différance, differing and deferring.

Derrida constantly reminds us that différance is not a word and not
a concept ("D," 3), indeed is not ("D," 6)—where to be is to be present[23]—but it is the condition for the possibility of lots of things: "the
possibility of the functioning of every sign" ("D," 5), "the possibility of
conceptuality" ("D," 11), "the possibility of "nominal effects" ("D," 26)
(i.e., the "structures that are called names" in chains of signifier substitutions), the possibility of "the presentation of the being-present"
("D," 6), etc. Furthermore, différance subtends or "remains undecided"

between activity and passivity ("D," 9), sensibility and understanding ("D," 5), existence and essence ("D," 6), in short, all the "founding oppositions" of the metaphysics of presence.

Derrida claims that the polysemic nature of *"différance"* allows it to "refer simultaneously to the entire configuration of its meanings" ("D," 8), as "difference" cannot. Specifically, it can accommodate the two senses of the French verb *differer* (from the Latin *differre*):[24] (1) to differ, "to be not identical, to be other, discernible" (which Derrida associates with spacing) ("D," 8); and (2) to defer, "the action of putting off until later" that "implies an economical calculation, a detour, a delay, a relay, a reserve, a representation" (which he associates with "temporalization" and sums up in the word "temporization") ("D," 8). In the essay at hand, "Différance," deferring is explicitly associated with the Freudian notions of sublimation and death instinct,[25] but, in "Freud and the Scene of Writing,"[26] written two years earlier, it is elaborated in terms of Freud's notion of *Verspätung* or the delay intrinsic to the operation of the secondary process or reality principle.[27] As I interpret this text, it says that we can have no direct experience of an origin. Or of any other presence. Everything present to consciousness is present only by virtue of having been deferred. In Freudian terms, every experience or excitation reaches us only after having suffered the transfiguration of secondary elaboration.

"Freud and the Scene of Writing" elaborates Freud's metaphorical representation of the psyche as a writing machine. The basic idea is that "psychical content" is "represented by a text whose essence is irreducibly graphic" ("FSW," 199). The point that is relevant here is that this metaphor precludes perception from being understood as a present origin or cognitive ground for truth because the perceived content is always the deferred/transformed trace of a prior inscription which, itself, was never originarily present but imbued with an essential secondarity.

Derrida concludes "that the present in general is not primal but, rather, reconstituted, that it is not the absolute, wholly living form which constitutes experience, that there is no purity of the living present— such is the theme, formidable for metaphysics, which Freud, in a conceptual scheme unequal to the thing itself, would have us pursue" ("FSW," 212).

Here is the problem of access, the problem of foundations, the denial of any grounding function to perception. Derrida is uncharacteristically straightforward about this claim: the deferred is the original, and it is irreducible. There is nothing (i.e., nothing accessible to us) prior to the transcription; no meaning prior to that which suffers symbolic transformation (condensation, displacement, overdetermination). "Since the transition to consciousness [i.e., the pathbreaking, Freud's *Bahnung*] is not a derivative or repetitive writing, a transcription duplicating an unconscious writing, it occurs in an original manner and, in its very secondariness, is originary and irreducible" ("FSW," 212).

This provides support for my claim[28] that Derrida is working within a reduced sphere of immanence, that is, that he refuses on principle to make any nonempty reference to a trancendent world. The principle is that all such access is mediated by the play of signifiers. The positive side of this thesis of immanence is stated in Derrida's doctrine of "transcendental writing," which he correlates with Freud's notion of dreamwork and conceives as erasing "the transcendental distinction between the origin of the world and Being-in-the-world" ("FSW," 212).[29] The world is transcendentally constituted by the work of the psyche/ writing machine upon pure traces of which we can never be conscious in their purity. It is essential to the trace to be erased. There is an originary distortion. The categories of Husserl's transcendental consciousness have been replaced by the categories of desire.[30]

The deferring of *différance* undermines the originality of the impression, of what is held to be present to the presence to itself of perceptual consciousness.

> The metaphor of pathbreaking . . . is always in communication with the theme of the *supplementary delay* and with the reconstitution of meaning through deferral . . . after the subterranean toil of an impression. This impression has left behind a laborious trace which has never been *perceived*, whose meaning has never been lived in the present, i.e., has never been lived consciously. ("FSW," 214)

In sum, the world we perceive is a text written by a machine laboring in impenetrable, primordial darkness.

Critique

Derrida's deconstruction of the metaphysics of presence proceeds from a critique of the conception of time that defines presence in our epoch. The burden of that critique is to show that presence is conceived in terms of an understanding of temporality which is, itself, inconceivable because it rests on a series of contradictions: time must be both real and unreal, eternal and passing, coincidental with space and nonspatial, etc. Derrida claims that the aporia of being and time is recapitulated in Heidegger's early work and interprets the difference between Being and beings or the ontological difference as an outgrowth of the difference between the eternal present and the present now-moment. But Derrida sees in Heidegger's later work a glimpse of the trace of something beyond presence in general (*Anwesenheit*), something which exceeds this Greco-Western-philosophical closure. The necessarily self-erasing trace Heidegger has glimpsed is the trace of *différance*. *Différance* is older than the ontological difference and underlies it. *Différance* is the condition for the possibility of that which was to have been accounted for by the ontological difference, namely, "the presentation of the being-present." The trace of *différance* has not been seen, indeed, cannot be perceived in the mode of self-presentation, because it erases itself by ceaselessly differing from and deferring itself. Deferral is the mode in which *différance* produces the traces from which it differs, the traces which, unlike itself, can be written or inscribed in present consciousness. What is present is therefore a representation that was never present, a presence that necessarily obscures that of which it is a trace.

What are we to make of this doctrine?

I take as my clue the terminology of "formal necessity" and "condition for the possibility of ———," which recurs regularly throughout the texts under consideration. These terms are taken from the lexicon of transcendental philosophy where they typically (e.g., in Kant, Husserl, and some of Heidegger's writings) appeal to a ground. Thus, for Kant, the condition for the possibility of temporal synthesis is the transcendental unity of apperception which serves as its ground.[31] Or, for Husserl, "the fundamental form of this universal synthesis [i.e., identification], the form that makes all other syntheses of consciousness possible, is the all-embracing consciousness of internal time" which is grounded in "the [transcendental] ego's marvellous being-for-himself," i.e., in "the being of his conscious life in the form of reflexive intentional relatedness to itself."[32] Derrida, however, explicitly refuses to appeal to a ground. The reason seems to be that for something $= X$ to serve as a ground, it must first *be,* and to be, for Derrida, is to be present or to be an absent presence. Since the possibility condition under consideration here, *différance,* cannot be presented, indeed, is erased by presence, it cannot serve as a ground. Yet, this consideration cannot be conclusive because, as shown in the example of Kant's transcendental unity of apperception, there are grounds which by formal necessity cannot be presented.[33]

Leaving aside the issue of Derrida's use of a strategy which permits him to employ a term and then disabuse himself of its implications
by putting the term under erasure, I confine myself to pointing out that
Derrida's appeal to "an 'originary' *différance*" ("D," 10) as a "playing
movement that 'produces' . . . differences [and] effects of difference"
("D," 11)[34] allows him to use the language of possibility condition and
formal necessity without making an overt ontological commitment to
grounds or origins. I will note, however, that there is a strong affinity
between the functions performed by *différance* and Kant's transcendental
unity of apperception: both name possibility conditions which are impossible presences or, to use another vocabulary, noumena lying beyond
the realm of temporal self-manifestation.

What does *différance* make possible that, without it, would be impossible? The short answer can be inscribed in a word: presence. A
longer answer has been inscribed in the words above, which trace the
reasoning through which Derrida seeks to demonstrate that presence is
inconceivable apart from the circular *gramme* which reconciles time with
itself and with space, and that the condition for the possibility of this
reconciliation resides in a play of differences without positive terms, that
is, in the play of *différance*. All the binary oppositions—the differences,
including the *ontologische Differenz*—which found the metaphysics of
presence originate in the nonorigin of *différance* which is the nonexistent
nonlocus of their provenance.[35]

"*Différance* is the . . . origin of differences" in two ways. (1) Language as the play of differences without positive terms is "produced" by
différance, and it is through language that these oppositions formulate
themselves. (2) *Différance* "produces" the binary oppositions by generating the privileged opposition—the unreal passing now versus the real
eternal now—which functions as the origin of presence and thereby
generates all the oppositions that grow out of the difference embodied
in presence. It is the second of these originating functions that most
concerns us here.

The being present presents itself on condition of presence to itself.
This is the thought—implicit in the Cartesian cogito, thematized in the
Kantian cogito (i.e., the "I think"), and explicitly developed in the Hegelian cogito (i.e., the self-consciousness that is the condition of consciousness or presentation of any object)—which Derrida identifies as
"phenomenology's principle of principles"[36] and sees as resting on the
aporetic conception of time informing our tradition from Aristotle
through Heidegger. To be is to be present in the now. The present now is
both the unreal terminator differentiating past and future and the pres-

ence to all times which defines the eternal reality of the theo-logical transcendental subject. The condition for the possibility of inner intuition is
momentary presence made present to itself through the synthesis of time
in an all-embracing or eternal unity. But this is also the condition for outer
experience: the spatial being adumbrated successively can be identified as
a unity by virtue of the coexistence of adumbrations in the appresentation
which spatializes time. The point here is that the deconstruction of presence rests on demonstrating its dependence on a notion of time that differs from itself, and hence cannot be thought through, but can be written
in the circular *gramme*. This conception of time "originates" in *différance*:
that is, its nonorigin is differing from itself in the dual modes of spatial
differing (the difference between the arbitrary finite temporal intervals
denominating the passing nows and the infinitely divisible circular periph-
ery which encompasses them while remaining incommensurable with
them) and temporal deferring (the difference between the deferred presence and its nonorigin in a presence which was never present). The deconstruction of presence rests on the critique of the now.

And the critique of the now rests on a mistaken assumption: the
assumption of the Eleatic conception of time and its relation to being.
Only if being is equated with immutability/eternity and becoming is rele-
gated to mere appearance on the grounds of the nonbeing of that which
changes, only then does the founding aporia of real eternal now versus
unreal passing now generate itself. The deconstruction of presence rests
on the assumption that there is a formal necessity that time in our epoch
be conceived in this Eleatic way.

This assumption is mistaken to the extent that it constitutes the
Eleatic conception of time as (1) the only conception of time to be found
in the metaphysical tradition or (2) the conception of time that this tradition has determined to be the true conception of time. Zeno was the first
to demonstrate the paradoxes or aporia generated by this conception of
time/space, and commentaries showing the mistaken nature of the Eleatic premise that restricts the real to the immutable can be documented
from Plato and Aristotle through the present. Indeed, the correlative
principle of the infinite divisibility of time has been disputed by several
of the thinkers Derrida cites as recapitulating the aporia. Although this is
not the place to present the textual evidence, Bergson's conception of *la
durée*, James' notion of the specious present, and Husserl's conception
of the now-moment as an indissoluble unity of retention and protention
are all aimed against the thesis of infinite divisibility. Mention might also
be made of the twentieth-century school of process philosophy which,
from Whitehead on, conceived process as reality.

Setting aside debate on the interpretation of the history of philosophy, I turn to the crucial philosophical issue: does the metaphysics of presence rest on Eleatic assumptions, or is the ontological privileging of presence compatible with the categories of becoming? The answer, of course, depends on how one defines presence. If one defines it as Derrida does, as resting on the aporetic conception of time, then his answer prevails. But if one defines the present moment, not in terms of a terminator that no person has ever experienced, a terminator that is the product of analytic thought, but rather in terms of a temporal gestalt that has indissoluble ties to past and future, as having the thickness of the living present in which motion can be perceived, then the phenomenon of passage is as real as any other and, indeed, far realer than the abstract reifications of instant and eternity.

In short, the claim being entered here is that the phenomenology of time, in articulating the primacy of becoming in terms of the irreducibility of perceptual unfolding, provides a conceptual matrix far more adequate to temporalization than a schema that would locate its non-origin in a noumenal or self-erasing trace that necessarily generates incompossible articulations and conceives perception in terms of a deferred/transformed inscription of a trace that never was present. The reduction of the perceptual world to a text forever relegates the question of the origin and referent of that text to darkness.[37]

Conclusion

Derrida sees the metaphysics of presence as founded on Eleatic principles and rebounds to a neo-Heraclitean nonposition of incessant differing/deferring within the immanent sphere of intertextuality.

I see the metaphysical tradition as contending with the tension between all the binary oppositions (although I would privilege the opposition of immanence and transcendence rather than that of permanence and change—while admitting a principle of nonequivalent translation among the oppositions) in the attempt to resolve them.

We agree that the oppositions sedimented in language can be resolved by appeal to a stratum beneath or prior to language and the dualisms it generates through the reification intrinsic to nomination.[38]

Derrida sees *différance* as the ungenerated generator of language, and the language of presence as the generator of metaphysical oppositions.

I see the phenomenon (admittedly defined as presence[39] and privileging the thickness of the living present) as the referent of language and summons to language—which has been afflicted by the very Eleatic antinomy (itself generated by language insofar as the illusion of permanence is instilled by the apparently unchanging nature of words regarded as linguistic essences) which Derrida takes up, affirms, and embodies in his notion of *différance*.

Derrida puts the dualism generator in an inconceivable *différance* beyond language—thereby raising contradiction to the level of principle—and I see dualism as generated by language generated in that manner.

We agree in associating presence with the positive content of signs taken as referring to a perceptual origin, but we disagree insofar as Derrida takes that positive content to be spurious and holds that "in language there are only differences without positive terms" ("D," 11). We agree that "these two motifs—the arbitrary character of the sign and the differential character of the sign—are inseparable [and that] there can be arbitrariness only because the system of signs is constituted solely by the differences in terms, and not by their plenitude" ("D," 10), but we disagree insofar as I hold that the system of signs is neither arbitrary nor grounded in an a priori necessity but historically generated from origins in which signs are originarily meaningful.

Finally, we agree that the metaphysical tradition has gropingly articulated itself through an ontology of presence conceived in terms of the primacy of the perceptual world, but we disagree insofar as he conceives this metaphysics in the categories of closure and I conceive it as a vital opening.

12

An Allegory of Modernity/Postmodernity: Habermas and Derrida

Richard J. Bernstein

D uring the past decade—in virtually every area of cultural life—there has been an explosion of discourses about "modernity" and "postmodernity." These discourses and the endless symposia dealing with this problematic have been at once heady and confusing. Heady, because they are signs of a prevailing mood—what Heidegger calls a *Stimmung*—one which is amorphous, elusive, protean. It is difficult to pin down and to characterize. Nevertheless it exerts a powerful influence. For there is a prevailing sense that something is happening that radically calls into question entrenched ways of thinking, acting, and feeling. Consider the following description of the postmodern movement as a movement of "unmaking" by the literary critic, Iban Hassan:

> It is an antinomian moment that assumes a vast unmaking of
> the Western mind—what Michel Foucault might call
> postmodern *epistēmē*. I say "unmaking" though other terms are
> now *de rigeuer:* for instance, deconstruction, decentering, dis-
> appearance, demystification, discontinuity, *différance*, disper-
> sion, etc. Such terms express an ontological rejection of the
> traditional full subject, the *cogito* of Western philosophy. They
> express, too, and epistemological obsession with fragments,

and a corresponding ideological commitment to minorities in
politics, sex and language. To think well, to feel well, to act
well, to read well according to this *epistēmē* of unmaking, is to
refuse the tyranny of wholes: totalization in human endeavour
is potentially totalitarian.[1]

Consider also the way in which Jean-François Lyotard defined
"modern" and "postmodern" in his polemical monograph, *The Postmodern Condition: A Report on Knowledge*—a tract that draws upon many
"postmodern" themes and which has provoked extensive discussion:

> I will use the term modern to designate any science that legiti-
> mates itself with reference to a metadiscourse of this kind mak-
> ing explicit appeal to some grand narrative, such as the
> dialectics of Spirit, the hermeneutics of meaning, the emanci-
> pation of the rational or working subject, or the creation of
> wealth. . . .

> Simplifying to the extreme I define postmodern as incredulity
> toward metanarratives. This incredulity is undoubtedly a prod-
> uct of progress in the sciences; but that progress in turn pre-
> supposes it. To the obsolescence of the metanarrative
> apparatus of legitimation corresponds most notably, the crisis
> of metaphysical philosophy and of the university institution
> which in part relied on it. The narrative function is losing its
> functors, its great hero, its great voyages, its great goal.[2]

Although these passages give some indication of the "postmodern"
mood, it is becoming increasingly evident that the terms "modern" and
"postmodern" are not only vague, ambiguous, and slippery, they have
been used in conflicting and even contradictory ways. Even when this
confusion is acknowledged there has been a strong temptation to go on
using them, to slide into a quasi-essentialism where we talk as if there are
a set of determinate features that mark off the "modern" from the
"postmodern." The trouble is that nobody seems to agree about what
these distinguishing characteristics are. My own conviction is that we
have reached a stage of discussion where these labels (and their cog-
nates) obscure more than they clarify—that it is better to drop these
terms from our "vocabularies," and to try to sort out the relevant issues
without reifying these labels.

So I want to do something different, but something that is relevant to these debates. I want to play off against each other two thinkers

whose names are frequently invoked in the so-called quarrel of
"moderns" and "postmoderns," a quarrel that seems to have displaced
the venerable quarrel of the "ancients" and the "moderns." Habermas,
for whom the concept of modernity is central, is frequently taken to be
the boldest defender of the unfinished project of modernity, a forceful
champion of the Enlightenment legacy. Derrida, who rarely even mentions "modernity" or "postmodernity," is nevertheless taken to be the
"postmodern" thinker par excellence.[3] Initially, the differences between
them—differences in focus, style, tone, and the legacies upon which they
draw, *seem* so striking that one wonders if they share any common
ground. When one turns to the ways in which they write about each
other, one may despair of bridging what appears unbridgeable.[4] It is all-
too-easy to think that an abyss separates them, that if ever there were
vocabularies that are incommensurable then the vocabularies of
Habermas and Derrida qualify as paradigmatic examples. I do *not* think
that there is some theoretical perspective in which their crucial differences can be reconciled, *aufgehoben*. They cannot. But I want to show
some of the ways in which they supplement each other, how we can
view them as reflecting two intertwined strands of the "modern/
postmodern" *Stimmung*. The "logic" of my argument is both/and rather
that either/or. This both/and exhibits unresolved, perhaps unresolvable
tensions and instabilities.

Drawing upon two metaphors used by Adorno—the metaphors
of a force-field and constellation—I intend to show how Habermas/
Derrida enable us to gain a deeper grasp of our present cultural and
philosophical situation. By a "force-field" Adorno means "a relational
interplay of attractions and aversions that constitute the dynamic, transmutational structure of a complex phenomenon."[5] By "constellation"—
a metaphor that Adorno borrowed from Benjamin—he means "a juxtaposed rather than integrated cluster of changing elements that resist reduction to a common denominator, essential core, or generative first
principle."[6] To refer to Benjamin once again, the force-field and constellation that I will be sketching may read as an *allegory* of the "modern/
postmodern" condition.

My approach to Habermas and Derrida may appear slightly unor-
thodox. I want to show what they are "up to." I share William James's
conviction when he shrewdly remarked:

> If we take the whole history of philosophy, the systems reduce
> themselves to a few main types which under all technical ver-
> biage in which the ingenious intellect of man envelopes them,

are just so many visions, modes of feeling the whole push, and seeing the whole drift of life, forced on one by one's total character and experience and on the whole *preferred*—there is no other truthful word—as one's best working attitude.[7]

I reject the approach to Habermas and Derrida that reads them as if they consisted only in a collection of disembodied texts with little regard to their flesh and blood experiences. We cannot gain a nuanced understanding of what they are "up to," to their "modes of feeling the whole push" unless we pay some attention to the vital formative personal experiences that have shaped even their most theoretical writings. Specifically, I am concerned with the ways in which they have experienced the threats, dangers, and challenges of the horrendous—almost incomprehensible—events of the twentieth century.

The Unfinished Project of the Enlightenment

For Habermas, one of these central formative experiences was his shock as a young adolescent to the revelations of the full horrors of Nazism. It is in the background of almost everything he has written. Habermas, who was born in 1929, tells us:

> At the age of 15 or 16, I sat before the radio and experienced what was being discussed before the Nuremberg tribunal, when others, instead of being struck by the ghastliness, began to dispute the justice of the trial, procedural questions, and questions of jurisdiction, there was that first rupture, which still gaps. Certainly, it is only because I was still sensitive and easily offended that I did not close myself to the fact of a collectively realized inhumanity in the same measure as the majority of my elders.[8]

The painful awareness of "the ghastliness," of "a collectively realized inhumanity," a sharp sense of "rupture" were the traumatic experiences of the young Habermas. A question began to take shape—a question that has haunted Habermas ever since: How could one account for the "pathologies of modernity"? How could one explain that rupture in the cultural tradition of Kant, Hegel, and Marx in which the ideals of reason, freedom, and justice had been so prominent? As a university student,

Habermas, like many of his contemporaries, experienced the intellectual power of Heidegger's *Sein und Zeit,* but he was also deeply affected by Lukács's *History and Class Consciousness,* and especially Horkheimer and Adorno's *Dialectic of Enlightenment.* Before he became Adorno's assistant, Habermas perceived the challenge posed by the *Dialectic of Enlightenment* when in its opening sentence the authors declared:

> In the most general sense of progressive thought, the Enlightenment has always aimed at liberating men from fear and establishing their sovereignty. Yet the fully enlightened earth radiates disaster triumphant.[9]

In the *Dialectic of Enlightenment* the authors relentlessly sought to highlight the "dark side" of the Enlightenment legacy and indeed all of social and cultural modernity—the way in which the Enlightenment gave rise to and promoted a "totalitarian" instrumental rationality that infected every aspect of cultural, social, and personal life—even reaching into the inner recesses of the human psyche. In this respect, Horkheimer and Adorno were deepening and extending the concept of reification that Lukács had so brilliantly analyzed in *History and Class Consciousness.* But contrary to Lukács, they categorically rejected the idea that a proletarian revolution would "solve" the problem of reification, or that with development of the proletarian class consciousness, there would be a "final reconciliation" of Subject and Object. Horkheimer and Adorno were at once much closer to and certainly more extreme than Max Weber—at least the Weber who was read as prophesizing that the twentieth century would be the epoch of the triumph of *Zweckrationalität* and bureaucratic normalization creating an "iron cage" from which there is no escape.

Habermas realized that one could not underestimate the growth and spread of instrumental, strategic, and systems rationality in the economic, social, and political structures of the modern world, and their powerful tendencies to reshape and colonize our everyday lifeworld. But at first, almost instinctively, and later, with increasing theoretical finesse, Habermas argued that this monolithic portrait of the totalitarian character of Enlightenment rationality was overdrawn. It failed to do justice to those philosophic and historical tendencies—also rooted in the Enlightenment—that gave rise to democratic public spaces in which a different type of communal rationality was manifested.[10] At a deeper level there was a failure to do justice to what Habermas first called symbolic interaction (and later called communicative action), and its distinctive type of rationality—the type of action that is oriented to mutual understanding and consensual action rather than to the goals of efficiency and success.

Gradually it became clear to Habermas that a proper response to all those—whether they were associated with the political left or right—who claimed that our modern destiny is one in which there is an ineluctable triumph of instrumental, technological "rationality" (what Heidegger called *Gestell*) is to reopen and rethink the entire problematic of rationality. In this rethinking—this reconstructive project—one needs to draw crucial and categorical distinctions between different types of action, rationality, rationalization processes, and their complex dynamic interrelations. Although Habermas's terminology has shifted and has become more differentiated, he has consistently maintained that there is a categorical distinction between the varieties of instrumental, strategic, systems, and technological rationality *and* communicative, dialogical rationality. Furthermore he has argued that instrumental rationality presupposes and is dependent upon communicative rationality. All attempts to reduce or translate communicative action to monological, teleological, goal-oriented action and rationality fail—or so Habermas argues. Once we make a categorical distinction between communicative and purposive-rational actions, we can sharply distinguish what the rationalization of these different action-types means.

"Purposive-rational actions can be regarded under two different aspects—the empirical efficiency of technical means and the consistency of choice between suitable means."[11] "Rationalization" as it pertains to purposive-rational actions means increasing efficiency or the consistency of "rational" choices. This is the type of rationalization that has been privileged by neo-classical economists and those influenced by models of economic rationality.

But "rationalization" of the communicative action has a radically different meaning.

> Rationalization here means extirpating those relations of force that are inconspicuously set in the very structures of communication and that prevent conscious settlement of conflicts. . . . Rationalization means overcoming such systematically distorted communication in which action supporting consensus concerning the reciprocally raised validity claims . . . can be sustained in appearance only, that is counterfactually.[12]

The position expressed in this passage is rich in its consequences. I want to emphasize that Habermas's theoretical reconstructive project of elucidating the universal conditions for communicative action is not merely "theoretical": it has strong practical consequences for orienting our ethical and political activity. It directs us to the normative task of overcoming those material obstacles that prevent or inhibit undistorted and noncoerced communication. Positively stated, it means working toward the cultivation of practices that bring us closer to the ideal of seeking to resolve conflicts through discourses where the only relevant force is the "force of the better argument." Habermas is frequently misread as if he were proposing an ideal form of life in which all conflicts would be settled by rational discussion—an ideal form of life where all violence would disappear. But this is a caricature. Our concrete historical forms of life are always shaped by traditions, social practices, and communal bonds that are more concrete, complex, and richer than our rational discursive practices. Without these traditions there would be no *substance* to our ethical and political convictions. Violence and distortion may be uneliminable, but they can be diminished. Habermas's limited but all important thesis is that:

> In action oriented to reaching understanding, validity claims
> are "always already" implicitly raised. Those universal claims
> (to the comprehensibility of the symbolic expression, the truth
> of the propositional content, the truthfulness of the intentional
> expression, and the rightness of the speech act with respect to
> existing norms and values) are set in the general structures of
> possible communication. In these validity claims communica-
> tive theory can locate a gentle, but obstinate, a never silent al-
> though seldom redeemed claim to reason, a claim that must be
> recognized *de facto* whenever and wherever there is to be con-
> sensual action.[13]

Habermas rejects any philosophy of history that is explicitly or implicitly committed to a grand teleological narrative. Nevertheless he does strongly affirm that, even though the claim to reason—to communicative dialogical reason—is silenced over and over again, it "develops a stubbornly transcending power, because it is renewed with each act of unconstrained understanding, with each moment of living together in solidarity, of successful individuation, and of saving emancipation."[14]

Habermas is a thoroughgoing fallibilist who rejects classical foundationalist and transcendental arguments. One of his criticisms of thinkers like Heidegger, Adorno, and Derrida is that they still write in the "shadow of the 'last' philosopher, as did the first generation of Hegelian disciples. They still feel the need to battle against those 'strong' concepts of system, totality, truth, and completed theory which belong to the past."[15] Ironically, much of the *pathos* of their writings gains its force from the specter of The Grand System. "They still think that they have to arouse philosophy from what Derrida calls 'the dream of its heart.' They believe they have to tear philosophy away from the madness of expounding a theory that has the last word."[16] Despite their protests to the contrary, they are still entrapped in the aporias and cul-de-sacs of what Habermas calls "The Philosophy of Subjectivity." Their failure, according to Habermas, is not to realize and fully appreciate that the "fallibilist consciousness of the sciences caught up with philosophy too, a long time ago."[17] When they declare that philosophy or metaphysics is over, their image of philosophy is still that of the Absolute System—the philosophy of "the last word." Each, in his way, wants to keep philosophy or thinking "pure"—pure from any contamination by empirical social scientific research.

Habermas's fallibilism is not incompatible with making universal claims and seeking to redeem them with the strongest arguments we can give. This is the way in which he conceives of his own theory of communicative action. In *this* respect, Habermas sees no epistemological difference between a theory of communicative action and any other scientific theory. For in advancing any theory we are always making universal validity claims which are necessarily open to ongoing criticism and revision.[18]

Throughout his intellectual career, Habermas has relentlessly sought to track down, expose, and defeat the varieties of nihilism, relativism, decisionism, historicism, and neo-Aristotelian contextualism that have been so fashionable in the twentieth century. Here too his motivations are not exclusively theoretical—they are motivated by his practical concerns. For he argues that the logic of all these "positions," when we think them through, undermines the possibility of critique that is rationally grounded and warranted. He criticizes all forms of totalizing critique, claiming that they lead to performative contradictions. What he says about Nietzsche applies equally to all those who work in his shadow (including Derrida): "Nietzsche's critique consumes the critical impulse itself." "If thought can no longer operate in the realms of truth and validity claims, then analysis and critique lose their meaning." One is left only with the seductions of a "bad" aestheticism that "enthrones *taste*, the 'Yes' and 'No' of the palate (BGE, p. 341) as the sole organ of knowledge beyond Truth and Falsity, beyond Good and Evil."[19]

Pervading all of Habermas's writings is his strong and unshakable commitment to democracy. No less than John Dewey, Habermas is the philosopher of democracy. This is one of the reasons why he has been so drawn to the American pragmatic tradition, especially Peirce, Mead, and Dewey. From Peirce he appropriates the idea of an ongoing self-critical community of inquirers always open to criticizing its validity claims. Following Mead, he develops a theory of the genesis of the social self in which democratic individuality, and postconventional morality are realizable achievements of practical intersubjectivity. With Dewey, Habermas believes in the normative ideal of a democratic society in which all share and participate. Like Dewey, who saw the most urgent problem of our time to be the cultivation of democratic public life, Habermas also believes that democratic participation is compatible with the complexity of advanced technological societies.

Habermas's entire project can be conceived of as a rethinking and rewriting of the *Dialectic of Enlightenment*. Habermas, like his mentors, has been alert to the self-destructive tendencies unleashed by the Enlightenment. But against them he argues that we need a more differentiated analysis of the conflicting tendencies of modernity and the Enlightenment legacy—one that does justice to the powerful tendencies of the growth and spread of systems rationality *and* those fragile practices in which we can still discern the transcending power of communicative rationality. Habermas is far more dialectical than Horkheimer and Adorno. For the overwhelming thrust of the *Dialectic of Enlightenment* is negative—it is a dark narrative of ineluctable self-destruction. But in a more dialectically nuanced manner, Habermas shows that our present situation, and the future possibilities open to us, are systematically ambiguous. Whether we will some day live in the cosmic night of nihilism *or* restore a proper balance between communicative and systems rationality is still an open question. The "colonization of the lifeworld by systems rationality" is the most powerful tendency of advanced technological societies. But this tendency is not the manifestation of a logic of history that is working itself out "behind our backs." The promise of modernity is still an unfinished *project*—a project whose realization is dependent upon our present *praxis*.

Once we get a sense of Habermas's mode of "feeling the whole push," his vision of "the whole drift of life" then many aspects of his thinking and actions fall into place. We can understand why he is so suspicious of the ways in which the talk of "postmodernity" and "post-Enlightenment" slip into "old" variations of countermodern or antimodern themes. We can understand his frequent political and journalistic interventions in a German context. For Habermas is hypersensitive to those aspects of the pernicious cultural tendency to separate

Germany's "spiritual destiny" from the moral and political achievements of Western democracy. Despite Habermas's acknowledgment that Heidegger—the Heidegger of *Sein und Zeit*—is Germany's greatest twentieth-century philosopher, he is scathing in his exposure and criticism of the ideological biases that infect Heidegger's writings from 1929 on.[20] We can even understand why Habermas is so critical and deeply suspicious of the major tendencies in post-World War II French cultural life. He reads Derrida as little more than a latinized disciple of Heidegger, who furthers some of the worst tendencies in the late Heidegger. For he thinks that Derrida seduces us into thinking we can confront contemporary political, ethical, and juridicial problems by endless deconstruction of texts. Habermas is impatient with anyone who disdains concrete empirical social scientific research—who still wants to keep thinking "pure."

Iris Murdoch once shrewdly remarked "it is always a significant question to ask of any philosopher: what is he afraid of?" The answer for Habermas is clear. It is "irrationalism" whatever guise it takes—whether ugly facists forms, disguised neo-conservative variations, or the playful antics of those who seek to domesticate Nietzsche. In a time when it has become so fashionable to attack, mock, ridicule the claim to Reason, Habermas is not afraid to appear "old-fashioned"—to insist on "the stubbornness with which philosophy clings to the role of the 'guardian of reason' "—a role that "can hardly be dismissed as an idiosyncrasy of self-absorbed intellectuals, especially in a period in which basic irrationalist undercurrents, are transmuted once again into a dubious form of politics."[21]

The Elusiveness and Threat of Otherness

Let me turn abruptly to Derrida. The turn is abrupt because initially it appears to be crossing an unbridgeable chasm. If one can speak of an experience of incommensurability and radical otherness, the turn to Derrida seems to transport us to a different world with few if any points of contact with the problems, theses, and concerns that so preoccupy Habermas. I have already suggested that the metaphors of a constellation and force-field are helpful to grasp the agonistic and antagonistic tensions between them. To show this I want to adumbrate a reading of Derrida that brings forth the ethical-political-juridical motifs that run through *all* his writings.[22]

Just as I began my analysis of Habermas by recollecting a formative experience in his intellectual development, I want to juxtapose this with what Derrida himself takes to be a crucial experience of his childhood. Habermas and Derrida are almost exact contemporaries (Habermas was born in 1929, Derrida in 1931). At the time when Habermas was growing up in Nazi Germany, Derrida was experiencing the war as a French Algerian Jew in El-Biar. In the fragments of his autobiography that Derrida weaves into his writings and from some of his interviews, we can gain a glimmer of his childhood experiences—or at least his *memory* of them.

> The war came to Algeria in 1940, and with it, already then, the
> first concealed rumblings of the Algerian war. As a child, I had
> the instinctive feeling that the end of the world was at hand, a
> feeling which at the same time was most natural, and in any
> case, the only one I ever knew. Even to a child incapable of an-
> alyzing things, it was clear that all this would end in fire and
> blood. No one can escape that violence and fear.[23]

Derrida came from a petit-bourgeois Jewish family which was partially assimilated. He was and was not a Jew. He was and was not an Algerian. As an Algerian Jew he was and was not a Frenchman. By his own testimony his primary experience was a "feeling of non-belonging"—of "otherness."[24] And this continued when he went to France as a student at the age of nineteen. For Derrida has always characterized himself as working at the margins of philosophy and literature. The motifs of alterity, difference, supplementarity, marginality that weave in and out all of his texts have their *correspondences* in those early experiences. He tells us:

> My central question is: from what site or non-site (*non-lieu*) can
> philosophy as such appear to itself, so that it can interrogate
> and reflect upon itself in an original manner? Such a non-site
> or alterity would be irreducible to philosophy. But the problem
> is that such a non-site cannot be defined or situated by means
> of philosophical language.[25]

The experience and obsessive concern with alterity, otherness—or more precisely, the singularity and otherness of the other—haunt all of Derrida's texts. Furthermore, his fascination with otherness (in all its modes) does have powerful ethical-political resonances—as we shall see. Deconstruction cannot be captured or reduced to a formula. But, if like Rabbi

Hillel, I were asked, while standing on one foot, to characterize deconstruction, I can think of no more apt description than the one given by
Derrida when he says "deconstruction is, in itself, a positive response to
an alterity which necessarily calls, summons or motivates it. Deconstruction is therefore a vocation—a response to a call."[26] Deconstruction is
"an openness towards the other."[27]

When I say that all the texts signed by Derrida are pervaded by
ethical-political-juridical motifs, I do not simply mean that Derrida
"has" an ethics and politics. I mean something much stronger. For I
want to argue that an ethical-political-juridical reading of all his texts is a
point of departure for understanding his "mode of feeling the whole
push." His ethical-political concerns shape and are shaped by his deconstruction of logocentrism, phonocentrism, phallogocentrism, and
especially what he—following Heidegger—calls "the metaphysics of
presence."[28]

Derrida is acutely aware that we cannot question or shake traditional ethical and political claims without at the same time also drawing
upon these traditional claims. The very dichotomy of "inside-outside" is
also deconstructed. We are never simply "inside" or "outside" metaphysics. Derrida has been read—I think seriously misread—as if he were
advocating a total rupture with metaphysics, as if some apocalyptic event
might occur that would once and for all release us from the metaphysical
exigency. But he mocks the very idea of such an apocalyptic happening.[29]
He tells us that "the idea that we might be able to get outside of metaphysics has always struck me as naive," and that "we cannot really say
that we are 'locked into' or 'condemned to' metaphysics, for we are,
strictly speaking, neither inside nor outside."[30]

According to Derrida, memory and promise, repetition and rupture always *come* together.[31] Concerning history and tradition, concerning the complex temporality of past-present-future, Derrida, in a
manner that is reminiscent of Benjamin, writes:

> My own conviction is that we must maintain two contradictory
> affirmations at the same time. On the one had we affirm the
> existence of ruptures in history, and on the other we affirm
> that these ruptures produce gaps or faults [*failles*] in which the
> most hidden and forgotten archives can emerge and constantly
> recur and work through history. One must surmount the cate-
> gorical oppositions of philosophic logic out of fidelity to these
> conflicting positions of historical discontinuity (rupture) and
> continuity (repetition), which are neither pure break with the
> past nor a pure unfolding or explication of it.[32]

There is another prevalent misreading of Derrida—claiming that he is guilty of some sort of linguistic idealism in his linkage of the history of signification, metaphysics, and the "West." The most common criticism of Derrida is that he "reduces" everything to texts (and/or language) and declares that there is nothing beyond the text. But the key question is: What does Derrida mean by a "text"? He answers this question in many places, but one of his clearest and most forceful statements occurs in his polemical exchange about apartheid, "Racism's Last Word." He tells us that "text" as he uses the term is not to be confused with the graphisms of a "book."

> No more than writing or trace, it is not limited to the *paper* which you can cover with your graphism. It is precisely for strategic reasons . . . that I found it necessary to recast the concept of text by generalizing it almost without any limit that *is*. That's why there is nothing "*beyond* the text." That's why South Africa and *apartheid* are, like you and me, part of this general text, which is not to say that it can be read the way one reads a book. That's why the text is always a field of forces: heterogeneous, differential, open, and so on. That's why deconstructive readings and writings are concerned not only with library books, with discourses, with conceptual and semantic contents. They are not simply analyses of discourse. . . . They are also effective or active (as one says) interventions that transform contexts without limiting themselves to theoretical or constative utterances even though they must also produce such utterances.[33]

Derrida claims that his "strategic reevaluation of the concept of text allows [him] to bring together in a more consistent fashion, in the most consistent fashion possible, theoretico-philosophical necessities with 'practical,' political and other necessities of what is called deconstruction."[34] He emphatically affirms that "deconstructive practices are also and first of all political and institutional practices."[35]

But what precisely does this mean? How are deconstructive practices "first of all" political and institutional practices? The following passage provides an important clue.

> [W]hat is somewhat hastily called deconstruction is not, if it is of any consequence, a specialized set of discursive procedures, even less the rules of a new hermeneutic method, working on texts or utterances in the shelter of a given and stable institu-

tion. It is also, at the very least, a way of taking a position, in its work of analysis, concerning the political and institutional structures that make possible and govern our practice, our competences, our performances. Precisely because it is never concerned only with signified content, deconstruction should not be separable from this politico-institutional problematic and should seek a new investigation of responsibility, an investigation which questions the codes inherited from ethics and politics. This means that too political for some, it will seem paralyzing to those who only recognize politics by the most familiar road signs.[36]

Let me step back in order to comment on this dense passage and the controversial claims that Derrida makes here. Derrida is always concerned (obsessed) with the question of the otherness of the other, with the differences that are presupposed by self-identity. He is always working on the margins, fascinated with the "logic of supplementarity." Metaphors of "exile" and "parasite" weave through his writings. Derrida is not only concerned with the receding limits that are presumably "discovered" or stipulated, he is deeply suspicious of all forms of boundary-fixing—including the boundary-fixing between theoretical and practical-political-institutional "domains." Here too one must be sensitive to Derrida's precise point if we want to grasp what he is "up to." Contrary to what many of his critics (including Habermas) claim, Derrida does *not* seek to deny all distinctions and reduce everything to one muddled confused homogeneous text. He does *not* deny there are important distinctions between philosophy and literature or logic and rhetoric. He scrutinizes the precise "points" where distinctions, dichotomies, dualisms break down and are called into question. His deconstructive practices would not even make sense unless we initially take distinctions, negations, and oppositions "seriously." It is nonreducible heterogeneity and heterology that he makes manifest. He consistently opposes a "logic of apartheid," radical separation into "natural" kinds—whether we understand apartheid "literally" or "figuratively." He sees the *logic* of apartheid at work not only in South Africa but in the "homelands of academic culture." In responding to the critics of his *appeal* concerning apartheid, he concludes with a declaration that has much broader significance:

> in the homelands of academic culture or of "political action" you would favor instead reserved domains, the separate development of each community in the zone assigned to it.
> Not me.[37]

There is no fixed boundary between theoretical and practical domains, between texts and institutional contexts. Willy-nilly, all deconstruction for Derrida is always and also political. But there is a problem here that needs to be squarely confronted. Deconstruction may be "too political for some" but why does it also "seem paralyzing to those who recognize politics by the most familiar road signs"? We need to probe further.

As a citizen, Derrida has taken strong, admirable stands on a variety of political and ethical issues. He has fought apartheid, written a moving homage to Mandela, actively participated in resisting the French government's attempt to reduce the teaching of philosophy in secondary schools, helped to start a new "open" university in Paris, been an outspoken critic of infringements on human rights, addressed feminist issues, and was even arrested and interrogated on a framed-up charge in Czechoslovakia. He has been an engaged intellectual. But what do these activities have to do with deconstruction? He speaks about this when he was asked: "Can the theoretical radicality of deconstruction be translated into a radical praxis?" He tells us "I must confess that I have never succeeded in directly relating deconstruction to existing political programmes."[38] The key terms here are "directly" and "existing," for Derrida declares "all of our political codes and terminologies still remain fundamentally metaphysical, regardless of whether they originate from the right or the left."[39] But this still leaves open the question whether it is even possible to imagine a "political code" that is not metaphysical—at least in the "objectionable" sense of metaphysical. Derrida himself is not clear whether this is possible. When asked again whether he thinks this implies inaction and noncommitment, he answers:

> Not at all. But the difficulty is to gesture in opposite directions
> at the same time: on the one hand to preserve a distance and
> suspicion with regard to the official political codes governing
> reality; on the other, to intervene here and now in a practical
> and *engaged* manner whenever the necessity arises. This posi-
> tion of dual allegiance, in which I personally find myself, is one
> of perpetual uneasiness. I try where I can to act politically
> while recognizing that such action remains incommensurate
> with my intellectual project of deconstruction.[40]

Although this is one of Derrida's most forthright statements on the relation (or nonrelation) "between" deconstruction and his politics, it is still open to different and conflicting interpretations. I want to suggest a reading that is consonant with many of his other texts. The danger with

any political code is that it can become rigidifed or reified—a set of un-
questioned formulas that we rely on to direct our actions. More important, no code is ever *sufficient* to justify or legitimate a decision in any
specific context. No code can close the gap or diminish the undecidability that confronts us in making an ethical-political decision or
choice. "*This particular* undecidable opens the field of decision or of de
cidability."

> It calls for decision in the order of ethical-political responsibil-
> ity. It is even its necessary condition. A decision can only come
> into being in a space that exceeds the calculable program that
> would destroy all responsibility by transforming it into a pro-
> grammable effect of determinate causes. There can be no
> moral or political responsibility without this trial and this pas-
> sage by way of the undecidable.[41]

Derrida is echoing and reinforcing a point made by many critics of the
modern bias that the primary task of moral and political philosophy is to
specify and justify the universal rules that ought to govern our decisions
and actions. But Derrida is also critical of those who think that an appeal
to judgment or *phronesis* gets us out of this bind.[42] He radicalizes the
openness that he takes to be characteristic of responsibility and decision
by emphasizing the *experience* of the undecidable. We have to think and
act without banisters and barriers—or rather with the realization that is
"we" who construct and deconstruct these barriers. Nevertheless, responsibility, action, and decision "here and now" demand that we at
least temporarily suspend constant questioning. (Otherwise we would
slip into inaction and noncommitment which are also modes action and
commitment.) This is his point about gesturing "in opposite directions."
We cannot escape from the responsibilities and obligations that are
thrust upon us—thrust upon us by the other. Given our radical contingency we can never know or control when we are called upon to respond.
We must always be prepared to confront new unpredictable responsibilities.[43] So when Derrida speaks of his "perpetual uneasiness" he is not
merely expressing an idiosyncratic subjective state of mind but rather
expressing a condition of undecidability which—to speak in a non-
Derridean manner—is built into "the human condition."

Derrida has an acute sense that, at least since the "rupture" we
call Nietzsche, we can no longer be content with self-satisfied appeals to
moral and political foundations, first principles and *archai*. We are compelled to question these. But he is equally acute in his realization that

such a questioning doesn't "solve" anything. We cannot assume a permanent frozen stance of *an-arché*. For this is another fixed metaphysical position. We cannot escape responsibility, decision, and choice. They are thrust upon us by the other. Furthermore, we cannot simply dismiss or ignore those ethical and political principles that are constitutive of our traditions. The problem—and it is a problem for which there cannot be any final or permanent "solution"—is how to live this perpetual uneasiness in a way in which we "gesture in opposite directions at the same time," where we keep alive the distance of questioning and are prepared to act decisively "here and now"—where we do not hide in bad faith from the double-binds that we always confront.

But still we want to know what sort of politics Derrida does favor. What is its substantive content? Derrida has been extremely tentative and hesitant, although not silent. Considering the subversive quality of all his thinking, and his questioning of all forms of authority (even the authority claimed by "guardians of reason"), it is easier to discern what he is "against" rather than what he is "for." One will not find in his writings a clear and explicit statement of a political program. But I do not think it is fair to say he is entirely negative—that his political views are nothing but a "negative theology" translated into a political register. Derrida himself declares, "Deconstruction certainly entails a moment of affirmation. Indeed, I cannot conceive of a radical critique which would not be ultimately motivated by some sort of affirmation, acknowledged or no. Deconstruction always presupposes affirmation."[44] What then is Derrida affirming?

Let me approach the question of Derrida's normative ethical-political vision in what may seem to be an oblique manner. Already in *Of Grammatology*, Derrida linked phonocentrism, logocentrism, and the metaphysics of presence with phallogocentrism. Phallogocentrism and the question of sexual difference have been persistent iterated motifs throughout his writings—explored with subtle nuances, wit, and sometimes with raucous humor. (Derrida's playfulness—a powerful deconstructive strategy—has infuriated many of his critics and provided ammunition for claiming he is "nonserious.") Derrida's concern with "sexual difference" has been a vehicle for exploring and elaborating what he means by *différance*, even for probing the blindness and insights of Heidegger's all important notion of "ontological difference." His analyses of "sexual difference" are intended to move us beyond the logic of binary oppositions so characteristic of metaphysics—or more accurately to complicate the logic of binary oppositions in a manner that makes us aware of differences that always elude our conceptual grids. In what may well be one of the most lyrical passages in his writings he dreams about what may be beyond our traditional gendered ways of thinking, acting, and feeling. He sketches the possibility of a different relationship with the other when he writes:

> This double dissymmetry perhaps goes beyond known or coded marks, beyond the grammar and spelling, shall we say (metaphorically) of sexuality. This indeed revives the following question: what if we were to reach, what if we were to approach here (for one does not arrive at this as one would at a determined location) the area of a relationship to the other where the code of sexual marks would no longer be discriminating? The relationship would not be a-sexual, far from it, but would be sexual otherwise: beyond the binary difference that governs the decorum of all codes, beyond the distinction masculine/feminine. . . . As I dream of saving the chance that his question offers I would like to believe in the multiplicity of sexually marked voices. I would like to believe in the masses, this indeterminable number of blended voices, this mobile of non-identified sexual marks whose choreography can carry, divide, multiply the body of each "individual," whether he be classified as "man" or as "woman" according to the criteria of usage.[45]

The syntactical construction of this passage ("shall we say," "if we were to reach," "I would like to believe," etc.) is itself a sign of Derrida's tentativeness in elaborating what is "beyond the binary difference." But it can be read as an allegory of Derrida's "ethical-political" vision. It also enables one to understand the power of Derrida's thinking for those—whether women, blacks, or others—who have experienced the pain and humiliation of being excluded and silenced. For whether Derrida writes about sexual difference, or the logic of apartheid, or a politics of friendship that is no longer infiltrated by fraternal metaphors, when he calls into question the dichotomy of friend and enemy that Carl Schmitt took to be the defining characteristic of all politics, he is envisioning the possibility of a state of affairs where the violence of discrimination—if not completely eliminated—is at least minimized, where difference is no longer taken to be a threat, but is affirmed and celebrated, difference where there is *both* symmetry and asymmetry, reciprocity and nonreciprocity.[46] He even speaks of this as "a democracy to come"—a democracy not to be identified with any of its existing institutional forms. Here too we can locate Derrida's double gestures. For his tentativeness and hesitancy in elaborating his dream is itself an expression of his conviction that we never quite eliminate violence from our language, institutions, and practices—that it is always a self-deceptive illusion to think this has been achieved—that we can "arrive at this as one would as a determined location." But we can—and Derrida takes this to be a perpetual demanding task to be renewed over and over again—

> try to recognize and analyze [violence] as best we can in its various forms: obvious or disguised, institutional or individual, literal or metaphoric, candid or hypocritical, in good or guilt conscience. And if, as I believe, violence remains in fact (almost) ineradicable, its analysis and the most refined, ingenious account of its conditions will be the least violent gestures, perhaps even non-violent, and in any case those which contribute most to transforming the legal-ethical-political rules.[47]

The *Polemos* of "Modernity/ Postmodernity"

In order to show how "the relational interplay of attractions and aversions" between Habermas and Derrida can be read as an allegory of our "modern/postmodern" condition, I want to consider how they exemplify conflicting strands in the modern/postmodern *Stimmung*. Habermas, as we have seen, is not a naive *Aufklärer*. He is profoundly aware of the ambiguities, conflicts, and treacheries of the Enlightenment legacy. He is not an uncritical champion of modernity. His project has been one of systematically analyzing social and cultural modernity in order to specify and do justice to its conflicting and ambiguous tendencies. The Enlightenment legacy cannot be smoothed out into *either* a grand narrative of the progressive realization of freedom and justice *or* the cosmic night of ineluctable nihilistic self-destruction. With a stubborn persistence, he seeks to keep alive the memory/promise and hope of a world in which justice, equality, and dialogical rationality are concretely realized in our everyday practices. He staunchly resists all those who claim this hope must be abandoned, that our most cherished dreams of creating and realizing norms of justice must inevitably turn into totalitarian nightmares. He rejects the all-too-fashionable view that discursive practices are only a meaningless displacement of power/knowledge regimes. He is a "guardian of reason," but the reason he defends is dialogical, intersubjective, communicative. He is a fallibilist, but argues this stance

is not only compatible with, but requires a serious attempt to ground
critique in universal validity claims, and to engage in political praxis directed toward the material achievement of the norms of social critique.
For Habermas, we cannot avoid the question, critique "in the name of
what?" His quarrel with many so-called "postmodern" thinkers is that
they either fail to confront this question, obscure it, or get caught in
performative contradictions. One reason why Habermas "speaks" to so
many of "us" and is so relevant to the "modern/postmodern" condition
is because however feeble and fragile this aspect of the Enlightenment
legacy has become, and despite the attacks on this legacy, it nevertheless
will not die—the demand for freedom and *claim* to dialogical reason-
ableness does have a "stubbornly transcending power," as recent events
from South Africa to Eastern Europe so vividly demonstrate.

Derrida, as I have tried to show, is not indifferent to this memory/
promise and hope. He even, in his way, calls for a new *Aufklärung*.[48] But
his "center"—his mode of "feeling the whole push"—is very different
from, but not necessarily incompatible with, Habermas's perspective.
What is "central" for Derrida is otherness, alterity, *différance*. His primary concern is with meticulously analyzing and deconstructing the ways
in which we consciously or unconsciously exclude, marginalize, suppress, and repress the otherness and singularity of the other—the other
that refuses to be contained, mastered, domesticated. This is the strand
of the "modern/postmodern" mood that Derrida has the genius for exhibiting.

Few contemporary thinkers have been as incisive and nuanced as
Derrida in tracking the varieties of otherness, in *showing* how otherness
ruptures, disrupts, threatens, and eludes our logocentric conceptual
grids. He seeks to show us why and how a "logic" of opposition and
negation requires to be complicated and supplemented by a "logic" of
différance. This "logic" is not quite a *logos* that can encompass and bind
together differences. For Derrida is also stubbornly persistent in analyzing and exposing the difference of difference. The "other" he speaks
about is not a "generalized other" that can be assigned a proper or common name. This is one reason he keeps returning to the question of naming. Translating this into an ethical-political idiom means that when we
turn our attention to the singularity of the other or *différance*, we must
focus on the differences that "make" a difference. Derrida avoids the
facile "postmodern" temptation to lump together all differences under
the general rubric of *the* "other."

Derrida "speaks to" so many of "us" because the question of otherness (in all its variations) has become a "central"—if not *the* central—

theoretical/practical question of our time.[49] How can we hope to be open to, and respond responsibly to the terror of otherness and singularity of the other? This is primarily an ethical-political question for which there is not and cannot be a "final solution." Derrida is much closer in style and temperament to Adorno and Benjamin than he is to Habermas. Like Adorno, Derrida also seeks to expose the violence of what Adorno called "identity logic"—the multifarious ways in which institutionalized forms of rationality and conceptual grids violate singularity. Like Benjamin, Derrida is also obsessed with fragments, detritus, and the fissures that rupture "smooth" historical continuities.

When we place Habermas/Derrida in a new constellation—view them as each other's other—then their strengths and weaknesses come into sharp relief. We can witness their symbiotic "interplay of attractions and aversions." For Habermas, communicative action and rationality are the powerful magnetic poles of his work. Everything he explores emanates from, and is drawn back to these poles. His reading of the philosophic discourse of modernity is that "postmodern" philosophic discourses are caught within the aporias of "a philosophy of subjectivity" which is now exhausting itself. These discourses—despite desperate protests to the contrary—have failed to break out of a philosophy of subjectivity or consciousness. They have failed to make the paradigm shift to a model of communicative dialogical action and rationality.[50]

Communicative action—action oriented to mutual reciprocal understanding—never becomes fully thematized in Derrida's writings. But his deconstructive practices bear on it. For Derrida, like Adorno and Benjamin, is far more sensitive to what Habermas acknowledges but does not closely analyze—the multifarious ways in which communication (even under "ideal" conditions) goes awry. He is alert to the ways in which "mutual understanding" so frequently turns into mutual misunderstanding, how appeals to dialogue can and do contain their own hidden violences, how communication—especially in the contemporary world—has become little more than an economy of commodity exchange of information bits. He warns us that even appeals to face-to-face spoken communication can repress the heterogeneity and asymmetry of the other.

Abstractly there is something enormously attractive about Habermas's appeal to the "force of the better argument" until we ask ourselves what this means and presupposes. Even under "ideal" conditions where participants are committed to discursive argumentation, there is rarely agreement about what constitutes "the force of the better argument." We philosophers, for example, cannot even agree what are the arguments advanced in any of our canonical texts, whether Plato, Aristotle, Kant, or Hegel, etc.—and there is certainly no consensus about who has advanced the better arguments. Furthermore there isn't even any agreement about the *role* the argument does or should play in a philosophic "vocabulary." We should not be innocent about the ways in which "tough minded" appeals to argumentation become ideological weapons for dismissing or excluding philosophical alternatives—for example, when analytic philosophers complain that continental philosophers (including Habermas) do not argue or indulge in "sloppy" argumentation. Who decides what is and what is not an argument, by what criteria, and what constitutes the force of the better argument? Who really believes that philosophers can achieve a rational consensus, or even that this is desirable? In raising these issues, I am not suggesting that "anything goes" or that there is never any way of sorting out better or worse arguments. On the contrary, we can and should debate about what constitutes an argument, how forceful it is, and how we are to evaluate competing arguments. But there are rarely (if ever) any algorithms or clear criteria for determining this in nontrivial instances.[51] Think how much more intractable the problems become when we turn to specific ethical and political disputes. Does it even make sense to think that there might even be a rational consensus about the force of the better argument in the current debates about abortion? Is the very idea of a "rational consensus" in such concrete conflictual contexts even intelligible? Any society must have some procedures for dealing with conflicts that cannot be resolved by argumentation—even when all parties are committed to rational argumentation. But what precisely is the determinate content (*bestimmt*) of declaring one ought to consider only the force of the better argument?

There are friends and foes of Derrida who think that he undermines and ridicules any appeal to rational argument—or that this is a consequence of his deconstructive practices. But this is a slander. It is not what he is doing when he analyzes the complex interplay of logic and rhetoric. He does *not* "reduce" all logic and argumentation to disguised rhetorical tropes.[52] Rather he is showing us just how difficult and complex it is to ferret out argumentation and rhetorical strands even in the most apparently "straightforward" and "serious" speech acts.

Habermas is certainly aware of the pervasiveness of plurality, heterogeneity, and difference. Those who think his insistence on universal validity claims means he has no understanding of contingency and plurality are caricaturing him. He even tells us the "pluralization of diverging universes of discourse belongs to specifically modern experience." There has been a "shattering of naive consensus."[53] For Habermas the primary question is how one is to *respond* to this intensified pluralization. His worry is that the celebration of plurality and difference all-too-easily degenerates into a self-defeating relativism, contextualism, and "bad" historicism. Habermas does provide an important corrective to those who uncritically celebrate contingency, plurality, difference, and otherness. There are manifestations of otherness that we *legitimately* seek to eliminate and destroy—when we are convinced the other we are confronting is evil—like the evil of apartheid and facism. One of the most obfuscating aspects of "modern/postmodern polemics" is the way in which universality is pitted against plurality and alterity. Even those who celebrate plurality and difference—like Lyotard and Rorty—make an implicit appeal to universality—when, for example, they advocate a world in which there is a *universal* "letting be" where difference is allowed to flourish.

Derrida is not guilty of some of these excesses. He is neither a relativist nor an irrationalist, but he is constantly showing us the treacheries of facile appeals to universals, principles, *archai*. Undecidability for Derrida is not indifference or a mask for nihilism, but rather a constant ethical-political reminder that "a decision can only come into being in a space that exceeds the calculable program that would destroy all responsibility . . . , [that] there can be no moral or political responsibility without this trial and this passage by way of the undecidable."[54]

Nevertheless, for all Derrida's affirmation that deconstruction intervenes, that it is a way of taking an ethical-political "position," and that it may be "too political" for some, there is a certain "abstractness" in his understanding of politics. Placing Derrida in constellation with Habermas helps to pinpoint this. Deconstruction, he tells us, "should not be separable from [the] politico-institutional problematic and should seek a new investigation of responsibility."[55] Derrida has shown, in a series of perceptive analyses ranging from Kant through Heidegger, how their discourses about the university cannot be separated from their discourses about the institutional structure of the modern university. He has developed a sharp and incisive critique of university institutions and practices. But suppose we step back and ask, what does Derrida mean by a "politico-institutional structure"? Of course, there is no univocal answer to this question. But Derrida never quite rises to the level of *necessary* generality (as he does in telling us what he means by a "text") where we can gain some perspective, some overview of the complex dynamics of institutional structures that shape politics and society in the contemporary world. We will simply *not* find in his writings anything resembling a social and political theory—as we do find in Habermas.

It is an important virtue to be vigilant—as Derrida is—about the ways in which *any* general social and political theory or code can go awry, how it can deconstruct itself. But it is just as important and necessary to seek, in a fallibilistic spirit, for a general understanding and explanation of the institutional dynamics of politics and society. Otherwise the specific ways in which we intervene "here and now" can lack any orientation. Derrida's claims about a "democracy to come" are powerfully evocative. He warns us against identifying this "democracy to come" with any of its present institutional forms. Like Habermas, he would insist that it is not the task of the philosopher or theorist—as some sort of "master" intellectual—to lay out blueprints for such a democracy. This can and should be decided by participants. But still it is fair to ask for some determinate content. We want *some* understanding of what kinds of institutions and practices should be developed for "a democracy to come." Or even more minimally, we want some orientation about what changes "here and now" are needed in our present institutional structures. Derrida, thus far, has very little to say about any of this.[56] Consequently there is a danger that, for all the evocative power of the very idea of a "democracy to come," the idea of such a democracy can become an impotent, vague abstraction.

There is another curious lacuna in Derrida's prolific writings. Earlier I indicated Derrida's deep suspicion of "boundary-fixing" and his incisiveness in exposing the precise points where boundaries and limits break down and/or recede. He has consistently maintained that philosophy itself is not a well-defined discipline or *Fach* neatly separable from other disciplines and discourses. But there is one lesson or consequence from this master strategy that he has not drawn—and this is the source of many of the sharpest differences between him and Habermas. Habermas argues that there is no fixed boundary between philosophy and the critical social sciences. There is—and ought to be—a symbiotic relationship between philosophy and the social sciences, although they are not reducible to each other. Pragmatically this means that the philosopher, especially the social and political philosopher, must be responsive and alert to what can be learned from the social disciplines. Whatever our final judgment of the ways in which Habermas uses and criticizes Weber, Durkheim, Parsons, Mead, Piaget, Kohlberg (and many other social scientists), he has consistently sought to develop a subtle dialectical interplay between philosophical speculation and social scientific theoretical-oriented empirical research. In his play, this to-and-fro movement between philosophy and the critical social sciences, he has *practiced* what one would think ought to be a consequence of Derrida's own deconstructive analyses.

Although Derrida does deal with what the French take to be the preeminent *sciences humaines*—linguistics and psychoanalysis—there are only casual references to the full range of the social disciplines. More important, Derrida's fundamental bias has been to move in one direction only—to show and expose the dubious "philosophic" presuppositions that infect the social disciplines, rather than to ask what, if anything, philosophy might learn from them. He tells us:

> To say to oneself that one is going to study something that is *not* philosophy is to deceive oneself. It is not difficult to show that in political economy, for example, there is a philosophical discourse in operation. . . . Philosophy, as logocentrism, is present in every scientific discipline and the only justification for transforming philosophy into a specialized discipline is the necessity to render explicit and thematic the philosophical subtext in every discourse. The principal function which the teaching of philosophy serves is to enable people to become "conscious," to become aware of what exactly they are saying, what kind of discourse they are engaged in when they do mathematics, physics, political economy, and so on. There is no system of teaching or transmitting knowledge which can retain its coherence or integrity without, at one moment or another, interrogating itself philosophically, that is, without acknowledging its subtextual premises; and this may even include an interrogation of unspoken political interests or traditional values.[57]

Habermas would agree with everything that is said here, but he would (rightly I think) ask: Should this not be a two-way street? Should we not also ask what philosophy can learn from critical social scientific research?

The issue here is not just metatheoretical. For it conditions the very way in which Derrida deals with social and political themes. When Derrida examines questions of justice, law, violence he does not *primarily* deal with specific institutional practices, but with the written texts, specifically the writings of those who have addressed these issues— Aristotle, Kant, Hegel, Kafka, Benjamin, Levinas, etc. I do not want to denigrate this way—this *methodus*. His analyses are extraordinarily perceptive and rich in their consequences. But surely—as Derrida himself acknowledges—they need to be *supplemented* by the theoretical and empirical study of societal institutions and practices. But this is not what Derrida does. There is nothing in Derrida's writings that seeks to rule out the importance of critical theoretical and empirical research into the structural dynamics of society and politics. On the contrary, such an endeavor is what his own questioning of boundary-fixing demands. Nevertheless, his neglect of dealing more directly and explicitly with political and societal institutions in their historical complexity does have the consequence of making his own understanding of society and politics sound rather "thin."

There are many aspects and problems in the writings of Habermas and Derrida that I have not explored here. But by now I hope the thrust of my argument is clear, and why I believe we can (and should) read them as an *allegory* of the "modern/postmodern" condition. I reiterate what I said earlier. I do not think there is a theoretical perspective from which we can reconcile their differences, their otherness to each other—nor do I think we should smooth out their "aversions and attractions." The nasty questions that they raise about each other's "project" need to be relentlessly pursued. One of the primary lessons of "modernity/postmodernity" is a radical skepticism about the possibility of a type reconciliation—an *Aufhebung*, without gaps, fissures, and ruptures. However, *together*, Habermas/Derrida provide us with a force-field that constitutes "the dynamic, transmutational structure of a complex phenomenon"—the phenomenon I have labeled "modernity/postmodernity." *Together* they form a new constellation—a "juxtaposed rather than an integrated cluster of changing elements that resist reduction to a common denominator, essential core, or generative first principle." I have spoken about Habermas/Derrida, but my primary concern here is not simply to focus on their texts—the texts that bear their signatures. The rationale for examining their texts is because, more rigorously and thoroughly than many others (including their "followers"), they *show* the tangled, intertwined strands of the "modern/postmodern" *Stimmung*. My reading of Habermas/Derrida is intended to be an allegory of this *Stimmung*. The "logic" of my allegory has been an unstable tensed both/and rather that a determinate fixed either/or. This is what I believe to be—to use an old-fashioned but not outdated expression—the *truth* of the *polemos* of "modernity/postmodernity."

13

Splitting the Difference: Habermas's Critique of Derrida

David Couzens Hoy

J ürgen Habermas and Jacques Derrida are arguably the living European philosophers who are best known to academics in the United States today. Each has a different audience, with Derrida receiving attention more from literary critics and Habermas from social theorists, for instance. This difference of audience is not merely a sociological feature, however, but it reflects the underlying philosophical differences between the two. I doubt that among those specialists who study both thinkers there are many who find both acceptable. Instead, there are "Habermasians" and "Derrideans," depending on whether their intuitions are that one or the other is wrongheaded. There is good reason for this response since each thinker represents not simply a different set of ideas, but more broadly, a different sense of what philosophy (or what is now called "theory") can be at the current stage of history. Or perhaps I should put the term "history" in scarequotes, since a crucial part of the debate is whether the idea of history can be taken seriously any longer.

But obviously "theory" must be put in scarequotes as well. Part of the debate is whether there can be "theory" that somehow transcends the phenomenon of historical change by stating conditions that are universal and therefore unhistorical. Another part of the debate is whether there is any such thing as "history," given that the unity required to tell a single story about complex events may merely be a fiction imagined by the historian. My own activity in this paper will be to take Habermas's critique of Derrida as a chapter in the history of late twentieth-century philosophy. Admittedly, then, my activity may seem to beg the question of history versus theory by assuming both that an understanding of history is indispensable to the formation of theory, and that the formation of theory ought to reflect on the history of its formation. Since I do think that history and theory are interdependent, and that Habermas's and Derrida's positions strike some critics as disconnecting history and theory, my own standpoint is neither Habermasian nor Derridean. I am therefore not begging the question in a fallacious way but am constructing a philosophical opposition for the further purpose of going beyond it.

I will therefore point out in advance that taking the Habermas/ Derrida debate as a chapter that is already part of a history, and therefore in the recent past, conflicts with another message of this paper, which is that the debate is really part of the present and will be constitutive of what philosophy becomes, especially since both thinkers are still alive and evolving. Any "history" I sketch will therefore be in the future perfect tense, projecting how things will have been. Writing the Habermas/Derrida debate as a chapter in the history of twentieth-century philosophy before rather than after the fact is a deliberate way of avoiding Habermas's emplotment, and especially its implication that we must take one side or the other. The point of constructing a fictional history in the future perfect tense is to suggest that the opposition is itself fictional. There may be other alternatives, and these alternatives may involve splitting the difference between the two. "Splitting the difference" is not the same, however, as synthesizing the two or of finding some third position between them.[1] Instead, it identifies philosophical possibilities that are left open instead of being closed off by two theoretical positions construing themselves as mutually exclusive.

Modernity vs. Postmodernity?

To write this history of the present I cannot avoid invoking two problematic terms, "modern" and "postmodern." I have doubts about the usefulness of these labels, but they feature in Habermas's book, *The Philosophical Discourse of Modernity*. These labels are more historical than theoretical, but they provide the general frame within which Habermas's particular criticisms are placed. I shall therefore question this historical frame in this section and leave the details of the theoretical arguments for the next section. Habermas sets himself as a modern and casts Derrida as a postmodern. The postmodern line begins with Nietzsche, who "renounces a renewed revision of the concept of reason and *bids farewell* to the dialectic of enlightenment."[2] As a defender of modernity Habermas stands in the tradition of philosophy from Descartes to Kant, but of course he cannot be modern in the same sense that they are. Habermas acknowledges that the modern philosophy of consciousness has reached a state of exhaustion by the nineteenth century, and the task ever since has been to find ways around this exhaustion.[3] Habermas's stance is later than the modern one, for it recognizes the failure of the modern philosophers to ground the possibility of knowledge in the self-certainty of subjectivity. The modern philosophers privilege subjectivity as the paradigm of philosophical efforts to discover the foundations of knowledge. Habermas claims to have moved beyond the philosophy of subjectivity into the philosophy of language. Doing so also means that he is not a foundationalist as the modern philosophers were. Instead, he thinks that philosophy must recognize that its claims are fallible instead of absolute. Having substituted language for the moderns' philosophy of the subject, and rejected their absolutism and foundationalism for empirical fallibilism means that in central ways he comes later than modernity. So it is tempting to think of Habermas himself as a postmodern. Yet, supposedly unlike the neo-Nietzschean French postmoderns, he has not abandoned modern philosophy's goal of formulating and defending rationality and universality. I would therefore characterize him as a *late* modern. But I wish to stress that both "late" and "post" suggest "after," and thus the contrast is not between modernity and postmodernity, but between a late-modern and a postmodern sense of what to do next, given that in central ways modern philosophy has reached a state of exhaustion, and not just recently.

These terms are more historical than theoretical, and are difficult to use precisely. As a result Habermas's account would be easy to deconstruct, if a Derridean wanted to turn the tables on Habermas's critique. Habermas characterizes Derrida as a postmodern, because Habermas sees Derrida abandoning modern philosophy's ambitions to be universal and thus to assure itself of its own rationality. But at the same time Habermas's message is that there is no successful postmodern stance and further that such a stance would be impossible anyway. So Derrida's theory is postmodern (says Habermas as historian of the present), and yet there really cannot be any postmodern theory (says Habermas as a theorist). Habermas then explains Derrida's motivation by suggesting that the postmodern effort to overcome modern enlightenment disguises a desire to return to a premodern anti-Enlightenment tradition. In Derrida's case the tradition influencing his thought is said to be Jewish mysticism.

The Derridean could object to this apparently ad hominem line of argument that explains and attacks Derrida's text by appeal to biographical features of Derrida's personal history. To the Derridean Habermas's reasoning would resemble the "kettle logic" that Derrida notices in Freud's account of the logic of dreams:

> In his attempt to arrange everything in his favor, the defendant piles up contradictory arguments: 1. The kettle I am returning to you is brand new; 2. The holes were already in it when you lent it to me; 3. You never lent me a kettle, anyway.[4]

Analogously, Habermas's argument seems to be: (1) Postmodernism represents a radical break with the history of modern rationalism; (2) To break with rationality and universality is impossible and philosophy without the aspirations of modernity would be unrecognizable, so Derrida is incoherent to the point of unintelligibility; and (3) Derrida is not doing anything new, anyway, since his moves are already familiar ones recognizable and intelligible from the tradition of Jewish mysticism, which is out-of-date because it is premodern.

In response to this attempt to deconstruct Habermas's critique of Derrida, a Habermasian could say that his argument is misinterpreted. Habermas's text is unfortunately vague about exactly what sort of explanation of Derrida's theory is being offered when Habermas writes that Derrida's stance "may have something to do with the fact that Derrida, all denials notwithstanding, remains close to Jewish mysticism."[5] The Habermasian could insist that Habermas is using the method of *Ideologiekritik*, adapted from the Critical Theory of the Frankfurt School. Habermas's argument is not ad hominem, appearances to the contrary, but depends on the difference between the *desire* to create a postmodern theory, and the success in doing so. If the desire fails and is frustrated, the critical theorist can give an account of the difference between what the desire seems to be on the surface, and what it really represents, given its failure and frustration. Thus, Habermas's analysis is that Derrida is attempting to break with modernity, and his desire is to be postmodern. But Derrida is unsuccessful in doing so, and his attempt at postmodernism is a failure. Derrida's desire to transcend the aspirations of modern reason is in reality a frustrated desire for a return to the premodern traditions where reason has not yet undermined the mystery of hidden religious authority. Since the quarrel is between the Enlightenment's faith in reason and the counter-Enlightenment rebellion against reason, what Habermas is objecting to is the vestige of Jewish mysticism (not because it is Jewish, of course, but because it is mystical to the point of being not only mysterious but also unintelligible).

A central point of this defense is that Habermas's goal is not simply to show that Derrida's theory is incoherent. Critical Theory differs from traditional theory in that the goal of the former is not simply to destroy a theory by showing its incoherence, but to *explain* how the adherents to the theory could have failed to perceive their own incoherence. This explanation depends on identifying how their real desires or interests were different from what the adherents thought they were. The explanation would also presumably be one that the adherents themselves could accept once their desires were unmasked.

So the conflict in theory today is also a conflict of methods. Textual deconstruction is one method, but the Critical Theory of the later Frankfurt School is another. Both claim to show what is really going on in a theoretical text, but the latter posits an extratextual reality (e.g., social conflict, real interests, frustrated desires, basic needs) as an explanation for the blindness of the text or the theory to its own inadequacy and inconsistencies.[6]

So Habermas's analysis of Derrida is not simply a form of kettle logic but can be properly understood only as the methodological consequence of the tradition of Critical Theory. With that much said in Habermas's favor, however, where I would also agree with my hypothetical deconstructivist defender of Derrida is that Habermas's use of the term "postmodern" does set the scene in his favor from the start. Derrida, as far as I know, does not see himself as a postmodern, so applying the label to him seems simply to use a term of abuse.[7] I would therefore like to offer a different model of what postmodernity might mean. This model is intended to be neutral, and thus "postmodern" will be a term neither of abuse nor of approbation. I adapt this account from Foucault (who is neutral in the exchange between Habermas and Derrida, although Habermas considers him to be a postmodern as well), but I hasten to point out that Foucault also does not claim to be a postmodern. (The label is explicitly adopted mainly by J.-F. Lyotard.)[8]

The fundamental drive of modernity, on Foucault's analysis, is to think the unthought. In particular, modern philosophy is obsessed with the question not of what sorts of beings can be known, but how knowledge itself is possible. So the unthought that modern philosophy tries to think is thought itself. This self-refectivity produces antinomies, which force successive modern theorists to redefine what about thought has been left unthought by their predecessors. While Foucault spells out these antinomies (or "doubles") at great length (in *The Order of Things*), I do not want to follow his exposition further, but will ask instead how we might construe postmodern thinking, given this characterization of modern thought.

Foucault himself seems to be beyond the modern thinking that he is describing, yet he too seems to be trying to think the unthought. Sometimes postmoderns are criticized for trying to think the unthinkable. If this is what they are doing, then Habermas is correct in rejecting their project as impossible. (Even to try to think the unthinkable is impossible, since one could not try to do what one knew one could not do, such as finding the last value of π.) Since this definition rules out postmodernity from the start, however, a more sympathetic approach is to see the postmoderns as continuing the modern project of thinking the unthought, but changing the enterprise such that the unthought is no longer some noumenal entity or an inexperienceable transcendental ego, but something more on the surface of things, and thus not in principle inaccessible. Nevertheless, the postmoderns do not share the desire of the moderns to make the unthought completely accessible.

For the postmoderns the mistake of earlier moderns lies not so much in their efforts to think the unthought, but in the moderns' belief that they could think the unthought completely. Moderns aim at *transparency* in a strong sense because they aim to attain self-transparency. In a weak sense transparency is the generally acceptable idea that how knowledge works or how ethical practices work should not be misunderstood by knowers or by moral agents. Enlightenment rationalism leads to the much stronger sense of transparency whereby we do not understand ourselves or our epistemological, moral, and social practices unless we can identify and state systematically the rules, principles, or beliefs that make them possible.[9] The postmoderns continue to try to think what has remained unthought, but they abandon the idea that the unthought can be made completely transparent. The difference, then, between moderns and postmoderns will not be in what they are doing so much as in their attitude toward what they are doing. Let me propose six features that typify the postmodern attitude.

(1) The first feature of the postmodern outlook is that it accepts rather than laments the inevitable inability to make completely manifest the unthought or unsaid. Moderns assume that a great unthought runs

throughout the world in all its forms and events, and we cannot claim really to understand anything about the world until we understand this unthought. For postmoderns, however, thinking can never be complete and self-transparent, but always generates further complexity and complications. Their acceptance of this point is not simply a nihilistic resignation to it, but because of the further features, it is a positive and liberating action.

(2) Postmoderns therefore do not give up trying to think the unthought altogether. The second feature thus concerns how they continue to try to think the unthought. They need not become idealists and deny the reality of what has been left unthought but still seems to be governing thought. They can accept that the kinds of unthought that they are trying to get at are real or genuinely operative, without believing that they can capture them in a theory that would make them completely transparent. The unthought might include background conditions and a general style of organization of a way of thinking, and thus will not be theorizable in the same way that particular objects, contents, or ideas are. (Thus, Foucault does not claim to have a "theory" of power, which is the unthought he pursues in some of his writings, and, as I will argue, Derrida also does not have a *theory* of writing, of the "trace," or of *différance*, the latter being neither a word nor a concept.)

These differences in how the unthought is to be approached lead to three further corollaries that explain the postmodern conception of what the unthought is like: (3) there is no single, privileged or uniquely paradigmatic way to think the unthought; (4) there is not a single, unique, "master" unthought running through every phenomenon; and (5) no unthought is itself a single thing (that is, capable of only one correct description or of one level of analysis). In short, postmoderns are pluralists, and can find more than one unthought to talk about. Foucault moves from analyzing discourse as the unthought, to power, to sexual self-fashioning. Derrida similarly addresses a different unthought with each text he analyzes (such as trace, supplement, graft, or parergon).[10] The postmoderns' pluralism contrasts with the drive of a late modern like Habermas to find in a single phenomenon—communicative competence—the unique a priori structure from which to derive the universal rationality to which the modern tradition aspires.

The final feature follows from these, and captures the difference in attitude between the late modern and the postmodern. The late modern thinks that the Enlightenment ideal of progress through the advance of reason cannot really be abandoned. The late modern will interpret the postmoderns' lack of belief in progress as a despair suggesting nostalgia

for a premodern age of innocence. But I interpret the postmodern attitude differently, and the final feature I suggest is, (6) that the
postmoderns realize that nostalgia only makes sense in contrast to the
hope for progress, so that truly abandoning this hope also leads them
beyond nostalgia. Thinkers like Heidegger and perhaps Adorno do seem
nostalgic in this sense, and thus do not strike me as genuine postmoderns
(despite Habermas's tendency to group them with Nietzsche, Foucault,
and Derrida). Like postmodern architecture, postmodern thought is
best understood not as nostalgic exhaustion, but as a more forward-
looking cheerfulness that manages to recombine and play with the elements of modernity in unanticipated ways.

One sign of a lack of nostalgia is a lack of interest in philosophical
self-legitimation. Of course, Foucault and Derrida do not want their
views and methods to be internally inconsistent. But they are not seeking
the foundations of thought so much as alternative methods for thinking
about and interpreting texts (and other worldly phenomena, such as
ourselves). I do not see either Derrida's strategy of dissemination or Foucault's genealogy as claiming to be the only correct method of interpretation. Methods are not "true" or "false," but only more or less useful,
and thus the main legitimation of a method of interpretation is its heuris-
tic value.

This lack of concern for self-legitimation may make postmoderns
seem playful even to the point of being unserious and irresponsible, especially about their own enterprises.[11] However that may be in particular
cases, I would suggest that it would be contradictory for them to be so
concerned with self-legitimation as to attack late modernism and to defend postmodernism as the only viable attitude in the present context.
Lyotard perhaps falls into a trap insofar as he does explicitly avow the
label of postmodernism, and defends it. However, if the postmodern attitude is as I have described it, then the postmodern would be inconsistent in thinking that postmodernism is the most advanced, most rational,
or in general, the only possible attitude. If there is no necessary progress
in history, the postmodern cannot claim a normative advantage in being
later in time or a sign of the future. Such a normative advantage is implied in the notion of "modernity," and is still assumed by the late modern. But the postmodern seems to have abandoned the idea that the
present is necessarily better than the past, as well as any nostalgia for the
past. So the postmodern should not claim to be better or more advanced
or more clever than the late modern, and has no argument that the late
modern should become a postmodern. Since the true postmodern could
not be an advocate of postmodernism, I think that the label is not really a

useful one. If there are genuine issues separating Habermas and Derrida, these issues can only be obscured by thinking that in resolving them we must be partisans of either modernity or postmodernity.

Deconstruction: Theory or Method?

I suggest, therefore, that the historical label of postmodernity is *not* the crux. Habermas may have been using the modern/postmodern contrast only as a convenient fiction, but when pressed, the device threatens to become counterproductive. Furthermore, the idea of progress is itself a red herring. If the postmoderns are accused of abandoning rationality because they do not believe that we are better off now than human beings were in the past, it should be noted that the postmoderns need not claim that there are *no* respects in which people are now better off. They need only affirm that in some particular respects (including crucial ones about which people often deceive themselves) people are not better off. So to the question whether the world never gets better, they can answer reasonably: never entirely.

To the further question whether history *as a whole* can be said to be necessarily progressive, their answer is that there is no possible standpoint from which this judgment can be made. So they are not denying the rationality and progressiveness of history as a whole so much as questioning whether the belief in the growth of reason makes sense, or has any content. On this point, even Habermas recognizes that progress can be spoken of only in some subsystem or other, and that there is no point to speaking of the progress of the whole of history. So the issue is not whether there is progress, but is instead to locate where the belief in progress in some areas of social life might be covering up insidious oppression in other areas.

Given this problem, there is a genuine question whether Derrida's method of dissemination or deconstruction can help. Habermas is not alone in arguing that Derrida's approach has not been and cannot be applied to such a concrete issue. Foucault also accuses Derrida of being overly preoccupied with texts and ignoring their social context. Foucault suspects that Derrida's method tacitly claims authority for itself as a result of the authority and primacy it grants to the text. Furthermore, Foucault believes that a text is not autonomous from the social practices to which it is tied both in its own time and in the time of its later interpretation. Foucault suggests that deconstruction is blind not only to the ways in which the text reflects social practices, but also to the extent to which deconstruction is itself a social practice.

I think that what may be troubling Foucault is that deconstruction may appear to have the status of being a philosophy, because it claims universal applicability. There is no form of text, no genre of discourse, nothing that can be said, thought, or done that escapes its purview. Yet this appearance of universality may be the result of its inability to apply itself to itself, even if only because it refuses to make any theoretical assertions. Unlike Foucault's own willingness to avow that his histories are the product of the needs of the moment, and therefore not objective or neutral studies (although Habermas thinks that they do aspire to such neutrality), Derrida's deconstructions take place as if in a vacuum, showing what could have been seen earlier and what will presumably have to be seen from now on. This vacuum probably seemed particularly apparent to Foucault and Habermas by the refusal (until more recently) to reflect on the social and political implications of the deconstructive method.

Habermas too thinks that Derrida's theory still looks like *Ursprungsphilosophie,* the search for what is really primary.[12] He finds this dimension particularly in Derrida's claims about arche-writing. More strongly than Foucault, Habermas accuses Derrida of being like Heidegger in maintaining that politics and history are merely ontic, everyday matters that can be ignored in favor of the more important ontological investigations. Unlike Heidegger, however, Habermas thinks that Derrida's practice is subversive and anarchistic, with no redeeming theory but simply a desire to blow up and trash tradition and continuity.[13] As Derrida says about *différance,*

> It governs nothing, reigns over nothing, nowhere exercises any authority. It is not announced by any capital letter. Not only is there no kingdom of *différance,* but *différance* instigates the subversion of every kingdom.[14]

But although Derrida denies claiming any authority, philosophical or otherwise, for *différance,* Habermas thinks that Derrida is suggesting that *différance* is really the primary feature of language. So Habermas believes that there is an appeal to authority after all, if not to the authority of Holy Scripture (expressing the direct voice of God, and thus phonocentric, onto-theology), then to that of an exiled Scripture (the Torah). Habermas thinks that the "a" in *différance* is to be understood as a mystical symbol, like the *aleph* with which the first commandment in the Hebrew text begins, and which is the only part of the commandments that the Hebrew people were supposed to have really heard, such that everything else is a matter of interpretation.

Habermas presses this point to show that Derrida fails in his attempt to take the linguistic turn and falls back into the paradoxes of philosophies relying on subjectivity.[15] Derrida's linguistic turn supposedly relapses into mysticism despite Derrida's intention of taking the linguistic turn precisely to avoid not only the later Heidegger's *Seins*-mysticism but also the earlier detour through *Sein und Zeit* that replaces subjectivity with *Daseins*-analysis. The philosophical issue separating them is Habermas's charge that Derrida's aesthetic contextualism ignores how the idealization procedures built into the communicative action of everyday practices require us to redeem and prove the validity of our claims. In seeming to deny that validity claims can be redeemed or proved, Derrida's view is blind to the social learning processes through which we change and improve our understanding of ourselves and our world. Because of this blindness, deconstruction implies that we are stuck in our context, and caught fatalistically in the forces of textual production. We are doomed to provincialism by the overpowering background of the arche-writing.[16] Derrida's Heideggerian privileging of the ontological over the ontic is seen by Habermas in the way Derrida denies or at least overlooks the point that judgments and experience require criticizable validity claims. Derrida focuses too much on the (ontological) question of whether texts can disclose the world, and forgets the (ontic) dimension of texts as solving problems and aiming at hermeneutical consensus (*Einverständnis*).

There are thus two basic charges against Derrida by Habermas. First, Derrida's linguistic turn is still a form of *Ursprungsphilosophie*, one that seeks the safety of pure theory. Second, Derrida's Heideggerian preference for the ontological over the ontic, philosophy over politics, is still a nostalgic desire to return to an archaic premodernism. Let me now discuss the first charge, leaving the second charge for the concluding section.

I agree that there is a tone in Derrida's earlier writings that does invite Habermas's first charge. Habermas's interpretation may thus be a possible one, but not the most favorable one, or the one that makes the best sense of many other elements in Derrida's text. Given my strategy of splitting the difference between Habermas and Derrida, I will offer a moderate hermeneutic reading of Derrida that is less radical than Habermas's, but also less radical than that of some Derrideans. A hermeneutical defender of Derrida has the option of showing that Derrida is not directly asserting philosophical claims, but alluding to them indirectly because he knows how problematic they are. Derrida may not even be offering a "theory," at least in the strong sense of theory that Habermas has in mind when he constructs his own theory of universal pragmatics as the best explanation of human communication. In the strong sense of "theory" that we inherit from the time since Galileo, a theory should have concepts, principles, and arguments based on evidence, and it should organize all the relevant phenomena in a single explanatory system. Deconstruction is not itself "theory" in this sense, but is more the general operating of resisting efforts at such theorization.

If deconstruction is not a theory, the term *différance* should not be taken as the essence or *origin* of language, as Habermas interprets it by seeing Derrida as falling back into the dream of *Ursprungsphilosophie.* Deconstruction is neither foundationalist nor antifoundationalist, Derrida asserts, since it should not be construed as a grounding or even as raising the question of grounds. Derrida therefore denies that *différance* is a master word or arche-synthesis that gathers everything into one word.[17] Habermas's interpretation does not take seriously claims in Derrida's essay, "Différance," that are intended to dispel the illusion of *Ursprungsphilosophie.* Derrida uses the image of a bottomless chess board to suggest that his remarks about trace and *différance* are not an attempt to ground writing or language. Neither a word nor a concept, *différance* is said not to be a name at all, let alone a substitute for a lost origin, for which Heidegger's master-name was "Being":

> What we know, or what we would know if it were simply a
> question here of something to know, is that there has never
> been, never will be a unique word, a master-name. . . . There
> will be no unique name, even if it were the name of Being. And
> we must think this without *nostalgia.*[18]

Habermas reads nostalgia back into Derrida's enterprise by dismissing these qualifications and seeing Derrida as pointing to the origins of language, when Derrida's point is instead to destabilize both the notion of an origin of language in this sense, as well as the enterprise of capturing that origin in a "theory" or "philosophy" of language.

Derrida is thus not well-served either by friends or by critics who read him as if he were attempting to offer a new theory of language, or as attempting to invent the traditional philosophical distinction between logic and rhetoric. This distinction between logic and rhetoric leads to the distinction between philosophy and literature, which Habermas defends in the face of attacks on that distinction by literary critics like Jonathan Culler. I think Habermas is right that there are some differences between philosophy and literature, but I think Derrideans could agree that these are differences *in degree*. Habermas maintains more strongly, I believe, that there is a difference *in kind* both between philosophy and literature and between logic and rhetoric. Here again I do not think that Derrida is best defended by interpreting him as collapsing entirely the difference between these terms. Instead, he can be interpreted as suggesting that the question whether there is a difference *in kind* is not answerable, or even fully intelligible. He can be *agnostic* about this question because his aim is to show that the traditional distinction between these terms is not simply a neutral distinction but a value-laden hierarchy. This hierarchy informs the philosophical tradition, where logic effaces rhetoric and philosophy asserts itself as the domain in which the relation between itself and literature is to be determined.

In challenging this distinction in kind, Derrida may give the impression that he rejects philosophy, truth, logic, and reason altogether, and turns everything into rhetoric. However, his style is designed to "show" the paradoxes following from any attempt to "say" these things. Contrary to Habermas's reading, then, Derrida does not deny truth, reason, or the seriousness of philosophical discourse. He knows he cannot deny that there is truth (or what Habermas would call validity claims), and he says of his enterprise,

> Finally, it goes without saying that in no case is it a question of
> a *discourse against truth* or against science. (This is impossible
> and absurd, as is every heated accusation on this subject.) . . . I
> repeat, then, leaving all their disseminating powers to the
> proposition and the form of the verb: *we must have [il faut]
> truth.*[19]

I interpret his nuanced view as suggesting that truth is a trivial notion, in that there are many statements that are true (e.g., "the grass is green," "the sky is blue," etc.). The question is why some statements are taken to be not only true, but more significant than others. Truths only ever appear in a context of interpretation, and interpretations select subsets of truths. Derrida therefore can question cogently whether any interpretation can claim to have captured "the truth" of a given text or author, where "the truth" means the single correct way in which to see all the things that are true.[20]

Similarly, Derrida denies being an enemy of reason. He may want to challenge the rationality of many established conceptual distinctions or institutional practices. The task of criticism involves a double gesture of formulating rationally questions about the limits of rational endeavors. Derrida explicitly acknowledges that his own efforts conform to the principle of reason, and he does not recommend that others who would share in these efforts try to contest reason: "Those who venture along this path, it seems to me, need not set themselves up in opposition to the principle of reason, nor need they give way to 'irrationalism.' "[21] Since philosophy has always been the "place" where reason must be respected, Derrida recognizes that his own discourse is subject to the constraints and rigors of philosophical (as opposed to those of "literary") expression. Early in his career he opposed the interpretation of deconstruction as advocating the death of philosophy.[22] More recently, he has acknowledged that his own discourse is institutionally framed by the philosophical profession. Although he wants to reflect critically on the institution of philosophy, he also admits (with a playful paraphrase on his famous earlier and controversial claim that "il n'y a pas de hors-texte") that "il n'ya pas de hors-philosophie."[23]

Can Derrida be interpreted as doing philosophy at the same time that he is denying that he is doing "theory"? Could the Habermasian urge that if Derrida is a philosopher, then he must tell us what the theoretical standpoint is from which he generates his deconstructive critique? Habermas formulates a theory of communicative action called universal pragmatics as a standpoint from which to do social theory and to generate social criticism. He thus sees Derrida's grammatology as a rival effort to do the same thing. For Habermas, only a theory can provide the conceptual clarity needed to explain and criticize. History, for instance, will not suffice, since from its standpoint developments are only ever contingent. On his view, only theory (for instance, a theory of cognitive or moral or social development, in the manner of Piaget or Kohlberg) gives us the principles to say why a particular stage represents an advance toward a more mature and reasonable position in comparison to previous stages. Theory thus tells us that developments are rational successes if there is a learning-process that results from solving problems.[24]

Habermas thinks that Derrida does not see that philosophy can recognize the problem-solving capacity of theory, and that as a result Derrida falls back into an older conception of philosophical theory as world-disclosing. He sees Derrida as holistically trying to get a global picture of how everything hangs together with everything else, and thus sharing in Heidegger's preference for the ontological over the ontic, philosophy over science, the speculative and poetic over the empirical and practical, world-disclosure over problem-solving.

A Derridean could try to turn the tables on Habermas by suggesting that a good deconstruction is a form of problem-solving, since it shows that a text has more than one side, and that problems in reading the text are best explained by the deconstructive exposure of its tensions. However, to say this would be to buy into Habermas's model. Another strategy would be to ask why problem-solving would be preferred to world-disclosure anyway. Even though this response suggests a different preference from Habermas's, it still accepts Habermas's distinction.

The best defense would therefore be for the Derridean to urge that Derrida is not taking the side of world-disclosure against problem-solving, but is challenging the distinction and splitting the difference. This separation, as that between history and theory, ignores the phenomenon of theory-formation by concentrating exclusively on the phenomenon of theory-verification. Habermas's emphasis on problem-solving draws on a narrow, late-empiricist conception of scientific method, whereas Derrida thinks of theory differently. Any observation, whether of physical events, historical actions, or textual features, will be theory-laden, but theory itself is conditioned by background assumptions and practices that are never completely articulated.

So again, Derrida's relation to "theory" is a double one (which is why the quotation marks around the word are necessary). On the one hand, deconstruction resists "theory" in the strong sense by constantly trying to destabilize it, and show it what lies outside its parameters. On the other hand, Derrida is not opposed to theory in a less strong sense (that therefore need not be put in quotes). Theory in this weaker sense should welcome deconstruction's efforts since theory must always remain open to what it has left unexplored, in the hope that it will confirm itself by explaining these further features, but always recognizing the possibility of being disconfirmed. Contrary to Habermas, Derrida believes, however, that what legitimates theory is not problem-solving. The phenomenon of theory change suggests that while from the inside a theory may seem to be viably solving problems, from the outside it may have stagnated and even degenerated. Derrida thinks that what legitimates theory is instead its ability to open a space, which should include opening up a multiplicity of problematics more than (as on Habermas's model) the elimination of particular problems.

The strategy of splitting the difference leads to the conclusion, then, that Habermas's distinction between world-disclosure and problem-solving is not an adequate "theory of theory," and does not capture either the complexity of theory-formation or Derrida's conception of deconstruction. Derrida's conception of theory as opening possibilities is as rich as world-disclosure (without being holistic in a Hegelian manner) and as determinate as problem-solving (without falling into verificationist difficulties).

Is deconstruction a theory, then? Or is it a method? The answer depends on which theory of theory gives sense to the word. Deconstruction is best construed, I believe, by suggesting that theories must always be on their guard against themselves, since they may close themselves off from possibilities to which they should be open. But Derrida insists that deconstruction is not a method. I believe he means that it is not a set of rules, like those postulated for the so-called "scientific method," to be applied algorithmically to every text. So again, I split the difference between the opposition, theory or method, by suggesting that deconstruction is an interpretive strategy or operation that can be performed on any particular "theory." The deconstructive operation puts the quotation marks around the theory in question by suspending the application of the theory and interrogating it instead.

If deconstruction is a strategy of interpretation instead of either a universal theory or an algorithmic method, can it always be applied successfully? Here I would think that the best answer is to admit that to claim universal applicability is to make a theoretical assertion, which deconstruction is not capable of if it is not a "theory" in the strong sense. If Habermasians object that Derrida does claim universality for deconstruction in asserting that *différance* can be found in all metaphysical texts, an appropriate response is to point out that deconstruction is not thereby claiming to be able to dissolve all texts, for instance, nonmetaphysical ones. Radical deconstructionists might believe that all texts are metaphysical, but I do not know how they could argue that. What I suspect is that texts that did not have some vestiges of metaphysics would not be of much interest either to Derrideans or to Habermasians. Hence, what both groups are doing can be described as "philosophy," whether they agree on what the term means or not.

Deconstruction: Philosophy or Politics?

More topical right now than the first general criticism raised by Habermas's reading of Derrida is the second one: Can deconstruction be used constructively in social and political contexts? Habermas believes that Derrida is like Heidegger in preferring the realm of pure philosophy to that of politics, except that unlike Heidegger's fascistic allegiance to authority, Derrida's stance is anarchistic. As in the contrasts of history versus theory, modernity versus postmodernity, and theory versus method, bifurcations between which I have tried to split the difference, Habermas's polemical opposition between philosophy and politics may be more of a problem than a solution. While I agree that the relation of deconstruction to social and political critique needs to be clarified, I think that its critical potential should not be underestimated. To make sure that the issue is presented fairly, let me first state what I take to be Habermas's legitimate worry, and then see whether more recent texts by Derrida than Habermas could have considered help dispel these worries.

Habermas and Foucault both allege that Derrida has not paid enough attention to the social practices that surround textuality. I would express their worry as follows. The practice of deconstruction appears to be subversive. But in reality it offers nothing to replace that which it destroys, and it suggests that nothing could serve as a replacement that could not be deconstructed and subvened in turn. At the same time, the deconstructionist's admission that we cannot think in any other terms than those metaphysically-laden ones being deconstructed, that we cannot get beyond metaphysics, seems to leave thought in the same situation, and not to change anything. So deconstruction is not even subversion, since subversion implies a desire to change, and deconstruction demurs from thinking about how things could be different, let alone better. (Foucault thinks that things will be different once genealogy reveals the arbitrariness of our present beliefs and norms, although he refuses to say that "different" necessarily means "better." Paradoxically enough, deconstruction seems to deny us the hope even for significant change or difference.)

To consider this charge I will take as an example of political deconstruction Derrida's remarks on the American Declaration of Independence.[25] Contrary to the way he is often interpreted, Derrida's deconstruction of this text is not a form of ideology criticism, or of finding substantive contradictions in texts or between texts and practices. He does not assert, for instance, that the Declaration of Independence is an indispensable hypocrisy, as the Frankfurt School might have. Instead, he is investigating the status of "declaration" as a linguistic act. He finds that it falls somewhere between a constative and a performative act. This act of declaration is neither a single act in itself, nor a third kind of act different from these other two, but is instead the undecidable play back and forth between these two kinds of act. This undecidability is not something philosophy should take as a challenge to resolve by deciding. Instead, Derrida is suggesting that we know (even if only implicitly) about the paradox of what declaration is, and that declaration as a linguistic act depends on this undecidability for its effect.

His larger point is that the act of declaring independence is an instance of a more general phenomenon of "founding" or "instituting." Some of his recent essays investigate institutions, especially academic ones, such as the university, or philosophy itself. "Institution" has a double sense, much like *différance*, which means both different and temporally deferred. Similarly, "institution" means on the one hand, the existing social edifice or structure, and on the other hand, the coming into being of that structure. The reason he chooses academic institutions is partly because he believes that deconstruction does have a political application in that it can bring out how in any text, discourse, seminar, or argument some conception of institution is at work.[26] This claim must be true about acts of deconstruction themselves, hence Derrida's own focus particularly on academic institutions. But Derrida does not believe that foundings are purely rational acts. The structure of *différance* is echoed in that the founding of a university is not an academic event (but presumably, a social event), and the founding of a state is not a legal event (at least, not in the same sense that the laws are legal once the state is founded). Derrida's point comes to more, therefore, than saying that acts of declaration or founding or originating are at once both constative and performative. He believes that more is involved than "speech acts" in the narrow, technical sense. Deconstruction is the enterprise of revealing the lack of clear boundaries between terms like "constative" and "performative," as well as the indeterminacy that lies at the beginnings of efforts to mark out the determinate boundaries of different kinds of texts and institutional discourses.

More problematically, however, he also states that the origin of the principle of reason is not in itself rational. I assume that he is not attacking the principle of reason (given his statement that I cited earlier), but what "origin" and "rational" mean is not clear. Insofar as he is engaged in a general critique of Enlightenment thinkers like Kant, he is probably urging that the founding cannot be "rational" in the sense of a purely cognitive and self-transparent act. Derrida is presumably agreeing with Kantians (like Habermas) that in any discursive act what is implied is an ideal conception of the conditions under which that discursive act should take place successfully. Against Kantians, however, Derrida thinks that there is more going on than constating what is true. He is not denying the constative element, but he thinks that other elements, such as the performative features, ought not to be ignored. Insofar as the discourse presupposes an institutional framework, and institutions have as much to do with power as with knowledge, Kantians are wrong to exclude power and authority in favor of ideal models of coercion-free truth.

Here is, I believe, the crux of the conflict between Habermas and Derrida. Habermas is not objecting to deconstruction because it is subversive. Habermas thinks that philosophy will always be subversive. In addition to philosophy's role of explaining the theoretical basis of science, morality, and law, Habermas believes that it "maintains just as intimate a relationship with the totality of the lifeworld and with sound common sense, even if in a subversive way it relentlessly shakes up the certainties of everyday practice."[27] Philosophical reflection must be able to show the irrationality of some practices, but it must also be able to see that others are rational. Habermas thinks that his own model of communicative interaction as attempting to reach understanding and consensus supplies a model for seeing the rationality as well as the irrationality of social practices, but he fails to find any basis for making this same discrimination from deconstructivist premises.

With this model Habermas thinks he can see the rationality of the separation of the domains of science, morality, and art from one another. He thinks that Kant was correct to argue for the differentiation of these spheres from one another, and he sees the deconstructivist attack on the separation of philosophy and literature as the beginnings of an attack on this Kantian separation of questions of truth, value, and taste. This rationalized differentiation is worthy of being preserved, according to Habermas. Derrida's analysis of foundings finds indeterminacy at the beginnings of such differentiation, and thus suggests that whatever the benefits of such differentiation, one cannot say that such differentiation is rational and therefore a necessary learning process, but only that it is contingent.

Habermas resists the suggestion of indeterminacy and contingency. He believes, for instance, that the deconstructionist claim that the same text can be open to different readings forgets that identical ascriptions of meaning must be possible for readers to talk to one another about the same text. Some readings must be right and others wrong, and "wrong interpretations must be in principle criticizable in terms of consensus to be aimed for ideally."[28] Consensus in the present is not enough, because our understanding of our reasons is never transparent, given the tacit background that conditions our utterances. Only the ide-alizations implied in communication, including what Habermas has called the ideal of arriving at consensus in a coercion-free speech situa-tion, will enable us to say that what looks *historically* like exhaustion is in reality (that is, according to the correct *theory*) "*deficient* solutions to problems and *invalid* answers."[29]

Several lines of rebuttal are open to Derrida here. First, on the point about identical ascriptions of meaning, I think that Derrida could ask Habermas for an argument for this claim that disagreement is possi-ble only when the words are understood in the same way by the parties to the dispute. This claim seems false about some disputes in which the op-ponents disagree about how to interpret a certain phenomenon because they contest the meaning of the central terms involved. There may be essentially-contested concepts on which consensus should not be ex-pected, but about which there could be genuine debate. For instance, as Ronald Dworkin has argued in *Law's Empire*,[30] to have genuine disagree-ments about how to interpret the law, differing lawyers do not need to use the same criteria for employing the term "law." Their disagreements are often theoretical, and what "law" means is precisely what leads to their differing interpretations, just as disagreement about whether to count a photograph as art may depend on different construals of what art is (and whether "art" can include the genre of photography). Simi-larly, in *Power: A Radical View*,[31] Steven Lukes argues that social theorists who disagree about whether a particular social power configuration has been analyzed properly disagree precisely because they understand power differently.

Second, even if meanings did have to be ascribed identically for genuine disagreement to be possible, Derrida could still ask Habermas whether the postulation of an ideal consensus follows. Why does Habermas draw such a strong conclusion about ideal consensus? My guess is that, in short, he is committed to the rationalistic transparency aimed at by "traditional theory," when Derrida is not. Third, the post-structuralists could ask whether Habermas's search for a guarantee that the paradigm of Enlightenment is not exhausted is not itself a sign of exhaustion. Postmoderns may be simply those who can live without such a guarantee. Stressing idealization will lead, Derrida might argue more specifically, to overlooking the institutional dimensions of texts, and to ignoring the contingency lurking behind the rationality that the texts might project but never achieve.

Finally, on the charge that Derrida is still caught in the philosoph-ical paradigm of subjectivity that deconstruction wants to overcome,

Derrida could ask in turn whether Habermas has really freed himself from the philosophy of the subject. Derrida might think that Habermas is still too theoretical in the Kantian sense, and that Habermas (especially in chapter 7 of *The Philosophical Discourse of Modernity*) privileges the constative, truth-telling function of language in his idealized speech situation.[32] Stressing idealization will lead, Derrida might argue, to overlooking the institutional dimensions of texts, and to ignoring the contingency lurking behind the rationality that the texts might project but never achieve. Furthermore, Habermas may have overreacted to Derrida in thinking that Derrida is dismissing subjects altogether from language, or turning language as a self-sufficient, self-stabilized system into an "event without any subject."[33] Models of communicative interaction may be intersubjective instead of subjective, but the appeal to many subjects instead of an isolated subject is still an appeal to subjects. To argue that an account of language is not necessarily the same as an account of communicative speech actions, Derrida need not assert that there could be language even if there were no speakers or writers. On this point, I believe that Habermas misinterprets Derrida's analysis of writing in the following passage:

> Writing guarantees that a text can always repeatedly be read in arbitrarily changing contexts. What fascinates Derrida is this thought of an *absolute readability:* Even in the absence of every possible audience, after the death of all beings with an intelligent nature, the writing holds open in heroic abstraction the possibility of a repeatable readability that transcends everything in this world. Because writing mortifies the living connections proper to the spoken word, it promises salvation for its semantic content even beyond the day on which all who can speak and listen have fallen prey to the holocaust.[34]

The page that Habermas cites need not be read as making this radical a claim. A more sympathetic reading would see it as suggesting, in the spirit of Wittgenstein's attack on private language, that writing must be legible by others than those to whom it is addressed.[35] Derrida's point would then be that we can say of any particular reader that the text could function in the absence of that reader. But this means only that some other readers could still read the text, not the nonsensical claim that the text could be read in the absence of all possible readers.

The difference can be split here by acknowledging that they are both saying something right. Habermas is insisting on context to say that meaning is not arbitrary. Meaning is tied to context, and contexts cannot be merely willed. The right theory will show us that the contexts in which we find ourselves have developed rationally as a result of learning processes, such that some parts are rational advances. In contrast, Derrida is insisting that texts can be taken up and interpreted differently in different contexts, so that no context is necessary or definitive. But this is not to say that the text could make sense in the complete absence of context (or in some "absolute context" that includes all possible contexts, since his absolute would be equally contextless). Derrida need not appeal either to a lost original or *Ur*-context to which all written texts point backwards in time, or to a contextless telos toward which any text points ideally. What *would* be contextless is the counterfactual, coercion-free, ideal speech situation.

Furthermore, Derrida need not deny the existence of speaking, writing, and communicating subjects. Thus, he does not deny that the intentions of subjects or agents play a role in contexts. He simply does not think that subjects are clear enough about what their intentions are, or that "intention" is a sufficiently clear notion, to make intention the decisive criterion for interpreting the range of possible meanings in a context or across contexts.

If I am right to read Derrida along these lines, deconstruction can be defended against the allegation that in principle deconstruction cannot be used effectively as destabilizing critique. There would be no reason to assume that such destabilization (the term I prefer to Habermas's term "subversion") is never justified or that it only ever leaves us with the status quo. We do not have to know what alternatives we would prefer to want to destabilize some of our present practices. If we deplore them, we can try through such indirect means (since we do not know what direct means to try) to shake up ways of thinking sufficiently so that we can start to see what would be preferable instead. We can try to see our practices in a different light so that we can become aware of other possibilities. That is how Nietzsche and Heidegger understood critical history, and Foucault's genealogy is also an example of one way of doing critical history. Another way is deconstruction, when informed by the critical attitude that Horkheimer contrasts to "traditional theory." The deconstruction of texts could thus become one more strategy to be used by critical philosophers. Specifying the universal categories of all thought need no longer be the primary task for critical philosophers who are trying to understand, both historically and theoretically, who we have become, where we are now, and what we can be.

Notes on Contributors

BARRY ALLEN teaches philosophy at McMaster University. Portions of his essay for this volume reappear in a chapter on Derrida in his forthcoming book, *Truth in Philosophy* (Cambridge, Mass.: Harvard University Press).

ROBERT BERNASCONI is Moss Professor of Philosophy at Memphis State University. He is the author of *The Question of Language in Heidegger's History of Being* and of a recently completed manuscript, *Heidegger in Question*, as well as a number of essays on various aspects of continental philosophy and the history of social thought. He is currently completing a book entitled *Between Levinas and Derrida*, is the editor of Gadamer's *The Relevance of the Beautiful*, and has co-edited works on Derrida and Levinas.

RICHARD J. BERNSTEIN is Vera List Professor of Philosophy at the New School for Social Research. Recent books of his include an edited collection of essays on Habermas (*Habermas and Modernity* [1985]) as well as *Beyond Objectivism and Relativism: Science, Hermeneutics and Praxis* (1983), *Philosophical Profiles* (1986), and *The New Constellation: The Ethical-Political Horizons of Modernity/Postmodernity* (1991).

JOHN D. CAPUTO is Professor of Philosophy at Villanova University and author of *The Mystical Element in Heidegger's Thought* (1978), *Heidegger and Aquinas: An Essay on Overcoming Metaphysics* (1982), and *Radical Hermeneutics: Repetition, Deconstruction and the Hermeneutic Project* (1987). He is currently completing a book on ethics and postmodernism.

DRUCILLA CORNELL is Professor of Law at the Benjamin N. Cardozo School of Law. She was a Visiting Member at the Institute for Advanced Study, Princeton, N.J., in 1991–92. In addition to numerous articles on critical theory, feminism, and "postmodern" theories of ethics, she is the author of *Beyond Accommodation: Ethical Feminism, Deconstruction and the Law* (1991) and *The Philosophy of the Limit* (1992). She is also co-editor, with S. Benhabib, of *Feminism as Critique: On the Politics of Gender* (1988).

M. C. DILLON is Professor of Philosophy at the State University of New York at Binghamton. In addition to having published essays on issues in contemporary continental philosophy, literary theory, and psychology, he is the author of

Merleau-Ponty's Ontology (1988) and editor of *Merleau-Ponty Vivant* (1991). He is currently finishing a book tentatively entitled *Semiological Reductionism: A Critique of Derrida.*

NANCY FRASER teaches philosophy and women's studies at Northwestern University, where she is also a member of the research faculty of the Center for Urban Affairs and Policy Research. She is the author of *Unruly Practices: Power, Discourse, and Gender in Contemporary Social Theory* (1989) and co-editor of *Revaluing French Feminism: Critical Essays on Difference, Agency, and Culture* (1992). She is currently working on a new book, *Keywords of the Welfare State,* co-authored with Linda Gordon.

DAVID COUZENS HOY is Professor of Philosophy (and of the History of Consciousness) at the University of California, Santa Cruz. His publications include numerous articles dealing with continental philosophy as well as an edited collection of essays on Foucault, *Foucault: A Critical Reader* (1986). He is the author of *The Critical Circle: Literature, History, and Philosophical Hermeneutics* (1978).

RICHARD KEARNEY is Professor of Philosophy at University College Dublin and Visiting European Professor at Boston College. His books include *Dialogues with Contemporary Continental Thinkers* (1984), *Modern Movements in European Philosophy* (1987), *Transitions* (1988), *The Wake of Imagination* (1989), and *Poetics of Imagining* (1991).

GARY B. MADISON is Professor of Philosophy at McMaster University. In addition to numerous articles on continental philosophy and the philosophy of the social sciences, he is the author of *La phénoménologie de Merleau-Ponty* (1973), *Understanding: A Phenomenological-Pragmatic Analysis* (1982), *The Logic of Liberty* (1986), and *The Hermeneutics of Postmodernity: Figures and Themes* (1988). He is a founding member and a former director of The Canadian Society for Hermeneutics and Postmodern Thought.

RICHARD RORTY is University Professor of Humanities at the University of Virginia. He has recently published two volumes of *Philosophical Papers (Objectivity, Relativism and Truth* and *Essays on Heidegger and Others)* with Cambridge University Press.

JOHN R. SEARLE is Mills Professor of Philosophy of Mind and Language at the University of California, Berkeley. His books include *Speech Acts; Expression and Meaning; Intentionality; Minds, Brains and Science;* and *The Rediscovery of the Mind.* A past president of the American Philosophical Association, he has been a member of the American Academy of Arts and Sciences since 1977.

DALLAS WILLARD has taught at the University of Wisconsin in Madison and, since 1965, at the University of Southern California. He has held visiting appointments at the University of California in Los Angeles and at the University of Colorado. He is the author of *Logic and the Objectivity of Knowledge* (1984), and he continues to work in the interface between theory of logic and philosophy of mind.

Notes

Gary B. Madison, Introduction

[1]Italo Calvino, *Mr. Palomar*, trans. William Weaver (San Diego: Harcourt Brace Jovanovich, 1985), p. 98.

[2]Jacques Derrida, *The Ear of the Other*, trans. Christie V. McDonald (New York: Schocken Books, 1985), p. 158.

[3]See Derrida, *Of Grammatology*, trans. Gayatri Chakravorty Spivak (Baltimore: The Johns Hopkins University Press, 1976), p. 158.

[4]Derrida, *Positions*, trans. Alan Bass (Chicago: University of Chicago Press, 1981), p. 63.

[5]See J. Laplanche and J.-B. Pontalis, *The Language of Psychoanalysis* (New York: W. W. Norton, 1973).

[6]Ibid., p. 489.

[7]For many of my remarks in this Introduction I am heavily indebted to my colleague Barry Allen for his many helpful suggestions. He should, in fact, be considered a coauthor of this text (though he should share none of the blame for some of my statements). I should mention as well that, as editor of this volume, I have sought to maintain a studied neutrality. The reader who might possibly be interested may find critical reflections of my own on Derrida in the following publications: "Beyond Seriousness and Frivolity: A Gadamerian Response to Deconstruction," in *Gadamer and Hermeneutics*, ed. Hugh J. Silverman (New York: Routledge, 1991) (published as well in my *The Hermeneutics of Postmodernity: Figures and Themes* [Bloomington: Indiana University Press, 1988]); "Gadamer/Derrida: The Hermeneutics of Irony and Power," in *Dialogue and Reconstruction: The Gadamer-Derrida Encounter*, ed. D. P. Michelfelder and R. E. Palmer (Albany: SUNY Press, 1989); and "Coping with Nietzsche's Legacy: Rorty, Derrida, Gadamer," *Philosophy Today* 36, no. 1 (Spring 1992).

1. Barry Allen, Difference Unlimited

[1]Jacques Derrida, *Speech and Phenomena*, (Evanston: Northwestern University Press, 1973), p. 103. Other references to Derrida's work are parenthetically abbreviated as follows: *G. Of Grammatology* (Baltimore: Johns Hopkins University Press, 1976). *L. Limited Inc* (Evanston: Northwestern University Press, 1989). *M. Margins of Philosophy* (Chicago: University of Chicago Press, 1982).

²Aristotle, *De Interpretatione*, 16a. For this and other references to Aristotle, see *The Basic Works of Aristotle*, ed. R. McKeon (New York: Random House, 1941).

³See N. Kretzmann, "Aristotle on Spoken Sound Significant by Convention," in *Ancient Logic and its Modern Interpretations*, ed. J. Corcoran (Dordrecht: Reidel, 1974), p. 3.

⁴Aristotle defines the sign in the *Prior Analytics*, 70a; cf. *Rhetoric*, 1357. Stoic semiology is reconstructed by T. Ebert, "Origin of the Stoic Theory of Signs," *Oxford Studies in Ancient Philosophy* 5 (Oxford: Oxford University Press, 1987). Augustine's important definition of the sign is in *On Christial Doctrine*, trans. D. W. Robertson (Indianapolis: Bobbs-Merrill, 1958) II.1.1. Peirce is an exception to many directions in this work; see D. Greenlee, *Peirce's Concept of Sign* (The Hague: Mouton, 1973). On this history generally, see J. Deely, *Introducing Semiotic: Its History and Doctrine* (Bloomington: Indiana University Press, 1982).

⁵Derrida, *Speech and Phenomena*, p. 51.

⁶L. Wittgenstein, *Philosophical Investigations*, 3d ed. (Oxford: Blackwell, 1953), section 1; F. de Saussure, *Course in General Linguistics*, trans. Roy Harris (La Salle, Ill: Open Court, 1986), pp. 65–67, 115–19; and *Cahiers F. de Saussure* 12 (1954), p. 63. On the objection to nomenclaturism, see Roy Harris, *Reading Saussure* (La Salle, Ill: Open Court, 1987), pp. 55–64. Harris compares this to Wittgenstein in *The Language-Makers* (Ithaca: Cornell University Press, 1980).

Saussure's *signifiant* (a signifier or a sign's signifying, signaling aspect) is not the real acoustic energy of enunciation but the sensation or perception it causes (an *image acoustique*); while the *signifié* or "signified" is a conceptual (rather than phonic) difference, and not a referent or nonlinguistic entity. Saussure says that differences of intralinguistic contrast make "sheep" and "*mouton*" distinct significations (*Course*, p. 114). Whether they "refer to the same thing" is a question Saussure does not ask, since he holds such extralinguistic reference to be of no consequence for the identity or linguistic value of signs.

⁷Saussure, *Course*, p. 115.

⁸Hans Aarsleff has observed that Taine's *De l'Intelligence* (1870) "contains all the elements of Saussure's doctrine of signs." This includes the distinctions between synchronic and diachronic, speaking (*parole*) and language (*langue*), and signifier and signified; also the comparison of sound and sense in a language to recto and verso faces; and a concept of linguistic value (*valeur*). Aarsleff concludes that "Saussure was working within the conceptual milieu of Taine's thought," and that "the concept of system or structure which a latter age found in Saussure was fully developed by Taine with the same broad implications and applications that have since been redeveloped from Saussure's linguistic thought" (*From Locke to Saussure* [Minneapolis: University of Minnesota Press, 1982], pp. 358–61). But Aarsleff may underestimate the innovation entailed by semiological difference. As Harris and Taylor observe, "It is this emphasis on *differences* which . . . [is] the distinctive signature of Saussurean structuralism" (*Landmarks of Linguistic Thought* [London: Routledge, 1989], p. 190).

⁹Plato, *Sophist*, 225c–d. Also: "to speak of 'something' is to speak of 'some *one* thing'" (237d); "whenever a thing comes into being, at that moment it has come to be as a whole" (245d); "each . . . [is] the same itself" (254d). *Collected Dialogues*, ed. Hamilton and Cairns (Princeton: Princeton University Press, 1961).

¹⁰Saussure, *Course*, pp. 14, 15, 80, 99, 113.

¹¹John Lyons observes that the "defining characteristic of modern 'structural' linguistics" is precisely that "linguistic units have no validity independently of their . . . relations with other units"; while Geoffrey Sampson observes that "with respect to the

notion of a synchronic language-state as a system whose elements are defined by their contrasts, it is approximately true to say that we are all Saussureans now." See Lyons, *Introduction to Theoretical Linguistics* (Cambridge: Cambridge University Press, 1968), p. 75; and Sampson, *Schools of Linguistics* (Stanford: Stanford University Press, 1980), p. 48.

[12]Aristotle, *Posterior Analytics*, 76b.

[13]For instance, Bloomfield says that "the important thing about writing is precisely this, that the characters represent not features of the practical world ('ideas'), but features of the writers' language" (*Language* [New York: Holt, Rinehart and Winston, 1933], p. 285). For Saussure, "the object of study in linguistics is . . . [the] spoken word alone . . . the natural and only authentic connection . . . links word and sound" (*Course*, pp. 24–26). Despite the authorities who can be cited, however, it is difficult seriously to maintain that writing is added to spoken language as an instrument for its representation; see Roy Harris, *The Origin of Writing* (London: Duckworth, 1986).

[14]Derrida, "Sending: On Representation," *Social Research* 49 (1982), p. 324.

[15]Nelson Goodman "prefer[s] to dismiss the type altogether and to treat the so-called tokens of a type as *replicas* of one another. An inscription need not be an exact duplicate of another to be a replica, or true copy, of it; indeed, there is in general no degree of similarity that is necessary or sufficient for replicahood." *Languages of Art,* 2d ed. (Indianapolis: Hackett, 1976), p. 131n.

One indication of how poorly Searle reads work he would criticize is that he does not consider whether Derrida might be less certain than he about "types." In the patronizing tone of his entire discussion he says, "As Derrida is aware, any linguistic element . . . must be repeatable. . . . To say this is just to say that the logician's type-token distinction must apply generally to all the . . . elements of language. . . . Without this . . . there could not be the possibility of producing an infinite number of sentences with a finite list of elements; and this, as philosophers since Frege have recognized, is one of the crucial features of any language" (p. 199). See J. R. Searle, "Reiterating the Difference: A Reply to Derrida," *Glyph* 1 (1977), pp. 198–208. This is not a crucial feature. Skepticism about this picture of language is a point on which Derrida can agree with Wittgenstein, Davidson, Bakhtin, and others.

[16]Martin Heidegger, "Modern Natural Science and Technology," in *Radical Phenomenology: Essays in Honor of Martin Heidegger,* ed. J. Sallis (Atlantic Highlands, N.J.: Humanities Press, 1978), p. 3; and interview in *Heidegger and the Path of Thinking,* ed. J. Sallis (Pittsburgh: Duquesne University Press, 1970), p. 10.

[17]"Sein *ist* nicht. Sein gibt Es als das Entbergen von Anwesen." Martin Heidegger, "Time and Being," in *On Time and Being* (New York: Harper and Row, 1972), p. 6; *Zur Sache des Denkens,* 2d ed. (Tübingen: Max Niemeyer Verlag, 1976), p. 6.

[18]Heidegger, "Science and Technology," p. 3; "The Anaximander Fragment," in *Early Greek Thinking* (New York: Harper and Row, 1975), pp. 50–51; "time and Being," p. 2; also see "The End of PHilosophy and the Task of Thinking," in *Time and Being,* and in *Heidegger: Basic Writings,* ed. D. F. Krell (New York: Harper and Row, 1977).

[19]Martin Heidegger, *The Basic Problems of Phenomenology* (Bloomington: Indiana University Press, 1982), p. 320; "The Way to Language," in *On the Way to Language* (New York: Harper and Row, 1971), p. 123.

[20]In *Of Spirit* (Chicago: University of Chicago Press, 1989), Derrida elaborates on the ambiguity or equivocity of Heidegger's relationship to the metaphysics he would overcome. Referring to the 1933 Rectorship Address, Derrida writes: "If its programme seems diabolical, it is because, *without there being anything fortuitous in this,* it capitalizes on the worst, that is on both evils at once: the sanctioning of nazism, and the gesture

that is still metaphysical. . . . Metaphysics returns. . . . Is this not what Heidegger will never finally be able to avoid? . . . this awesome equivocality" (pp. 40–41).

[21]Derrida translates Hegel's *Aufhebung* as *la relève;* see "The Pit and the Pyramid: Introduction to Hegel's Semiology," in *Margins.*

[22]David Holdcroft, *Saussure: Signs, System and Arbitrariness* (Cambridge: Cambridge University Press, 1991), pp. 119, 130. In his presentation, Holdcroft calls T₁ (T) and T₂(T1).

[23]Ibid., p. 126. For similar criticism of Saussure (and Derrida), see Norman Bryson, *Vision and Painting* (New Haven: Yale University Press, 1983), pp. 67–86. (I should note that Holdcroft does not claim that his criticism of Saussure has implications against Derrida, whom he does not discuss in this connection.)

[24]Holdcroft, *Saussure,* p. 133.

[25]Saussure, *Course,* p. 13.

[26]Derrida, *The Truth in Painting* (Chicago: University of Chicago Press, 1987), p. 11.

[27]V. N. Vološinov, *Marxism and the Philosophy of Language* (Cambridge: Harvard University Press, 1986), pp. 54, 68–69.

[28]Bakhtin, in Tzvetan Todorov, *Mikhail Bakhtin: The Dialogical Principle* (Minneapolis: University of Minnesota Press, 1984), p. 57. On this point there is no difference between Saussure and Chomsky; see my paper, "The Historical Discourse of Philosophy," *Canadian Journal of Philosophy,* supplementary volume (1991).

[29]Ludwig Wittgenstein, *Philosophical Investigations,* 3d ed. (Oxford: Blackwell, 1967), sections 66, 108.

[30]Roy Harris, *The Language Machine* (London: Duckworth, 1987), p. 122.

[31]Ibid., pp. 113–14. On the nationalist politics of language in eighteenth- and nineteenth-century Europe also see R. Breton, *Geolinguistics* (Ottawa: University of Ottawa Press, 1991), pp. 69–72. On the singular role of the dictionary, unknown to antiquity but dating from early modern times, see Harris, *The Language-Makers,* pp. 128–33.

[32]Donald Davidson, "A Nice Derangement of Epitaphs," in *Truth and Interpretation,* ed. E. LePore (Oxford: Blackwell, 1986), p. 446.

[33]Davidson, "Nice Derangement," pp. 434, 440–41, 445. In a discussion of Davidson's paper, Ian Hacking suggests that while "there can be lots of systematic relations which a listener must bring to a hearer," there is "no necessity for one monolithic whole," while the "recursivity" widely supposed to be essential to a language can and should drop out of the picture. See "The Parody of Conversation," in *Truth and Interpretation,* esp. pp. 455–56.

[34]See Alfred Tarski, "The Concept of Truth in Formalized Languages," in *Logic, Semantics, Metamathematics* (Oxford: Oxford University Press, 1956).

[35]Donald Davidson, "The Structure and Content of Truth," *Journal of Philosophy* 87 (1990), p. 285; and "On the Very Idea of a Conceptual Scheme," in *Inquiries Concerning Truth and Interpretation* (Oxford: Oxford University Press, 1984), p. 194. Also see B. Ramberg, *Donald Davidson's Philosophy of Language: An Introduction* (Oxford: Blackwell, 1989), p. 47.

[36]Derrida, *Positions* (Chicago: University of Chicago Press, 1981), p. 27; cf. *Writing and Difference* (Chicago: University of Chicago Press, 1978), pp. 178–79.

[37]This was not always entirely clear in earlier work. For example, it is not impossible to read the following passage as one in which the value of truth is at least contested if not destroyed:

> I wished to reach the point of a certain exteriority in relation to the to-
> tality of the age of logocentrism. Starting from this point of exteriority,
> a certain deconstruction of that totality . . . might be broached. The
> first gesture of this departure and this deconstruction, although sub-
> ject to a certain historical necessity, cannot be given methodological or
> logical intraorbitary assurances. . . . It proceeds like a wandering
> thought on the possibility of itinerary and of method . . . an attempt to
> get out of the orbit, to think the entirety of the classical conceptual op-
> positions, particularly . . . the opposition of philosophy and
> nonphilosophy . . . being produced as truth at the moment when the
> value of truth is shattered. (*G*, 161–62)

What is contested here is the "Truth of the Philosophers," the vicegerent, the ministe-
rial mimic of being, Paremenides' "still heart of Truth unconcealed and committed"
(frag. 1), not Opinion, not what *passes* for true.

[38]Michel Foucault, *The History of Sexuality* (New York: Vintage, 1980), p. 100.

[39]Michel Foucault, *Power/Knowledge* (New York: Pantheon, 1980), p. 131.

[40]Jacques Derrida, Roundtable on Translation, *The Ear of the Other* (New York: Schocken Books, 1985), p. 140.

[41]Jacques Derrida, "Punctuations: The Time of a Thesis," in *Philosophy in France Today*, ed. A. Montefiore (Cambridge: Cambridge University Press, 1983), pp. 44–45.

2. Richard Kearney, Derrida's Ethical Re-Turn

[1]"Interview with François Ewald," *La Magazine Litteraire* 286 (1991), p. 29.

[2]Jacques Derrida, "Comment ne pas parler," in *Psyche* (Paris: Galilée, 1987), p. 587. Hereafter cited in text as "Comment."

[3]Christopher Norris, "On the Ethics of Deconstruction," in *Derrida* (London: Fontana, 1987), pp. 194f.

[4]Subsequently published under the title, "Deconstruction and the Other," in my *Dialogues with Contemporary Thinkers* (Manchester: Manchester University Press, 1984). Hereafter cited in text as *Dialogues*.

[5]On Derrida's post-Heideggerian version of deconstruction, see also Dermot Moran, "The Destruction of Destruction" (forthcoming).

[6]Jacques Derrida, "Violence and Metaphysics," in *Writing and Difference*, trans. Alan Bass (Chicago: University of Chicago Press, 1978). Hereafter cited in text as *WD*.

[7]See Geoffrey Bennington, *Derridabase* (Paris: Seuil, 1991), pp. 154–56. Hereafter cited by name in text.

[8]See Bill Reading's discussion of this point in *Introducing Lyotard* (New York: Routledge, 1990), p. 37.

[9]See Jacques Derrida, *Of Grammatology*, trans. Gayatri Chakravorty Spivak (Baltimore: Johns Hopkins University Press, 1976), pp. 442–43. Hereafter cited in text as *G*.

[10]First published in a special issue of the *Cardozo Law Review* 11, nos. 5–6 (1990), pp. 919–1047, entitled "Deconstruction and the Possibility of Justice." Hereafter cited in text as "Force."

[11]Jacques Derrida, *De l'esprit: Heidegger et la question* (Paris: Galilée, 1987), p. 179. Hereafter cited in text as *E*.

[12]Jacques Derrida, *Schibboleth: Pour Paul Celan* (Paris: Galilée, 1986). Hereafter cited in text as *Schibboleth*.

[13]Jacques Derrida, "Circonfession," in *Derrida* (Paris: Galilée, 1991). Hereafter cited by name in text.

[14]Jacques Derrida, *D'un certain ton apocalyptique adoptè naquère en philosophie* (Paris: Galilée, 1983).

3. Nancy Fraser, The French Derrideans: Politicizing Deconstruction or Deconstructing the Political?

[1]See Jean-Luc Nancy and Philippe Lacoue-Labarthe, eds., *Les fins de l'homme: A partir du travail de jacques Derrida* (Paris: Galilée, 1981); hereafter cited as *Fins*.

[2]See, especially, the essay whose title provided that of the conference: Derrida, "The Ends of Man," trans. Edouard Morot-Sir, Wesley C. Piersol, Hubert L. Dreyfus, and Barbara Reid, *Philosophy and Phenomenological Research* 30, no. 1 (September 1969), 31–57.

[3]See Jacques Derrida, "Positions: Interview with Jean-Louis Houdebine and Guy Scarpetta," in *Positions*, trans. Alan Bass (Chicago: University of Chicago Press, 1981), 37–96.

[4]The present account covers only the first two years of the center's existence.

[5]*Rejouer le politique* (Paris: Galilée, 1982); hereafter cited as *Rejouer*.

[6]*Le retrait du polique* (Paris: Galilée, 1983); hereafter cited as *Retrait*.

[7]See, for example, Michael Ryan, *Marxism and Deconstruction: A Critical Articulation* (Baltimore: The Johns Hopkins University Press, 1982). Related work by Gayatri Chakravorty Spivak will be discussed below.

[8]Gayatri Chakravorty Spivak, "Il faut s'y prendre en s'en prenant à elles," in *Fins*, pp. 505–15; hereafter cited parenthetically, by page numbers, in my text. The translations are my own.

[9]Derrida, "The Ends of Man," p. 56. I have altered the translation slightly.

[10]Discussion transcribed in *Fins*, pp. 515–16.

[11]Jacob Rogozinski, "Déconstruire la revolution," in *Fins*, pp. 516–26; hereafter cited parenthetically, by page numbers, in my text. The translations are my own.

[12]Jacques Derrida, "Semiology and Grammatology: Interview with Julia Kristeva," in *Positions*, p. 24.

[13]Discussion transcribed in *Fins*, pp. 526–29; hereafter cited parenthetically, by page numbers, in my text. The translations are my own.

[14]Jacques Derrida, "D'unton apocalyptique adopté naguère en philosophie," in *Fins*, pp. 445–79.

[15]Jean-Luc Nancy, "La voix libre de l'homme," in *Fins*, pp. 163–82.

[16]Christopher Fynsk, "Intervention," in *Fins*, pp. 487–93.

[17]See Hannah Arendt, *The Human Condition* (Chicago: University of Chicago Press, 1958).

[18]Philippe Lacoue-Labarthe, "Intervention," in *Fins*, pp. 493–97; hereafter cited parenthetically, by page numbers, in my text. The translations are my own.

[19]Martin Heidegger, "The Question Concerning Technology," in *The Question concerning Technology and Other Essays*, trans. William Lovitt (New York: Harper and Row, 1977), and "Overcoming Metaphysics," in *The End of Philosophy*, trans. Joan Stambaugh (New York: Harper and Row, 1973).

[20]Discussion transcribed in *Fins,* pp. 497–500.

[21]Jean-Luc Nancy and Philippe Lacoue-Labarthe, "Ouverture," in *Rejouer,* pp. 11–28; hereafter cited parenthetically, by page numbers, in my text. The translations are my own.

[22]See n. 19 above.

[23]See Friedrich Nietzsche, "European Nihilism," in *The Will to Power,* ed. Walter Kaufmann, trans. Walter Kaufmann and R. J. Hollingdale (New York: Random House, 1968); and Heidegger, "Overcoming Metaphysics." See also Heidegger, *Nihilism,* trans. Frank A. Capuzzi, vol. 4 of *Nietzsche* (New York: Harper & Row, 1982).

[24]Cf. Karl Marx, "On the Jewish Question, Part 1," and "Contribution to the Critique of Hegel's *Philosophy of Right,*" both in *The Marx-Engels Reader,* 2d ed., Robert C. Tucker (New York: W. W. Norton, 1978).

[25]Several of the formulations in this paragraph and in the preceding one were suggested to me by John Brenkman.

[26]Jean-Luc Nancy, "La jurisdiction du monarch hegelien," in *Rejouer,* pp. 51–90; an English translation by Mary Ann Caws and Peter Caws appears in *Social Research* 49, no. 2 (Summer 1982), pp. 481–516.

[27]Philippe Lacoue-Labarthe, "La transcendence finit dans la politique," in *Rejouer,* pp. 171–214; an English translation by Peter Caws appears in *Social Research* 49, no. 2 (Summer 1982), pp. 405–40.

[28]Denis Kambouchner, "De la condition la plus générale de la politique," in *Retrait,* pp. 113–58.

[29]Philippe Soulez, "La mère est-elle hors-jeu de l'essence du politique?" in *Retrait,* pp. 159–82.

[30]Claude Lefort, "La question de la democratie," in *Retrait,* pp. 71–88.

[31]Philippe Lacoue-Labarthe and Jean-Luc Nancy, "Le retrait du politique," in *Retrait,* pp. 183–200; hereafter cited parenthetically, by page numbers, in my text. The translations are my own.

[32]Nancy and Lacoue-Labarthe credit group member Jean-François Lyotard with this notion; they cite his book *La condition postmoderne: Rapport sur le savior* (Paris: Éditions de Minuit, 1979).

[33]Pierre Clastres, *La société contre l'état* (Paris, 1974)

[34]See Aristotle, *Politics,* book 1, trans. Ernest Barker (Oxford: Oxford University Press, 1958).

[35]Recent (but not wholly successful) attempts to address such questions include André Gorz, *Farewell to the Working Class,* trans. Michael Sonenscher (London, 1982); and Michael Walzer, *Spheres of Justice* (New York: Basic Books, 1983).

[36]Among the many works one could cite here, see Alison M. Jaggar, *Feminist Politics and Human Nature* (Totowa, N.J.: Rowman and Allanheld, 1983); Susan Moller Okin, *Women in Western Political Thought* (Princeton, N.J.: Princeton University Press, 1979); Linda Nicholson, *Gender and History: The Limits of Social Theory in the Age of the Family* (New York: Columbia University Press, 1986); Lorenne M. G. Clark and Lynda Lange, eds., *The Sexism of Social and Political Theory: Women and Reproduction from Plato to Nietzsche* (Toronto: University of Toronto Press, 1979); Carol Gilligan, *In a Different Voice: Psychological Theory and Women's Development* (Cambridge, Mass.: Harvard University Press, 1982); Nancy Hartsock, *Money, Sex, and Power: Toward a Feminist Historical Materialism* (Boston: Northeastern University Press, 1983); and Iris Young, "Impartiality and the Civic Public," Seyla Benhabib, "The Generalized and the Concrete Other," and Maria Markus, "Women, Success, and Civil Society," all in *Feminism as Critique: Essays in the Politics of Gender in Late-Capitalist Societies,* ed. Seyla Benhabib and Drucilla Cornell

(Minneapolis: University of Minnesota Press, 1987). For my own take on these issues, see chapter 8 of my *Unruly Practices: Power, Discourse, and Gender in Contemporary Social Theory* (Minneapolis: University of Minnesota Press, 1989).

4. Drucilla Cornell, The Violence of the Masquerade: Law Dressed Up as Justice

[1]Jacques Derrida, "Force of Law: The 'Mystical Foundation of Authority,' " *Cardozo Law Review* 11, nos. 5–6 (1990), pp. 919–1047.

[2]Dominick LaCapra, "Violence, Justice, and the Force of Law," *Cardozo Law Review* 11 (1990).

[3]Walter Benjamin, "Critique of Violence," in *Reflections*, ed. Peter Dementz (New York: Schocken Books, 1986).

[4]Ibid., pp. 281–83.

[5]Ibid., pp. 277–79; Derrida, "Force," pp. 41–43, 46.

[6]Benjamin, "Critique," p. 277.

[7]Derrida, "Force," p. 41.

[8]LaCapra, "Violence," pp. 19–20.

[9]Derrida, "Force," p. 1.

[10]Ibid., p. 17.

[11]Ibid., p. 47.

[12]Ibid., p. 48.

[13]Ibid., p. 16.

[14]LaCapra, "Violence," pp. 4–5.

[15]See Stanley Fish, *Doing What Comes Naturally: Change, Rhetoric, and the Practice of Theory in Literary and Legal Studies* (Durham: Duke University Press, 1989).

[16]Ibid., pp. 328–31.

[17]In his essay "Working on the Chain Gang," Fish notes:

> Paradoxically, one can be faithful to legal history only by revising it, by redescribing it in such a way as to accommodate and render manageable the issues raised by the present. This is a function of the law's conservatism, which will not allow a case to remain unrelated to the past, and so assures that the past, in the form of the history of decisions, will be continually rewritten. In fact, it is the *duty* of a judge to rewrite it (which is to say no more than that it is the duty of a judge to decide), and therefore there can be no simply "found" history in relation to which some other history could be said to be "invented." (Ibid., p. 395; note omitted, emphasis in original)

[18]478 U.S. 186 (1985).

[19]While discussing Mark Kelman's essay, "Interpretive Construction in the Substantive Criminal Law" (Stanford Law Review 33, p. 591 [1981]), in his own essay "Dennis Martinez and the Uses of Theory," Fish notes that Kelman thinks

> "It is illuminating and disquieting to see that we are nonrationally constructing the legal world over and over again." In fact, it is neither. It is not illuminating because it does not throw any light on any act of

construction that is currently in force, for although your theory will tell you that there is always one (or more) under your feet, it cannot tell you which one it is or how to identify it. It is not disquieting because in the absence of any alternative to interpretive construction, the fact that we are always doing it is neither here nor there. It just tells us that our determinations of right and wrong will always occur within a set of assumptions that could not be subject to our scrutiny; but since everyone else is in the same boat, the point is without consequence and leaves us exactly where we always were, committed to whatever facts and certainties our interpretive constructions make available. (Fish, *Doing What Comes Naturally*, p. 395; note omitted)

[20]See 478 U.S., pp. 192–94.
[21]760 F.2d 1202 (1985).
[22]478 U.S., p. 189. The Ninth Amendment reads:

The enumeration in the Constitution, of certain rights, shall not be construed to deny or disparage others retained by the people. (U.S. Const., amend. IX)

The Due Process Clause of the Fourteenth Amendment provides that:

No State shall make or enforce any law which shall abridge the privileges or immunities of citizens in the United States; nor shall any State deprive any person of life, liberty, or property, without due process of law. (U.S. Const., amend XIV, cl. 1)

[23]*Griswold vs. Connecticut*, 381 U.S. 479 (1985).
[24]*Roe v. Wade*, 410 U.S. 113 (1973).
[25]*Carey v. Population Services International*, 431 U.S. 678 (1977).
[26]478 U.S., pp. 190–91.
[27]See notes 23, 24, and 25 above.
[28]478 U.S., p. 191.
[29]478 U.S., pp. 192–94 (footnotes and cites omitted).
[30]Ibid., p. 194.
[31]See "Institutionalization of Meaning, Recollective Imagination and the Potential for Transformative Legal Interpretation," *University of Pennsylvania Law Review* 136 (1988); "Time, Deconstruction, and the Challenge to Legal Positivism: The Call for Judicial Responsibility," *Yale Journal of Law and Humanities* 2 (1990).
[32]See Fish, *Doing What Comes Naturally*, pp. 93–95.
[33]Derrida, "Force," p. 51.
[34]478 U.S., p. 191.
[35]See note 28, above, and accompanying text.
[36]478 U.S., p. 199, quoting, *Olmstead v. United States*, 277 U.S. 438, 478 (1928) (Brandeis, J., dissenting).
[37]Ibid., quoting, Holmes, "The Path of the Law," *Harvard Law Review* 10 (1897), pp. 457, 469.
[38]Derrida, "Force," p. 17.
[39]LaCapra, "Violence," p. 7.
[40]Benjamin, "Critique," p. 286.

41See LaCapra, "Violence," pp. 11, 19–20.

42Derrida, "Force," p. 36.

43See note 19, above.

44Derrida, "Force," p. 17.

45See note 22, above.

46760 F.2d, pp. 1211–13.

47See Derrida at 28–30.

48See note 37, above, and accompanying text.

49Derrida, "Force," p. 29.

50Ibid., p. 36.

51478 U.S., pp. 187, 199.

52Derrida, "Force," p. 25.

53LaCapra, "Violence," p. 6.

54Derrida, "Force," pp. 48–49.

55Benjamin, "Critique," pp. 297–98; Derrida, "Force," pp. 71–72.

56Benjamin, "Critique," p. 294.

57See LaCapra, "Violence," p. 8.

58See Benjamin, "Critique," pp. 286–87.

59Monique Wittig, Les Guérillères, trans. David Le Vay (Boston: Beacon Press, 1985).

60LaCapra, "Violence," p. 1070.

5. Robert Bernasconi, Politics beyond Humanism: Mandela and the Struggle against Apartheid

1Marges de la philosophie (Paris: Minuit, 1972), p. 134; Margins of Philosophy, trans. Alan Bass (Chicago: University of Chicago Press, 1982), p. 113. Henceforth M, followed by French pagination/English pagination.

2De la grammatologie (Paris: Minuit, 1967), pp. 167–68; Of Grammatology, trans. Gayatri Spivak, (Baltimore: Johns Hopkins University Press, 1976), p. 114. Henceforth G.

3Positions (Paris: Minuit, 1967), pp. 54–65; Positions, trans. Alan Bass (Chicago: University of Chicago Press, 1981), pp. 37–47. Henceforth P. Note particularly the remarks about formalization at P, 63/46.

4More recently Derrida has attempted to correct this impression, for example, when he wrote that "Deconstruction is inventive or it is nothing at all; it does not settle for methodical procedures, it opens up a passageway, it marches ahead and marks a trail." Although this statement is important as a warning against a mechanical deconstruction which would be lacking in radicality and would be out of touch with what, I shall argue, gives rise to deconstruction, or calls for it, it leaves the place of the methodical procedures intact. "Psyché. Invention de l'autre," in Psyché (Paris: Galilée, 1987), p. 35. Henceforth Ps. Trans. Catherine Porter as "Psyche: Inventions of the Other," in Reading de Man Reading (Minneapolis: University of Minnesota Press, 1989), p. 42.

5For a slightly less simplistic attempt to characterize some of the different ways in which Derrida is being taken up, see my "Deconstruction and Scholarship," Man and World 21 (1988), pp. 223–30.

6Richard Bernstein, "Serious Play: The Ethical-Political Horizon of Jacques Derrida," The Journal of Speculative Philosophy 1, no. 2 (1987), p. 112. Henceforth JSP.

7This is a somewhat existential interpretation of Derrida, but leaving that aside, it can hardly be denied that attention to "the individious and pernicious tendency toward hierarchy, subordination and repression" on the part of the metaphysical tradition informs Derrida's rhetoric. See *JSP*, 97.

[8]Cited at *JSP*, 106 from *L'écriture et la différence* (Paris: Seuil, 1967), p. 208; *Writing and Difference*, trans. Alan Bass (Chicago: University of Chicago Press, 1978), p. 141. Henceforth *ED*. In fact other sentences from Derrida's discussion of Levinas might have served better, such as these: "According to the indication present in the notion of *archia*, the philosophical beginning is immediately transposed into an ethical or philosophical command. From the very first, *primacy* indicates principle *and* chief. All the classical concepts interrogated by Levinas are thus dragged toward the *agora*, summoned to justify themselves in an ethico-political language that they have not always sought—or believed that they sought—to speak, summoned to transpose themselves into this language by confessing their violent aims" (*ED*, 144-45/97). These sentences might be thought preferable to the one selected by Bernstein because, especially when taken out of the context of "Violence and Metaphysics" it might seem to propose the ideal of a liberation from violence which Derrida would also find oppressive.

[9]R. Bernasconi, "Deconstruction and the Possibility of Ethics," *Deconstruction and Philosophy*, ed. John Sallis (Chicago: University of Chicago Press, 1987), p. 136. Henceforth *DP*.

[10]"Admiration de Nelson Mandela ou Les lois de la réflexion," in *Psyché*, pp. 453-75; trans. Mary Ann Caws and Isabelle Lorenz in *For Nelson Mandela*, ed. Jacques Derrida and Mustaph Tlili (New York: Seaver Books, 1987), pp. 13-42. Henceforth *NM*.

[11]Derrida is even more insistent about the link between the discussion of politics at the beginning and the more conventionally philosophical portion that follows in 1972 when the following remark was added: "Thus the transition will be made quite naturally between the preamble and the theme of this communication, as it was imposed upon me, rather than as I chose it" (*M*, 135/114). The first version of the essay was published in *Philosophy and Phenomenological Research* 30, no. 1 (1969), pp. 31-57. Henceforth "EM."

[12]"Envoi," in *Psyché*, pp. 109-143, esp. 134-36; trans. Peter and Mary Ann Caws as "Sending: On Representation," *Social Research* 49, no. 2 (1982), pp. 294-326, esp. 320-23.

[13]M. Heidegger, *Wegmarken* (Frankfurt: Klostermann, 1967), p. 153; trans. F. A. Capuzzi in *Basic Writings*, ed. D. F. Krell (New York: Harper and Row, 1977), p. 202.

[14]"Mais c'est bien comme inséparabilité qu'on a *ensuite*, dans la métaphysique, pensée les rapports de l'etant (substance, ou *res*) et de con prédicat essentiel" (*M*, 160/132). I have slightly altered the translation to bring it more closely into line with the original version, which is only available in English.

[15]A more detailed reading of "The Ends of Man" would be obliged to show not only how the essay retains a humanist vocabulary but also, for example, and most obviously, a sexist one—so that the term "man" is not put in question on these grounds *here*, although of course Derrida does so elsewhere. The point of such an analysis, however, would not be critical in the conventional sense, but rather confirmation of an inevitability that Derrida himself constantly insists upon about the power of what language imposes on one, irrespective of one's desire to escape it (*M*, 157-58/131).

[16]For a brief sketch of the history of humanism that explores the complicity of the concept of *humanitas* with educational elitism, see my "Love of Humanity, Love of the

266

NOTES TO PAGES 103-13

Other" in *Eco-ethica et Philosophia generalis,* Festschrift für Tomonobu Imamichi (Tokyo: Academic Press Enterprises, 1992).

[17]"Le dernier mot du racisme," in *Psyché,* p. 357; trans. Peggy Kamuf as "Racism's Last Word," in *"Race," Writing Difference,* ed. Henry Louis Gates, Jr. (Chicago: University of Chicago Press, 1986), p. 333. Henceforth *RWD. RWD* also includes Derrida's "But, beyond . . . (Open Letter to Ann McClintock and Rob Nixon)" (*RWD,* 354–69), as well as "No Names Apart," by McClintock and Nixon (RWD, 339–53).

[18]M. Heidegger, *Zur Sache des Denkens* (Tübingen: Niemeyer, 1969), p. 62; trans. J. Stambaugh in *On Time and Being* (New York: Harper and Row, 1972), p. 56.

[19]What this might mean is exhibited clearly in the postscript Derrida adds to his Open Letter to Anne McClintock and Rob Nixon. Having recognized that apartheid is an American problem not just in the sense that is calls for American pressure, but because apartheid might bear "too great a resemblance" to a segregation "whose image continues at the very least to haunt American society," Derrida makes a pertinent observation about American society. He observes the way that segregation may have become less immediately racial as it has become more urban, industrial, and socioeconomic, but it is evident in the frightening percentage of young black unemployed (*RWD,* 369). Segregation therefore continues to haunt American society as more than a memory. Segregation remains after the end of segregation. And, I add this in 1991, for the same reason, nothing that has happened in South Africa since this essay was written, specifically what has been hailed as the official end of apartheid as a legal system, diminishes the urgency or relevance of Derrida's discussion. Apartheid remains.

[20]Nelson Mandela, *The Struggle is My Life* (New York: Pathfinder Press, 1986), p. 13. Henceforth *SL.*

[21]Letter of 4 February 1985. Cited in Winnie Mandela, *Part of My Soul Went with Him* (New York: Norton, 1985), pp. 148–49.

[22]See "Déclarations d'indépendance," in *Otobiographies* (Paris: Galilée, 1984), pp. 13–32; trans. T. Keenan and T. Pepper as "Declarations of Independence," *New Political Science* 15 (1986), pp. 7–15. On the same question in Rousseau see my "Rousseau and the Supplement to the Social Contract: Deconstruction and the Possibility of Democracy," *Cardozo Law Review* 11 (1990), pp. 501–24.

[23]J.-J. Rousseau, *Du contract social, Oeuvres complètes,* vol. 3 (Bibliothèque de la Pléiade, Paris: Gallimard, 1964), pp. 571–72; *On the Social Contract,* trans. Judith R. Masters (New York: St. Martin's Press, 1978), p. 61. Henceforth *CS.* Only once does the Freedom Charter refer to "the people as a whole" and then with respect to the ownership of mineral wealth, banks, and monopoly industry (*SL,* 53). Usually it refers to "all the people," "all people," "all national groups and races," "all national groups," "all South Africans," "men and women of all races," phrases which leave some room for multiplicity and diversity.

[24]I added this sentence after a discussion about my paper with Nahum Chandler, who encourages me to emphasize the strategic importance of this point.

[25]Nelson Mandela, "Statement to President P. W. Botha," in *Mandela, Tambo, and the African National Congress,* ed. Sheridan Johns and R. Hunt Davis, Jr. (Oxford: Oxford University Press, 1991), p. 218.

[26]Derrida cites *L'apartheid,* (Paris: Minuit, 1965–1985). The only works by Mandela which it contains are transcripts of the statements that he gave at the trials in Pretoria in 1962 and in Rivonia in 1963–1964.

[27]The fact that similar problems of exclusion (in terms of American Indians, black slaves and more generally, albeit in another respect, women) can be raised about the American Declaration of Independence cannot be denied and may account for a reluc-

tance to entertain them. There is in social contract theory also, as is already clear from Locke, a contradiction between the intention and a humanist language that seems to be universalist (apart from occasional markers, like property qualifications). Such tensions seems to be endemic to metaphysical humanism in modernity.

[28]*Pour Nelson Mandela,* avant-propos de Dominique Lecoq (Paris: Gallimard, 1986).

[29]Jacques Derrida, *De l'espirit* (Paris: Galilée, 1987), pp. 86–87; *Of Spirit,* trans. Geoffrey Bennington and Rachel Bowlby (Chicago: University of Chicago Press, 1989) p. 55. Henceforth *E.*

[30]"Choreographies," trans. Christie McDonald, in *Diacritics* 12 (1982), p. 70.

[31]Jacques Derrida, *"Geschlecht:* différence sexuelle, différence ontologique," in *Psyché,* p. 395n; trans. R. Berezdivin as *"Geschlecht:* Sexual Difference, Ontological Difference," *Research in Phenomenology* 13 (1983), p. 65n.

[32]Jacques Derrida, "Le main de Heidegger *(Geschlecht II),"* in *Psyché,* p. 444; *"Geschlecht II* Heidegger's Hand," trans. John Leavey, Jr., in *Deconstruction and Philosophy,* p. 186.

[33]An earlier version of this paper was delivered as the 8th Annual Spiegelberg Lecture at Washington University, St. Louis, on 22 March 1990. It is an attempt to take up in a somewhat different setting some of the questions raised at the end of my essay "No More Stories," which will appear in *Derrida. A Critical Reader,* ed. David Wood (Oxford: Basil Blackwell, forthcoming). I am grateful to my colleague Len Lawlor for sharing with me his essay "From the Trace to the Law: Derridean Politics," which has since appeared in *Philosophy and Social Criticism* 15, no. 1 (1989), pp. 1–15.

6. Dallas Willard, Predication as Originary Violence: A Phenomenological Critique of Derrida's View of Intentionality

[1]Emmanuel Levinas, *À quoi pensent les philosophes,* ed. Jacques Message, Joël Roman, and Étienne Tassin (Paris: Autrement Revue, 1988), pp. 53–54.

[2]Henri Bergson, *Laughter: An Essay on the Meaning of the Comic,* trans. C. Brereton and F. Rothwell (New York: The Macmillan Co., 1921), pp. 151ff.

[3]Ibid., p. 154.

[4]Trans. Joseph P. Fell in the *Journal of the British Society for Phenomenology* 1 (1970), pp. 4–5.

[5]Jean-Paul Sartre, *Being and Nothingness,* trans. Hazel Barnes (New York: Philosophical Library, 1956).

[6]Jacques Derrida, *Writing and Difference,* trans. Alan Bass (Chicago: University of Chicago Press, 1978), p. 135.

[7]Edmund Husserl, *Ideas,* trans. W. R. Boyce Gibson (New York: Collier Books, 1962).

[8]Husserl, *Logical Investigations,* 2 vols., trans. J. N. Findlay (London: Routledge and Kegan Paul, 1970). Sixth Investigation, subsection 10.

[9]Ibid., Second Investigation, subsection 37.

[10]Jacques Derrida, *Positions,* trans. Alan Bass (Chicago: University of Chicago Press, 1981), p. 3. Hereafter referred to as *P.*

[11]Jacques Derrida, *Of Grammatology,* trans. Gayatri Chakravorty Spivak (Baltimore: The Johns Hopkins University Press, 1976), p. 284. Hereafter referred to as *G.*

¹²Cf. Jacques Derrida, *Margins of Philosophy*, trans. Alan Bass (Chicago: University of Chicago Press, 1982), p. 12. Hereafter referred to as *M*.

¹³Cf. Rodolphe Gasché, *The Tain of the Mirror* (Cambridge, Mass.: Harvard University Press, 1986), pp. 6–7, 242.

¹⁴Richard Kearney, *Dialogues with Contemporary Continental Thinkers: The Phenomenological Heritage* (Manchester: Manchester University Press, 1984), p. 125. Cf. *Positions*, p. 88.

¹⁵Ibid., p. 123. Cf. Ynhui Park, "Derrida ou la prison du language," in *Philosophy* (Seoul, Korea, 1983), pp. 151–62.

¹⁶Kearney, *Dialogues*, pp. 123–24.

¹⁷Discussed in my *Logic and the Objectivity of Knowledge* (Athens: Ohio University Press, 1984), chapter 4.

¹⁸Jacques Derrida, *Speech and Phenomena* (Evanston: Northwestern University Press, 1973), p. 49. Hereafter referred to as *SP*.

7. Richard Rorty, Is Derrida a Transcendental Philosopher?

¹Jonathan Culler, *On Deconstruction* (Ithaca: Cornell University Press, 1982), p. 28. Hereafter cited as Culler.

²See my "Deconstruction and Circumvention," in Culler.

³Culler, p. 85.

⁴See Norris's "Philosophy as *Not* Just a 'Kind of Writing': Derrida and the Claim of Reason," in *Redrawing the Lines*, ed. R. W. Dasenbrock (Minneapolis: University of Minnesota Press, 1989); and my "Two Meanings of 'Logocentrism,' " in the same volume.

⁵Culler, p. 153.

⁶For a partial list of those who make this sort of charge, and my attempt to reply to it, see my "Thugs and Theorists: A Reply to Bernstein," *Political Theory* 15 (Nov. 1987), pp. 564–80. A fuller reply can be found in my *Contingency, Irony, and Solidarity* (Cambridge: Cambridge University Press, 1989). In that book I claim that "theory" cannot do much to bring the excluded in from the margins—to enlarge the community whose consensus sets the standards of objectivity—but that other kinds of writing (notably novels and newspaper stories) can do quite a lot.

⁷Christopher Norris, *Derrida* (Cambridge: Harvard University Press, 1987), p. 156. Hereafter cited as Norris.

⁸See, especially, chapter 6 ("From Ironist Theory to Private Allusions: Derrida") of *Contingency, Irony, and Solidarity*. The original title of this chapter, which I sometimes wish I had retained, was "From Ironist Theory to Private Jokes."

⁹Norris, p. 183. Also: "[D]econstruction is a Kantian enterprise in ways that few of its commentators have so far been inclined to acknowledge" (p. 94).

¹⁰Rodolphe Gasché, *The Tain of the Mirror* (Cambridge, Mass.: Harvard University Press, 1986), p. 8. Hereafter cited as Gasché.

¹¹There is no interesting least common denominator of, for example, Rawls, Croce, Frege, Nietzsche, and Gödel—no feature which makes them all representative of the same natural kind. One can only explain why all five are studied with a single academic department by developing a complicated historico-sociological story.

¹²Another way of putting this point is to note that each important figure in the tradition in question has had to invent his own "central problem of philosophy" rather than work on some issue previously agreed to be problematic. Consider, in this light,

Gasché's claim that "Arche-writing is a construct aimed at resolving the philosophical problem of the very possibility (not primarily the empirical fact, which always suffers exceptions) of the usurpation, parasitism and contamination of an ideality, a generality, a universal by what is considered its other, its exterior, its incarnation, its appearance, and so on" (p. 274). Nobody knew *that* was a "philosophical problem" before Derrida came along, any more than we knew that "the conditions of the possibility of synthetic a priori judgments" was a problem before Kant came along

¹³See Jürgen Habermas, *The Philosophical Discourse of Modernity* (Cambridge: MIT Press, 1987); Rudolf Carnap, "The Overcoming of Metaphysics through the Logical Analysis of Language," in *Logical Positivism,* ed. by A. J. Ayer (Glencoe: The Free Press, 1963).

¹⁴Consider Gasché's claim that Derrida has "demonstrated" that "the source of all being beyond being is *generalized,* or rather *general,* writing" (p. 176). This is just the sort of claim which inspired the logical positivists to say that metaphysics lacked "cognitive status." Their point was that such a claim cannot be "demonstrated," unless "demonstration" means something very different from "can be argued for on the basis of generally shared beliefs."

¹⁵For Tugendhat's Wittgensteinian working-through of Frege's holistic dictum ("only in the context of a sentence does a word have meaning"), see his *Traditional and Analytic Philosophy* (Cambridge: MIT Press, 1984) and my review of that book in *Journal of Philosophy* 82 (1985), pp. 220–29. For his use of the resulting repudiation of the non-propositional to criticize "the philosophy of reflection," see his *Self-Consciousness and Self-Determination* (Cambridge: MIT Press, 1986), especially the claim that "the phenomenon of justification and the question of justifying what is considered true is actually nowhere to be found in Hegel" (p. 294). On the attempts of "the philosophy of reflection" to work at a subpropositional level, to get behind sentences to "the conditions of possibility" of sentences, see my "Strawson's Objectivity Argument," *Review of Metaphysics* 24 (Dec. 1970), pp. 207–44. In that paper I try to show how Kant's search for "conditions of the possibility of experience" requires him to violate his own claim that we cannot know anything that is not a possible experience. I argue that the temptation to go transcendental (i.e., to search for noncausal conditions of possibility) is lessened (though not, alas, eliminated) once the "linguistic turn" is taken. Gasché, by contrast, believes that "the method of reflection" (the one common to Hegel, Heidegger and, on his view, Derrida) can survive the linguistic turn; he claims, for example, that Austin "hinged the entire representational function of language . . . on a constituting self-reflectivity of the linguistic act" (p. 76). I criticize the idea of transcendental argumentation at greater length in "Verificationism and Transcendental Arguments," *Nous* 5 (1971), pp. 13–14, and in "Transcendental Argument, Self-Reference, and Pragmatism," in *Transcendental Arguments and Science,* ed. Peter Bieri, Rolf-P. Horstmann, and Lorenz Krüger (Dordrecht: D. Reidel, 1979), pp. 77–103.

¹⁶ For Tugendhat, and the analytic tradition he represents, knowledge
and truth can only be propositional. . . . [But] by eliminating altogether the ontological dimension of self-identity in self-consciousness
(and, for that matter, in absolute reflection), one deprives oneself of
the possibility of thinking the very foundations of propositional knowledge and truth, as well as of the very idea of epistemic self-consciousness. . . . Without the presupposition of ontological or formal-ontological identity of being and thought, of subject and object, of the
knower and what is known, there is no ground for any propositional attribution whatsoever. (Gasché, p. 77)

On the "analytic" view I share with Tugendhat and Habermas, the very idea of a "ground" for "propositional attribution" is a mistake. The practice of playing sentences off against one another in order to decide what to believe—the practice of argumentation—no more requires a "ground" than the practice of using one stone to chip pieces off another stone in order to make a spear-point.

[17]Gasché, p. 122.

[18]Ibid., p. 136.

[19]Ibid., p. 139. Gasché thinks that the confusion of Derrida's enterprise with such a *Verflüssigung* is one of the "dominant misconceptions" of deconstruction. He views American Derrida-fans as especially prone to such misconceptions, in particular to the misconception that Derrida "literarizes" philosophy.

[20]Ibid., p. 45. For a discussion of Davidson's work as a break with the notion of language as medium, see the first chapter of my *Contingency, Irony, and Solidarity*.

[21]See Henry Staten, *Wittgenstein and Derrida* (Lincoln: University of Nebraska Press, 1984): "The deconstructive critique of language could even be phrased as a *denial that there is language*" (p. 20).

[22]I have criticized Derrida's tendency to adopt this tone in "Deconstruction and Circumvention." For a more general criticism of the Heideggerian, un-"playful" side of Derrida, see Barbara Hernstein Smith, "Changing Places: Truth, Error and Deconstruction," in her *Contingencies of Value* (Cambridge: Harvard University Press, 1988). Smith argues that " 'the metaphysics of Western thought' *is* thought, all of it, root and branch, everywhere and always" and that "as figure and ground change places, the unravelling of Western metaphysics weaves another Western metaphysics" (p. 118). I agree, and take the point to be that each generation's irony is likely to become the next generation's metaphysics. Metaphysics is, so to speak, irony gone public and flat—liquefaction congealed, providing a new ground on which to inscribe new figures. From my angle, the attempt to make Derrida into somebody who has discovered some "philosophical truths" is a premature flattening-out of Derrida's irony. I think that he ought to be kept fluid a while longer before being congealed (as eventually he must be) into one more set of philosophical views, suitable for doxographic summary.

[23]Gasché himself expresses doubt (p. 4) that his way of reading Derrida works for some of Derrida's later writings.

8. John D. Caputo, On Not Circumventing the Quasi-Transcendental: The Case of Rorty and Derrida

[1]Richard Rorty, *Contingency, Irony, and Solidarity* (New York: Cambridge University Press, 1989), p. 197. Hereafter cited in text as *CIS*.

[2]Rorty came to the defense of the "natural attitude" in the discussion which followed a presentation of "Two Meanings of 'Logocentrism': A Reply to Norris" at a Conference sponsored by the Greater Philadelphia Philosophy Consortium in October 1988. I found this defense singularly enlightening about Rorty's views. My commentary on Rorty's and Norris's paper that day was the first draft of the present study. "Two Meanings of 'Logocentrism' " was subsequently published in *Redrawing the Lines: Analytic Philosophy, Deconstruction, and Literary Theory*, ed. Reed Way Dasenbrock (Minneapolis: University of Minnesota Press, 1989), pp. 204–216.

[3]Still, there are curious tendencies in his work toward a naturalistic reductionism

which turns everything over to charged particles migrating through empty space. See *CIS*, 17.

⁴Jean-Francois Lyotard, *The Postmodern Condition: A Report on Knowledge,* trans. G. Bennington and B. Maussumi (Minneapolis: University of Minnesota Press, 1984), pp. xxiii–xxiv.

⁵That is also how Rorty reads Davidson. Davidson's critique of the very idea of a conceptual scheme, on Rorty's view, is not primarily that it would cut off communication between the users of different schemes. That would make Davidson look too much like Apel and Habermas, viz., like a defender of transcendental conditions of communication. Rorty takes Davidson to be objecting that the "very idea" is a *philosophical* one and makes language into some kind of magical mystical something, some sort of unknown somewhat, another Transcendental Object = X. And who needs that? All a pragmatist needs are the physical causes of particular beliefs; everything else is a redundant backup. See Richard Rorty, "The World Well Lost," in *Consequences of Pragmatism* (Minneapolis: University of Minnesota Press, 1982), pp. 3–18. This talk of physical causes is what I mean by physicalistic reductionism.

⁶Rorty's first piece on Derrida was entitled "Philosophy as a Kind of Writing," in *Consequences of Pragmatism,* pp. 90–109.

⁷Edmund Husserl, *Ideas Pertaining to a Pure Phenomenology and to a Phenomenological Philosophy,* first book, trans. Fred Kersten (The Hague: M. Nijhoff, 1983), sec. 30, pp. 55–56: Husserl would never have been able to formulate the principle *of* the natural attitude in this section without having already implicity *made* the *epoché* which is not announced until sec. 31.

⁸Friedrich Nietzsche, *Twilight of the Idols,* trans. R. J. Hollingdale (Baltimore: Penguin Books, 1968), pp. 40–41. Martin Heidegger, *On Time and Being,* trans. Joan Stambaugh (New York: Harper and Row, 1972), p. 24.

⁹"Apart from his incredible, almost Nabokovian, polylingual linguistic facility, he is a great *comic* writer—perhaps the funniest writer on philosophical topics since Kierkegaard." "Two Meanings of 'Logocentrism,' " p. 209.

¹⁰Jacques Derrida, *Glas* (Paris: Galilée, 1974). Eng. trans. *Glas,* John Leavey and Richard Rand (Lincoln: University of Nebraska Press, 1986); *Glassary,* ed. Gregory Ulmer and John Leavey (Lincoln: University of Nebraska Press, 1986).

¹¹Rorty, "Two Meanings of 'Logocentrism,' " p. 208.

¹²Richard Rorty, "Deconstruction and Circumvention," *Critical Inquiry* 11 (1984), pp. 1–23.

¹³Rorty, "Two Meanings of 'Logocentrism,' " pp. 209ff. See Paul De Man, *The Resistance to Theory* (Minneapolis: University of Minnesota Press, 1986).

¹⁴Norris criticizes Rorty in "Philosophy as a Kind of Narrative: Rorty on Postmodern Liberal Culture," in *The Contest of Faculties* (London: Methuen, 1985), pp. 139–66; and "Philosophy as *Not* Just a 'Kind of Writing': Derrida and the Claim of Reason," in *Redrawing the Lines,* pp. 189–203. See also Richard Rorty's review of Rodolph Gasché, *The Tain of the Mirror* (Cambridge: Harvard University Press, 1986), in "Is Derrida a Transcendental Philosopher?" *Yale Journal of Criticism* 2 (1988).

¹⁵Norris, "Philosophy as *Not* Just a 'Kind of Writing,' " p. 193; cf. p. 195.

¹⁶Christopher Norris, *Derrida* (Cambridge: Harvard University Press, 1987), pp. 142ff.; cf. pp. 150–55.

¹⁷"Norris, "Philosophy as *Not* Just a 'Kind of Writing,' " p. 198.

¹⁸See my review of Gasché: "Derrida: A Kind of Philosopher," *Research in Phenomenology* 17 (1987), pp. 245–89.

[19]See Jacques Derrida, *Of Grammatology*, trans. Gayatri Spivak (Baltimore: Johns Hopkins University Press, 1974), pp. 57–63.

[20]See Jacques Derrida, "A Number of Yes" (*Nombre de Oui*), trans. Brian Holmes, *Qui Parle* 2, no. 2 (1988), pp. 118–33.

[21]Rorty, "Deconstruction and Circumvention," p. 18.

[22]Christopher Norris, *Deconstruction: Theory and Practice* (London: Methuen, 1982).

[23]Rorty, "Two Meanings of 'Logocentrism,' " p. 212.

[24]I have complained about this before, in an earlier piece on Heidegger and Rorty. Cf. "The Thought of Being and the Conversation of Mankind: The Case of Heidegger and Rorty," *The Review of Metaphysics* 36 (1983), pp. 661–85; cf. pp. 672–74 where I argue that the notion of language as freely invented by human subjects for their own use belongs to the most classical metaphysical idea of language. It is not a neutral nonphilosophical idea (*CIS*, 14–15), but philosophy's most classical gesture, as Heidegger shows (e.g., in "Language," in *Poetry, Language, Thought,* trans. A. Hofstadter [New York: Harper and Row, 1971], pp. 187ff.). Like Rorty himself, I think the main value of this earlier piece of mine is the way it differentiates Rorty from Heidegger. And I have to confess that I am now more in sympathy with Rorty's more Derridean skepticism about how Being itself comes to words in human talk, about which Rorty, as I now think, rightly complains in response to my earlier treatment (*CIS*, 122–23, n. 4). I am much more sympathetic now—via Derrida—with a lot more of what Rorty—via Derrida—is up to. Nonetheless, I still think he is steadfastly stuck in metaphysics when he treats language as a man-made tool, as I hope to show here.

[25]Which is the point of Rick Roderick in "Reading Derrida Politically (Contra Rorty)," *Praxis International* 6 (1987), pp. 442–49. For Derrida's politics, see Norris, *Derrida*, pp. 155ff.; and my "Beyond Aestheticism: Derrida's Responsible Anarchy," *Research in Phenomenology* 18 (1988), pp. 59–73.

[26]This is a point on which Mark Taylor takes Rorty to task. See "Paralectics," in Mark Taylor, *Tears* (Albany: SUNY Press, 1990), pp. 123ff.

[27]The notion that language is a tool is, in my view, separable from the theory of autonomy. I think—contra Heidegger—that language is like a tool, but a tool—this is a little more Heideggerian—forged not by autonomous subjects but by communities, slow historical tendencies, erratic and contingent circumstances, collective-impersonal impulses, structural and unconscious forces. Language is filled with inertia, is a culture-wide phenomenon, is not subject to individual volitions or subjective fiats. When Derrida speaks of "prag-grammatology," he is also I think trying to appreciate the pragmatic point, which is that language is a way of coping with the world, of getting through the day. But I must say the notion of "tool" leaves a lot out for me.

[28]Jacques Derrida, *Margins of Philosophy*, trans. Alan Bass (Chicago: University of Chicago Press, 1982), pp. 319–20; cf. *Speech and Phenomena*, trans. David Allison (Evanston: Northwestern University Press, 1972), pp. 97–99. For a further account of this example, see my "The Economy of Signs in Husserl and Derrida," in *Deconstruction and Philosophy*, ed. John Sallis (Chicago: University of Chicago Press, 1987), pp. 99–113; and *Radical Hermeneutics* (Bloomington: Indiana University Press, 1987), pp. 138–45. Husserl discusses "Green is or" in sec. 15 of the *Logical Investigations*, vol. 1.

9. John R. Searle, The World Turned Upside Down

[1]Jonathan Culler, *On Deconstruction: Theory and Criticism after Structuralism* (Ithaca: Cornell University Press, 1982). Hereafter cited by page numbers in my text.

[2]Perhaps the reason that Derrida and Culler have such an odd reading of Plato's and Aristotle's remarks about the relation of speech and writing is that they are unaware that the Greeks of antiquity usually read aloud. Our practice of reading silently with the mouth closed was a "rare accomplishment" until the Middle Ages. (See W. B. Stanford, *The Sound of Greek* [Berkeley: University of California Press, 1967], and B. M. W. Knox, "Silent Reading in Antiquity," *Greek, Roman and Byzantine Studies* 9, no. 4 [Winter 1968].) Aristotle's claim that "spoken words represent mental experience and written words represent spoken words" should be understood in light of this fact.

[3]Ferdinand de Saussure, *Course in General Linguistics*, trans. Roy Harris (La Salle, Ill.: Open Court, 1986), p. 119.

[4]Ibid., p. 120.

[5]On the question of truth, Culler wants to have it both ways. He says that truth is a kind of fiction (p. 181) and that "truth is both what can be demonstrated within an accepted framework and *what simply is the case, whether or not anyone could believe it or validate it*" (p. 154; my italics). The italicized phrase is not consistent with the idea of truth as fiction, nor is it in the spirit of deconstruction.

[6]I said that deconstruction had found little appeal among professional philosophers. But there are some notable exceptions, much prized by deconstructionists. They tend to be ambiguous allies. One of these characterized Derrida as "the sort of philosopher who gives bullshit a bad name." We cannot, of course, exclude the possibility that this may be an expression of praise in the deconstructionist vocabulary.

10. John R. Searle, Reply to Mackey

[1]Mackey's letter and this reply appeared under the title "An Exchange on Deconstruction," in *The New York Review of Books*, 2 Feb. 1984.

[2]Mackey is guilty of precisely the sort of misrepresentation that he accuses me of. I point out that in *Of Grammatology* Derrida discusses only three major philosophers in his effort to prove that the history of Western philosophy is dominated by the attempt to suppress writing in favor of the privileging of speech. Mackey interprets my remark as the absurd view that Derrida has never discussed any other philosophers on any other subjects in any other of his works. Again, near the end of his letter, Mackey claims that I imply that the issue of foundationalism has been decided. I make no such suggestion. He also supposes that I hold the view that we should simply "relax our (epistemic) criteria in order to disarm the difficulties" (of skepticism). I don't know where he got that, but it is certainly not to be found in anything by me.

11. M. C. Dillon, The Metaphysics of Presence: Critique of a Critique

This paper was presented at the 1988 meeting of the Society for Phenomenology and Existential Philosophy at Northwestern University.

[1]Martin Heidegger, *Being and Time*, trans. John Macquarrie and Edward Robinson (New York: Harper and Row, 1962), p. 44.

[2]Rodolphe Gasché, *The Tain of the Mirror* (Cambridge, Mass.: Harvard University Press, 1986), pp. 13–15.

³ In the broadest sense, evidence denotes a universal primal phenome-
non of intentional life, namely—as contrasted with other conscious-
ness-of, which is capable a priori of being "empty," expectant, indirect,
non-presentive—the quite preeminent mode of consciousness that
consists in the *self-appearance*, the *self-exhibiting*, the *self-giving*, of an af-
fair, an affair-complex (or state of affairs), a universality, a value, or
other objectivity, in the final mode: "itself there," "immediately intuited," "given originaliter." For the Ego that signifies: not aiming con-
fusedly at something, with an empty expectant intention, but being
with it itself, viewing, seeing, having insight into, it itself. (Edmund
Husserl, *Cartesian Meditations*, trans. Dorion Cairns [The Hague:
Nijhoff, 1960], sec. 24, p. 57. Note the indirect correlation of self-
givenness with presence.)

Compare Heidegger, *Being and Time*, sec. 7A, pp. 51–55: "the expression '*phenomenon*' signifies *that which shows itself in itself*, the manifest."

⁴Jacques Derrida, "*Ousia* and *Gramme:* Note on a Note from *Being and Time*," in
Margins of Philosophy, trans. Alan Bass (Chicago: University of Chicago Press, 1982).
"Ousia et Grammè: note sur un note de Sein und Zeit," in *Marges de la philosophie*
(Paris: Minuit, 1973). Hereafter abbreviated as "OG."

⁵"Eternity is another name for the presence of the present" ("OG," 46).

⁶"Aristotle, in his [aporia concerning the being of time], picks up Zeno's argu-
ment" ("OG," 50). Also see "OG," 43, n. 16.

⁷"Having recalled why it may be thought that time is not a being, Aristotle leaves
the question in suspense" ("OG," 47).

⁸"Because time, in its Being, is thought on the basis of the present, it is also
strangely thought as nonbeing (or as an impure, composite being). . . . And past and future are thought as attenuating affections overtaking the presence which is known to be
the meaning or essence of what is (beings). This is what will not budge from Aristotle to
Hegel" ("OG," 52).

⁹Derrida argues that the Aristotelian aporia concerning the nonbeing or unreality
of time underlies the Kantian conception of time as a pure form of sensibility, that is,
"the nonsensuous sensuous." Time is not a being, but is the condition for the possibility
of the appearance of beings. And this condition is then located in transcendental subjectivity: time is the form of *inner* sense. Derrida sees an anticipation of this move to
subjectivity as the substratum (my word) of time in Aristotle. "Aristotle unites time and
movement in *aisthesis*. And does so such that no sensory exterior content, or objective
movement, is necessary. Time is the form of that which can occur only [in the soul]. The
form of inner sense is also the form of all phenomena in general" ("OG," 49).

This conception of time (which Derrida contends will be recapitulated in *Being and
Time* and in *Kant and the Problem of Metaphysics*) "takes off from the possibility of the
analogy constituted by *what is traced* determined as *line (gramme, Linie)*." Support for this
is provided in the following quote from the *First Critique*.

Time is the form of inner sense . . . and because this inner intuition
yields no shape, we endeavor to make up for this want by analogies. We
represent the time-sequence by a line progressing to infinity in which
the manifold constitutes a series of one dimension only; and we reason
from the properties of this line to all the properties of time, with this
one exception, that while the parts of the line are simultaneous the

parts of time are always successive. From this fact also, that all the relations of time allow of being expressed in an outer intuition, it is evident that the representation is itself an intuition. (Immanuel Kant, *Critique of Pure Reason,* trans. Norman Kemp Smith [New York: St. Martin's Press, 1965], 77. Quoted at "OG," 49, n. 28)

10 This impossibility, when barely formulated, contradicts itself, is experienced as the possibility of the impossible. This impossibility implies in its essence, in order to be what it is, that the other now, with which a now cannot coexist, is also in a certain way the same, is also a now as such, and that it coexists with that which cannot coexist with it. . . . The impossible comaintenance of several present nows is possible as the maintenance of several present nows. Time is a name for this impossible possibility. ("OG," 55, emphasis added)

It is worthy of noting that, in the phrase I have emphasized above, Derrida makes an appeal to phenomenal experience in order to ground a transcendental argument in support of the position he is articulating. To rephrase his argument: space and time *are experienced* as compossible, therefore, colliding a prioris notwithstanding, they must *be* compossible.

[11]A different argument to the same conclusion maintains that the points constituting space cannot be thought as simultaneous—because time is required to think, e.g., the two points constituting a line (as Hegel argued in describing the *Aufhebungen* through which space constitutes itself) ("OG," 40–42). Similarly, to think time as the impossibility of the coexistence of nows, one has to think of the two incompossible nows at the same time, i.e., simultaneously, i.e., in their (spatial) differing.

[12]Derrida suggests that Heidegger's distinction between authenticity and inauthenticity names another metaphysical opposition that derives from the original opposition of now and eternity. The fall into now recapitulates the Christian fall into finitude and is but another fall from eternity. What is *eigentlich* (proper, ownmost) is full presence to self. This complete or final self-consciousness is equivalent to the circular coincidence of consciousness with itself which names Hegel's absolute. It is from this that we fall into the moment and are caught up with what is now present ("OG," 60, 63).

[13]"The now . . . is (1) a constitutive part of time and a number foreign to time; (2) a constitutive part of time and an accidental part of time. It can be considered *as such* or *as such.* The enigma of the now is dominated in the difference between act and potentiality, essence and accident, and the entire system of oppositions that follows from them" ("OG," 61).

[14]Derrida, "Différance," in *Margins of Philosophy,* p. 11. "La différance," in *Marges de la philosophie,* p. 11. Hereafter abbreviated as "D."

[15]"The play of difference . . . , as Saussure reminded us, is the condition for the possibility and functioning of every sign" ("D," 5).

[16]Call it "vulgar," "exoteric," ordinary, natural, or taken-for-granted, it is this aporetic conception of time that underlies the metaphysical tradition from Aristotle to Heidegger because, as Derrida argues, "nothing other has ever been thought by the name of time" ("OG," 60). Or, in other words, "there is no 'vulgar concept of time' " because there is no other concept of time that can be opposed to it which is not reducible to it ("OG," 63).

[17]Martin Heidegger, "The Anaximander Fragment," in *Early Greek Thinking,* trans.

David Farrell Krell and Frank Capuzzi (New York: Harper and Row, 1975). "Der Spruch des Anaximander," in *Holzwege* (Frankfurt am Main: Klostermann, 1963).

[18]According to Derrida, a further discrimination appears in Heidegger's use of *"Präsenz"* as "another narrowing of *Anwesen* under the heading of subjectivity and representation" ("OG," 64).

[19]"OG," 65, emphasis added. I have stressed "text" here because it attests to Derrida's characteristic reduction of world to writing.

> [20] If Being, according to the Greek forgetting which would have been the
> very form of its advent, has never meant anything except beings, then
> perhaps difference is older than Being itself. There may be a difference
> still more unthought than the difference between Being and beings.
> We certainly can go further toward naming it in our language. Beyond
> Being and beings, this difference, ceaselessly differing from and defer-
> ring (itself), would trace (itself) (by itself)—this *différance* would be the
> first or last trace if one still could speak, here, of origin and end.
> ("OG," 67)

> *Différance*, in a certain and very strange way, (is) "older" than the onto-
> logical difference. ("D," 22)

[21]"Presence, then, far from being, as is commonly thought, *what* the sign signifies, what a trace refers to, presence, then, is the trace of the trace, the trace of the erasure of the trace" ("OG," 66).

[22]Derrida acknowledges that his own language is drawn from "the text of metaphysics," but points beyond itself to its "own transgression" ("OG," 66).

[23]"*Différance* is not. It is not a present being" ("D," 21).

[24]*Differre* is richer than the Greek *diapherein* because the latter lacks the sense of deferring which is included among the meanings attaching to the Latin term ("D," 7–8).

[25]In his description of the death instinct, Derrida emphasizes the idea of expenditure without reserve, the squandering of presence or energy ("D," 19)—an idea that Lingis has developed under the heading of "excess" in a book oriented around that topic. See Alphonso Lingis, *Excesses: Eros and Culture* (Albany: SUNY Press, 1983), esp. pp. 71–74.

[26]Jacques Derrida, "Freud and the Scene of Writing," in *Writing and Difference*, trans. Alan Bass (Chicago: University of Chicago Press, 1978). "Freud et la scène de l'écriture," in *L'écriture et la différence* (Paris: Seuil, 1967). Hereafter abbreviated as "FSW."

> [27] [Freud] complies with a dual necessity: that of recognizing *différance* at
> the origin, and at the same time that of crossing out the concept of
> *primariness*: we will not, then, be surprised by the *Traumdeutung*, which
> defines primariness as a "theoretical fiction" in a paragraph on the
> "delaying" (*Verspätung*) of the secondary process. It is thus the delay
> which is in the beginning. Without which, *différance* would be the lapse
> which a consciousness, a self-presence of the present, accords itself. To
> defer (*différer*) thus cannot mean to retard a present possibility, to post-
> pone an act, to put off a perception already now possible. That possi-
> bility is possible only through a *différance* which must be conceived of in
> other terms than those of a calculus or mechanics of decision. To say

the *différance* is originary is simultaneously to erase the myth of a present origin. Which is why "originary" must be understood as having been *crossed out,* without which *différance* would be derived from an original plenitude. It is a non-origin which is originary. ("FSW," 203)

[28]See "Beyond Signifiers," in *The Future of Continental Philosophy and the Politics of Difference,* ed. Hugh Silvermann and Donn Welton (Albany. SUNY Press, 1988)

[29]Hence, the world as transcendentally written erases the distinction between the objective world-in-itself and the world as correlate of experience.

[30]"Desire," here, is my term. Derrida refers to force or energy in the context of this essay on Freud:

> Psychic writing does not lend itself to translation because it is a single energetic system . . . , and because it covers the entirety of the psychical apparatus. Despite the difference of agencies, psychical writing in general is not a displacement of meanings within the limidity of an immobile, pregiven space and the blank neutrality of discourse. A discourse which might be coded without ceasing to be diaphanous. Here energy cannot be reduced; it does not limit meaning, but rather produces it. *The distinction between force and meaning is derivative in relation to an archi-trace.* ("FSW," 213, emphasis mine)

The point at stake here is that the energetics (desire) is constitutive of meaning. It is not as though one could separate a specifiable meaning which is then transformed by energy/desire/locus within Freud's topography. (Incidentally, we have precisely this thought informing the basic theses of Lacan: everything passes through the defiles of the signifier, and the signifier defiles by transformations dictated by desire.) See my essay "Desire: Language and Body," in *Post-Modernism and Continental Philosophy,* ed. Hugh Silvermann and Donn Welton (Albany: SUNY Press, 1988).

[31]"All necessity, without exception, is grounded in a transcendental condition. There must, therefore, be a transcendental ground of the unity of consciousness in the synthesis of the manifold of all our intuitions. . . . This original and transcendental condition is no other than *transcendental apperception." Kant's Critique of Pure Reason,* trans. Norman Kemp Smith (London: Macmillan, 1963), A 106–107, pp. 135–36.

[32]Edmond Husserl, *Cartesian Meditations,* trans. Dorien Cairns (The Hague: Nijhoff, 1970), sec. 18, p. 43.

[33]*Kant's Critique,* B 131–32, pp. 152–53; B 157–59, pp. 168–69.

[34]The scarequotes around "originary" and "produces" allow Derrida to suggest that *différance* functions as a ground—i.e., that it produces "effects"—without holding himself accountable for the ontological presuppositions implicit in that function. "To say that *différance* is originary is simultaneously to erase the myth of a present origin. Which is why 'originary' must be understood as having been crossed out. . . . [*Différance*] is a non-origin which is originary" ("FSW," 203).

[35]"*Différance* is the non-full, non-simple, structured and differentiating origin of differences. Thus the name 'origin' no longer suits it" ("D," 11). Derrida leaves it to his reader to determine why the name "origin" no longer suits *différance.* Apart from the issue of presence—origins are traditionally conceived as absent presences, beings that once *were* present—I would suggest that Derrida's thinking here parallels Kant's when he argues that that which accounts for the unification of time in experience cannot appear in experience: *différance* cannot be a term in one of the binary oppositions (begin-

ning versus end, ground versus consequent, cause versus effect, etc.) because it is held to "produce" them all. In both cases, the ground cannot present itself without generating an infinite regress, hence must be treated in the categories of ultimacy as a noumenal *causa sui*.

Speaking of the differences of language (which differences have already been identified as made possible by *différance*), Derrida writes that these "differences have been produced, are produced effects, but they are effects which do not find their cause in a subject or a substance, in a thing in general, a being that is somewhere present, thereby eluding the play of *différance*" ("D," 11).

36"Phenomenology's principle of principles [is] the principle of presence and of presence in self-presence, such as it is manifested to the being and in the being that we are." Jacques Derrida, "The Ends of Man" in *Margins of Philosophy*, p. 125. "Les fins de l'homme," in *Marges de la philosophie*.

37"Derrida maintains that outside a text there 'is' no origin—historical, metaphysical, or transcendental—if by 'origin' is meant something having the kind of determinate presence often attributed to veridical perception. Just as 'there never was any 'perception'* once we deconstruct the idea of such presence, so there never was any origin either—*except in (and as) a text*." Edward S. Casey, "Origin(s) in (of) Derrida/Heidegger," *The Journal of Philosophy* 81, no. 10 (1984), p. 602. (At* Casey cites Jacques Derrida, *Speech and Phenomena*, trans. David Allison [Evanston: Northwestern University Press, 1973], p. 103.)

"One cannot get *around* a text so as to locate its extratextual origin because in the very effort to do so one meets yet another text; any *soi-disant* 'origin' is always already pre-inscribed in a text. In short, there *is* only the re-inscription of one text in another, the re-marking of one by the other—the tracing of intertextuality" (ibid., p. 608, emphasis on *is* added).

38Derrida would put the notion of "a stratum beneath or prior to language" under erasure: "language . . . has not fallen from the sky, its differences have been produced, are produced effects," but there is no cause resident in "a being that is somewhere present" ("D," 11). Terminological differences notwithstanding, Derrida is committed to a doctrine of the primacy of *différance* to language (it is "the play that makes possible nominal effects" ["D," 26]), and is equally committed to asserting that the language of our epoch is permeated with the oppositions generated by its latent metaphysics.

39In a letter to me postmarked 27 September 1988, David Levin wrote:

> I . . . think that, in order simultaneously to rescue presence and acknowledge the validity in (some of) Derrida's critique of metaphysics, you have to distinguish more sharply than you have between a concept of presence that remains caught in the discourse of metaphysics where it *is* reified, totalized, and fixated, and a concept of presence that we can twist free of this traditional discourse.

Levin's criticism is apt: this distinction needs to be made explicit, and I have made an effort to do that in an essay—"Temporality: Merleau-Ponty and Derrida" in *Merleau-Ponty: Hermeneutics, and Postmodernism*, ed. Thomas Busch and Sean Gallagher (Albany: SUNY Press, 1992)—I wrote as a sequel to the one at hand. However, the point developed there is anticipated here: it is in the coherence of the specious, lived present that Derrida's Eleatic antinomy is resolved. It is intrinsic to language to reify experience: Derrida's mistake is to make the sign constitutive of the phenomenon upon which it is parasitic.

12. Richard J. Bernstein, An Allegory of Modernity/Postmodernity: Habermas and Derrida

[1]This passage from Iban Hassan is cited by Albrecht Wellmer, "The Dialectic of Modernity and Post-Modernity," *Praxis International* 4 (January 1985), p. 338.

[2]Jean-François Lyotard, *The Postmodern Condition: A Report on Knowledge,* trans. G. Bennington and B. Massumi (Minneapolis University of Minnesota Press, 1984), pp. xviii–xxiv.

[3] I have never been very happy with the term "modernity." Of course, I feel that what is happening in the world today is something unique and singular. As soon, however, as we give it the label of "modernity," we describe it in a certain historical system of evolution or progress (a notion derived from Enlightenment rationalism) which tends to blind us to the fact that what confronts us today is *also* something ancient and hidden in history. I believe that what "happens" in our contemporary world and strikes us as particularly new has in fact an essential connection with something extremely old which has been covered over [*archi-dissimulé*]. So that the new is not so much that which occurs for the first time but that "very ancient" dimension which recurs in the "very modern"; and which indeed has been signified repetitively throughout our historical tradition, in Greece and in Rome, in Plato and in Descartes and in Kant, etc. No matter how novel or unprecedented a modern meaning may appear, it is never exclusively *modernist* but is also and at the same time a phenomenon of *repetition*. ("Dialogue with Jacques Derrida," in *Dialogues with Contemporary Continental Thinkers,* ed. Richard Kearney [Manchester: Manchester University Press, 1984], pp. 112–13)

[4]Habermas's most sustained discussion of Derrida occurs in *The Philosophical Discourse of Modernity,* trans. F. Lawrence (Cambridge, Mass.: MIT Press, 1987). See chap. 8, "Beyond a Temporalized Philosophy of Origins: Jacques Derrida's Critique of Phonocentrism," and "Excursus on Leveling the Genre Distinction between Philosophy and Literature." Derrida has not systematically discussed Habermas's work. But see his brief and sharp reply to Habermas, p. 156, footnote 9, *Limited Inc.,* ed. Gerald Graff (Evanston: Northwestern University Press, 1988).

[5]Martin Jay, *Adorno* (Cambridge, Mass.: Harvard University Press, 1984), p. 14.

[6]Ibid., p. 15.

[7]William James, *A Pluralistic Universe* (Cambridge, Mass.: Harvard University Press, 1977), pp. 14–15.

[8]Jürgen Habermas, "The German Idealism of the Jewish Philosophers," *Philosophical-Political Profiles,* trans. Frederick Lawrence (Cambridge, Mass.: MIT Press, 1983), p. 41.

[9]Max Horkheimer and Theodor W. Adorno, *Dialectic of Enlightenment,* trans. John Cumming (New York: Continuum, 1972), p. 3.

[10]See Habermas's early book on the public sphere, which has recently been translated into English by Thomas Burger and Frederick Lawrence, *The Structural Transformation of the Public Sphere: An Inquiry into a Category of Bourgeois Society* (Cambridge, Mass.: MIT Press, 1989).

[11]Jürgen Habermas, "Historical Materialism and the Development of Normative

Structures," in *Communication and the Evolution of Society,* trans. Thomas McCarthy (Boston: Beacon, 1979), p. 117.

[12]Ibid., pp. 119–20.

[13]Ibid., p. 97.

[14]Jürgen Habermas, "A Reply To My Critics," in *Habermas: Critical Debates,* ed. John B. Thompson and David Held (London: MacMillan, 1982), p. 221.

[15]Habermas, *The Philosophical Discourse of Modernity,* p. 408.

[16]Ibid.

[17]Ibid.

[18]Habermas does think there is a categorical distinction between the natural sciences and the reconstructive critical social sciences. But both types of sciences are fallibilistic and make universal claims open to ongoing criticism.

[19]Jürgen Habermas, "The Entwinement of Myth and Enlightenment: Re-Reading *Dialectic of Enlightenment,*" in *New German Critique* 26 (1982), pp. 23, 25, 27.

[20]See Jürgen Habermas, "Work and Weltanschauung: The Heidegger Controversy from a German Perspective," *Critical Inquiry* 15 (Winter 1989).

[21]Jürgen Habermas, "Questions and Counterquestions," in *Habermas and Modernity,* ed. Richard J. Bernstein (Cambridge, Mass.: MIT Press, 1985), p. 195.

[22]Derrida himself frequently uses such hyphenated expressions as "ethical-political-juridical" or "ethical-political." The point of these hyphenated expressions is to mark the inseparability of the issues examined. In this respect Derrida acknowledges the ancient (Greek) tradition in which questions concerning *ethos, polis,* and *nomos* are intertwined. This does not mean that one can ignore important differences between ethics, morality, and politics. For the purposes of this essay I will stress the interrelatedness of these "domains" rather than the crucial differences and distinctions among them.

[23]"An Interview with Derrida" in *Derrida and Différance,* ed. David Wood and Robert Bernasconi (Evanston: Northwestern University Press, 1988), p. 74.

[24]Ibid., p. 75.

[25]Kearney, "Dialogue with Jacques Derrida," p. 108.

[26]Ibid., p. 118.

[27]Ibid., p. 124.

[28]See "Serious Play: The Ethical-Political Horizon of Derrida," in Bernstein, *The New Constellation* (Cambridge: Polity Press, 1991), pp. 172–91, where I argue that an ethical-political orientation is a point of departure for reading virtually everything Derrida has written. During the past decade the "themes" of violence, justice, law, and responsibility have become even more prominent in his writings.

[29]See Jacques Derrida, "Of an Apocalyptic Tone Recently Adopted in Philosophy," *Oxford Literary Review* 6 (1984).

[30]Kearney, "Dialogue with Jacques Derrida," p. 111.

[31]"I never separate promising from memory," Jacques Derrida, "But beyond . . . (Open Letter to Anne McClintock and Rob Nixon)," *Critical Inquiry* 13 (Autumn 1986), p. 160.

[32]Kearney, "Dialogue with Jacques Derrida," p. 113.

[33]Derrida, "But beyond . . . ," pp. 167–68. See also Jacques Derrida, "Racism's Last Word," trans. Peggy Kamuf, *Critical Inquiry* 12 (Autumn 1985).

[34]Derrida, "But beyond . . . ," p. 168.

[35]Ibid.

[36]Jacques Derrida, "The Conflict of Faculties: A *Mochlos*" (forthcoming).

[37]Derrida, "But beyond . . . ," p. 170.

[38]Kearney, "Dialogue with Jacques Derrida," p. 119.

[39]Ibid., p. 120.

[40]Ibid.

[41]Derrida, "Afterword," *Limited Inc.*, p. 116.

[42]For a critical discussion of recent appropriations of the concept of *phronesis*, see Richard J. Bernstein, *Beyond Objectivism and Relativism: Science, Hermeneutics and Praxis* (Philadelphia: University of Pennsylvania Press, 1983).

[43]Almost every text of Derrida's touches on questions of response, responsiveness, and responsibility. In his writings during the past decade the explicit discussion of responsibility has become more and more prominent. See "The Principle of Reason: The University in the Eyes of its Pupils," *Diacritics* 13 (Fall 1983); "The Conflict of Faculties"; and "Like the Sound of the Sea Deep within a Shell: Paul de Man's War," *Critical Inquiry* 14 (Spring 1988). Few commentators on the latter essay have noted that it is not only an essay dealing with "Paul de Man's War" but also a meditation on the question, ambiguities, and double binds of *responsibility*.

[44]Kearney, "Dialogue with Derrida," p. 118.

[45]Jacques Derrida, "Choreographies," *Diacritics* 12 (Summer 1982), pp. 66–67. See also "Voice ii: Jacques Derrida et Verena Andermott Conley," *Boundary 2* 12 (Winter 1984); and "*Geschlecht*—Sexual Difference, Ontological Difference," *Research in Phenomenology* 13 (1983).

[46]See Jacques Derrida, "The Politics of Friendship" (unpublished manuscript). See also "Violence and Metaphysics: An Essay on the Thought of Emmanuel Levinas," in *Writing and Difference*, trans. Alan Bass (Chicago: University of Chicago Press, 1978).

[47]Derrida, "Afterword," *Limited Inc.*, p. 112.

[48]See Derrida, "The Principle of Reason."

[49]The "problem" of the other is just as fundamental for Habermas as it is for Derrida. Here too their approaches supplement each other. Harbermas's primary concern is with the personal other as it appears in communicative action, i.e., with reciprocal communication in achieving mutual understanding. All communication is dialogical where the *right* of the other to assent freely to professed validity claims should prevail as a binding universal norm. Derrida typically focuses on the ways in which the other eludes understanding and provides a site (nonsite) for questioning that which strives to assimilate and master the other. Whereas Habermas emphasizes reciprocity, symmetry, and mutual recognition, Derrida focuses on nonreciprocity, asymmetry, and the faults in mutual recognition.

[50]See Habermas, *The Philosophical Discourse of Modernity*.

[51]For a development of this point see my book *Beyond Objectivism and Relativism*. See also my criticism of Habermas's understanding of his project of reconstructive science of communicative action in "Interpretation and Solidarity: An Interview with Richard Bernstein by Dunja Melcié," *Praxis International* 9, no. 3 (October 1989).

[52] Deconstruction, as I have practiced it, has always been foeign to rhetoricism—which, as its name indicates, can become another form of logocentrism—and this despite or rather because of the interest I have felt obliged to direct at questions of language and at figures of rhetoric. What is all too quickly forgotten is often what is most massively evident, to wit, that deconstruction, that at least to which I refer, *begins* by deconstructing logocentrism, and hence also that which rhetoricism might owe it. Also for the same reason I never assimilated philosophy, science, theory, criticism, law, morality, etc., to literary fictions. (Derrida, "Afterword," *Limited Inc.*, p. 156)

[53]Habermas, "Questions and Counterquestions," p. 192.

[54]Derrida, "Afterword," *Limited Inc.,* p. 116.

[55]Derrida, "The Conflict of Faculties."

[56]See Thomas McCarthy, "The Politics of the Ineffable: Derrida's Deconstructionism," *The Philosophical Forum* 21 (1989–90).

[57]Kearney, "Dialogue with Jacques Derrida," pp. 114–15.

13. David Couzens Hoy, Splitting the Difference: Habermas's Critique of Derrida

[1]Splitting the difference is an interpretive operation used by Richard Rorty in "Habermas and Lyotard on Postmodernity," in *Habermas and Modernity,* ed. Richard J. Bernstein (Cambridge, Mass.: MIT Press, 1985).

[2]Jürgen Habermas, *The Philosophical Discourse of Modernity,* trans. Frederick Lawrence (Cambridge, Mass.: MIT Press, 1987), p. 86.

[3]Ibid., p. 296. Habermas hopes that the symptoms of exhaustion will dissolve with his own shift from the philosophy of consciousness to his paradigm of mutual understanding.

[4]Jacques Derrida, "Plato's Pharmacy," in *Dissemination,* trans. Barbara Johnson (Chicago: University of Chicago Press, 1981), p. 111.

[5]Habermas, *The Philosophical Discourse of Modernity,* p. 182. Habermas suggests further that

> Derrida's grammatologically circumscribed concept of an archewriting whose traces call forth all the more interpretations the more unfamiliar they become, renews the mystical concept of tradition as an ever *delayed* event of revelation. Religious authority only maintains its force as long as it conceals its true face and thereby incites the frenzy of deciphering interpreters. Earnestly pursued deconstruction is the paradoxical labor of continuing a tradition in which the saving energy is only renewed by expenditure. The labor of deconstruction lets the refuse heap of interpretations, which it wants to clear away in order to get at the buried foundations, mount ever higher. (p. 183)

Habermas is here varying a famous image of Benjamin's to make fun of deconstructionist literary critics.

[6]These are not the only methods currently employed in contemporary philosophy, or even in continental philosophy alone. A third competitor is genealogy, a method normally attributed to Nietzsche and Foucault, but which goes back to British moralists like Hume. I have discussed the genealogical method in several papers, including "Nietzsche, Hume, and the Genealogical Method," in *Nietzsche as Affirmative Thinker,* ed. Y. Yovel (Dordrecht: Kluwer Academic, 1986); and "Power, Repression, Progress: Foucault, Lukes and the Frankfurt School," in *Foucault: A Critical Reader,* ed. D. C. Hoy (London: Basil Blackwell, 1986).

[7]At a conference on "The States of 'Theory' " at the University of California, Irvine (24–25 April 1987), Derrida distanced himself from the use of the prefix "post," as in, for instance, "poststructuralism" (but also, by implication, in "postmodernism"). He thinks deconstruction should not be identified with any such *-ism* because terms like "af-

ter," "new," and "post" imply a global rewriting of history (which is what we should have learned to avoid from Derrida's earlier readings of Nietzsche and Husserl).

[8]For a more detailed discussion of whether Foucault is a modern or a postmodern, as well as of the differences between Foucault's and Lyotard's postmodernism, see my essay, "Foucault: Modern or Postmodern?" in *After Foucault: Humanistic Knowledge, Postmodern Challenges*, ed. Jonathan Arac (New Brunswick: Rutgers University Press, 1988).

[9]In *Ethics and the Limits of Philosophy* (Cambridge: Cambridge University Press, 1985), Bernard Williams challenges theorists like Rawls for such a strong notion of transparency:

> One significant point is that while transparency is a natural associate of liberalism, it falls short of implying rationalism. It is one aspiration, that social and ethical relations should not essentially rest on ignorance and misunderstanding of what they are, and quite another that all the beliefs and principles involved in them should be explicitly stated. That these are two different things is obvious with personal relations, where to hope that they do not rest on deceit and error is merely decent, but to think that their basis can be made totally explicit is idiocy. (p. 102)

[10]While I derived these particular categories in thinking about Foucault, I found them confirmed by Derrida's remarks at the meeting of the American Philosophical Association in March 1987. In a discussion of Heidegger, who believes great thinkers each have one central thought (which eludes them and which remains unthought, until it is revealed by a later great thinker like Heidegger himself), Derrida rejected three central premises of Heidegger's way of reading the history of thought: (1) the idea of the great thinker; (2) the idea that there is only one thought for any such thinker; and (3) the idea that there is only the one unthought that runs through the earlier great thinker but that can necessarily not be thought except by the later great thinker.

[11]For instance, Derrida suggests that his own interpretation of Nietzsche's undecidability is itself undecidable. See *Spurs: Nietzsche's Styles*, trans. Barbara Harlow (Chicago: University of Chicago Press, 1979), pp. 135–39.

[12]Habermas, *The Philosophical Discourse of Modernity*, pp. 179, 296.

[13]Ibid., p. 182.

[14]Jacques Derrida, *Margins of Philosophy*, trans. Alan Bass (Chicago: University of Chicago Press, 1982), p. 22.

[15]Habermas, *The Philosophical Discourse of Modernity*, p. 166.

[16]Ibid., 205.

[17]Derrida made these remarks in response to Rodolphe Gasché and Stanley Cavell at the March 1987 meeting of the Pacific Division of the American Philosophical Association. On "arche-synthesis," see Rodolphe Gasché, *The Tain of the Mirror: Derrida and the Philosophy of Reflection* (Cambridge, Mass.: Harvard University Press, 1986), p. 273.

[18]Derrida, "Differance," in *Margins of Philosophy*, p. 27.

[19]Jacques Derrida, *Positions*, trans. Alan Bass (Chicago: University of Chicago Press, 1981), p. 105.

[20]See Derrida in *Spurs:* "there is no such thing either as the truth of Nietzsche, or of Nietzsche's text. . . . Indeed there is no such thing as a truth in itself. But only a surfeit of it. Even if it should be for me, about me, truth is plural" (p. 103).

[21]Jacques Derrida, "The Principle of Reason: The University in the Eyes of its Pupils," in *Diacritics* 13 (Fall 1983), p. 17.

²²Derrida, *Positions,* p. 6.

²³Jacques Derrida, "Les Antinomies de la discipline philosophique: Lettre préface," in *La Grève des philosophes* (Paris: Osiris, 1986), p. 12.

²⁴See Habermas, "Geschichte und Evolution," in *Zur Rekonstruktion des Historischen Materialismus* (Frankfurt: Suhrkamp Verlag, 1976). I discuss Habermas's claims at greater length in "Two Conflicting Conceptions of How to Naturalize Philosophy: Foucault versus Habermas," in *Metaphysik nach Kant?,* ed. Dieter Henrich and Rolf-Peter Horstmann (Stuttgart: Klett-Cotta Verlag, 1988).

²⁵Jacques Derrida, *Otobiographies* (Paris, 1984), pp. 13–32. For a more extensive discussion of his analysis of the Declaration of Independence see my article, "Dworkin's Constructive Optimism v. Deconstructive Legal Nihilism," *Law and Philosophy* 6 (1987), pp. 321–56, especially pp. 333–37.

²⁶See Jacques Derrida, "The Conflict of Faculties: A Mochlos," trans. Cynthia Chase, Jonathan Culler, and Irving Wahlfarth, in *Institutions of Philosophy,* ed. Deborah Esch and Thomas Keenan (Cambridge, Mass.: Harvard University Press, 1992).

²⁷Habermas, *The Philosophical Discourse of Modernity,* p. 208.

²⁸Ibid., p. 198.

²⁹Ibid., p. 206.

³⁰Ronald Dworkin, *Law's Empire* (Cambridge, Mass.: Harvard University Press, 1986), pp. 31–46.

³¹Steven Lukes, *Power: A Radical View* (London: Macmillan, 1974).

³²Certainly Habermas deals at length with the performative dimensions in chapter 3 of his *Theory of Communicative Action,* vol. 1, trans. Thomas McCarthy (Boston: Beacon, 1984). In the chapter on Derrida in *The Philosophical Discourse of Modernity,* however, the focus is primarily on truth, which Derrida could interpret as an implicit privileging of the constative, cognitive dimension, as well as of the "theoretical" in general.

³³Habermas, *The Philosophical Discourse of Modernity,* p. 178. See Derrida, *Positions,* p. 88: "I have never said that *there is not* a 'subject of writing.' . . . It is solely necessary to reconsider the problem of the effect of subjectivity such as it is produced by the structure of the text."

³⁴Habermas, *The Philosophical Discourse of Modernity,* p. 166.

³⁵Derrida, *Margins of Philosophy,* p. 315.